To Betty with love from

24th Nov. 1958.

JOHN WHITE

J. Mortimer, sculpt.

This plaque was unveiled and dedicated in the John White Chapel in The Barony Church of Glasgow on 21st April, 1953. Replicas were later placed in the churches of Dr. White's former parishes, Shettleston and South Leith; in the Assembly Hall, Edinburgh; and in sixteen Church Extension buildings.

JOHN WHITE
C.H., D.D., LL.D.

by

AUGUSTUS MUIR

Foreword by

H.R.H. THE DUKE OF GLOUCESTER
K.G., K.T.

HODDER AND STOUGHTON

FOREWORD

BY

H.R.H. THE DUKE OF GLOUCESTER, K.G., K.T.

WHEN I was asked to become associated with the John White National Memorial Fund I was pleased to learn that a Biography of this great Scottish Churchman was to form part of the Memorial to him.

The life and work of Dr. John White form an indivisible part of a long and notable chapter in the history of the Church in Scotland; in particular, the union of the Church of Scotland and the United Free Church of Scotland in 1929 is one of the great milestones in the ecclesiastical story of our land, and that dramatic achievement will always be associated with his name.

His great work in the Church Extension Movement has already been fittingly commemorated by the setting up of replicas of the original plaque, unveiled in the John White Memorial Chapel in The Barony of Glasgow, in no less than sixteen churches in new housing areas in Scotland. Now this excellent biography by Mr. Augustus Muir has been completed.

Amongst the duties I performed on behalf of my brother, King George VI, I look back with especially happy memories on my term as Lord High Commissioner to the General Assembly of the Church of Scotland in 1949. It was there, listening to the debates in the Assembly, that I obtained a deep insight into the life and work of the Church with her width and splendour of vision, her dynamic vigour and her selfless and devoted service to mankind. It was there, too, that I was privileged to meet and listen to Dr. John White, who seemed to embody those same qualities in his person; that he was a man of fine gifts of mind and heart was plain for all to see, and to them he added good humour and kindliness.

Scotland and Scotland's National Church may indeed be proud to have nurtured such an one.

PREFACE

THE John White archives filled many a capacious cupboard in his house at Partickhill in Glasgow, and with high hope I began my study of them. The pleasantly discursive letters, self-revealing and full of humour and by-play and human touches: of these I had expected to find many and I found none. It was plain to me that no picture of John White's rich personality could be built up from his correspondence. Out of a full heart he would write to one in sorrow—this we know from those he comforted—and he wrote at length to wife and family as the occasion called. But most of his work-a-day letters were as terse as telegrams, and in them you will look in vain for the opinions you would wish to hear on half a hundred things, from fly-fishing to foreign travel, from Prime Ministers to kirk sessions—opinions that would flow from him in his weekly hour of relaxation at his study fire of a Sunday night, with his own and other men's assistants forming a blithe fraternity of the cloth, individually perhaps a little difficult to distinguish through the tobacco smoke.

Nevertheless, in these immense archives, we find notes on all the events in which he took part—notes that illumine nearly every important movement in the Church of Scotland since the beginning of this century. He had always been a student of Church history, and his papers show how his knowledge of the turbulent story of the Kirk in Scotland gave him perspective and helped him in every decision he made. In writing of his life and work, I find that I have in fact been showing Presbyterian Church government and discipline in action. This is perhaps no bad thing at a time when so much is in the melting-pot and there is talk even of constitutional change. I have shown, too, how the *Credo* of the Church of Scotland, as embodied in the first of her Declaratory Articles, was hammered out prior to the union of 1929—with what fervour and even fury did friends battle with each other to put into words an epitome of their faith! Seldom were John White's emotions more touched than in some of these tussles: but, as a good friend of his once said to me, however warmly John White's feelings were involved, he managed to keep his brain on ice.

His achievements can be appreciated to the full only when we reckon on the forces deployed against him. At one time or another, he had to contend with obstructive lawyers, recalcitrant statesmen, pig-headed bureaucrats, but perhaps his hardest fights were with his fellow Christians in the Church—the men who were convinced that he was wrong and they were right. In the struggle for union, which lasted for twenty years, he was more concerned with dissentients in his own Church than with opponents of union in the other. And of course he made enemies; but none of the greathearts among those he battled with could withhold from him the hand of friendship.

When I was asked by the late Professor J. Gervase Riddell, chairman of the John White National Memorial Committee, to undertake this biography, I appreciated the extent and importance of the task; and I was emboldened to accept it by the many offers of help from those who had been close to John White in his home and his work. Such help has been given in overwhelming measure. In addition to the documents I have referred to, Mrs. White placed at my disposal all her husband's private papers and diaries, and for this and for her continual encouragement I am profoundly grateful. The Rev. W. Roy Sanderson, successor to John White at The Barony of Glasgow, became chairman of the Memorial Committee on the death of Professor Riddell, and he devoted many laborious hours of his busy life to making smooth my path: his patience and kindness are among the happiest memories of my work on this book. Another who fills an old pulpit of John White's, the Rev T. D. Stewart Brown of South Leith, has given me his support in so many ways that I find it hard to express my appreciation.

Of that brotherhood or freemasonry composed of John White's assistants, many have been glad to tell of their association with their "bishop". I remember with pleasure the illuminating talks with Dr. David Scott of Kinclaven, with Dr. William MacNicol of Longforgan, with the late Rev J. R. Spence of Southdean, with the late Rev. John Swan of Ramshorn, Glasgow, and with the late Rev. John Munro of Strathbungo. Dr. James M'Cardel, formerly of New Kilpatrick, Dr. J. C. M. Conn of Kilmarnock, and Dr. William Barclay, Vice-Chairman of the Presbyterian Church of Canada, all of them old assistants, put on paper for my benefit their recollections; and the Rev. J. Anderson, minister of Shettleston, John White's first charge, helped me to recreate the atmosphere of those days in the eighteen-nineties when a short chapter of Church history was made in his parish. To the late Dr. W. White Anderson of St. Cuthbert's I am indebted for much good advice; and his colleague, Dr. Adam Burnet, gave me glimpses of John White without which I would have been the poorer. Dr. J. Hutchison Cockburn, of Dunblane Cathedral, told me of his association with John White in the work of the Church, and from him I learned something of the ardours of those thrilling months before the great convocation of October 1929 when the Church union was sealed. To Dr. Charles L. Warr, K.C.V.O., Dean of the Thistle and Chapel Royal, and to Professor J. Pitt Watson of Trinity College, Glasgow, I am indebted for much wise counsel. At the Church Offices in George Street, Edinburgh, I received many kindnesses, in particular from Dr. Robert Mackintosh, the Rev. Horace Walker, Miss A. C. Veitch, Mr. Hay Downie, C.A., and Mr. Mercer Robertson, S.S.C. Nor must I omit to put on record my appreciation of the work of the Rev. David Gourlay of Glasgow University who carried out the onerous task of arranging and indexing the John White archives. For great kindness, my thanks are due to the Rev. David Rutherford of Aberdour in Fife, to the Rev. Ronald Falconer of the British Broadcasting Corporation, and to three librarians who located for me a prodigious number of books, biographical and historical, the moment I put out a call of need—Dr. John Campbell of the General Assembly Library and Record Room, Dr. John A. Lamb of New College Library, Edinburgh, and Mr. K. J. Lace of the County Library of Essex. Sir Randall Philip, Q.C., D.D., late Procurator of the Church of Scotland, would have been John White's biographer but for his failing health; his death in 1957 was an immense loss to the Church and to his numberless friends; and for myself, I should like to add that I never sought his advice but it was gladly given, and the care with which he weighed every sentence of the chapter in which I dealt with the notorious Shettleston Church Case left me deeply in his debt. Correspondence on Church Extension in the possession of Sir James Simpson was generously put at my disposal. For the help and support of the Rev. A. Ian Dunlop I am grateful; and finally I must record the two years of work so devotedly and tirelessly given to this book by my personal research assistant, Miss Mair Davies.

I was welcomed at the homes of John White's daughter and of his son, Mrs. Glen of Houndwood and Mr. J. B. White of Middleton Tyas; and they helped to build up a picture of their father in his earlier days at Shettleston and South Leith. To their talk of those robust years, Mrs. White's memories of the last days at Partickhill was a fit and gentle conclusion: they spanned, between them, the best part of a long lifetime joyfully dedicated to the service of Christ's Kirk in Scotland.

AUGUSTUS MUIR

ACKNOWLEDGMENTS

THANKS are due to the Trustees of New College Library, Edinburgh, for permission to quote from the late Principal Martin's letters; to the Hon. Mrs. Maclean for permission to quote from the letters of her husband, the late Dr. Norman Maclean; to Miss Wallace Williamson for permission to quote from the letters of her father, the late Dr. Wallace Williamson; to Sheriff J. Wellwood Johnstone for permission to quote from the letters of his father, the late Lord Sands; to Professor Robert Candlish Henderson for permission to quote from the letters of his father, the late Dr. Archibald Henderson; to Mrs. Matthew White for permission to quote from writings of her late husband, John White's elder brother; to the Very Rev. Dr. R. F. V. Scott of St. Columba's, London, for permission to quote his words; to the Very Rev. Dr. George F. MacLeod for permission to quote from documents and letters; to Sir Hector Hetherington for permission to quote from his speech to the Presbytery of Glasgow on the occasion of John White's Jubilee; to Sir James Fergusson, Bt., of Kilkerran for permission to quote from a broadcast talk; and to Lord Balfour of Burleigh for permission to quote letters written by members of his family. Special acknowledgment is due to the General Administration Committee of the Church of Scotland for permission to quote from official papers, the copyright of which is vested in the Church.

CONTENTS

xiii

CONTENTS

LIST OF ILLUSTRATIONS

Chapter I

THE YEARS OF INCREASE

I

JOHN WHITE was born on 16th December 1867 in The Barony parish, with which his name was to be permanently associated. His forebears had been millers for many generations, and the most familiar sound of his boyhood years was the soft gush of water in the lade and the thud of the millwheel. An eighteenth-century Matthew White who farmed and milled at Garnieland, in the Renfrew parish of Inchinnan, was John White's great-great-grandfather. A son of his took over Scotstoun Mill on the Kelvin, the river that loops round Glasgow University, and worked there on the lands of the old Archbishopric of Glasgow. This White of Scotstoun had a son who followed him, and the next descendant was the Matthew White who was to become John White's father. Matthew struck out for himself, took over Dalgarven Mill, two miles north of Kilwinning, and it was there that he met and married John White's mother.

Kilwinning, a town in Cunninghame of ancient foundation, is renowned in the annals of freemasonry. Traditionally its name was taken from a St. Winning who came from Ireland and founded a church in the eighth century. Four centuries later, monks from Kelso built a fine abbey there; and in the village, once called Saint's-toun, a St. Winning's Well inspired awe in the local folk. It was a place of weavers when Matthew White went there. Muslins and shawls, woven for the Glasgow markets, earned bread for the villagers until the Eglinton Iron Works were established near the middle of the century. Matthew White's mill lay in a gentle hollow within a bend of the River Garnock, and a number of cottages were part of the little property. Not far across the fields was the farm of Gateside, the home of the worthy James Kennedy, with whom Matthew occasionally had business to transact. They were both pious men; the Kirk meant much in their lives: but while Matthew was a faithful member and later became an elder of Kilwinning Abbey, the parish church, James Kennedy and his wife had left the Church of Scotland at the Disruption of 1843, and James had long been an elder and one of the pillars of Kilwinning Free Church. The Disruption was still a bitter memory, and the two Churches were not given to tolerance; but that did not deter Matthew White from courting James Kennedy's daughter Marion, and he married her in the spring of 1861. If the young man ventured to argue with his father-in-law, it did not lessen his respect for him, and he left it on record that "he was indeed a man of God, and his every act was the outcome of a vital Christian faith. . . . There was never need of a minister at a death-bed or a funeral if folk had James Kennedy of Gateside."

James's wife was held in an equally high esteem. And her repute in no way depended upon her being the chatelaine of Gateside. A woman of fine dignity and charm, she had a will of her own, and James Kennedy was proud of her. He had her portrait painted; and in the carriage of her head and the strong yet delicate lineaments of her face one may see, without perhaps being fanciful, something of an inherited distinction in the features and general aspect of her grandson. She had "one of the finest strongest womanly faces that I can recall," wrote John White of her. "As a child I remember how she awed me as she sat in queenly state, a piped mutch on her head, in the great chair in that large, roomy, cosy kitchen at Gateside."

Matthew White prospered and his family increased. Of the four sons born to him, the eldest died just before the birth of a fifth, an event that took place in Glasgow. In a fashion not uncommon in those days, the deceased boy's name was transferred to the infant. "My brother died shortly before I was born, and I got his name," wrote John White. "That is supposed to be an unlucky christening, but I have survived the risks. I was often told by those who knew us both that I was 'not a patch on the first John'." The later advent of a couple of girls brought a touch of gentle femininity into a household which had been preponderantly male.

Looking back on his younger days at Dalgarven, John White said that the strongest influence on him was the sweet, tolerant, loving, religious atmosphere of the home. Dark threats of eternal Hell-fire as the certain punishment of sin were not shaken over the heads of the children at the Mill: rather, for them, was virtue made a thing of beauty. The daily reading of the scriptures was entrusted to each child in turn, and at meals it was the custom of the family to join hands around the table while the blessing was asked. Each Sunday a little cavalcade set out on the two-mile walk to the Abbey kirk at Kilwinning. In front were the children, James, Matthew, William, John and the two little girls, Marion and Jane, with their parents following doucely behind them. As they topped the brae, the towers of the ancient Abbey came into view, a pleasant sight against the sky of a quiet Sabbath morning. John White has left it on record that his father took special delight in creating and stimulating a love of God's out-of-doors. There was much for John to learn on the little farm; one of his later recollections was of his joy when he was given a lamb of his own to look after. He fished in the Garnock, a river that rises in the green Mistylaw hills of Cunninghame and flows into the Irvine a short distance from the sea. The mill at Dalgarven was in two parts. Water from the lade turned the flour mill, then passed under the road to work the meal mill on the other side. If the Garnock was low and the flour mill was going at full speed, there would not be a great enough head of water to turn the wheel of the meal mill across the road, and it had to be worked at night. A huge hopper filled with oats would usually keep the stones supplied with grist until morning. John White has often told how he and his brothers took turns at sleeping beside an open window. If anything went wrong with the hopper, the noise of the mill would alter, and the sharp change of pitch would always awaken the sleeping boy, whose duty was then to hurry out and discover what was amiss. The old Dalgarven mill, now the property of the National Trust, is still in running order.

Among John White's teachers at Kilwinning was Mr. MacMorland, who used to say that he was a very difficult pupil—"not because he would not do his work but because he would insist on doing it in his own way". An old lady, alive a few years ago, remembered the White boys and would tell of how John was in the habit of bringing pigeons to the Kilwinning butcher and getting twopence each for them: he was a doughty wielder of the catapult. The twopences, or part of them, were handed over to "Lizzie Manners who had a wee shop beside the school, for John had an awfu' weakness for her Black Man toffee". Of his pranks, which were many, she said, "it wouldna be fair to clype".

From the tuition and the tawse of Mr. MacMorland, John went on to the Academy at Irvine about half a dozen miles away. The fees paid were a couple of pounds a quarter. Since John's brother William was at school there, they set out together each morning in a milk cart that left the mill at half-past six. The two older brothers had joined their father in the mill; but at the back of the mother's mind was the ambition that her two younger sons should enter the professions. She would have greatly liked William to become a minister and John a lawyer. At last she told of her dream.

The family purse could provide for William at the University; but since there would not be enough to pay for both of the boys, John must win bursaries. She did her best to help him to study at home. "This brought us very close together," said John White, looking back on her efforts, "and there was a great understanding between us. . . . I think she was a little sorry for me. I was not supposed to be so bright as William—he was to be the shining luminary of the Whites of Dalgarven." When the two brothers one day went in for an open essay competition, the rest of the family sat speechless when it was John who brought home the prize in triumph. His brother Matthew, looking back over a full seventy years, said of him: "John was always a thinker. He would go off and think a thing out. He got into the way of thinking quickly." But it was probably true to say of him, at one period, that he was more fond of fishing than of thinking, and his brother's words may be worth recalling:

> "I can mind fine one morning when John didn't turn up to join the milk cart with William at half-past six. The cart was kept waiting, for it would never do for John to miss a day at school. And then he came up from the river. He was trailing a big salmon. He knew he was late, but it had been a sore job for him to land the fish. He would rather have missed school than missed that fine salmon."

John White was to be a fisherman all his life; and second to fishing, among the sports and games he took to with pleasure was the playing and watching of football. Professor A. M. Hunter has said that John White once told him he had played inside left for Monkcastle United, a famous football team at Kilwinning: "The outside left of that team was capped for Scotland and John White assured me it was only his entering the ministry that stopped him from playing for Scotland too."

The earliest family sorrow known to John White was the death of the younger of his sisters. Marion had eaten a herb she had found while out playing in the fields, and her death from poisoning followed shortly after.[1] And then, when the boy was fourteen, his father died. The widowed mother looked into the future years with sorrowing but fearless eyes. Her splendid courage deeply impressed her family. The two elder boys

---

[1] The other sister, Jane, died several years later after catching a chill at a church service where her eldest brother William was being inducted. John White wrote of her: "She was the youngest of the family, and was spoiled by her four brothers. We were her slaves and allowed her to join in all our sports, in which she excelled. Her death was a great blow to all of us. It was inexpressibly sad to see the sun sink at noon. Jane was a young woman of many and great gifts."

had gone to manage another mill which Matthew White had bought, so their way was straight; but William had just gone up to Glasgow University with a view to entering the ministry, and the mother made plans for John to follow in November 1883. She decided to go with him, and took rooms in Glasgow not very far from where John had been born nearly sixteen years before, in the home of relatives. The two had become closer companions than ever. John White wrote afterwards:

> "If I cannot speak much of my father, who passed from the home at the age of fifty-one, I can say that he was a wise and understanding man. Looking back and thinking on many things that I then accepted, I can understand why everyone turned to him for advice—and how it came to pass that the whole neighbourhood, particularly his employees at the mill, esteemed him so highly and trusted him. . . . Of my mother I can speak more freely. She was Mother in the fullest sense of that most sacred word. . . . She had great wisdom and a knowledge of the world—an inheritance from her mother at the farmhouse of Gateside."

In those days, the University session ran from November to Easter, with a short break at Christmas. Since classes began at eight o'clock, students made their way to the University in the dark of winter mornings. Bowler hats with narrow curly brims were the headgear, long dark coats were worn, and winged collars with enormous ties were the fashion: altogether a quaint grown-up garb for a fifteen-year-old. But he now felt like a man and intended to satisfy his mother's ambition and become a lawyer. The first step, he decided, would be to take his Master of Arts degree.

II

There were no easy "options" in those days; the curriculum was as hard as the paving-stones on Gilmorehill. Latin, Greek, English literature, mathematics, logic, moral philosophy, natural philosophy: these were the common lot of all Arts graduates. "I entered the University at too early an age," John White said later; "a boy can make more of his first year's study if he goes under university discipline when he is a little more mature. In my first two years I had to give constant and strenuous attention to my classical reading. But every year after that, I felt I was adding a cubit to my stature." A fair comment: his record of study bears it out. Not until the session of 1885-6 did he begin to shine. He carried off first prize in the junior division of logic and rhetoric, and in the summer he won the vacation prize. During the summer of the next year he got a first-class honours certificate in forensic medicine. He then read civil law, for he still had the Law in view as his life's work, and he decided to article himself to a solicitor. He was offered a post with a lawyer whose business was so small that he employed no clerk, and John White hoped this would mean that he would be given more responsibility than would have come his way in a larger office. But he found to his disgust that the solicitor was in the habit of being absent from the office for inordinately long spells, particularly after the luncheon interval. Time and again John would arrive to find the door locked and a notice hung upon it which announced: "*Back in half an hour.*" At first he was merely bored with hanging about, and then he became exasperated. One day when the solicitor returned to his office he found his own card removed and a large notice hung in its place: "WON'T BE BACK AT ALL—JOHN WHITE." That was the end of his work in a solicitor's office; it was also the end of his legal career.

His thoughts had been deflected in a new direction. He had fallen under the influence of Professor Edward Caird, who was later to become Master of Balliol—and not the least in that distinguished lineage of Masters. Under Edward Caird, he read moral philosophy and political economy and took first prize.

"Through the award of two gold medals," he said, "and the Henderson Prize for special studies on many themes (from Locke and Leibnitz and the French Revolution to Pre-Christian Institutions analogous to the Sabbath) I gained much needed confidence. Edward Caird was one of the great teachers of higher thought, acknowledged by all his pupils to be one of the richest sources of light and leading for their lives."

Later, when he looked back upon himself in those days he said he must have been "a very precocious young philosopher", and he told of an incident that amused him:

"In the summer of 1887, my mother took a house at the seaside so that my brother and I might have a right good holiday after our university terms were finished. I had taken first place in philosophy and was about to take Caird's higher classes, and I felt compelled to do some reading for the coming session. I had filled a trunk with Hegel, Kant, not to mention Zeller's volumes, and a dozen other heavy tomes. . . . One day a minister came to look over the house—

he wanted to rent it later in the season—and when he saw this collection of books he asked my mother, 'Who reads these?' My mother answered: 'My son, John, who is studying philosophy.' His answer was expressive—'What holiday reading—my God!' . . . When I think of his answer," said John White, "I smile my approval. I'm not sure that, behind that collection of books, there was not a little bit of unconscious self-importance. Still, I did read them. As a result, I was awarded two more gold medals. But I must say no more, for even *that* savours of pride. Yes, indeed—my God!"

About Edward Caird's influence on him at this time, he wrote:

"A spiritual atmosphere pervaded Edward Caird's class-room. In the presence of the threatening forces of materialism, men were taught to interpret life in spiritual terms. . . . There was nothing of the dogmatic theologian about him; nothing of the agnostic either. He held that it was possible to maintain a critical spirit without agnosticism —and a reasonable faith without dogmatism. The one thing necessary was devotion to God and humanity. 'However important it is that our thoughts about God and about Christ, about the relations of God to man and of man to God, should be as adequate as we can make them, yet the root of the matter lies in the spirit of Christ, not in doctrines about him—in the living realisation of the nearness of the finite life to the infinite, not in the theological exactness of our creed.' Caird never imposed his beliefs on anyone. He urged men to think for themselves."

He urged John White to go on to Cambridge and read history, then left him to ponder the proposal and make up his own mind. John White decided to stick to Glasgow.

Long before he had any thoughts of the ministry, he used to visit church after church in the Glasgow area.

"I expected to find some spiritual help," he said, "but everything I wanted was pre-supposed. There was no footing for a beginner. I always found myself in an advanced class when it was an elementary one I was looking for. The fault lay with myself, chiefly. I was asking for the impossible. The existence of God cannot be established by logical truths."

John was trying to re-think the faith taught by his mother. He was passing through that stage in which youth questions the validity of a spiritual universe. He was trying, as he said, to find logical proof of the existence of God. He tells how he had gone in his early teens to an evangelistic meeting at Kilwinning, and the preacher called out, "Hands up those who are saved!" Then he asked, "Hands up those who are *not* saved." John White was the only one in that audience who did not raise his hand at all, and the evangelist made for him at the end of the meeting. "Look here," he said, "you must either be saved or not saved—which are you?" John White replied that it was hard to say, and the evangelist tried to make his point clear: "I'm in Kilwinning tonight. Tomorrow I'll be in Saltcoats. I must be in one place or the other." John White shook his head. "Not at all. You might be somewhere in between. That's where I am. In between." It seems that no further progress was made that night.

Search for yourself, Caird told him, and John White followed this advice. He kept up his church-going: that was part of the search. Often he went to sit under Dr. John Hunter at Trinity Congregational church:

> "I valued John Hunter's great powers of getting his message across. He made a strong spiritual appeal to all men who were thinking deeply on religious matters. His merit was that he took you out of the rut—he placed your feet on the open road. . . . In after years I was honoured by several invitations from him to take his pulpit; I wish I had been free to accept."

Another minister also named Hunter was to influence him—David Hunter of St. Mary's, Partick—under whom he made the great decision. He realised then that the whole self must be given and that until the self was given without reserve there was no dedication. He stepped across the line from "no" to "yes" and became a communicant for the first time at St. Mary's on 12th April 1889; he was twenty-one years of age. He knew at once what his life's work was to be: it was as if a hand had come down on his shoulder. By the following November he was a student at the Divinity Hall preparing to become a minister of the Church of Scotland.

III

Altogether, John White spent nine years at the University, and during that unusually long period one distinction after another fell to him. He won the Armagh Bursary offered by the Senate to the "most distinguished graduate in Arts of the year"; he had already held an Exchequer bursary, and for three years running he won a bursary at the Glasgow Presbytery examination. In prizes, his firsts had included those for Logic, Higher Metaphysics, Moral Philosophy, Political Economy, second and third year Divinity, Biblical Criticism, Ordinary and Senior Church History. He won the Coulter Prize and both the Ewing and Gartmore gold medals. From the time when he went to the Divinity Hall he was a prizeman in every class except Hebrew. He said he had never applied himself to it as he should have done because he considered Hebrew a sadly uninteresting subject, but he thought "Rabbi Robertson was one of the most likeable of men, a conscientious teacher who did his best to make his pupils take to Hebrew". He never greatly regretted that Professor Robertson had, in the case of at least one student, failed in his appeal.

If the personality of Edward Caird had captured his imagination far more fully than had the subjects Caird taught, there could be no question about John White's passion for Church History. He threw himself into it with zeal. To the end of his days, Church History was to enthrall him, and in particular the history of Christ's Church in Scotland. This study on which he then entered was to prove, over a period of twenty years that were among the most fruitful of his life, a pilgrim's staff to support him on a hard journey.

Professor Herbert Story then held the Chair of that subject at Glasgow: later he was to become Principal of the University. He was a man of deeply devotional mind, a man who was saddened by the onset of humanism and the attacks of some scientists upon the ancient tablets of faith.

> "He was a great figure," John White said, "a great churchman with uncommon powers of dialectic. I found him one of the kindliest of men, although not so regarded by those who did not know him. Because there were no lectures on pastoral work, I went to him with a couple of others and asked if he would give us some lectures on Church Law and Procedure. This he did. The result was that W. G. Black was appointed lecturer in this subject."

John White was already seeing things that were needed and making a drive for them. But his next request to Story was given short shrift. He asked if something could be done to give divinity students an idea of the practical work of the ministry. Story listened with interest and approval, but when John suggested that probationers should be admitted to kirk-session meetings to see how they were run, Story's answer was emphatic: "No! You can't be admitted to a kirk-session meeting, White, unless you are summoned to one for defection." When he heard that Boyd Carpenter, then Bishop of Ripon, was coming north to preach in the Bute Hall, he went to Story to ask if any member of the Senate had drawn the attention of the Glasgow Presbytery to it. "I haven't," said Story. "Nor shall I. Anyone who can sign the Thirty-nine Articles can sign our Westminster Confession of Faith."

In John White's time, it was John Caird, Edward's brother, who was Principal of the University, "our revered chief whose addresses and sermons were an inspiration beyond many class lectures—a great orator and great Hegelian scholar". He sat at the feet of Professor Dickson, "a man of vast biblical lore, a man we all loved and revered—a positive dungeon of learning". And there was Professor William Stewart, who held the Chair of Biblical Criticism:

"We called him Zaccheus because of his tiny stature. Stewart was famous for his lectures on the Sibylline Oracles. I recall an incident when he discovered in class that I was not listening but checking proofs of the University magazine. . . .

"'Will Joannes White please take the next portion and translate,' he said blandly.

"The portion turned out to be the fifth chapter of St. Mark, the twenty-fifth verse, about the woman that suffered much and doctors failed to heal. I successfully translated it.

"'Have you anything to say with regard to the passage?' he asked me.

"I knew well that Dr. Stewart's claim to fame was his theory that the gospel of St. Mark was a summary of what St. Luke and St. Matthew had already written, so naturally I replied that the passage proved conclusively that St. Mark wrote later than St. Matthew and St. Luke. Dr. Stewart seemed to think I was poking fun at him. He demanded proof.

"'It shows,' I said, 'the humour of the writer.'

"Dr. Stewart was horrified. 'Humour—in what way?'

"'Well,' I said, 'St. Mark not only adopted St. Matthew's brief account of the incident of the sick woman, but he also took up St. Luke's reference to physicians who had failed to cure her. Since St. Luke was himself a physician, St. Mark had no doubt added with a quiet chuckle, that the physicians had not only failed to cure her but had made her a good deal worse.'"

Of the great Lord Kelvin, he said:

"He was the brightest ornament of Glasgow University—and quite easily the worst teacher. . . . His was one of the greatest intellects and personalities of the century—and I never met a man of such strong simple faith in the great Christian truths. Well do I remember what he said one day—it was something like this—'When you're up against an impossibility, you are often on the edge of a discovery.'"

Kelvin meant this in terms of science; John White was often to develop it in terms of faith.

If there were outstanding teachers at Gilmorehill at that time, there were many lads of parts among the students. Some became professors themselves, among them David Smith (author of a notable life of Christ, *The Days of His Flesh*, and other works), James Gemmill, Ernest F. Scott, Alfred Garvie, Evan K. Evans. Hugh Black was to become one of Scotland's most popular preachers before he was called to a chair in the Union Theological Seminary of New York, and John A. Hutton became the editor of *The British Weekly*.[1] A special friend of John White's was Robert S. Horne, whose political career was crowned when he became Chancellor of the Exchequer. He had gone up to the University intending to become a minister, but had turned aside to take up Law: John White's college career in reverse. They were reckoned to be the most brilliant students then at the University. The day came when there was to be a test of personality between the two friends. Robert Horne stood as President of the Students' Representative Council. With a reputation such as his, nobody dreamt of standing against him, and it looked as if he would go in unopposed. But John White said he did not believe in anyone getting anywhere unopposed, so he got himself nominated, and an election was duly held. It was John White who was appointed President. In the recollection of his contemporaries, there was only one student whom John White challenged without success. John Campbell, later to be known throughout the Church of Scotland as librarian and keeper of Kirk records at the Tolbooth in Edinburgh, was his antagonist in a battle over a librarianship in the University. It had been the custom in the Divinity Hall for a third-year student to be appointed librarian in the

---

[1] Another Glasgow student who rose to eminence was Cosmo Gordon Lang, who became the Archbishop of Canterbury. A son of Dr. John Marshall Lang, Minister of The Barony, he left the University the year before John White entered it. While John White got on well with his fellow students, liked them, drew the best out of them, Cosmo Gordon Lang looked back upon his contemporaries and said that most of them were but "Scottish boors".

theological library; and Campbell, a third-year man, applied for the post. When John White heard of this, he said it was a preposterous rule that the librarianship should be reserved for third-year men, and he applied. Dr. Campbell, looking back over a vista of sixty-five years, would tell the story and add with a gentle smile, "It was the only time I ever bested John White. He was never an easy man to best. He was aye the first among us all."

His duties as the President of the Students' Representative Council took up but part of his spare time. He was appointed President of the Philomathic Society, the Philosophical Society, the Independent Club, the Theological Society, and he was Vice-President of the Missionary Society. A letter from a fellow student, Dr. A. Boyd Scott, written a quarter of a century later, gives a hint of how he was regarded: "I sat at your feet, a humble and somewhat recalcitrant member of the S.R.C., when you were President—and I admired that grave poise and inevitable wisdom which marked you in office. As all prophesied with assurance, it would (with your other great gifts) carry you on to the highest things."

There was one of the higher things, however, to which his gifts did not carry him. When John White sat the honours examinations in Mental Philosophy, he was clearly marked out for a First. The decision lay in the hands of two professors, Edward Caird and John Veitch. Caird was a strong neo-Hegelian; but Veitch, the last of the Scottish school of philosophy, was notorious for his attacks on some of Hegel's conceptions. "Veitch could say nothing bad enough about Hegel," said John White, and this was well known by all who took his class of Logic and Rhetoric. In one of the honours papers there was a question about Hegel, and John White answered it. If he had left it at that, all might have been well, but he could not refrain from hurling a stone into the pond and making a splash. At the end of his answer, he added a defiant footnote: *The man who set this question knows nothing about Hegel.* Many might have said there was a touch of truth in his comment. But it was Professor John Veitch who had set the question. In the seclusion of an ante-room there was a considerable rumpus. Veitch insisted that John White be failed out of hand. Edward Caird protested that White was an outstanding man, a man of such intellect that they could not do less than give him a First. Veitch held out that he must be ploughed for this piece of gratuitous insolence and defiance of all order and academic authority. At last they came to a compromise. John White found his name on a paper pinned to the notice board. It was among those who had been awarded Second Class honours.

The experience shook him a little, and he never forgot it. When his son James went up to Cambridge he told him of the wicked joy it had given him to sting Veitch to anger, and he said: "The student who fails to make an effort to put himself in the place of the examiner is a tactless fool."

IV

Being very much a Caird man himself, it was almost inevitable that Hegel's ideas should dominate a good deal of John White's thinking in those years. To the Philosophical Society he delivered a paper on Hegel that caused some stir.

"It was a most ambitious paper," he said afterwards. "I composed it when I had just left the Arts Faculty. In youth we are more confidently omniscient than in later years, when the mysteries of life deepen and our boundaries of knowledge widen. On looking over this lecture now, I feel glad I did not spend my life talking this jargon. I don't use the word 'jargon' in a derogatory sense. Science has its jargon, so has politics. Jargon saves time when your hearers know the jargon language. But it is not easily intelligible to the ordinary man, and it is mostly with ordinary men that one passes one's life."

Some of his speeches were on more practical subjects. At the University Union, he was asked to open a debate in favour of the thesis "that the Church is losing its hold on the people". He agreed on condition that the thesis was altered. Because he insisted, it was instead proposed, "that the Church is *at present* losing its hold on the people". It was a packed meeting. When word went round that John White was to lead in a debate, the students crowded in to enjoy the fireworks. And fireworks there were that night. He was well trounced by his critics, but fought back in his best style. He maintained that the Church was most certainly—*at present*—losing its hold on the people:

"The Church is not—*at present*—ready to meet the changing demands of the world in which science is creating a revolution in thought—a world that is being changed, too, by a great social movement. The world calls for something more than a religious faith that merely begins and ends with the individual life. The Church has a permanent side—and a changing side. The Church, in its faith to Him Who is the Rock of Ages, must be the same yesterday, today

13

and for ever. But there is also a law of adaptation that the Church must obey. The Church of three hundred years ago could not meet the needs of men and women in the nineteenth century. . . . As for the divisions in the Christian Church, here is a weakness you will see everywhere. I am of Paul, I of Apollos, and I of Cephas. It is not many men, many minds; it is many men and not a mind among them. And some governing mind is needed to show that the Church must unite to meet the spiritual need of all kinds of people. . . . The Church has lost its hold on the multitude. As for the fundamental truths, the dogmas of religion, the Church has failed to restate them in language that can be understood by the people of today."

John White challenged the Church because it had not welcomed the widening of the modern mind. Many scientific movements had been unheeded by the Church and were sometimes condemned as conducive to sheer materialism.

"People have been so charmed with the splendour of our new knowledge that, lacking guidance from the Church, they have allowed it to separate them from their former faith. True it is that science has been far from sympathetic with the Church, forgetting that the Church has to serve other provinces of life for which science has no message. Science has been too confident in its triumphs. Science has concluded that its discoveries are revealing absolute and final truth. But there will come a day when science and religious teaching will be harmonised. The reconciliation can be seen in some of our great scientists who have strong religious faith. The Church of tomorrow must—and will—readjust itself to the new world that is being ushered in. The hold that has weakened—at present—will again be strong."

As he looked back on that debate after many decades, John White added the comment that he was then a young man untroubled by any doubts: "I thought I had the wisdom of all the ages. But at least I had got hold of one thing. I was eager for the Church to regain its leadership in thought and action." This was to be a theme of his throughout all his life, and tied up with it in his fledgling speeches was an ideal that was to dominate and inspire him:

"A disunited, disorganised Church—a Christendom with hostile factions—cannot conquer the heart and mind of the world. Unity was never more urgent than at the present hour, *when the Church is at the beginning of one of the most searching trials it has ever undergone.* An irresistible stream of events is rushing us into a new Age. A like problem faced the Church with the coming of the printing-press— and again with the advent of the New Learning in the fifteenth and sixteenth centuries. . . . And in this world of ours it is only a re-united Church that can hold the people."

His notes for other university speeches show how again and again he spoke of the urgency of Church reunion: a foreshadowing of the great task to which he was one day to bend his energy.

Classes, examinations, debates, committee meetings: with these and a happy concourse of like activities, the Divinity terms raced by. With the coming of the final examinations, he realised that his student life was at an end. Gilmorehill would see him no longer; the high tower above the River Kelvin would cease to be the most familiar landmark in a little academic world. He had enjoyed his university days—enjoyed them more than he had thought possible when he had gone for the first time to sit at the feet of a professor. Now he was twenty-five: nine years of lecture-rooms and debates and tobacco-fragrant talks at midnight—a long tale of contemplative years for one who was by nature made for action and the dust of battle. Many had envied their fellow student because in mind and body his stature had been greater than theirs; because success had come to him, it seemed, without effort, because of his quick laughter, his continual high spirits, the glitter of his devastating wit. Only his more intimate friends had realised that, in the first six of those nine years, he had been on a quest of his own. He had been searching, often upon his knees, to find himself. And he had failed: failed utterly. But he had found something else. He has told, in a few tense words, what he discovered at the end of a long road. That meeting, that discovery, changed his life. "I met a MAN," he said. And in that meeting with Christ, his quest was ended. To God's work his strength was to be dedicated. And now, at the close of his last session in 1891, he was beginning the great adventure.

V

All that summer he worked as a student missionary in the parish of New Kilpatrick, and became assistant to the minister, Dr. J. W. King. The task specially allotted to him was to conduct the mission at Drum-chapel and Blairdardie in what were then gentle green uplands with little farms and cottages, between Bearsden and Clydebank. At Drumchapel, he preached in a "but and ben" hall at the end of a row of miners' cottages. In a short time, he seems to have been as popular among the villagers and countryfolk as he had been among his fellow students at the University. A minister who was there after he had left said: "I have heard an old parishioner describe what a fine sight it was to see the youthful minister come striding across the fields to Drumchapel on a Sunday morning to preach." It was agreed that he left his mark on Drumchapel, and his bent for efficiency soon came into play. The singing in the little building he found to be far from good: perhaps this was because he had to lead the praise himself. He has told of his chagrin one Sunday morning when he found that when he reached the end of the second line of a hymn he was singing a different tune from the one on which he had started. He must get an organ; that was essential. A copy of a circular dated 27th May 1892 is still in existence: "All acquainted with the mission admit that a small harmonium is a necessity and urge the purchase of one. The sum required is not more than £15. We are sending out 300 circulars, and so limit the subscription to one shilling." Commenting on the young minister's drive, one writer said: "This was John White's first scheme for raising money for the Church, and it was successful. The organ we bought served Drumchapel till 1911, and its canopy still stands above the vestry fireplace."

At the little mission station he began to find his feet as a preacher. In the pulpit, his approach to worship was evangelical. To save souls, comfort the distressed, and inspire the weary: this mandate he kept continually in front of him. He made an unusually strong impression on the members of the Presbytery of Dumbarton who examined him for licence, and Dr. King has left it on record that "John White possessed a singular power of influencing young minds". One of these young people was the minister's own daughter, Jessie M. King, who became a well-known artist. To her, he was always "Brother John" or "Big Brother", and she was to turn to him on all occasions when she needed help and comfort. Many years later, she wrote to him that she remembered a prayer he had offered up at New Kilpatrick: "And if, for us who dwell here, Thy Kingdom may never come in all its fullness and glory, may we at least be cheered by some rays of its rising dawn."

VI

John White was so thirled to his work that some of his family thought he was paying them scant attention; there were times when they wondered

The Young Probationer.

what was happening to him—or even whether he was well in health. When his mother took a house at Kirn near Dunoon, in the summer of 1892, his sister wrote to him: "Where have you got to? We have been expecting you down for some time, and when you did not come we expected a letter." His sister added: "The Gardners are down, and they stay not far from us." She felt sure that if anything would bring John to Kirn it was the proximity of that family. Mr. Gardner was a prosperous farmer and flesher—he had large contracts to supply meat to some of the big Atlantic liners—and at a social John White had met Margaret, the eldest daughter. There is no record of John White's reply to his sister's gentle bait: it was more than likely that, by this time, he was very well posted in the movements of Margaret Gardner, for they were wed by the autumn of the following year. She was a girl of quite unusual charm, happy and vivacious, wise beyond her years, with a gentle courage and firm faith that were to be a wellspring of inspiration to the young minister. In that same summer of 1892 there was talk of his going to The Barony as assistant to the famous Dr. John Marshall Lang, but he remained at New Kilpatrick till the turn of the year. The death of the minister of Shettleston parish created a vacancy there, and at the end of January 1893 John White was chosen from among seven candidates, and the call came to him.

To his great satisfaction this call was declared unanimous. He had spent nearly two strenuous years in New Kilpatrick, and he had continued to study, reading some Christian Ethics and much Church History. The grave yet radiant story of the Christian Church was never to lose its appeal to him for the rest of his days. There were moments when he toyed with the thought of serving the Church in the academic field. Indeed, at one point he did more than toy with it: he was persuaded to apply for the Chair of Church History at Glasgow. Professor Story, then Principal-Elect of the University, would have liked to see the young minister succeed him, and he recorded his opinion that he "never had a better student in the Church History classes—one who did all the work in a more thorough, intelligent and conscientious way—and he always showed his possession of a clear and powerful mind. . . ." John White felt at that time that it would be good to share his enthusiasm for Church History with younger minds—to inspire them, as he was inspired, by its splendours. But he was destined to be a maker of Church History rather than an exponent of it—and in a manner he little dreamed of when he accepted the call to the Parish of Shettleston.

JOHN WHITE

Long before he had reached the age of thirty, his name was to become familiar in religious communities and legal circles throughout Scotland. In the last decade of the nineteenth century, to mention John White to Scottish kirkfolk—particularly in the West country—was to bring to mind the "Shettleston Church Case" and to evoke the picture of a young minister who was fearless, high-spirited, a passionate defender of the rights of his congregation—and who triumphed in an almost miraculous way over vested interests. White of Shettleston became known as a bonny fighter. In the course of long-drawn-out battles, many names were to be hurled at him—young firebrand, a fomenter of trouble, even a thumping liar—but he cared not a jot. He knew he was in the right; he knew that strong forces were banded against him; and he drove ahead. Many a stout blow was to be given and taken before the end of a campaign which was to last for the whole period of his ministry in the parish.

Chapter II

THE SHETTLESTON CHURCH CASE

I

"We have a debt of gratitude which we owe to the forefathers of Shettleston folk who built this old kirk in which we worship, and we will honour that debt to the past by rearing a new fabric to the glory of God for the worship of many generations yet to be born."

THESE words, spoken by John White to his own people at what he called a private meeting of the congregation, were to throw light upon the work of many years to come, and their splendour was never to be tarnished even by disputes that were described at the time as worldly, odious, and warranted to bring into disrepute the work of extending God's kingdom.

Shettleston, now a part of greater Glasgow, was at the time of John White's advent a long straggling little town of rather dingy aspect beyond the eastern suburbs of the city. The parish included the hamlets of Old Shettleston, Middle Quarter, Eastmuir, and Sandyhills, as well as the greater part of the villages of Millerston and Hogganfield and nearly the whole of Tollcross. It was crossed by three main roads and two railways from Glasgow. It had a population of over ten thousand when he came to it, but, he recorded,

> "there were no trams or buses in 1893. One or two of us set ourselves to secure for our folk a share in the comforts of the city. We got horse buses as a great favour. Then we got horse trams. After some agitation, we even got street lighting. Last, but not least, we got pavements instead of mud walks so that the workers could get to their factories with dry feet. I can recall how all these efforts brought Shettleston to a consciousness of itself as a separate community."

Once it had been a place of weavers, but the clack of looms could no longer be heard at half-open cottage doors. In 1786, the Clyde Iron Works had been established by the side of the river, little more than a mile from Shettleston town, and many coal-pits were sunk in the neighbourhood.

It was a mixed community to which John White came to minister, and many of his members were colliers and farm-workers. The congregation was by no means an affluent one, although the stipend was considered good in those days—about six hundred pounds a year. The population was growing quickly; new houses were lining roads and lanes; and it seemed that here was a rich field for a man zealous to win souls and quicken the religious life of the community.

John White threw himself into the work with fine vigour, and his Communion Roll began to lengthen. The kirk was seated for barely eight hundred, and it was evident that soon the place would be too small. But there was a worse problem than that of accommodation. The building was condemned as insanitary; and the gallery, unduly large for the size of the kirk, was reported to be so unsafe that it might collapse, with a tragic outcome. Anxious to know exactly how the church could be repaired, the young minister took expert advice. The cost, he was told, would be out of all proportion to the value of the building. There was only one thing to be done. He must build another kirk. And in doing this, he put into motion a train of events that was to take him into both the ecclesiastical and civil courts and was to cause him, as he sadly recorded, "many years of constant worry and anxiety".

II

He had not been long in Shettleston before he learned that the decay in the fabric of the church had already been discussed in the Presbytery of Glasgow. In 1886, the Presbytery had been warned that it must soon be rebuilt. But the question of who must bear the burden of the cost had never been settled. Counsel's opinion had been taken; the Procurator of the Church, Mr. William Mackintosh, later Lord Kyllachy, had said that in his view the heritors were liable to contribute to the expense of building a new church for Shettleston parish when such had to be built. The heritors in Scotland, it may here be said, are the "landholders who are liable to public burdens". At that time they included feuars, who hold land in perpetuity but pay feu-duty therefor to a feudal superior. There had been good reason why the Presbytery had taken Counsel's opinion, for the problem of responsibility had ancient roots.

Shettleston had originally been part of The Barony parish, and many of the folk at its south-eastern end had felt themselves to be "disadvantage-ously situate for the means of Grace" because of the distance they had to travel to The Barony kirk—and in the middle of the eighteenth century many roads in winter were often no better than impassable quagmires. It was therefore decided that a preaching station should be built in Shettleston, and a subscription list was opened. A site for a new church at the side of the road that ran eastward out of the village was given by the proprietors of Budhill, and the only stipulation made by James and George Reston was that they be granted a pew in the kirk and a lair in the kirkyard. The Bogle family, also landowners in the district, were among the chief supporters; and as a mark of gratitude, the crest of the Bogles—a three-masted ship in full rig—was duly displayed on the spire of the church.

Begun in 1751, the church had stone walls two and a half feet thick, and in the front were three tall romanesque windows: it was a forthright and not uncomely specimen of eighteenth-century architecture. In 1788, Glasgow Presbytery constituted the church a Chapel of Ease under its parent, The Barony. Immediately after the Disruption, the Graham Act gave Parliamentary sanction to the dividing up of very large parishes. As the population of The Barony parish numbered one hundred and twenty thousand, it came well within the scope of this Act, and Shettleston was the first parish in Scotland to be proposed for disjunction. Thus it was that

> "in 1847 it was decerned and ordained that the district of Shettleston should be disjoined and erected into a new and distinct parish, and that the inhabitants of the district should repair to the church of Shettleston as their proper parish church for hearing the Word of God, receiving the sacraments and partaking in all other public acts of divine worship, and subject themselves to the minister of the said church and parish of Shettleston as proper parishioners thereof, in all time coming."

The decree provided for a constitution which included both sections of the Graham Act, and made Shettleston a parish *quoad omnia*. The church was given some of The Barony endowments, and its managers were entitled to levy seat-rents. The salient point was that the decree relieved the heritors in the new parish of their responsibilities to The Barony but did not saddle them with any responsibilities for the fabric of the church already built at Shettleston. That was a burden that rested only on the church managers.

Had Shettleston been merely a *quoad sacra*, the heritors would not even have had any responsibility for the building of a new church; but John White had before him the opinion of an eminent lawyer that the *quoad omnia* character was predominant and it had come under the *quoad sacra* section of the Graham Act merely as an added privilege. He did not want to appeal to the heritors for a single penny and he was anxious to avoid trouble of any kind. At a meeting of the members and adherents of his congregation, he said: "We have met as Christians earnest to do our best in a quiet peaceful and kindly way free from all heat and acerbity, for the welfare of God's people." Promises of money flowed in until he was sure of at least twelve hundred pounds. For a congregation drawn from a community largely composed of colliers and farm-workers, this was not illiberal, and many gave promises of further support, so that the minister thought he would be able to count on about three thousand pounds. But it was soon apparent to him that he would be laying a burden upon his flock from which they would be relieved only after a long struggle. The estimated cost of building a church large enough for his increasing membership was some nine or ten thousand pounds, and there was a wide gap between this sum and the amount he felt the kirk session could raise even with help from Endowments and Trust Funds. Reluctantly he decided to apply to the main section of the heritors, the proprietors of land in the parish.

He made the approach in as friendly a way as he could. At a meeting held in February 1895 the heritors expressed interest in the project; but they pointed out that they could do nothing legally without bringing in what was termed the "real-rent" heritors, which included the feuars of land as distinct from the "valued-rent" heritors. They asked John White to lay his scheme before a meeting of both classes of heritors, and this was held on 12th June. It was then that the minister asked the heritors to contribute in the neighbourhood of one-third of the cost of building a new church. The clerk to the heritors put before them "a statement bearing on their liability in the peculiar circumstances of the parish and recommended that they should raise a third of the money required, as suggested by the Minister of Shettleston". The heritors decided to obtain a report on their own behalf from an architect on the condition of the old church, and the meeting was adjourned for three weeks.

These were fateful weeks for the young minister's project. Two days before the meeting was due, a public protest was organised, and feuars and ratepayers crowded into the Hill Street Hall on 1st July to hear what might be said against the proposal of the minister and his kirk session.

By the time the various speakers had had their say it was passed almost unanimously that "this meeting of heritors, feuars and other ratepayers in Shettleston protest against the proposed tax to be levied on us for the purpose of building a new church for the people worshipping in Shettleston Parish Church on the grounds that we believe it to be illegal as per the constitution of the said Parish Church". It was maintained that the congregation was well able to pay for a new church, and the meeting recommended "the Rev. John White and his people to follow the example of the Rev. Dr. Marshall Lang of The Barony Church, in similar circumstances, and appeal to the liberality of the general public". The atmosphere of the adjourned meeting of heritors on 3rd July was very different from that of the meeting three weeks before. Far from there being any friendly interest in the project, John White found hostility on almost all sides. The clerk to the heritors placed before them the architects' report which had been made at their bidding.

Messrs. Steel and Balfour said that to repair the church would be a formidable undertaking:

> "The back wall must come down, the roof be taken away, the building entirely gutted, the area excavated and run in with asphalt; new flooring, joists, modern seats, choir and pulpit arrangements, put in; new gallery and seating installed; also new roof, a proper system of heating and ventilation, and if possible more space to take in the rooms and offices belonging to a church."

They pointed out that this would reduce the seating accommodation considerably, and they summed up that it would be "unwise to deal with the old buildings at all, which, in our opinion, seem to have served their day and generation".

This report, which amply confirmed the previous survey obtained by John White, seemed to leave only one course open—to build a new church. But the minds of the majority of the heritors had already been made up. There was a good deal of talk, but no real discussion. One speaker repeated what had been said at the protest meeting two days before, that if the Rev. John White wanted a new church let him pass round the hat for public contributions.

> "When Moses built the Tabernacle in the wilderness, he asked for a free will offering from the Children of Israel, and so freely was the response given that he had to issue another proclamation not to bring any more. It would be a good thing for the Rev. Mr. White and his

session to try the experiment in Shettleston. He sometimes preaches from Moses; it might be a good thing for him to act from Moses."

A proposal that a new church should be built was rejected by almost three-quarters of those present. Many a young minister would have left that meeting in great depression; but John White, with his resilient spirit, fought back without delay. He sat down and penned a pamphlet which was rapidly printed by James Clark of Glasgow and was distributed to all whom it might concern. The first three paragraphs ran as follows:

"A Disestablishment stratagem has been carried out in our midst. An attack on the Church of Scotland has been made under cover of an organised opposition to the new church in Shettleston.

"To expose the artful dodge, as well as to state the facts of the case, will be interesting and instructive.

"The question has been asked, who are liable to be assessed for the erection of a Parish Church? And the uncertainty that existed in the minds of some has been increased by confusing and fallacious answers."

John White pointed out that only the heritors were liable to erect and maintain ecclesiastical buildings. "But unfortunately," he added, "it has become a habit of some to play on the hopes and fears of those who are unacquainted with the law on this subject." Many ordinary ratepayers had attended the protest meeting under the impression that they would be forced to contribute to the building of a new church. The protest was made in a ferment of indignation at a burden which ratepayers could never have been legally asked to shoulder. The John White pamphlet, issued from The Manse of Shettleston on 5th July 1895, was a hard-hitting declaration. In his accusation that there had been a deliberately organised manœuvre, he was but adding one more voice to the clamour of complaint which had for many years been raised by clergymen and laymen of the Church of Scotland.

III

To bring into a correct perspective the dispute which became known as the Shettleston Church Case, it is necessary to understand how the mention of the word "Disestablishment" was apt to touch off a train of gunpowder. During the previous twenty years, the battles which had been fought round this matter had been too many to count. Immediately after the Disruption of 1843, there had been no talk of disestablishment in the courts of the newly formed Free Church of Scotland. That Church had not left the parent body because of any conscientious objection to Establishment being an appropriate expression of the principle of National Recognition of Religion: on the contrary, her members had left on the ground that the State had interfered in spiritual matters where by Statute it had no jurisdiction. But the passing of the years brought great changes; a new generation grew up to whom Establishment was not an essential in a Christian country; and by 1877, the General Assembly of the Free Church officially declared its support of Disestablishment. In dissenting Presbyterian Churches in Scotland, this became something like a war-cry —and the cry echoed through the House of Commons when an ill-contrived Bill for the Disestablishment and Disendowment of the Church of Scotland was introduced in 1886 by Mr. J. R. Dick Peddie, a Scottish member. But this Bill made little progress in Mr. Gladstone's short-lived Liberal Government. Sir Charles Cameron's Disestablishment Bill of 1893 had the support of the leaders of the Free Church; but this Bill too came to nothing.

A straight fight between the Churches on a plain issue would have been one thing; but unfortunately the Disestablishment cause had become a weapon in the hands of many whose interest in the Church in Scotland was slight. Principal Tulloch of St. Andrews University, himself a strong Liberal, had deplored the manner in which "sectarian and dogmatic forces" had used Disestablishment in Scotland as the thin end of the wedge which had nothing whatever to do with the Scottish Church.

"The chief home of these forces is in England," he said. "The Church of England is the real object of offence. The money which promotes the agitation in Scotland comes almost all from England, and is given by men or societies who hate the English Church for its social privileges and the very largeness of the power which it exercises. They think comparatively little of the Church of Scotland, save as a means for the overthrow of the more powerful institution."

Worse still, Disestablishment in Scotland later on became a pawn in a political party game where it was difficult to discern where statesmanship ended and chicanery began. In the popular ferment over Irish Home Rule, the Liberal Party had been split. In 1887, the leader of the Unionist section of that party denounced the Home Rulers for using the promise of Scottish Church Disestablishment as a bait to capture votes:

"I do not think it is possible to call to mind anything so cynical as the manner in which these questions of great national and imperial importance, as well as of supreme local interest, were put up the other day for auction to the highest bidder. . . . In Scotland, to tell conscientious advocates of Disestablishment that the settlement of their question shall depend, not upon the merits of the case, but upon the amount of support which Scotland can be prevailed upon to bring to the cause of Home Rule in Ireland—what is that but the holding out of a bribe?"

On Scottish Disestablishment, Mr. Gladstone himself had been "sitting on the fence and with great difficulty preserving his balance", as his enemies put it, or "had been giving the matter long and conscientious thought", as his friends preferred to describe it. In the correspondence of Dr. John Brown, we find that in 1877 Mr. Gladstone was writing to ask the worthy author of *Rab and His Friends* whether he had made up his mind about the Disestablishment of the Church of Scotland: if so, Mr. Gladstone said, he was anxious to have the Doctor's advice on the matter. In the end Mr. Gladstone did "declare for Disestablishment", and when he became Prime Minister again in 1892 it seemed to many of the disestablishers that the day was as good as won. Hopes were raised still further when he gave his official blessing to the Cameron Bill. But another storm blew up over Irish Home Rule, which had become almost an obsession with the Grand Old Man—he was over eighty-three when he had taken office for this the last time—and the Bill never became law. The Gladstonian Liberals received their *coup de grâce* in the election of 1895, and a Tory government took office.

The results of this election had been announced just in time for the protest meeting against John White to be organised at Shettleston. The advent of the Tories relieved the Church of Scotland of all anxiety that a Disestablishment Bill could be passed through Parliament for some time to come. Thus the Shettleston protest meeting was held in the midst of political turmoil. John White stated in his pamphlet that popular feeling had been whipped up by Disestablishment zealots. Now that the results of the election had for them darkened the political horizon, there would still be opportunities of impeding the normal processes of the law and either relieving the heritors of their obligations or, if there was no loophole, acting generally as dog in the manger. John White concluded:

"This disguised attempt to attack the Church of Scotland, by giving a local colour to the question of disestablishment, is, however, too patent to succeed, and will doubtlessly drive many to reconsider their connection with a Disestablishment party which can adopt such tactics."

It was in a much calmer frame of mind that he met his parishioners at a congregational meeting. He pointed out that there had never been any question of forcing an assessment on the heritors, and he was only asking a third of their legal obligation. "I have been anxious to have this question decided definitely—gently but firmly—in as just and as amicable a fashion as possible." But nobody could blink the fact that a very different spirit now existed from that which had been shown at the first meeting of heritors when they had expressed a friendly interest in the young minister's proposal.

IV

The breach between heritors and congregation widened during the autumn and winter, and early in the new year the heritors met in the church to deliberate upon a petition which John White had been forced to present to the Presbytery of Glasgow "craving them to ordain that the Parish Church of Shettleston be condemned as unsafe for public worship and that a new church be built according to such plans as might be approved by the Presbytery". At this meeting, two new architects employed by the heritors reported that the church could be put into a proper state of repair at a cost of six hundred and fifty pounds. Here was a flat contradiction of the survey made at the instance of the heritors themselves in the previous summer. One heritor declared that they had no intention of allowing themselves to be taxed merely to gratify the vanity of the minister.

"Of course it may be difficult," he went on, "to teach them Christian liberality, for I am sorry to say the Reverend Mr. White seems to have a low opinion of the liberality of his members. When he said that even Moses could not build a Tabernacle in Shettleston, I do not know whether he was more disparaging to Moses or to his own congregation. However, I think it will be safe to leave the Reverend Mr. White meditating among the tombs until a Joshua arises to lead the people to the erection of a new church."

Another speaker described John White as "a young man with large ideas who wanted not a church but a cathedral". A committee was formed and given full power "to take such legal steps as may in their judgment be necessary to vindicate the contention of the heritors that they are not liable for the maintenance and repair, or for the renewal and rebuilding, of the Parish Church, and to prevent the present church being condemned and a new church being erected at the cost of the heritors". Before the heritors dispersed, they were comforted by the assurance of one of their number that their two new architects "could go into any court of law and simply knock into a cocked hat anyone who offered an opinion contrary to theirs about the structural condition of Shettleston kirk".

From the start, however, a group of heritors had been anxious to come to a friendly settlement with John White and his congregation. Deploring the trend things had taken, they had formed themselves into a Conciliation Committee. They had held meetings with the minister, kirk session and managers, and came to a provisional agreement, of which the following was the first of fourteen clauses:

> "That the Heritors shall assess themselves in the sum of £3600 sterling as their contribution towards the cost of building a new Church, including Heating Apparatus, Walls, value of new Site, Seating Fittings, and necessary Offices and Furnishings, and all incidental expenditure, and that the Kirk Session and Managers for the Congregation shall accept the same in full payment of all claims against the Heritors in connection with the present rebuilding."

This draft was laid before the heritors by the Conciliation Committee. Sir David Carrick Buchanan pressed his fellow heritors to agree to it, saying that they would be very foolish indeed to throw away the chance of getting a new church for £3600. He was convinced that they were, in law, liable for the whole cost of a new church, whereas this draft agreement reduced their liability to less than half. But a majority of the heritors rejected the proposal. The minister was present at this meeting, and he said he would gladly adjourn with representatives of both committees in the hope of coming to an agreement, but the heritors rejected this suggestion also. The words of Sir David and others had, however, shaken their confidence about their legal position. The committee which they had formed to protect their interests was reappointed, but its terms of reference had one notable change: "If an order for rebuilding is pronounced, the Committee will see that no greater burden is placed upon the heritors than is necessary to fulfil the requirements of the law." To their dismay, on 18th February 1896, the Presbytery did ordain that the heritors pull down the old church at Shettleston and build a new one.

Much was to happen before the foundation stone could be laid. Mr. William Borland, Writer, the eminent and ingenious Glasgow lawyer who represented the heritors, served his clients well, and every stumbling-block that could be legally created was placed in the path of his opponents. Mr. J. L. Gemmill, Writer, served the minister and kirk session equally well and tried to press matters to a conclusion. Meanwhile, the Concili-ation Committee did not relax its efforts to close the breach between the majority of heritors and the minister and congregation. At last, on the first day of June 1897, the whole dispute came into open court.

V

The heritors had already applied to the Sheriff-Substitute "praying the Court to recall or alter the ordinance of the Reverend the Presbytery of Glasgow", and had failed. Now John White and his kirk session and managers were obliged to raise an action to compel the heritors to take down and rebuild the church. The case had wide publicity in many newspapers. It stirred up much interest not only in Scotland but south of the Border, and the London press took it up. The enterprising editor of the newly established *Daily Mail*, then fighting hard to build its circulation, picked upon the Shettleston Case as "a striking object lesson showing how people of all denominations are fleeced for the upkeep of the Established Church". The newspaper had, of course, a political axe to grind, and it was ground with much noise and a great shower of sparks. Entitled "The Pauper Kirk", one leading article ran:

> "The Established Church does not pay for its own buildings, but makes other churches pay. The law gives it the power and it exacts its pound of flesh, without shame and without compunction. It is quartered like a pauper on the people, and it demands its dole, though its pockets may be full. . . . Legality there is of course in this robbery of the public by a privileged sect; but where is the morality which should be an essential part of religion?"

The case was tried before Sheriff Strachan and some of the evidence was of so macabre a kind that it might have formed part of a gruesome story by Edgar Allan Poe. The County Medical Officer of Health stated that the known graves of the kirkyard came within less than five yards of the church wall and some were probably nearer than that, while a number of the coffins were only two feet six inches from the surface of the ground. He spoke of the air being polluted by decomposing remains in the churchyard, for in the loamy soil it took ten or eleven years for a body to dissolve. The stone of the church building was porous and so drew up damp from the soil. The ventilation was defective, and the great quantity of dry-rot fungus was most unhealthy, particularly for children. There was no drainage, and water had for many years seeped into the foundations of the building. Other expert evidence was given to the effect that the front wall was cracked, the back wall was in serious structural condition with an outward bulge; and as for the gallery, it was hanging together by nails, and the timbers were rotten. Iron pillars had been put up to support the roof, but that was sagging and it was only a matter of time before it would fall in. The cubic air space per person, if the church were well filled, was less than a quarter of what was necessary. If the church were to be repaired, the only woodwork that could be utilised in the new building would be the doors of the pews. The vestry, nearly twenty-five yards distant from the church, was damp and dilapidated. The proceedings were evidently becoming so oppressive that the Sheriff decided to liven them up with a touch of facetiousness. When one witness said there was no adequate heating apparatus, His Lordship remarked that "it was not customary in old Scottish churches to have a heating apparatus: the preaching kept folk warm".

The case, which had opened on 1st June, did not come to an end until the second week in August. Sheriff Strachan declared that "nothing could be more unsatisfactory than the voluminous evidence that had now been piled up in this case". He had heard the reports of no less than twenty experts, including those of architects employed by the heritors, who had given a comparatively favourable report about the state of the church.

"I have never known," said the Sheriff, "a more striking instance of the unreliability of expert evidence. It would be very surprising, if it were not so common, to see the extent to which men of high character and ability can, when acting as experts, entertain and express the most conflicting and irreconcilable opinions regarding matters with which they must be familiar in their own everyday experience."

Sheriff Strachan had no hesitation in pronouncing that "in accordance with the law as at present existing it is inexpedient to repair the church, and that a new edifice must be erected". In a leading article, the *Glasgow Herald* remarked that "any person who read with care even the evidence of the experts employed by the heritors themselves might well be surprised that they ever allowed the case to go into Court at all". When the verdict was given for John White and his kirk session and managers, the *Daily Mail* made a political point: "There is but one small consolation in this matter, and that is that the sectarian favouritism and injustice of the law as demonstrated by the Shettleston case will increase the majority of the Scottish people who are convinced of the equity, the wisdom, and the need of Disestablishment."

VI

However near the truth John White may have been in his belief that the dispute had been started and was largely being sustained from a political motive, it is certain that the fight was waged by the heritors with an ardent zeal. No doubt this ardour had led them to take the step which was, in the event, to be heavily to their disadvantage. When they had had the chance of shedding a large part of their responsibilities, as John White proposed, by paying one-third of the cost of a new church, the warmth of their indignation had caused them to throw it away. They had a bitter pill to swallow when Sheriff Strachan ordered them to pay the full cost of a new church. Thereafter, they fought a strenuous rearguard action as the young minister advanced and captured one position after another.

The heritors tried to quibble about the question of a site for the new church. They argued that the decision of the Presbytery that they must take down the old church and rebuild it, without any reference to the site, implied that it must be rebuilt *on the old site*. They knew very well that this would be contested by John White and his congregation, but they pressed home their point with all possible ingenuity. Mr. Borland argued their case adroitly in front of the Sheriff, and again there was a cloud of witnesses on both sides. When the last witness had left the Court, Mr. Borland said with some sarcasm:

"My Lord, there is another witness the minister has not called. Are you aware that he has within the sacred precincts of this Court the Shettleston grave-digger as a witness?"

"The grave-digger!" exclaimed the Sheriff. "Why a grave-digger, Mr. White—and why have you not called him?"

John White's retort came in a flash: "I am keeping the grave-digger, my Lord, until Mr. Borland's case is presented, in order that it may have a decent burial."

31

The case for the heritors was buried by the Sheriff himself, whose patience was soon put to the test by a war that seemed to have no end. The heritors disputed the size of church that John White had asked for. He had said it must have seating for twelve hundred. The only law on this point was that a parish church should be capable of seating two-thirds of the "examinable persons in the parish"—i.e. persons not under twelve years of age. The heritors' lawyer retorted that this law had been formulated at the end of the eighteenth century when the population was small, and with a wry smile he added that if the Rev. Mr. White chose to rely on that law, the new church would have to seat more than seven thousand. But, since the actual church membership was then one thousand, he maintained that if the heritors built a church large enough to accommodate that number they were doing very well; a possible increase in the membership was not their concern.

All through the winter and the following year (1898) objections were raised and countered. It was not until 14th February 1899 that Sheriff Strachan could issue an interlocutor on the site for the new church. Mr. Bell, an architect from Glasgow, functioning as Judicial Reporter to the Court, repeated what had so often been stated, that the old site was unsuitable, and the site he recommended was some five or six hundred yards to the south. At last, four years after the dispute had started, it looked as if the building of the new church was to begin. The Sheriff was forced to pronounce "an order on the heritors for the production of the necessary plans of the church". But it would not have required a cynic to prophesy that, when the plans were at last delivered, the proposed church would be found by the Court to be inadequate in many ways. The area was too small to give adequate seating accommodation for twelve hundred people. The entrance vestibule was cramped; the stairs to the galleries were badly planned; there was no room allowed for an organ and insufficient room for the choir; the church tower was described as a miserable affair; and "externally the design is cheap looking and quite unsuitable for such an important building". The Judicial Reporter gave it as his considered opinion that the heritors had restricted the architect in his work. Back went the plans for revision. The Sheriff was moved to say in open court that he had great sympathy for John White and his congregation.

And still no detailed specifications were forthcoming; no plan of the road giving access to the church. In November the Sheriff ordained that the heritors must within six weeks lodge these specifications and produce

During his Shettleston ministry John White, on his horse
Victor, was a familiar figure in the remote parts of his large
parish.

a road plan. Still manœuvring for delay, the heritors maintained that the Sheriff had not the power to order them to submit a plan of the road: but once again they failed to gain their point. In January 1900, there was another dispute about the quarries from which the stone must be got, whether from Ballochmyle or Locherbriggs or the Gatelaw Bridge Quarries; there was trouble about the slates, whether they should be green or West Highland. On 8th February 1900, Sheriff Strachan at last approved of the site and the plans and specifications, and ordered the heritors to have the new church built and "ready to be open for public worship on or before the first day of June 1901". The heritors protested against a time limit being placed upon them, but once more they were overruled. In the middle of March, John White announced to his people that he hoped that the building of the new church would begin in a few weeks' time.

> "The delay has been long continued," he said, "and one has to go back to the tenth century to find a parallel to the present unwillingness to build a new church—and to the attempt to build a church devoid of architectural features. At that period, a belief prevailed concerning the immediate revelation of anti-Christ and the approaching end of the world, with the result that there was an unwillingness to build new churches or to restore those that were old and dilapidated. Whatever be the eschatological beliefs of the present heritors, it has now been decided by an impartial judge that a church to seat twelve hundred, a church of good architecture, must be erected and ready by 1st June for public worship."

VII

The church was not, in fact, open for public worship on 1st June 1901. Nor was it open by June of the following year. Even in November 1902 John White was complaining to the Sheriff that the work was not finished nor the road made up. Sheriff Strachan ordained that all must be ready on or before 20th December and the road completed. He stated that, as the remaining work could be done within a matter of ten days, it was obvious that the heritors were purposely delaying it because they did not wish to have the church open for public worship, and he added: "No ulterior motive can entitle the heritors either to thwart or delay the completion of the church in terms of the order of the Court." He rejected the plea that it could not be open until a current dispute regarding the allocation of seats was settled. Whoever had the power to allocate seats would of course be in control of a considerable revenue.

The dispute about the church sittings went before Sheriff Scott Moncrieff. His pronouncement was that, since the heritors had built the church, they must control the seat-letting according to the usual custom. Representing the minister and congregation, Mr. Gemmill pointed out that the number of heritors was about seven hundred, and this would allow for only a fraction more than one sitting to each heritor. He pressed for an arrangement suitable to everyone. One-tenth of the seats was usually allotted for the free use of poor folk, and he suggested that a certain number be made available for the heritors and the remainder to be under the supervision of the kirk session or managers, with the seat-rents used by them to relieve the heritors of the burden of maintaining the fabric of the church. His suggestions were not acceptable to the heritors, and the church continued to stand empty.

It had been ready for use in December 1902: and by June 1903 the minister and congregation were still pressing for it to be opened for public worship. In the last seat-letting of the old church, applications for four hundred seats had had to be held over because of the lack of room. The Presbytery ordered the heritors to throw the church open, but they appealed to the Synod, and when the minister took the matter to the civil court, Sheriff Scott Moncrieff said:

> "The state of affairs in the parish of Shettleston is much to be deplored. . . . If the object of the heritors is to prevent unseemly wrangling over the sittings in the future, I question the wisdom of the course they are pursuing. It is clear that heritors cannot keep a church closed for an indefinite period."

At the beginning of July, when the matter was again taken to court, Sheriff Strachan ordained the heritors to deliver the keys of the new church to the beadle. This was hailed by all, except perhaps the heritors, as the final victory for the minister and his congregation. The press joined in the paean of triumph. In a leading article under the title "The Heritor Obstructionist" one newspaper referred to "the stubborn and unreasoning temper of the parties to the dispute" and said:

> "The contention of the heritors that a new church ready for occupancy, and urgently required, should not be opened because the sittings have not been allocated, would not be seriously maintained by these gentlemen, as individuals presumably endowed with ordinary

commonsense. But heritors, engaged in a deadly feud with the Session and Minister, will take up any position which promises good 'cover', no matter how absurd."

As to the dispute among the heritors themselves about the allocation of seats, the leader writer went on to say that

"even in their present temper the heritors will scarcely attempt to capture the best seats by physical force and drive out the intruders by a well-directed fire of hassocks and hymn-books. Shettleston folk," the writer concluded, "will be early at the door of the new kirk next Sunday. The 24th Psalm, from the 7th verse, will be specially appropriate to the occasion: and no doubt the minister will preach an eloquent sermon upon the text, *Knock and it shall be opened unto you*."

VIII

Over the years, some had watched the delays and divagations of this case in sorrow; some had followed it in anger; some had regarded with cynical mirth a dusty battle fought over a Christian place of worship. Many wondered if the heritors would try still further to postpone the opening of the church. At any rate, those who were confident that it would at last be opened on Sunday, 12th July, were disappointed; for the heritors appealed to the Lord Ordinary on Teinds against the court order to hand over the keys, and firmly retained possession of them. The doors remained locked on 12th July and the Shettleston congregation worshipped in the old church.

On behalf of John White and his flock, Mr. Gemmill applied to the Sheriff for *interim* possession of the new church. On 30th July Sheriff Strachan gave the heritors three days, and three days only, to deliver the keys to Thomas Edwards the beadle—and if they failed to do so, officers of the court must "make the doors of said church open and patent in order that it may be used by the minister and inhabitants". The Sheriff added in a Note to his interlocutor:

"Speaking from an intimate knowledge of the circumstances, I said that the necessity for the opening of the church was of a clamant character, and I expressed surprise that the heritors should compel the parishioners to worship in an old musty and unhealthy building, while a new church was standing empty. The answer of the heritors to this was the presenting of a petition to the Lord Ordinary on Teinds, which might hang up the proceedings and exclude the parishioners from the church until at least the month of November. This I regard as a somewhat ungracious act on the part of a public body dealing with a matter from which all personal feeling should have been excluded."

It was wryly remarked that the words "ungracious act" constituted the most magnificent piece of understatement made throughout the entire Shettleston Case.

The heritors were advised by their law agent to hand over the keys, which they did. But the transfer of the keys to the beadle was by no means the end of the trouble. In May 1904, Sheriff Strachan was hearing arguments about legal expenses incurred over the years by both parties. This phase of the dispute also ended in John White's favour, for it was ruled that the heritors must shoulder nearly the whole of that immense burden of legal costs. For the church building alone they had to meet bills amounting to £11,158—and had also to pay for the ground on which it was erected. But for the minister and his congregation, the thing that mattered most was that, on the morning of Sunday, 9th August 1903, the doors of the new church had indeed been unlocked and thrown open by the beadle, and divine service for the first time had been held within its doors.

Some who took part in that service recalled the words spoken by John White so many years before, when they had united in an access of spontaneous enthusiasm to follow him in his fine ideal—"We have a debt of gratitude which we owe to the forefathers of Shettleston folk who built this old kirk in which we worship, and we will honour that debt to the past by rearing a new fabric to the glory of God for the worship of many generations yet to be born."

A silent procession of folk followed the minister from the old church to worship for the first time in the new. The opening ceremony was a deeply moving service which the minister himself conducted. Those who thought that a joyful flourish of trumpets would be appropriate were disappointed. For the last thing John White wanted was the faintest hint of any glorying in the defeat the heritors had suffered in the courts of the Church and the State. His policy throughout had been: "Peace if possible in God's name—but if you are forced to fight, fight hard." There were no words but those of peace spoken from the pulpit on that tranquil Sunday morning in August. John White had come home from a spell of convalescence at Crieff to open his new church with as little display as possible. In the Session Records there is not even a special minute about an event so important in the history of the parish. Indeed, it is mentioned only in a terse parenthesis: "It was agreed to continue the three services in the New Parish Church (*which was opened by the Rev. John White M.A. Moderator on the 9th August* 1903) until the Communion."

It might be said that John White's decision to open his new kirk in the way he did was typical of the man: for in him there never had been, and never was to be, any of the corroding acid of venom or resentment. A year after the opening of the new church he uttered these words in public: "There are few of my six hundred heritors with whom I am not today in as close terms of friendship as I was at first, and in some cases our mutual respect has been strengthened."

The Shettleston Case left its mark in more than one way on John White. Under its impact he matured in worldly wisdom. It is true that he had not rubbed shoulders with his fellows at the University for nine years without learning something of character development, and he had acquired the knack of summing a man up quickly. But the Shettleston Church Case, with all its intrigue and frustration, gave him a harsh experience of some strange aspects of human nature, how envy and ill-feeling can be like a fire that parches the soul, how good men under ungoverned and ungenerous impulses can fall into courses of action far below their own highest standard. Moreover, the Shettleston Case made him an ecclesiastical lawyer. He was asked in confidence to guide the University Court of St. Andrews on a situation which had elements similar to that in Shettleston; and in after years, from time to time, he was answering letters from ministers who sought his advice because, as they said, they were about to approach their heritors, and there was some point on which he would be able to give expert counsel. This knowledge of Church law and procedure was to serve him well when he came to direct policy and shape events in those great projects of the Church with which his name was to be associated.

Chapter III

THE MAN AND THE PARISH

I

IT might seem to have been quite impossible that a young minister, deeply involved as he was in harassing litigation, could have been able to throw himself with full energy into his day-to-day pastoral work: yet, most providentially, that is what he was able to do.

In accepting the call to Shettleston, he had no illusions about the task he was taking up. A good deal more than the fabric and furnishing of the kirk was in a poor state. His predecessor, who had been in the parish for twenty years, had been in failing health long before his death, and there had been a lack of vitality in some departments of the church life. The session clerk told him frankly that things were "in a backward state": but both the kirk session and members of the congregation were to learn that, in the clerk's own words, "Mr. White meant business, and before he had been a year in the parish he had appointed two missionaries, and meetings were begun in kitchens and rooms." Recalling his earliest days in Shettleston, a member of another church described how his mother recalled John White's visit to her:

"When she opened the door to his knock, he said, 'Will you receive the visit of a clergyman?' 'With pleasure,' said my mother, 'will you come in?' He then said, 'I am the new parish minister, and I am visiting every house in the parish to find if every family in it has a church connection.' My mother told him that we sat under Mr. Allan at the Carntyne Free Church. He then said, 'You are in good hands, and I'll not be back again.' My mother asked him if he would take a cup of tea. He said he had been out all morning and a cup would be most acceptable. His later actions in the parish provoked some criticism of the Reverend gentleman, but my mother would never listen to a word of it."

When he visited the outlying parts of his parish in earlier years he went on horseback, and folk became accustomed to see the minister's mount, Victor, tied up outside a house. Faithful pastoral visitation had a good deal to do with the lengthening of the Communion Roll. The church became so crowded in the morning that he had to hold an additional service immediately afterwards. He had not been two years in the parish when it was evident that he needed the help of an assistant. Between 1893 and 1898 he doubled the membership.

II

A few months after he had been installed in the manse at Shettleston, John White had married Margaret Gardner of Muirpark. The young bride had at once taken her share—often more than her share—in the work of the church. With a candour that was seasoned by gentle humour, she gave advice which her husband quickly learned to value. She made it her special task to provide for him a home-life where he could—although he seldom would—forget the travails of the day. A colleague of his wrote to him: "May I say that my admiration for your dear partner has grown with the months. She is truly a fellow-labourer in the Lord who needeth not to be ashamed. Would that all the wives of ministers were such helpmeets!"

She did much to put new life into the Church Guild, which he counted a powerhouse of good. Every member of it, he insisted, must be eager to work; and throughout his entire ministry in the parish it was to support him at every turn—and was indeed to become one of the largest in the Church of Scotland. He was a supporter of the Boys' Brigade, and a Shettleston company soon was flourishing. With enthusiasm he fostered the Literary Society, and did all he could to improve the quality of lectures and discussions, for he knew how these would help to open new vistas to young folk eager to improve themselves. During his years at Shettleston he went abroad several times and visited Germany, Greece Turkey, Palestine, Egypt, Canada, and the United States. On these journeys it was his practice to jot down each night what he had seen and heard, and his notebooks were the basis of informative lectures delivered to his folk at Shettleston. Some who came to his lectures had joined the new socialist party, and he did nothing to dissuade them. He preferred to pass on the advice of Professor Edward Caird: "Think it out for yourselves." Although he was a stout Tory all his life, he could never have been called a bigoted one, and when several of his young men later became socialist Members of Parliament he was proud of them. After the General Election at which one or two of them had won Labour seats, he was at an evening meeting and he spoke to a friend about them: "I see from the paper they're leaving for London on the night train. I wish I could get away from here and run down to the Central Station to wish my laddies godspeed."

Another of the young men who attended the lectures was to become Lord Provost of Glasgow. More than a quarter of a century later he wrote to John White:

"If you only knew the large part you played in the formation of my character you would be proud indeed. I was born of very poor but thrifty parents who shared their all with a family of six. This did not rise above a Board School education, which for me finished before I was twelve years of age. I sacrificed a good deal to train as an engineer, and when I could from my own earnings pay for a little more education it had to be on the technical side of my business. And this is where you come in. Your sermons and your Sunday evening lectures were to me a great general education, from which I received much encouragement and lasting benefit. Today I am Lord Provost of what is to me the most wonderful city in the world; I control some of the largest concerns in this country, and to you, sir, I am greatly indebted, as I feel that your teaching and encouragement has done much to make me what I am. I thank you for all you have been to me in the past."

III

During the years when the Shettleston Church Case was being argued and fought, the Communion Roll continued to lengthen, and in the end the session clerk was able to say that it was "treble the length it had been when Mr. White came". Because the parish was large, John White knew many of his people had a long way to come to church. Just as the Shettleston parish church had been built for the convenience of those in the great Barony parish who had been "disadvantageously situate for the means of Grace", so he wished to bring means of grace nearer to two outlying places in Shettleston where the population was quickly increasing—Tollcross and Carntyne. During the early stages of the Shettleston Church Case, it will be remembered, John White had told the heritors that he would undertake, if they agreed to his proposals, to raise part of the necessary building fund. By rejecting his terms, the heritors had of course made themselves liable to build the new parish church out of their own resources, and John White's building fund had lain intact. He had augmented it in every way he could. With the avowed object of "church extension within the parish", he had inspired his people to organise the largest church bazaar ever held in the Glasgow area, and the amount of money it brought in—between four and five thousand pounds—was considered a prodigious sum for an effort of the kind in those days. He boldly went ahead and built two new churches: St. Margaret's at Tollcross and St. Michael's at Carntyne. By the law of the Church of Scotland, he was obliged to raise money to endow the stipends of both ministers, and this he did. The kirks he built and endowed at Tollcross and Carntyne were his earliest achievements in a nation-wide movement to which he was to devote many years of vehement effort.

If the Shettleston Church Case had brought notoriety to the parish, the success of John White's pastoral work had added lustre to its name throughout the Presbytery of Glasgow—and indeed much further afield. It was acknowledged that the parish kirk with its two satellites had made Shettleston a place of spiritual vigour. But John White's eyes were continually peering out beyond the kirkyard wall into the wilderness around him. His frequent visits to Barlinnie prison as chaplain revealed to him the degradation to which men could fall in the squalor of city back-streets.[1] Even as he walked through his own parish on his visitations, he was conscious that little more than one generation had seen the green fields and country lanes blotted out by houses, shops, workshops, factories. Shettleston was becoming part of the city of Glasgow.

"We are faced with a social problem of great magnitude." These words he uttered often in Shettleston, and he knew that the social problem was primarily a spiritual problem. By how much, he asked himself, had he extended God's Kingdom since he had come there? Communion Rolls at Shettleston and Carntyne and Tollcross might be lengthening: but was it enough that the snug world of religious activities included the respectable church-going poor if the others were left without a thought? He

---

[1] One of his parishioners asked John White what he preached to the prisoners at Barlinnie at ten o'clock each Sunday morning. "The same as I preach to you at twelve," was the reply. "Why that?" asked the parishioner. "Because," said John White pointedly, "the only difference between them and us is that we haven't been found out." These words have been subsequently attributed to several other men, but Shettleston folk held that they were first spoken by their minister.

John White undertook the work at Barlinnie at the request of Lord Balfour of Burleigh. "I strongly favoured a more humane approach to the prisoner," he wrote afterwards. "I introduced for the first time in prison the Magic Lantern with slides of places I had visited in America, Canada, Europe, the Holy Land. Even the Governor attended and remarked on the excellent discipline. The Prison Commissioners thanked me and sent me a bill of expenses for 18s. 6d. as no provision had been made in the estimates for gas."

talked it over with those closest to him. Remembering the effect of his
house-to-house visitation in his first year, he felt convinced he had found
a plan that would bring the straying, kirkless folk of his parish under the
healing and saving influence of the Church. And so, in 1901, he launched
a new campaign.

He placed the facts before his congregation. He spoke of the blatant
defiance of God which they could see on all sides. He painted a true picture
of what most folk could see for themselves if they cared to look search-
ingly: drunkenness, gambling, Sabbath desecration, the spiritual languor
of those who had drifted from the churches, children who were growing
up without ever having been inside a Sunday School. It was a parish
crusade he was proposing. The motto on its banner might have been "Tell
Shettleston", for it was an early prototype of the "Tell Scotland" movement of today. John White said he would not rest till he had enlisted every
Christian man in his church who was ready to give him a promise of
help. Shettleston he was determined to save for Christ.

"A city is the centre of civilisation," he said, "and Shettleston will
soon be part of a great city. Our Lord did his mighty works in the
cities of men. He commanded his disciples to begin in the cities and
towns. After the Ascension, the disciples followed his divine strategy
to preach the gospel to the world, beginning at Jerusalem, reaching
out to Athens, Rome, Ephesus, Thessalonica, Corinth. And in the
midst of the city today stands the Church of Christ. Yet, under its
very shadow, masses of men take no thought of it or its gospel. When
we walk through the crowded streets, we are forced to acknowledge
that, between multitudes of human beings and the Church, there is a
great gulf fixed.

"And how can we bridge that gulf? We can do so, as it was done
in the first century, *by human sympathy*. Those of us who are prepared
to make our faith a living thing must go out like the seventy of old.
We must preach a gospel of compassion to the many who are scattered
and faint. If we would find the lost sheep, we must seek them. A
heart of love draws men. We need warm, loving, missionary hearts.
We need a love that will seek out and find those who are living away
from Christ's Church and *show them that the Church is yearning for
them*.

"No method of work will avail unless it is accompanied by a
revival of apostolic zeal. Our object is not to preach another gospel

42

but simply to bring the old gospel of Jesus Christ fully within the knowledge of everybody in Shettleston. The minister is not appointed to a kirk but to a parish. His duty is to look after all within his territory. Here is our base for evangelising the whole parish—and not merely a centre of local religious pride."

He still further developed his argument. John Knox had deemed that a parish of a thousand souls was of a goodly and convenient size, and later twice that number or perhaps a little more had been reckoned within the ability of a minister to serve. But John White pointed out that the folk in Shettleston now exceeded twenty-two thousand and said:

"With such a number, how can the parochial system have a fair chance? The Church of Scotland has added about five hundred parishes to the territorial system—but this is still inadequate. The increase of population is greater than the increase of our means to cope with it. The eternal money question comes up. But if we are not rich enough to pay a number of dedicated workers in this cause, there is another way to carry out the aggressive work. We must resort to the unpaid work of every Christian man and woman.

"Is this a revolutionary proposal? No; the aggressive work of the Church belongs to the laity as well as to the clergy. To *every* Christian it is said: 'Go and preach the gospel to every creature.' The Church is not the clergy. The laity have work to do in the church. I propose we adopt the methods of Our Lord as recorded in the tenth chapter of Luke. Seventy were sent forth, two by two. The work of the disciples was supplemented by this new band of workers. The conditions of the world are different today from what they were when Our Lord sent out the seventy. The Church of Christ is established. But Christianity is still a missionary religion. It is only fulfilling part of its duty when it obeys the command, 'Feed my sheep'. It has also to obey the command, BE YE FISHERS OF MEN. And the main work and activity of the workers we propose to organise must be among the multitudes that swarm around us."

John White said that the number of their workers would be limited to seventy, the number that Our Lord sent out. The name chosen for this band was the Septuagint. Since most of the Shettleston church-workers were women, the membership of the new band would for the time being be confined to men:

"I seek now to stimulate the zeal of our men to work for God's glory and their brothers' welfare. The duties of members of the Septuagint will be very simple. Two by two, they will visit a small district allocated to them. To their work they will devote not less than one hour a week. A religious census of the district must be made, and members of the band will draw to the minister's attention all cases of sickness, suffering, poverty, and indeed anything which they feel he ought to know. They will give a warm personal invitation to every non-churchgoing family to come and hear the gospel preached, and they will offer them seats in their own pew or in some other convenient one.

"Our great aim is to reveal the sympathy of the Church with those who consider the Church unsympathetic. By our deeds we must declare that the Church is ready and anxious to help the outcasts of society. The great social problem of the day will not be solved by argument but by labour and love. The world wants men and deeds— the psalm of labour and the psalm of love!"

IV

The sermon with which he launched the Septuagint was remembered as one of the most compelling he had preached in Shettleston. He had no wild dream of a sudden revolution in the spiritual life of the parish—of a rounding up and a quick regeneration of the lost and strayed. By its very nature, the work he was starting was of a slow and persistent kind. He was ready for disappointments, and he warned his workers to expect them and to use them as a spur to more fervent effort. Slowly but steadily, all the homes of the parish were visited. Here and there, folk were brought in, one or two at a time. A new light shone into some homes. Children came to Sunday School from the lanes and the backyards; at Sunday School treats, the organisers had to plan for an attendance of over fifteen hundred children. There were new recruits in the Bible Class. The success of his crusade brought home to John White how sore was a need that had been felt for a long time. There was no adequate meeting place for the activities of the church members. For want of a better place, they had for a time been using the old insanitary parish kirk. Alongside the new church there must be erected another building, with a great hall and other meeting rooms under one roof.

He set to work on this project with confidence. His people had never failed in any call he had made on them, and before long he was able to congratulate them. He was proud of them and of his new church—he thought it "one of the most beautiful modern kirks in all Scotland"—and the buildings now built alongside it he acclaimed as a handsome partner.

"With the opening of these halls," he said, "our scheme of church extension and hall provision is complete. A church without halls is handicapped in its Sabbath School, its Bible Class, its Boys' Brigade, and in all work auxiliary to the Sanctuary. It is handicapped in its sociableness. Friendliness towards each other is essential to healthy co-operation in church work. Every church ought to have a parlour that is the centre of the religious-social life of the congregation. I pray that much good work will be done in these halls in the years to come; I pray they may become the rallying place, the headquarters, of a large army of devoted soldiers of Jesus Christ. . . . All my work up to now in Shettleston," he said, "has been a work of preparation. Only now is the parish fully equipped."

He had completed the task of creating a place where they could worship together and mingle in friendship. But that is where the chapter ended for John White in Shettleston. His work was to be taken up by other hands.

Many a time he had been asked to let his name go forward as a candidate in vacant churches. He had even been asked if he would consider a call from a large and prosperous Free Church. He had brushed aside these suggestions. The most attractive of all offers had come from one of the largest parish churches in Scotland—that of South Leith—which had fallen vacant when Dr. James Mitchell had retired after a ministry of forty years in the parish. But John White had rejected even this. He had no ambition in the sense that he had no urge "to better himself" in status: but he did have a keen desire that his talents should be used to the full. That he might become the minister of South Leith, after he had rejected an invitation to stand as a candidate, was the last thought in his mind. But in a manner he did not foresee, the injunction was to come to him—and with an urgency that was imperative. .

Chapter IV

THE MINISTER OF SOUTH LEITH

I

IT was at a burnside in Arisaig, on the west coast of Scotland between Moidart and "blessed Morar", that John White had his first inkling of the call to South Leith. A messenger came running upstream to him with a telegram. It was from Dr. Archibald Scott of St. George's, Edinburgh, at that time one of the foremost men in the Church of Scotland. John White reeled in his line and read the telegram with astonishment:

"Presbytery have unanimously appointed you to Leith and have adjourned till Saturday very urgent that we proceed without delay I can wait for you here tomorrow or meet you in Glasgow on Friday in Baird Trust office at twelve."

It seemed to him preposterous that he should in this way have received information of so important a matter. Dr. Scott had, in fact, written to him five days before; but because he had addressed the letter to the Shettleston Manse, it had not yet reached him in Arisaig, where the letters were delivered by a postman who made his rounds on the back of a sturdy Highland garron. Dr. Scott wrote again on the same day as he sent off the wire:

"I know you would be surprised by the contents of my telegram; but if you had been with us in the Presbytery today, you would have appreciated the promptitude with which we came to our decision. Events moved more rapidly than I expected, but quite as I desired. It is a great compliment to you that we offer you the appointment of so important a charge without negotiating with you as to your acceptance. This we have done because we are conscious of your thorough qualifications in ability and experience to serve the Church with distinction and success—and because we believe that you will be inclined to co-operate with us in putting a happy end to a state of matters in Leith which threatened the peace and honour of the Church. If you accept the appointment, I think honestly that the mischievous agitation will speedily subside, and that all parties will acquiesce and give you a welcome."

46

JOHN WHITE

Of the mischievous agitation John White had already heard. Under the ministry of Dr. James Mitchell, begun in 1864 and lasting forty years, the congregation of South Leith had become a great and powerful centre of Christian activity. The people had been devoted to their minister and had been united in all things. The kirk session had been controlled by good men and true, men strong and indeed stubborn in their opinions. When Dr. Mitchell had retired, that strength—that stubbornness—had unfortunately divided them. Some had considered that the senior assistant, the Rev. A. J. Fleming, should be given the charge; others had been convinced that Mr. Fleming was unable to undertake such heavy work and responsibility. Of the three thousand two hundred members of the church, nine hundred had petitioned the vacancy committee to appoint the assistant. The committee had rejected this and had nominated a man whom the majority of the congregation had refused to consider. By this time, more than five months had passed since the resignation of Dr. Mitchell, and according to Church law the sand in the glass was running out. Anent the South Leith vacancy there had been public talk and private gossip. After much trouble, the large vacancy committee— it had over eighty members—had produced a short leet of three names. When Mr. Fleming's supporters had seen that his was not on it, their anger had risen and contentious letters appeared in the press. At the end of June, the committee had asked the Presbytery for an extension of the statutory time of six months so that the congregation could proceed to the election of a minister. The Presbytery, wisely led by Dr. Archibald Scott, had refused. They had seen that the good folk of South Leith were divided by a rift that time would have widened. The Presbytery had used their powers under *jus devolutum* and appointed a commission to go into the matter. The result might have been foreseen. A minister was to be "intruded" upon the congregation. It was the only way to make peace. But the quality of that peace would obviously depend upon the minister whom the Presbytery placed in spiritual authority over the divided people.

When John White read the telegram in Arisaig, he had little inclination to accept. Had he not already refused to allow his name to go forward among the candidates for this vacancy? As he travelled south to meet Dr. Scott, he could think of several good reasons why he should turn down the offer. But at their meeting, the whole case was laid before him in detail. The Presbytery of Edinburgh was depending upon him to bring peace to a community of sorely troubled souls; the majority of the

47

kirk session and a large number of the seat-holders had threatened to sever their connection with South Leith and quietly annex themselves to churches nearer their homes, "leaving the congregation practically in the hands of raw lads and harbour folk". John White had a clear picture of the duty before him. To be an "intrusion" minister was the last thing he relished: but there could be no other way of it. It was plain that every day the affairs of the congregation were worsening.

On the first Sunday in August 1904, John White stood in their midst. He went in apprehension to preach to them. How would they receive him? For any minister, young or old—John White was thirty-six—the ordeal was of a peculiarly formidable kind. It recalled the old uneasy days of patronage when the holder of a living thrust a man of his own choice into a benefice whether the congregation wanted him or not, and the Presbytery was now doing the thrusting. Would he look into hostile faces and hear a low deep mutter of protest, as had many an unhappy minister in the old days? Something far different happened. John White said afterwards that it was as if a miracle had been wrought—as if a warm wind of reconciliation had blown upon them. In one sudden access of relief, the whole of the folk of South Leith rallied round him. Their ranks closed as if in obedience to a word of command they had been aching to hear. When John White made his farewell speech to the Presbytery of Glasgow on the last Wednesday of the same month, he was able to say:

"The hearty reception given to me by the people of South Leith dispelled all my apprehensions—they made me feel as much at home as if I had been the unanimous choice of the congregation."

II

He was astonished at the congratulations he received. The minister who had been first nominated by the vacancy committee wrote with special warmth to say that if there was one man who could heal the division it was John White. Another, whose name had been on the short leet, wrote to say how greatly he was relieved by the decision of the Edinburgh Presbytery and how delighted at the wise choice: "I do hope the people will remain and be loyal to you; I feel sure they will. I have urged some personally. They are a kind-hearted folk." As soon as he had received the call, John White had written to his mother, who lived with her son William, parish minister at Crosshouse, and she had quickly

Margaret Gardner became the wife of John White in 1893
and died in 1942.

replied: "Surely you would not have two thoughts about accepting it. I have got what I have long wished for, that you would get another church without preaching against other candidates." He was glad also to have had a letter from the assistant whose popularity among so many of the congregation had caused the first division. Mr. Fleming said how glad he would be to serve under John White as he had served Dr. Mitchell in the past:

> "It will no doubt take some little time for feelings to die down between the hitherto contending sections, but I have not the slightest doubt that your advent among us will act as a salve to all dissensions. The general feeling on both sides is one of genuine relief at the ending to the prolonged period of tension. Every facility will be given to accomplish your task as peacemaker in the congregation so long riven by faction." [1]

Folk were indeed eager to forget what had happened since the beginning of that year. The day when he was officially inducted to the parish by the Presbytery of Edinburgh was described by one newspaper as "a day of days in the history of the parish church of South Leith". Ministers of many denominations were present, and the preacher was a well-known Edinburgh figure, the Rev. Thomas Burns of Lady Glenorchy's. The ceremony of induction, always impressive, was thus recorded in the minutes of the Presbytery of Edinburgh:

> "The Presbytery Clerk produced the attested Edict; then the officer was ordered to go to the most patent door of the church and give notice that the Presbytery had now met, and were ready to hear any objections to the life or doctrine of Mr. White. But there was no compearance. Whereupon, the congregation having assembled, Mr. Burns went to the pulpit and conducted public worship. Thereafter, he represented that the church and parish of South Leith, having become vacant . . . and the congregation having failed to elect a minister in the prescribed time, the Presbytery had appointed Mr. John White, minister of Shettleston, to supply the vacancy. . . . This day had been fixed for his admission, and after due notice had been given, and none had compeared to object to his life or doctrine, the

[1] As some indication of how popular was Mr. Fleming in Leith, it might be mentioned that he was immediately appointed to another vacant church in the same burgh. This was the church of St. Thomas, the first of the "daughter" churches of South Leith parish church. Mr. Fleming was ordained and inducted to this charge on the day following the induction of John White.

Presbytery were now to proceed to his admission. Mr. Burns then called Mr. White and put to him the questions annexed to Act XVII 1889.[1] Mr. White, having given satisfactory answers to all the same, was solemnly admitted to be minister to the church and parish of South Leith, and he received from the brethren the right hand of fellowship. . . . When the congregation was dismissed, the Presbytery resumed; and Mr. White, having signed the Formula, his name was added to the Roll. The sederunt was closed with prayer."

To read in the local press of the "induction dinner" that was held in the Queen's Hotel after the ceremony is to travel back into another era. It was recorded that

"one hundred and fifty gentlemen assembled to do justice to the eight course meal which had been prepared for them, the menu including fried smelts, sirloin of beef, roast grouse. A dozen toasts were drunk, beginning with 'The King' and continuing with 'The Church of Scotland', 'The Town Council', 'The Shettleston Kirk Session' and 'The Newly Inducted Minister'. That evening, in a church uncomfortably crowded, the congregation again had an opportunity to meet the man whose intrusion upon them had already been forgotten. Dr. Mitchell himself was there to welcome John White. He recalled that he, too, had been intruded upon the congregation of South Leith, although in different circumstances. Neither he nor John White had ever thought of being minister to that congregation. 'Indeed, when it was put to me,' he said, 'I regarded it with the very direst dismay. I came, as did Mr. White, because it had been urged upon us as a duty. He was brought, as I was, to promote peace, goodwill, and unity. I do not think it was any disadvantage, in either case, that we were not the choice of the people.' He went on to express an opinion still strongly held at that time among some of the older ministers in the Church of Scotland, if not also among the younger ones: 'When a minister comes as the choice of the people, it often happens that he is indebted to one or two members of the church more than others for the interest they took in bringing him forward. His relations to those two or three are afterwards different from his relation to the congregation as a whole. These people were the minister's patrons. I

[1] These were the usual questions, put to ministers before ordination, to ensure that they were sound in doctrine; were ready to submit themselves to the admonitions of the brethren of the presbytery; had "used no undue methods to procure this call"; and other questions on which the presbytery required full assurance before proceeding with the service.

felt it a mighty advantage, when I came to South Leith, to be under no obligation to any man or woman for my being there at all. I am persuaded that the Presbytery never made a more faithful appointment than they did when they selected Mr. White to be my successor. God has led you all in a mysterious way, yet He is already beginning to make all things plain. . . .'"

John White preached in South Leith at the evening service on Sunday, 2nd October, to a congregation that included the Town Council. He spoke of the wrench it had been to leave his people in Shettleston and the large and growing church:

"But that is past. Last Sabbath morning I closed that page—a page filled with success and failure, joy and sorrow, cloud and sunshine—and tonight with trembling hands I turn over another, not knowing what in the days to come may be written thereon, but knowing that it will be one page nearer the end of the volume, the number of whose pages no man knows. With fear and hope in our hearts, what else can we do but go tonight together to God's throne of grace, so that you strive in your prayers for me and I in my prayers for you."

III

It was to a parish of thirty-eight thousand souls he had come. Built in the latter half of the fifteenth century, and originally known as St. Mary's Chapel, the kirk of South Leith was situated within the ancient parish of Restalrig. Built upon one of the first Christian sites in Scotland, the old Restalrig church was famous for its images. Because folk continued to worship these after the Reformation, the General Assembly ordered it to be "razed and utterly destroyed" and folk were instructed to resort for worship to the Kirk in Leith, which in 1609 was given the status of a parish church. Its first Protestant minister had been David Lindsay, a close friend of John Knox's, and he had been no less than six times Moderator of the Assembly and had become the titular Bishop of Ross with a seat in Parliament. When James VI had returned from Perth, after his alleged escape in what became known as the Gowrie Conspiracy, he joined the large congregation met together to give thanks. The minister, David Lindsay, had felt it to be his duty to refer in his sermon to the King's promise that justice would be impartially done; and the monarch who was to be called the wisest fool in Christendom thought fit to smirk and jest audibly with those around him while the minister spoke from the pulpit. The building had been desecrated at different times. In the sixteenth century Hertford, in one of his terror-spreading raids from across the Border, turned the place into a prison for Scottish nobles. A century later, Cromwell ousted ministers and congregation and used the kirk at one time as an arsenal and at another as a stable.

Within its walls there had been drawn up, between members of the Privy Council and ministers of the Church of Scotland, the famous concordat appointing Protestant bishops—the cause of storms of contention in the Church.[1] In August 1692, the church for the last time was used as an episcopal place of worship. Under the orders of the Presbytery, the magistrates of Edinburgh and Leith descended upon it and demanded the keys so that they might banish the episcopal minister. On being asked to produce their warrant from the Privy Council, they admitted that they had none, and they were ordered to be off. Whereupon, the magistrates and the Presbytery "with a confused company of people entered the church by breaking open ye windows, breaking off ye lock of ye doors of ye church, and putting on new ones, and so caused guard the church doors wt halberds". They then rang the bell and duly installed a Presbyterian minister: which was the end of prelacy for the Lady Kirk of Leith.

John White's interest in the history of the church increased as his study of it took him into some fascinating by-paths. The family of Robert Louis Stevenson's mother, the Balfours of Pilrig, had their burial place in South Leith, and members of the church would point to a certain tombstone in the kirkyard on which, they suggested, the eyes of the young R.L.S. must surely have lighted and the name carved thereon lingered in his memory until a wet August day in 1881 when, in the Castleton of Braemar, he was planning his most popular tale: thus, "John Pew, Maltman in Leith", as scoundrelly a fellow, they said, as Stevenson's own creation, gave his name to blind Pew of *Treasure Island*. The Rev. John Home, of Athelstaneford, author of *Douglas* and other plays, had been born in Leith and was buried in the kirkyard. John White was later to print a short biographical study of this minister who had caused so much

[1] When John White recounted to his own people some of the history of South Leith, he told of the Concordat of Leith, which he called the Discordat, and of the so-called Tulchan Bishops that had been created as a result of this convention: "These Protestant bishops were humorously described as tulchans because, in the old Scots tongue, a tulchan is a calf's skin stuffed with straw and set beside a cow to deceive her and make her yield her milk. These bishops had an outward form but were only as a skin stuffed with straw. While the bishop had the title, it was my lord who drew the milk of the benefice."

commotion by his interest in the theatre that he was forced to leave the Church. He then became tutor to the Prince of Wales, afterwards George III, who settled a comfortable pension on him. Another minister with a literary bent had been inducted to the second charge at South Leith. The author of some of our finest Scottish paraphrases, John Logan was friend and patron of the young Loch Leven poet, Michael Bruce, and today Logan's memory is reviled by a small but fervent band of Michael Bruce enthusiasts who, from time to time, remind the public that it was the Loch Leven lad and not the rascally plagiarist of South Leith who wrote *Ode to the Cuckoo*. Some consider the poem a poor little jingle, yet it sent Edmund Burke into such raptures that he called it the most beautiful lyric in the English language: but that it was composed in the South Leith kirkyard one summer evening by John Logan has never been satisfactorily disproved by the Michael Bruce partisans. In the records of his new parish, John White found a wealth of matter to interest him, and with pleasurable anticipation he prepared to settle down in his new domain.

IV

Some men seem to have been born with a gift for domesticity, but John White was not one of them. In his own home, he took things happily as they came: and come they always did, thanks to the contriving of a most capable and devoted wife. The settling down in the new manse at Leith was planned and carried out by her in every detail, except the arrangement of John White's growing library of books. The Manse, 12 Hermitage Place, was a large square house of four storeys looking across the Links of Leith. It was in the library, which was conveniently at one's left hand as one entered the hall, that the minister interviewed his callers. All his desk work was done in his study on the first floor. Behind the house was a terraced garden, over which John White cast a critical eye and regretted the loss of his factotum at Shettleston. Old Tom Edwards had not only kept the garden there in fine trim, but had driven the minister's pony trap and had been the beadle of the kirk. With the children, the word of Tom Edwards had been law; this benevolent autocrat had seemed to them a much more important man than their father.

As some compensation for the loss of Tom Edwards, the young folk had the thrill of moving to a new home on the other side of Scotland—a home, moreover, in a seaport town with great docks and the shore of the Firth of Forth not far distant. The three boys carried the family names of

Matthew, John, and James; the elder of the two girls, Lily, was able to join her brothers in their ploys; Margaret, bearing her mother's name, was the baby of the family. They had the whole of Leith Links as their playground, and one of their sharpest recollections of those days was the edict of their mother that they must keep an eye upon a certain dormer-window on the top floor of the manse. If they could see a towel hanging from that window, they knew that another meal-time had come round, and this became the signal to scores of young folk on Leith Links that they should disperse to their homes. The Rev. John R. Spence, one of John White's assistants, wrote:

"Mrs. White's hands were so full with domestic duties that she was not able to take nearly as large a part in congregational work as she would have liked. But all the church workers knew they had her sympathy and support—and her wise advice. Mrs. White never appeared to make any fuss, whether with a poor person or one of the quality; I never once saw her flustered when visitors arrived without warning and were pressed by the minister (without any thought of a crisis in the kitchen!) to stay for a meal. It was an elastic dining-room table they had. The 'bishop' would give a most expert exhibition of carving a roast or a fowl so that everyone got a fair helping. To an assistant living in digs, it was a wonderful experience to be allowed to join in the happiness of that home. Mrs. White was *officially* At Home to all parishioners on the first Tuesday and Wednesday of each month, but it was an 'open house' every day, as I well remember. . . . It was from this background, organised to make everything smooth for him, that the minister went forth to his strenuous and absorbing public life."

V

Because the congregation had over three thousand on the Communion Roll, John White said it would take him a long time to visit every family. He was eager to know his people as soon as possible, to know them in person and as friends; also, he wanted them to know each other. To this end, he divided the congregation into groups, taking them by districts, and organised a series of At Homes in the church hall. The point of these informal meetings was not that folk should enjoy some music and refreshment but that there should be general post—for John White told them he would allow no person to remain in the same place for more than ten minutes. "Perhaps you don't know it," he said, "but somebody else wants to talk to you!" Many admitted after the meetings that they were surprised to learn what a friendly lot of folk were to be found in South Leith. At once, John White set about the pastoral visitation with his three assistants, and one member, looking down a long vista of years, said: "He was soon a welcome visitor in the homes of the poor as well as the rich. You could find many of both in an old seaport town like Leith. What a way he had of adapting himself to all kinds, all ages, all classes." He continued to preach about the need of friendliness among members of the congregation, and quoted the case of one (not a member of South Leith) who had written: "I have been sitting near some folks for years in the kirk, and we meet every Sunday in the aisle or the vestibule, but they have never said Good-morning or Good-evening—never smiled at me, never looked as if they even knew me. I tried more than once to get a smile of recognition, but gave it up." John White suggested that perhaps the writer was a little to blame: could he not himself have made a more active attempt to be friendly? Barriers of shyness must be broken down; so must barriers of indifference. The kirk session found in him a kindliness that greatly sweetened the vitalising spirit he brought into their meetings. He told them of a minister at the Assembly who asked one of his brethren from the Highlands how he got on with his kirk session. "Grand," said the Highland minister. When he was asked how many elders he had he replied: "None—thank God." John White reminded them that he had thirty in South Leith, and he intended to get on as well with his session as the Highlander had got on with his.

He brought fresh enthusiasm into the Literary Society and Young Men's Guild; he started a Boys' Brigade before he had been many months in Leith; and later there was a cycling club that explored the Lothian countryside once a week in the summer months. He had two, and subsequently three, Bible Classes. These and the Sunday School he considered vital church work. To his delight, he found there had been a long tradition in Leith of what had once been called the Sabbath Evening School, begun exactly one century before. It had first met in the old King James VI's Hospital, and an immeasurable amount of good had been done among boys of the seaport. John White spurred the teachers on:

"To be the means, in God's hands," he said, "of imparting moral and spiritual life to the young is a sacred privilege. I make three rules. Firstly, a teacher must be a church member. In the second place, the text books must be the Bible, the Psalms, and the Catechism.

55

Lastly, no Sunday School must be regarded as something that takes the place of worship in church, so must never be held during the hours of the church services."

On these three points he was emphatic.

He distrusted many of the so-called modern aids to teaching in the Sunday School; he would have no pseudo-scientific nonsense taught—no talk, for example, of some of the miracles being merely natural phenomena which had struck wonder into credulous people. He had many meetings with the teachers, and he never left them in any doubt about his views on the way to lead young folk to Christ. He said there were six primary truths that must be patiently and continually impressed on the minds of the young. No boys or girls should leave the South Leith Sunday School without having the six truths indelibly impressed on their minds as part of their philosophy of life. They must, he said, have—

A clear conviction that, behind all this world, is a living Person—God our Father.

A clear conviction that, behind all the suffering and woe of life, there is One Who worketh righteously, and He will bring the good thing to pass. We can only see as through a glass darkly, and hence we often despair, but all things work together for good to them who love God.

A clear conviction about the forgiveness of sin. Every child must know the message of the Atonement—peace with God through Jesus Christ.

A clear conviction that life here is a probation, a passing day compared with the deathless spaces of eternity.

A clear conviction of the reality and strength of God's grace, the gift of God to enable us to attain salvation—to raise man from his low estate to heavenly glory, which he could not attain by his own efforts.

A clear conviction of the value of membership in Christ's Church. Admitted into the Church by Baptism, we need grace and an increase of spiritual strength for the active service of God in the world. This increase is ours when we come forward to confirm our baptismal vow and sit at the Table of Holy Communion.

It was a proud day for John White when he was able to announce that South Leith had the second largest Sunday School in the Presbytery of

Edinburgh, with nine hundred and twenty-one children and seventy-two teachers.

If he spoke his mind plainly to his loyal and enthusiastic staff in the Sunday School, he was no less forthright in his sermons. There were those who said he hit too hard when he said such things as: "I attend meeting after meeting and find work being done by the same faithful few, and I begin to wonder whether one should allow matters to go on as they are."

A thing he rigidly insisted on was an annual purging of the Communion Roll. He saw that his kirk session removed the names of all who had been absent from Holy Communion for three consecutive years without good reason. The first purging was done not many months after he had come to South Leith, and from the Roll several hundred names were struck.

Continually he preached the duty of taking Communion. In his early years at South Leith, the sacrament of the Lord's Supper was dispensed thrice annually, but later the Communion service was held four times a year. So great was the number of those who wished to communicate that two services were held in the morning and two again in the afternoon. He taught his people the value to their spiritual lives of partaking of the Lord's Supper with a humble, contrite, and grateful heart. To the young people in particular, he gave tender guidance:

> "Some young communicants," he said, "expect a thrilling and almost magical sensation of happy feeling at the Lord's Table. They are grievously disappointed when they do not experience it. Such delightful emotions are sometimes felt as we lean on Jesus' bosom. All our sorrows, cares, even our sins, seem to be driven away. Our souls are so filled with Jesus that there is room for nothing else. But less than this may be a very profitable Communion. If our faith is made stronger, if our love and gratitude are quickened, if our purpose to serve Him better is deepened, even if only our sense of unworthiness and sinfulness is increased, then we may surely conclude that we have communicated with profit. . . . Let your soul be filled with the thought of Jesus and His undying love. It matters little if you think of your sins and duties at all so long as you sit at Jesus' feet, like Mary of Bethany, and drink in His Love. *One earnest gaze upon Christ is worth a thousand scrutinies of self.*"

One of his assistants, greatly impressed by the way he spoke to young communicants, said that "his talks to them were always based on the

Shorter Catechism and the Creed. Unlike some ministers, he did not strain to be *modern* in his teaching." And certainly his talks to parents about their sons and daughters were straight from the shoulder:

"Your boys and girls are growing up. *Are they Communicants?* They ought to be. They are members of the Church by their Baptism. But perhaps you say you leave your children to themselves in these things. Was there ever anything so absurd? Do you not influence them in other things of less importance? You must be a useless parent if you do not. In this weightiest matter of all, do you leave them unhelped, unguided? Perhaps you hope that the minister or some earnest teacher will influence them. Whose business is it if not yours? For God's sake, and for your own sake, and for your children's sake, put away such nonsensical cant! Tell them they are baptised members of Christ, and now it is their privilege to take His vows upon themselves. Open up the matter with them. Help them to know their own minds. Very likely they have been expecting you to speak. Perhaps they have wondered why you did not. Is it that you have a difficulty in speaking to your children about their souls and their life in Christ? Better to begin now than to be condemned for utter unfaithfulness. Or are you *ashamed* to speak of it? Is your own life so careless, your own member-ship of Christ so slack, that your son or your daughter would not respect your advice on this matter? You may have tried and failed. Then you have need for humility and penitence. Try again after a prayer for wisdom. Try wisely and gently. Tell them of the need of grace. Tell how, at the Lord's Table, the baptised receive more grace and always more. Tell of the baptismal inheritance—of the joy in claiming it. The age for becoming a communicant is put far too late in modern custom among us. For a long time after the Reformation, lads and girls became communicants while still in the Sunday School. Set it before your children as a hope and reward for faithfulness. Do this in such a way that they may the earlier go to the Holy Table and receive the gifts of God."

VI

At the end of the first year of his ministry in South Leith, John White paused to take stock. He declared to his people that he was not satisfied with what had been done: "The work we have started is but a tithe of what we have yet to do." He announced that one minister and three assistants did not suffice to maintain regular contact with the members of the congregation:

"I look forward with confidence to your willingness to help. The work of the parish needs your sympathy, your prayers, your financial support—and your personal help. I now talk of that help. I wish to engage the services of *two hundred willing workers* from among the women of the congregation. Each will have six families allotted to her. These families must be visited at least once a month."

And so John White launched his plan of keeping in touch with every family through his team of lady visitors, and so successful did it prove that the same scheme still operates and flourishes in the parish of South Leith.

Upon the kirk session he pressed the need of a Church Sister, and they agreed to appoint one. Thus it was that Miss Maclean came to work with him, and she was at his side throughout his ministry there. Every week she held a gospel meeting, conducted a large sewing class, helped with the Mothers' Meeting, ran a special Sunday School as well as a girls' Bible Class, and made between two and three hundred visits to families each month. Although John White had said from the pulpit that he was far from satisfied with what had been achieved during his first year in the parish, the records indicate that he had found out for himself what was lacking in the congregational life and had come to grips with every parochial problem in which he felt it was his duty as parish minister to put out a helping hand. Within that first year he had found out, too, that in every instance where he had called upon his people for support, it was given with overwhelming generosity.

VII

There was one great and distressing thing he discovered during that first year; indeed he saw it only too plainly soon after he had settled there. This was the amount of poverty within the parish. In that old seaport town, there could be no doubt that trade was in a poor way. Many men were unemployed, many families underfed. The rather ponderously self-titled Association for the Improvement of the Condition of the Poor received hundreds of applications for help every month. Other organisations, such as the Destitute Sick Society, were active.[1] But the homes

[1] The two named societies were recently amalgamated in the Leith Benevolent Association.

where the suffering was keenest were often those in which the folk were too independent to make any appeal. Many looked forward with misgiving to a spell of bitter winter weather: the ancient human problem of keeping warm in the cold struck something like terror in the hearts of mothers with young children. The local papers seized eagerly on news of business concerns that made plans to expand, for this gave some promise of work for those who had none. The extension of the tramway was hailed as a boon for the unemployed; even orders for the building of a couple of yachts in a yard beside the docks were published as an item of hope in the local press. Soon John White found himself organising an intricate system for the relief of poverty and distress. He even started what became an unofficial employment agency. All who were out of work were asked to come and see him, and he appealed to members of his congregation who were employers to provide what work they could. One notice in the parish magazine ran: "Among applicants for work are women prepared to do washing, etc., and men who are qualified as grooms, etc., *but are ready to do anything.*" Before he had been very long in South Leith, he was in the thick of the battle against want. In many cases of distress he had made arrangements for coal and groceries to be sent at once. On his first Christmas in the parish he decided to give in the church hall a breakfast for poor and lonely folk. Between two and three hundred came, including some children, and each went away with a parcel. John White took the opportunity to speak words of comfort to them. It might have been a doleful affair, with the reek of condescending charity about it: but in his hands, and with the help of his kirkfolk, it turned out to be such a happy occasion that it became a regular feature of the Christmas activities of the church.

Meanwhile, Mrs. White was conducting a Mothers' Meeting for poor women who felt that they had not clothes good enough to wear in church on Sunday, and this inspired her husband to start an afternoon Sunday service for both men and women in the same state of poverty. Later, he went a good deal further. He perceived in the course of his work that many mothers were not having adequate food, and he arranged to provide a dinner for them every day of the week except Saturdays and Sundays, and they were invited to bring with them their children under school age. Members of the congregation cooked and served the food, and donations for the Dinner Table became part of the givings of the church. The Mothers' Meeting and Clothing Society made clothes for the children of widows, and necessitous mothers with large families were helped.

"Outside of our Communion Roll," said John White one day from the pulpit, "outside of our own church, under the shadow of the walls within which we worship, are many weary hearts that need comforting, many the little ones that need shepherding. The Church must grope its way into alleys and courtyards, up the broken staircases, into the bare room to the chair or the bedside of the loathsome sufferer." He took his people in imagination into some of the darkest and foulest corners of the seaport town, and then he took them far beyond the confines of the parish: "The Church must go down into the pit with the miner, into the fore-castle with the sailor, into the shop with the mechanic, into factory and field, into the counting-house. Like the sea, the Church must flow into every nook of the shoreline of humanity—and, like the sun, it must shine on things foul as well as fair."

When the new Town Council of Leith was elected, the Provost, Magistrates, and Councillors came to be kirked, as was the custom, and John White preached a sermon that none of them was likely to forget. His text was from Luke: *For the Son of Man is come to seek and to save that which was lost.* Well-worn words, he said—words bright with the wear of time. But he reminded his hearers that the "lost" included the outcasts, the degraded ones, and Christ had had fellowship with them, had sat at table with them—and had drawn upon Himself the withering scorn of those in high places.

"Remember, he took one of these despised sinners with Him into the presence of the Father. Social wreckage! That is what quickly strikes a visitor to great cities like London and Glasgow; but it is present, too, in the burgh of Leith. Progress has brought poverty as its dark companion. Wealth has heaped up destitution. Croesus stands and wonders at the starving household. What can be done? Must the strong survive, the weak go to the wall? . . . No! No! a hundred times no! The Son of Man is come to seek and to save that which is lost."

In another sermon he preached before the Provost, Magistrates, and Councillors, he told of some of the cases he had personally dealt with:

"Here is one partly due to intemperance. A man of sixty, savings gone, his good clothes gone, no work. He is not so much unemployed as unemployable. His own fault? Of course it is. But what do you propose to do? Perhaps you have no sympathy with him. Do *you*

61

wish to be judged by that standard—do *you* wish to be taken on your own merits by God? . . .

"Here is a mother and a young family of four. The home is almost bare of furniture—it was sold to buy food. But the floors are scrupulously clean. The woman is a heroine. Her husband, a poor weak man, deserted her. What do you say? 'Sorry, but to help her would be simply easing the husband of his responsibility.' I know it would, but I am thinking of these four children—the babies that 'suckle dry breasts of want'. I am thinking of the weary, worn mother. I can see Christ laying His hands on these little ones.

"I have striven to tell of the Christian work that is waiting to be done here," said John White, "and you will join in this work the moment you have had a vision of the real Christ, the living Christ, the Christ in the heart."

With this in mind, John White had not been long in South Leith before he had been pointing out to his congregation the need for larger church halls. Both the work of the congregation and the mission work in the district were being cramped by the lack of space. What he had done at Shettleston, could he not do again here? The need was as great; he sometimes thought it was greater. Before long he was pushing ahead with plans, and he carried the kirk session and congregation with him. By the end of 1907, the premises in Duke Street had been reconstructed. The main hall, which John White said, "would previously have answered well enough as a barn", had been transformed; and the new session house had been lavishly equipped, the gift of a member of the congregation. He had not yet asked the congregation for a penny: but he had no qualms. In his study of the history of South Leith kirk, he had found that the tercentenary of its constitution as the parish church fell in 1909. Would it not be a glorious thing to let his folk look back on these three centuries of life in the burgh? As a feature of the celebrations, why not hold a bazaar which would pay for their new church halls? One Sunday morning he put this to his people: "Could there be a grander offering to the Christ on our Tercentenary than the spiritual uplift of this neighbourhood? Dare we stand idle in the presence of that great need? I ask you this morning to give of your time, your energy, your prayers, your substance." His rousing sermon fired the congregation. The kirk session became enthused by his zeal: 1909 must be made an *annus mirabilis* in the history of South Leith.

VIII

The minister's challenge was quickly answered. A committee was formed. Schemes were drawn up. Out of a chaos of suggestions there appeared a sharply defined picture of the bazaar in being. And the magnitude of the project made folk catch their breath.

To be well prepared was half the battle, said John White, when someone pointed out that they had almost a year in hand. He told about Count Von Moltke—how he was in bed when they burst in and cried that war had been declared between France and Germany. Von Moltke told them quietly that all the orders would be found in a certain drawer in his bureau, and he turned over and went to sleep again. "In this complete preparation lay the secret of German success in the Franco-Prussian War. Preparedness is the high road to success—it will be the prime factor in the success of our bazaar." The thirty districts of the church were divided into groups, and to each was given a task. Even a bazaar bank was started, and collectors went round taking weekly payments even of single pennies so that the subscribers would have money to spend. "Watchman, what of the bazaar?" John White said one day to a member of the committee, and the reply was that they were not getting enough help from people outside the congregation. Not enough help from outside? Then it must be found. For big battles, big battalions were needed as well as brave men. "When a Highland chief went to war he sent out the Fiery Cross, charred in the fire, dipped in blood, passed from glen to glen—a summons that brought every clansman to the muster place. Far and near, let us send out the message—South Leith has need of you!" said John White. "Let us muster all the willing friends we can and make our victory a triumph."

And a triumph it became. The celebration service in the church created more interest and excitement in the burgh than any ecclesiastical occasion the old could recall. John White saw to it that there was no lack of appropriate pomp and ceremony. The great procession that formed up near Trinity House was composed of the Provost and Town Council, representatives of the Presbytery of Edinburgh, of Trinity House, of the Parish Council, of the Dock Commission, of the Chamber of Commerce, the Leith High Constables, and other bodies. The ministers of many other churches helped in the service, and John White himself occupied the pulpit. His Tercentenary sermon was read in newspaper and magazine columns by many thousands more than the church could have held on that Thursday, 24th June 1909. He spoke of "the subtle fascination by which that ancient kirk held the affections of all who at any time had been associated with it". He told how it had been important in the annals of the seaport, how it had played what he called "its little side part in the history of the nation, and had been a place of worship for kings and queens. . . . Think of your forefathers! Think of your own posterity! Today we think reverently of the former that we may think sensibly of the latter. It is divinely wise to listen to the echoes that survive when the voices of the past are hushed." He sketched the history of the church, taking his hearers back to its beginnings: "It was being built when Luther was born, when Leonardo da Vinci saw the light of day, one hundred years before the University of Edinburgh was founded." He spoke of the bullets from the guns of the Reformers smashing through the east window while the priest was celebrating High Mass at the altar, of the struggles of the Lords of the Congregation, of the Stuart and Commonwealth periods. . . . "From these old unhappy things and battles long ago, we shall reach a happy stage of peace when we strive with mutual zeal in acts of benevolence and love. . . . And the best tercentenary offering of gratitude that the church can make will be to engage more unitedly than ever to bring the power of the gospel of Christ to the many living under the shadow of our own walls." At the end of the service a version of "God Save the King" composed by John White himself was sung. And since it seemed that a suitable way to round off the celebrations was to join together in a festive meal, a great luncheon was held, with a long string of toasts and many speeches. Of its success there could be no doubt; and no finer fanfare could have been devised for the bazaar that followed.

This was held in the Music Hall and Assembly Rooms, which were to be made the social centre of the Edinburgh Festival. Huge canvasses, hung on the walls, were painted with scenes of the Shore of Leith, the South Leith kirk, the old chapel it replaced, and other spirited pictures of the seaport. They had aimed at a sum in the neighbourhood of two thousand pounds, and when everything in the coffers had been counted it was found that the total was seven hundred pounds more—a sum that may be reckoned to have the purchasing power of some twelve thousand pounds today.

"I think I am expressing your mind as well as my own," said John White in a sermon after it was over, "when I declare that clever hands, ardent hearts, and an ungrudging spirit have been very manifest.

Our bazaar broke down many barriers, reduced many partitions, so that members who had worshipped together as strangers are now able to shake hands over the lowered walls. We are proud of the old church of Leith that has borne witness to the deep things of God for so many centuries, that has stood through the storm and stress of years, and has a deep place in the affections of all who worship within these hallowed walls."

IX

John White had thrown himself into the project with a characteristic disregard for his health. "A Hercules for work," one of his helpers described him. It was only because of his exceptionally tough constitution that he had been able to take the strain without breaking, but afterwards he needed the attentions of his doctor. What gave him special joy was the suggestion that a Tercentenary memorial, with which his name would be permanently associated, should be put up in some prominent position in his church. It seemed odd that a church with such traditions should have been so bare of memorials of its past. Searching among the archives, John White had ascertained the reason why on its walls and pillars were displayed neither the arms of nobles and patrons of the church, nor anything that marked the place reserved for ancient incorporations and crafts. Of these the Kirk had once been rich. The arms of Leith had been represented in the large east window; those of Trinity House could have been seen on the gallery; those of the Hammermen and the Cordiners and other craftsmen were carved on pillars and elsewhere, as well as the arms of the Earl of Moray, once an important heritor and the patron of the church. But all had fallen into decay in the early part of the last century. Now, in their desire to bring into the sanctuary more records of their past in stone and brass and wood, the kirk session and members decided that for their Tercentenary memorial they would erect a new organ-gallery screen that contained the arms and motto of Leith, the arms of Edinburgh and of past patrons of the church: and prominently upon it there would be carved the initials of David Lindsay, minister in 1609, and of John White, minister in 1909. The screen was formed out of nine hundred separate pieces of oak, and the work was carried out with skill and artistry. John White was delighted to see also some of the old incorporations of the burgh commemorated by coats of arms: the Maltmen's was now there in its former position; that of the Carters was a tablet that showed their sittings at the south-west end of the church.

But before the Tercentenary organ-gallery screen had been installed, forces were at work which were to give a new direction to John White's life in the service of the Church.

He was invited to fill the pulpit of one of the most important churches in Canada. Other approaches had been made to him, but this was of a different order. It had the thrill of service to Christ in a great and growing Dominion. A deputation from the Canadian church had been in Scotland to choose a minister; they had heard several prominent men preach, and John White had been their choice. At the same time, The Barony of Glasgow had become vacant, and the choice of its committee had also fallen upon John White. He found himself in that state of mind which can be perplexing and even agonising to a minister. That a call from the Lord is a call to a better stipend is one of the oldest of all clerical jests. These two invitations, of which John White had been made aware, were to spheres of greater influence and wider responsibility. Stipend was the last thing to which he gave a thought. To those who knew him best, it was agreed that he was at fault in the lack of thought he gave to money: brusquely he would declare that the work of the Lord must be carried out and the money certainly would be found. When challenged he would say that he took little thought of it, for if one lacked faith in the splendour of tomorrow's adventure one was indeed lost. The story of John White's call to The Barony is still recounted with relish by his friends. The deputation were told by someone at the Church Offices in Queen Street that it might be difficult to see him next morning because the Canadian deputation had an appointment with him at eleven o'clock. But the men from The Barony were not to be beaten. One of their number telephoned to the manse at South Leith and made an appointment for ten o'clock. A few minutes early, they climbed the stone steps to the front door of the manse and were ushered into the library. They told John White how the vacancy committee had resolved unanimously to offer him the charge; they spoke of their last meeting when all had been so moved with enthusiasm that they had risen to their feet to acclaim the decision; and now they had come to get the man of their choice. Their ardour was touching; it was infectious. What hope had the Canadians, due on the stroke of eleven? . . . John White had been brought up in the West country. For nine years he had studied in the University of Glasgow; he had won his spurs as a student-missionary in the northern confines of that city; his first charge had become a part of the great and rapidly growing metropolis that straddled the Clyde; and it was homeward he felt he was going when he found the call too strong to resist and the opportunities of service too great to reject.

X

By 1911, John White had become deeply engaged in work for the Church of Scotland. For five years he had been convener of the Church Extension Committee of the Presbytery of Edinburgh. For four years he had been on a committee appointed to consider the filling of vacant pulpits. He had been a member of the Presbytery Law Committee, convener of the Session Records Committee, a member of the committee to consider social problems within the Presbytery area. In addition, he had for three years been a member of the General Assembly's committee on social work throughout Scotland. Most onerous task of all, he had been clerk, from the day of its foundation, of the Assembly's committee on union with the United Free Church. These tasks might well have drawn off much of the strength he had expended during his ministerial work in South Leith; but in spite of some warnings that there is a limit to the strain that can be put on even the strongest constitution, he worked in the parish with what seemed to be unquenchable intensity. He had dedicated himself to the well-being, spiritual and material, of the poor folk in his parish. They were his people; but perhaps it would be nearer the truth to say he looked upon them as his children. Long afterwards he wondered whether his time had been divided to the best advantage; and he recalled that, very reluctantly, he had given up a piece of special study on which he was engaged. The subject had been sociology, and it had been based to a large extent on his own experience in the parish. But Dr. Archibald Scott, convener of the Business Committee of the Church, had asked him personally to undertake an important mission. He had gone to London to brief the Secretary of State for Scotland on a Bill that dealt with the ecclesiastical assessment of heritors, and it had been largely due to his efforts that the matter had had a successful issue. But the negotiations had cut heavily into his time; and with other tasks falling to his hands, he had been forced to put aside his study on sociology. If completed, it might have been a valuable work: it would certainly have been of interest as showing John White's method of approach to the vexing problems of poverty and distress. "Any study of sociology that I might have published," he wrote, "would, I am certain, have been of less value than what I was providentially able to achieve in other ways."

In his farewell sermon to his people at South Leith, preached on the morning of 4th June, he spoke with great earnestness of prayer. He believed with a deep conviction that the prayers of those whose own lives were attuned to the Divine Will brought a wealth of spiritual blessing:

"It is the upholding power of spiritual life. I recall how even our Lord and Master looked to His disciples for the support of their prayerful sympathy—*Tarry ye here and watch with me.* I have had your intercessions and your prayerful sympathy to help me in the great and responsible work of this parish.

"As I look back today over my ministry in South Leith and consider the work that has been done, I thank God for you, my brethren. I thank you for the charity of every one of you, for your blindness to my faults, for your readiness to appreciate my well-meant efforts, however feeble. As I look forward to the work that awaits me in the Church and Parish of The Barony, I have no word but that best and simplest word of St. Paul—to ask for your prayer."

John White left his mark on South Leith. Some of the things he instituted there still exist, as the present parish minister, The Rev. T. D. Stewart Brown, has testified. Since Mr. Brown began his ministry as one of John White's Barony assistants, he takes pride in maintaining the tradition of a great servant of the Church whom he came to know so intimately and for whom he had such deep affection. Looking back to the time when he received the call to South Leith, he tells how he turned to John White to seek his advice.

"That was in 1942," he said, "and I was rather reluctant to tackle so huge a task. I knew what it would mean, and I was concerned about my own fitness to shoulder such responsibilities in one of the largest congregations in the Church of Scotland—a congregation which has now become the largest. Dr. White listened to what I had to say. Well do I remember the twinkle in his eye as he silenced my objections with these words: 'You have all the qualifications necessary. Were you not trained under John White? . . . So was South Leith!' "

Chapter V

JOHN WHITE OF THE BARONY

I

THE Barony of Glasgow has an unique history. It was created a few years after the Reformation, when it was separated from the ancient parish of St. Mungo. The congregation had then no kirk to worship in, and used the crypt of the Cathedral for nearly two and a quarter centuries. The best-known description of Barony folk holding a service in their eerie underground sanctuary can be read in Sir Walter Scott's *Rob Roy*.

"We descended . . . as if into the funeral vaults beneath the church. . . . Conceive an extensive range of low-browed, dark, and twilight vaults, such as are used for sepulchres in other countries, and had long been dedicated to the same purpose in this, a portion of which was seated with pews, and used as a church. . . . In those waste regions of oblivion, dusky banners and tattered escutcheons indicated the graves of those who were once doubtless 'princes in Israel'. . . . Surrounded by these receptacles of the last remains of mortality, I found a numerous congregation engaged in the act of prayer."

These Barony folk did not have a kirk of their own until 1800. Designed by one of the Adam brothers, it was described by Dean Stanley as "quite the ugliest church I have seen—except one". The Dean was entitled to his opinion: but we are entitled to wonder what he thought beautiful. It was generally agreed to be stuffy and ill-lit, and poor Dr. Norman MacLeod had difficulty in heaving his huge bulk up the narrow pulpit stair. It was demolished after the present Barony kirk had been built in 1889 by Dr. John Marshall Lang, later Principal of Aberdeen University. The list of ministers of the congregation forms a roll of honour that might be warranted to daunt anyone upon whom the mantle of these patriarchs might fall, and John White left nobody in any doubt of his feelings when he went to take up his duties.

"I realise how unworthy I am of following in the footsteps of men like Zachary Boyd, Donald Cargill, Lawrence Hill, John Burns, William

Black, Norman MacLeod, John Marshall Lang. . . . I can but say that I shall do what I can with any powers God has given me."

Each in his own way had been a man of fine distinction; some of them were what the Scots call "worthies". The stout-hearted Zachary Boyd had not been shaken by the military fame of Oliver Cromwell when the English dictator marched north, defeated the Scots at Dunbar, and came thundering across the country to subdue the city on the Clyde. Cromwell, that pious man, attended the Cathedral church on Sunday. The magistrates had discreetly withdrawn from Glasgow and the minister had gone with them, so Zachary Boyd had come up from the church in the crypt to occupy the pulpit. He fixed Cromwell with a glittering eye and preached a sermon so charged with home truths that one of Oliver's lieutenants asked him, "Shall I pistol this scoundrel?" Perhaps Cromwell decided it would not be a seemly thing to do, for the pistol was not drawn, although some might not have considered a pistol shot a more heinous desecration of the sanctuary than the storing of munitions therein and the fall of horse-dung upon the altar. Cromwell is said to have invited the preacher to dinner, and prayed fervently thereafter for what seemed an interminable time: but neither the dinner nor the prayer won him over. As for Donald Cargill, he was the Covenanter who, with Richard Cameron, founded that famous Scottish regiment, the Cameronians. He had snapped his fingers at Charles II and denounced him as a tyrant, perjurer, and usurper. When he dared to excommunicate Charles and his even more dissolute brother, the reward placed on his head was raised from three thousand to five thousand merks. While in his teens, John White had been familiar with the more violent episodes in the long story of The Barony's ministers, and in his later studies in Church History he had noted their part in the making of the Church of Scotland. Dr. John Burns, grandfather of the first Lord Inverclyde, had been minister for sixty-five years, and in 1775 had established the first Sunday School in Scotland. The great and good Norman MacLeod had always been a hero of John White's; he referred to him as "the prince of Home missionaries and the apostle of foreign missions", and in 1912 he organised the centenary celebrations of the birth of his great predecessor. Norman MacLeod had come to The Barony a few years after the Disruption—a hard time for the Old Kirk, bereft as it was of so many vigorous ministers and stout-hearted folk—and he had opened and set going again many a church in his parish that had been closed, and then had taken all Scotland for his parish and had built more churches in the newly populated industrial areas than any other man of his time. Many a kirk he planted within the wide Barony parish, where the need had been acute. Since Shettleston had once formed part of that parish, John White now felt like a man coming home—coming home, as he often said, "to share again in the pulsating life of the great city of Glasgow".

Since Norman MacLeod's day, the aspect of that part of Glasgow had greatly changed. A walk of a few hundred yards to the canal would then have brought one out into green fields, but by 1911 the city had crept far northward. In those earlier days, folk had said that The Barony congregation had been unique.

"Its uniqueness," explained John White, "had consisted in its being at once rural and urban. But three decades have altered all this. It is no longer 'a country church in a busy street'. It is a city church ministering to a congregation gathered in from north, south, east, and west, and it faces problems that are only to be met with in the busy quarters of a great modern city."

And one of the most difficult problems of all was the keeping together of a congregation of three thousand people many of whose homes were separated from their kirk by two miles and more of city streets. For these folk there were places of worship nearer their own doors, Sunday Schools which the companions of their children attended, and only a strong sense of loyalty held them thirled to the historic kirk which their fathers had attended in days gone by when they had dwelt within the confines of the parish.

II

From The Barony it was a good two miles to the manse at 15 Dundonald Road in Kelvinside. At South Leith, the manse had been easily accessible, and it had been the same at Shettleston; but The Barony folk were so far scattered over a great city that fewer folk would drop in to see the minister's wife. John White had regular Vestry Hours at the church, but he was anxious to know as many of his people as would come to him in person, and he at once began to hold a series of social gatherings in the church hall, as he had done at South Leith. Mrs. White was made president of the women's organisations, and the position was not a nominal one, for the Woman's Guild included more than half a dozen active societies: a large Girl's Club, a Girls' Guildry (formed that year "to induce girls to become followers of Christ and to develop in them womanly helpfulness"), a Mothers' Meeting, Work Parties, a Clothing Society to provide garments for poor members, an Association for Foreign Missions, and soon Mrs. White had started a Mothers' Union to stimulate women in the "training of our children in the fear of God and to be of service to their fellows". By her zeal for all of these, she became the friend of an increasing number of The Barony women. Long years afterwards, one of John White's assistants, Mr. Stewart Brown, said he was astounded at the number of eager and kindly enquiries made about Mrs. White by old folk when he was visiting in Glasgow: "In the poorest of homes she was remembered." In the words of Dr. David Scott, another assistant, "Mrs. White, bright-eyed and quick of step, soon was on the closest and friendliest terms with an enormous number of her husband's folk."

John White, as he had always done, took a warm interest in Bible Class work. There were two classes at The Barony, and he taught one of them himself. Under the aegis of the Sabbath School Society, there were two schools for children of the church and a Mission Institute school held in Black Street. The total number in Bible Class and Sunday School was nearly thirteen hundred, with eighty-four teachers and twenty-one monitors. The Band of Hope met in the same Institute; and the Boys' Brigade, with a membership roll of forty, paraded weekly in the church hall. John White was appointed one of the trustees of the three Penny Savings Banks run by The Barony members and open every Monday evening throughout the year; they were put to such good use that more than twenty-three thousand transactions were recorded in the year 1911. But to John White nothing was more important than the Parish Mission. The Institute had been opened in 1874, soon after Dr. Marshall Lang had begun his ministry. "At one time or another," said the convener who was in office when John White came, "there has flourished in our Institute every agency designed to bring men to a saving knowledge of the gospel of Christ. We invite everyone to be members and helpers, and we encourage communicants to become members of the kirk itself." Soon after his coming to The Barony, John White helped in an exhaustive visitation of the whole mission district. Nearly twelve hundred families were called upon by a team, and visits by the ministers and parish sisters followed. At the end of his first year, John White spoke to a large gathering of all the women's organisations and said that "every member of the Guild should try and get to know one poor family who are non-churchgoers. They should visit and take an interest in them in every possible way—until, through kindness, they have been won back to the Church." Under his supervision, seven Mission Study Circles came into being, and The Barony took the leading place in Glasgow in this method of spreading a knowledge of the Church's work overseas. A leader of one of these circles, Miss Euphemia Bain, became so inspired by what was being done in the mission field that she decided to go out to teach in a mission school at Madras, where The Barony paid a portion of her salary. A long letter John White wrote to her parents about her decision included these words:

"Her whole heart has been in the work of the mission field for years, and this seems a clear call to her to enter upon the work. . . . It is a great honour to have a daughter who has consecrated herself in this way. There comes a time when we must all make some sacrifice for the sake of our Master—and the greater the sacrifice, the greater the joy that accompanies it. . . . I thank you both for the help and stimulus your daughter has given to us, and I feel assured she will have great happiness in her new and sacred work."

There is today in the Cunliffe Chapel in The Barony a memorial window to her memory.

Every week, no less than thirty-five meetings of one kind or another were held in connection with the church, and there was not one in which John White did not take an interest. His complete knowledge of all that was afoot was noted with surprise both by his own people and by those from other churches who came to seek his help or advice.

His impact on civic affairs was soon felt; both he and his wife came of Glasgow families; and many calls upon his time were made in the interests of the city. Nor was he ever free from demands for his services in the ceremony of reopening churches, dedicating new ones, the opening of halls, the installation of new organs. He did what he could, and was glad to do it: but he knew it was little in comparison with what he might have done if his hands had been more free.

He applied to his life the same rule as he had followed at South Leith. He planned, he looked ahead, he arranged his tasks, parochial and otherwise, like a business man with a heavy engagement diary, and with the same care he organised the work of his assistants.

III

Throughout the whole of his ministry, John White counted himself greatly blessed in his assistants. He was blessed indeed; but one need not look very far to find the reason. From among the many who were eager to join him, he sought always for the young man who would glory in hard work: a young man with zeal and initiative, with humour and loving-kindness. He once said with a smile he always chose a young man that he thought would be able to put up with John White! Possessing these qualities in varying degree, his assistants were men of different types, but they had one thing in common: all had loyalty and respect for the man who took them by the hand and taught them their rudiments. To them it was an experience without price. Throughout his ministry, John White had more than forty assistants, and they formed a fraternity that was closer than any link of sentiment made at school or college.

"Even now in 1957," said Dr. William MacNicol, leader of the General Assembly, "there is still a tremendous bond between John White's men. Though we have not known each other personally, immediately we meet there is a tie of friendship between us, and we take an interest in each other's welfare and talk about old days and the man himself." Dr. MacNicol, senior assistant at The Barony when John White went there, described those early days:

"He found time somehow for regular pastoral visitation, and he made it his own special task to visit the members who lived in the most outlying parts. He would go round them by taxicab. He felt this was only fair to his assistants, for their time would be wasted by long journeys by tramcar and on foot. You can see his kindness in this—and his efficiency. He left the afternoon service on Sunday to an assistant, but always took the morning one himself. At Communion time, and when there were other special services, we spent all day with him at the kirk. We ate our sandwiches together in the vestry, the bishop acting like an elder brother to us. In that vestry of his you would find him without fail every Wednesday evening. He sat there and made himself available to anyone—ready to give help not only to the members of his congregation but anyone who needed him. Some folk came for money, and he would send one of us to investigate. If there was need, help was always given. When sternness was called for, how stern he could be! In many of those tenements around The Barony, we had to visit regularly; the folk may not have been members of the kirk, but John White counted them his parishioners. Before his time, the elders were supposed to do the visiting, and John White was told of some who had simply left a card—sometimes on people who had been dead for years. That was stopped. Under a new rota system there would be no more of that kind of thing; and if an elder was found to be slack, woe betide him! The poverty in some places was pitiable. Stairs and landings were so dark you could never climb them without an electric torch, and we had difficulty in reading the names the postmen had put on the wall beside the doors. In those tenements, I well remember, the only furniture in many a room was a mattress on the floor. . . . But what a fine training it was for a young minister. The life was hard, but you knew exactly what your duty was. . . ."

To know exactly what their tasks were—that simplified life for the assistants. Dr. David Scott said of his own share in the work:

"Every Monday morning, without fail, a letter arrived from the bishop at my lodgings to give me a list of the people I was to visit. The other two assistants each had a list, and these had to be returned at the end of the week with a report on every visit we made. We had to make a note whether or not further visits had to be paid to any sick person. With his usual precision, the bishop graded the amount we had to do according to whether we were to have a particularly heavy Sunday. The thought he must have given to this! These visiting lists were long enough, but we knew the bishop would have a longer list than any of us. We had to take our turns with funerals. All our 'marching orders' were written out by hand. He knew everything that was going on. That was a remarkable thing, but it was a great comfort to his assistants."

Some folk said they could not understand how John White got through all the work he did at that time.

"We assistants understood this well enough," said Dr. J. C. M. Conn. "For one thing, he was always *punctual*. I never knew him to be late for any appointment—and he wouldn't allow anyone else to be late if he could help it. If he had another appointment, he had a wonderful knack of bringing an interview to an end. I wish I could describe that gracious smile and the kindly push on the shoulder towards the door. . . ."

John White worked his assistants hard, but he helped them to play hard too. Their few weekly hours of leisure were hours of real relaxation —a forgetting of all cares. He enjoyed a first-rate football match, and they

75

enjoyed going with him. He insisted on their all wearing soft collars: "I don't like to spoil the enjoyment of the people round me," he always said. "When a really good goal was scored, you would have thought he was going to throw his cap over the heads of the crowd." Dr. Scott gives us another glimpse of John White in high spirits. He tells how every Sunday evening, all the assistants were expected at the manse for supper—and often they were joined by assistants from the Cathedral. It was a joyful gathering. One of the Manse children was excused from going to the evening service in order to be at home to welcome whoever arrived first, for as a rule the assistants would be coming in from different places. The meal that awaited them was usually a bowl of soup, followed often by a kedgeree dish, and there was always the huge tea urn. After supper, the children were allowed to sit listening to the exchange of stories amid a haze of tobacco smoke, then they were sent off to bed. No shop talk of a worrying kind was allowed.

"We just made a happy social occasion of it," said Dr. Scott. "Sometimes we kept it up till midnight. One winter night stands out in my memory. All the children were home from school. We sallied out, the lot of us, with big tea trays and tobogganed down the snow on the steep slope of Dundonald Road. J. W. took his turn on a tray. If a passer-by caught a glimpse of the 'cloth' thus engaged, well, it couldn't be helped. Were the neighbours scandalised at the minister of The Barony permitting these ongoings—even taking a hand in them? Perhaps they were. But they had the good sense to hold their tongues about it. . . .

"After the great kindness shown to me," continued Dr. Scott, "I vowed that if ever I had an assistant, he should be made welcome to my house every Sunday evening. I ought to say that the lot of many assistants in those days was very different from ours. Their relation with their bishops was much more distant than ours with the great John. They weren't the friends of their bishops as we were. I remember I had had a serious operation just before I joined him—and how careful he was that I should not be overburdened with work till I was quite fit again. Of all his personal characteristics, I think I would put kindness first. That meant more to me in those days than all his great powers of organisation and gifts of leadership."

Mr. Stewart Brown, who came later in that long succession, has told of the first interview he ever had with John White:

"My diary for that day records my impression of 'a very quiet man, unassuming, kindly. Courteous to a very young probationer. Direct and to the point. Asking few but very penetrating questions. I thought his mind had already been made up about me. He was seeing me merely to satisfy himself. . . . No sign of unctuous affability —but a very genuine interest.' He outlined my work and gave me three rules. First, loyalty to the staff—'You are not my assistant, but my colleague.' Second, a sense of responsibility—'A man who is licensed to preach the Gospel of Christ need not wait for orders from his bishop. When he sees a need he must meet it.' Third, no worry— 'Plenty of work but no worry, for even God Himself can't ask you to do better than your best, and the worst probably won't happen anyway!' He added, 'Try it; even if you make mistakes. I may correct you, but I'll also commend you.' And I never had one unkind word from him."

Dr. William Barclay, Vice-Chairman of the Presbyterian Church in Canada, has told how his assistants would plague him to tell them how they should deal with a difficult situation that had come along: "I went to him, like the others, time without number. He was always very patient, very wise and helpful. He may have thought I was a little sensitive, for one day he gave me a word of advice in which I have never ceased to find comfort—'Barclay, remember this, you won't please everyone, so don't try.' "

Few of his assistants ever took an important step without seeking the guidance of their chief.

"If we heard of a vacancy," said Dr. Scott, "and thought we would like to try for it, he was the first one we consulted. He knew our failings better than anybody. He knew exactly what we were capable of, he knew what we had yet to learn. Sometimes he would head us off from putting in for a parish if he thought we would not fit. If he did approve, he did everything he could to help us—and his influence was immense. I can remember when I put in for a parish to which I afterwards went. I was very eager to get it and he thought I would suit. He took me aside and said, 'Now, look here—if you don't get this, there's to be no remorse. It will just mean that that parish was not meant for you, and the place for you lies somewhere ahead.' When I got the parish he was delighted. He said he particularly wanted me there. It was within a reasonable distance of The Barony."

Among the first of his assistants had been the Rev. John R. Spence, who had come to him at South Leith. He had been brought up in Shettleston, had been a member of the parish church there, and he became one of John White's closest friends.

"Our bishop forgot none of us after we had left him for a charge of our own," said Mr. Spence. "All of us could tell the same story. He came to my induction at Southdean, he married me, he christened my boy. In fact he said he would have been very annoyed if I had failed to ask him, although it meant a long journey down into the Border country to our Southdean manse. What red-letter days his visits were! He was always eager for a tramp over the hills, a day's fishing on the Jed, even a game of croquet on the lawn (he was a Terrible Ivan with the mallet), and he revelled in preaching to good Border folk in our Souden kirk. . . . A great friend, a great minister, a great leader. His was a dedicated life. He could have risen to the heights in any profession, but never for one single moment—I am certain of this—did he regret his choice to serve in the Church of Christ."

John White took particular care to give his assistants "a good send-off" when they were beginning work for the first time in a parish of their own. He liked to preach in their pulpit on the Sunday morning service after the ordination and induction, and he would give the congregation some straight advice.

"Refrain from making trifling demands on your minister's time," he said in one of these sermons. "Help him to husband his strength for the more important work of his ministry. Pray for him that he may be strong and enabled, through all distractions, to keep a firm grasp on spiritual realities. Remember that ministers are not made at a university. They are made—or unmade—by congregations: by sympathy or the lack of it. He needs you as you need him. There will be no end to the spiritual prosperity in this parish if you are at one with your minister in your affections—if your hearts burn with fire for the same Holy Love. . . . Judge your minister by his best, never by his worst. None of us would care to be judged by our feeblest effort. No one can live on the hilltop every day. . . . Help your minister to preach well. It takes two to make a sermon—the preacher and the hearer. . . . In his pastoral work, don't all of you expect to be visited first. Somebody must be first, somebody last. But whether

rich or poor, all will be equal in the pastoral regard of your minister. . . .
Be not sermon-hearers only, but be labourers together in the work of
the Lord. Many of you have more experience than he, experience
bought by sorrow, and I ask you to lay this at his service. . . . God grant
that the trembling hopes that have filled his heart, as he faces his work
here, may be more than fulfilled. May he live in peace and honour
among you, strong in the Lord and in the power of His might."

IV

In looking at John White through the eyes of his assistants, one finds a
striking unanimity in the impression he made upon them all as a comforter
in time of sorrow.

"At humble Glasgow funerals," said Dr. David Scott, "I used to
be deeply touched by the way he repeated the fifth verse of the sixty-
seventh Paraphrase: 'His gracious hand shall wipe the tears from every
weeping eye . . .,' and then he would repeat the last line with a wonderful tenderness—'Death itself shall die.' Always when we were leaving
the cemetery, I can remember how he would seek out the most
stricken one and give comfort in the gentlest way. At a funeral in a
poor tenement, a small girl was crying bitterly because her grand-
mother had died. John White went straight to that bairn and took her
on his knee. He spoke to her very quietly until she had dried her tears."

Dr. Conn wrote of his chief:

"He had a most gentle way of dealing with the poor mission folk
at the Black Street Institute, and it was the same in giving Communion to the dying. There was a simplicity, a brevity, a homeliness,
a dignity, about him at such times. Dr. White liked to be present, if
he could, at every funeral, even when one of his assistants had been
detailed to take the service. He always gave me an order to begin at
the appointed time whether he had then arrived or not, but only once
do I remember him to have been late; his punctuality was remarkable
since he often had to get right across Glasgow at the peak period of
traffic. I have known him, when he was almost crippled with lumbago,
dragging himself out to the funeral of some poor person, and climbing
three flights of steep stairs with the help of a stout stick and the hand-
rail. No one who heard him could fail to be touched by the words he
would repeat when the burial was of a little girl: 'Death is a going

home. Death is a sleep. *She is not dead but sleepeth.* And because it is a sleep, there must be an awakening. *Talitha cumi* . . . wee lassie, rise up.' One can never forget things like that. Who would want to? Then came the radiant smile, the warm handshake, the very quiet kindly goodbye. There was never any outward display of emotion at a funeral service conducted in the house by Dr. John White. How could there be in the presence of such faith and fortitude as he possessed?"

Mr. Stewart Brown gives another little glimpse of the man:

"I still see him, a tall figure, standing half-stooped, hands on the table, without a book or scrap of paper, going through a funeral service that was moving yet inspiriting. His emphasis was always on the future, on the great Christian hope, 'that this was not an end but a beginning, not a door closing but a door opening on a life far finer and more fair and full than anything we can know here'."

After every funeral, a visit was paid to the house to give comfort to those grieving for the lost one. A letter in his own hand reveals his sympathy with all in sorrow:

"May you be upheld and comforted by the grace of Him Who alone can keep and sustain us at such an hour of trial. Any word from me can only assure you of the deep sympathy of the wide circle of friends whose hearts will be sore for you in your loss and loneliness. And yet there is a word I would add. It is a grand thing that we hold a faith which assures us that death has no dominion over our loved ones and that they still live, still love, still serve. What a dark tragedy life would be without this great hope of Christ to lighten and comfort us."

The Very Rev. Dr. R. F. V. Scott, who had been a colleague of John White's, said:

"One had but to see him in touch with sorrow to know how close he lived to God. Once I was with him at the funeral of an old Barony member, where I had asked him to take the prayers at the service in the house. He prefaced the prayers with just a word or two addressed to that sorrowing household. The memory is not so much of *what* he said but of the sense of comfort flowing like a benediction from the man. It was not the type of sympathy that brings a ready tear to the eye, but real comfort springing from the blessed assurance of the faith. Here was revealed the true source of all his sympathy and kindness.

John White, for all his greatness, assumed no throne because in all his life of thought and action God was enthroned."

V

John White's relations with his kirk session at The Barony were in some ways unusual. With most of his elders he was on terms of cordial friendship. But he was not the man to sit mute when he felt that there was a tendency for the discussion to stray in the wrong direction. It has been said that he often acted as if he had no elders at all, but this is an exaggeration. He would lead his elders when he felt they needed leading, and he did so at times with tremendous verve, at times with adroit persuasion. Some of his assistants tell of how he would ponder over a problem and come to a decision, then he would call together the members of his session after a Sunday morning service.

"He would explain carefully to them that he was not holding a session meeting; they were only having an informal talk together. He then would announce the decision he had made and ask if there were any criticisms or suggestions. If there were any, he would duly dispose of them. Later, at a properly constituted session meeting, it is not surprising that his decisions were homologated. Only a man who was a born leader and had the absolute confidence of his fellows could have risked such authoritarian methods. . . . One might describe his attitude to his session as that of a company director to his executives. For the most part, his elders responded splendidly. But in a very large kirk session, such as that of The Barony, it was inevitable that there would be a little unevenness of quality, and it was not always possible to inspire everyone with such zeal that all his plans were carried out fully. There were occasions when he was brusque. These were not frequent, but they were never forgotten."

Among the incidents still told of him is the occasion when, during a spell of bitter winter weather, he summoned an emergency meeting of the kirk session. The members duly gathered and he stalked into the midst of them and constituted the meeting, then said: "Gentlemen, I am not going into that pulpit again until you have improved the heating of the church." That was all he had to say, and having said it he closed the meeting with prayer. There was consternation. But the kirk session were bound to agree that it had been uncommonly cold in the kirk that morning, and a number of gas radiators were hastily installed in the course of the week. During the services on the following Sunday the radiators hissed and whistled, and gave off such noxious smells that they had to be removed as hastily as they had been installed. (It is not on record whether faulty ones had been chosen by a whimsical elder.)

Some there were who went away disgruntled from a kirk session meeting, and they were usually the ones who had not ventured to speak up; but for most of the time, the great majority of his elders and deacons were glad that they had a minister whose decisions, nine times out of ten, were wise and practical. He was not as other men: but it was better to have a John White than someone whose heart was not as large as his and who lacked his sagacity and enthusiasm and drive.

VI

In calling him to The Barony, the congregation fully understood how heavily he was engaged in important tasks for the Church of Scotland. In South Leith, he had undergone excessive strain by maintaining his work in the parish at full pressure and at the same time serving the Church in a wider sphere. He could see that his activities outside his own parish would be likely to increase, especially in the union negotiations with the United Free Church. He had had a particularly strenuous time before the Assembly of 1911 drawing up one of the most important statements of policy in the union movement. And as the movement gathered impetus, he feared the calls upon him would be even more insistent.

What he had foreseen was to come true. Often he was forced to turn over to an assistant a task he himself would normally have taken without a thought. He had lived in Leith when the union movement had begun; now the committee work meant frequent journeys by train from Glasgow to Edinburgh. But there was at least one compensation for his being located in the West country. He became a member of the Presbytery of Glasgow and of the Synod of Glasgow and Ayr. The "turbulent West" was the name that one of the leaders of the Church applied to that great area: turbulent, because in loyalty to the Old Kirk many feared that some of the things that were part of their ancient heritage were being bargained away in the committee rooms at Edinburgh. As a member of the Presbytery and the Synod, it was to fall to John White to allay their fears and lead his brethren forward "to the larger union of Christ's Church on earth which all our hearts desire".

Chapter VI

THE TRAGEDY OF DISUNION

I

ON 5th August 1915, while John White was under orders to go to France and take up his duties as chaplain to a battalion of Cameronians, the minister of St. Giles' wrote a revealing letter to him. Dr. Wallace Williamson, joint convener of the Reunion Committee which had been in existence since 1909, begged for a loan of the immense dossiers John White had compiled on Church Union which included memoranda of every step taken since the movement had begun. It was then uncertain how long he would be absent at the front, and Wallace Williamson was naturally anxious for the Committee to have the full records at their disposal. "So long as we had you at our elbow," he wrote, "there was always a living Encyclopaedia at hand!"

Among the private papers of John White, it was found after his death that by far the largest section dealt with Church Union. His meditations on this subject must have been frequent and deep, for he recorded many of his thoughts, sometimes in brief notes, sometimes in developed arguments and disquisitions. If Church History was not his first love in his studies at the Divinity Hall, it was the most abiding; and he left the Hall with such zeal to pursue it that he applied a few years later, as we have seen, for the Chair of Church History in the Divinity Faculty at Glasgow University. As his thoughts played around the prospect of a reuniting of the Kirk of Scotland, he studied in detail the many splits and unions of Scottish Presbyterianism. He analysed what had caused them, and this took him back to the Reformation and earlier, and sent him probing below the surface of events and into the motives and designs of men. The long string of Acts on ecclesiastical matters passed by the Parliament of Scotland, and later by that of Great Britain, came under his review. With his gift of rapidly tearing the heart out of a problem, and with the aid of that prodigious memory of his, it would have been strange if he had not become expert in the history and law of Scotland's Kirk. Wallace Williamson had good ground for his description of his friend as a "living Encyclopaedia" on these cognate subjects.

JOHN WHITE

It was a turbulent history John White had mastered. For the most part, Parliamentary enactments and legal judgments on Church cases form a long record of battle: of striving and frustration, of Erastian suppression, of wrong-headedness and hard-heartedness, all of it too seldom softened by Christian charity. Between the Revolution Settlement in 1690 and the end of the nineteenth century, there had been no less than thirteen splits in the Presbyterian Kirk.[1] Of these, more than half involved the formation of a separate body; the others were caused by a minority who refused to enter a union along with their brethren. The dismay felt by John White was often tinged with admiration for the stout hearts of men who held so doggedly to their opinions on matters which they counted vital. The first group to bind themselves into a separate body had been the old Cameronians, who had hived off to form a sect of their own because the Covenants had not been made an integral part of the Revolution Settlement of 1690 which ratified the Confession of Faith and regulated Presbyterian Church government. Up to 1863, if any member of this body, the Reformed Presbyterian Church, dared to take the oath of allegiance to the Sovereign, or to exercise his Parliamentary vote, he was ruthlessly excommunicated. John White assessed the causes of the other secessions from the Church of Scotland that had taken place before the Disruption of 1843—those of men who formed the Associated Synod and the Relief Synod, the two bodies that were to come together in 1847 to form the United Presbyterian Church. He noted that no dissenting body had ever returned to the fold of the Established Church: "no straying daughter had ever come home" except those few that formed part of a minor sect called the Old Light Burghers. The men who went out, it was evident, stayed out: but although they stayed out, it was not "in unison to dwell". For it was among those dissenting bodies that most of the splits took place, and a diagram of the intricate severings and joinings is apt to remind one of a plan of the complicated London Underground Railway system. John White was familiar not only with these movements but with the constitution and testimony of the different Presbyterian bodies—and to promulgate their testimony they all seemed to regard as a cardinal duty. During most of the nineteenth century in Scotland there were as many as six Presbyterian denominations, and each reckoned itself to be the true representative of the Reformed Church. John White's

---

[1] These took place in 1690, 1733, 1747, 1761, 1799, 1806, 1820, 1839, 1843, 1852, 1876, 1893, 1900. The serious splits and schisms in the Scottish Episcopal Church are outside the scope of the present work.

84

studies revealed to him that common to all was an inherent love of liberty in matters spiritual: it was on a definition of spiritual liberty that they differed. Their desire for reunion was as warm as their love of liberty, but it could not be reunion at the expense of a principle held so dear. With no disparity in essential doctrine, the dissenting Presbyterian Churches failed to find common ground for a comprehensive union.

The Established Church had her own internal dissensions, but she suffered no split in her body politic after the Disruption. Leaders worked and prayed for the day when the many rents in the fabric of Scottish Presbyterianism would be repaired. Some of them indeed went beyond Presbyterianism and bewailed the fact that the Scottish Episcopalians were outside the Established Church—"the onely trew and haily Kirk of Jesus Christ within this realme". A corporate union with all Protestant Churches in Scotland was the clearly avowed ideal of men whose words carried weight in the General Assembly. John White was one of these: but he was able, which some were not, to look upon the dismembered Kirk and acknowledge that this was an ideal that only a miracle could bring to fulfilment in the lifetime of any of them. Not that he considered that this in any way blunted the sharp edge of that Divine challenge to all Churches to come together in a union both spiritual and temporal. On the contrary, he declared that no effort, the motives of which had been clarified and fortified by prayer, would be made in vain even if only a partial reunion were at first achieved; it would be at least one good firm step forward. But his passionate conviction was that the larger effort should be made and that it was the task of the Church of Scotland to make it.

II

From the start of his ministry John White had been a reunion man. Brought up in the Old Kirk, he had roots also in the Free Church through his maternal grandparents: at her marriage, his mother had transferred to the Church of her husband. His wife had also been of the Free Church, and it was not until she became his bride and went to Shettleston that she had "lifted her lines" and joined the Old Kirk. He had had sympathetic tuition from these two pious and highly intelligent women on the spirit and activities of a dissenting Church. Many a minister has left it on record how mutual help was the exception rather than the rule between the different denominations: but John White counted it his duty to fraternise with the clergy of all Christian Churches within his own parish—and indeed with those outside it when their paths happened to cross. He preached in their pulpits; he gave encouragement and support where it was welcomed. Picking at random a letter from his files, one may read the words of the Episcopal minister in Leith, written in 1906, that show how the reopening service of his church, after alterations, would not be counted complete without the presence of John White, the parish minister who had shown such friendship towards his Episcopalian brethren; one may read a letter written in 1907 by a member of the Roman Catholic church at Shettleston recalling the material support John White had given to the work of the Catholic community there; one may read a letter from the man who had been a Congregational minister in South Leith—"with your many and great kindnesses in the old days at Leith ever in mind, every new indication of your wide usefulness adds to our pleasure and evokes our warm wishes. . . . With the passing of the years, my gratitude to you, who were so kind and good to me, at times pressing favours on me of which I felt myself unworthy, has steadily increased. . . ."

There were dissenting ministers who spoke of what they called the stimulus of sectarianism. Erskine of Linlathen's words had been too easily forgotten: "I doubt not that a certain kind and degree of good may arise among certain persons out of our Scottish kirk separation—more awakened thought, more zeal—but I fear also *more judging: more spiritual pride.*" Whatever stimulus it may once have given, nobody knew better than John White that separation was now often at the root of rivalries and tensions in both local administration and trade. In small communities, with leaders on each side who were narrow and stubborn men, it caused the severing of old friendships, the splitting of families related by marriage ties, and the befouling of social life. And some of the growing ills of the time were rendered the more tragic by the religious state of the land. Men of vision had only to look about them to discern things that made the heart ache. In towns large and small to which countryfolk had been drawn by the lure of the better wages to be earned in industry, thousands of men and women lived beyond the influence of church-life and thousands of children had no Sunday School. While in country parishes, two or more Presbyterian kirks had each their handful of folk worshipping in spiritual isolation, often with a dour sense of rectitude that was mingled with pity for those in the kirk across the road, a few hard-pressed ministers in nearby towns were making a pitifully inadequate effort to carry "the means of grace" to the quickly multiplying denizens of slums and near-slums. The triumphs and failures of the Church in Scotland are bound up

with the history of the Industrial Revolution, and with the developments
that sprang from the loins of that revolution, which so drastically altered
the way of life of thousands who grew to manhood in surroundings from
which their grandfathers would have recoiled as from a new and alien
world.

The churchless thousands: this was to be a dark thought that drove with
a furious and sacrificial compulsion the energies of John White into two
great channels, one of which was Church Reunion. Surely the ministers
who could be spared from depleted country districts, where often three
were doing the work of one, would find a fresh impetus for service among
folk now huddled together in tenements or rows of tiny cramped houses!
And when the inevitable swing of the industrial pendulum brought a
recession of trade, there would follow weeks and months of destitution
in these squalid communities, where it was the children who suffered most
sharply. John White's voice rang out from the pulpit in many a resounding
challenge to his fellow Christians:

> "The poor are always with us, and the scanty employment of
> past months has not enabled them to save much to tide over this
> period of winter slackness. . . . This is a question that should find a
> sympathetic hearing in the Churches—and find there a sympathetic
> answer. Let the Churches delay for the winter months all questions of
> spiritual and ecclesiastical independence and unitedly engage in
> upholding family independence; by this truce to the present denomin-
> ational asperities, they would be more spiritually qualified to answer
> with success the question of Church federation or union."

These words were uttered in 1904, soon after he had gone to South
Leith. Four years previously, the Free and United Presbyterian Churches,
after a travail that had persisted for nearly forty years, had achieved
corporate union. At an important meeting in Shettleston, in speaking of
that Union in 1900, he had given it his full-hearted blessing:

> "We trust it will prove a stimulus to religious life of the members
> of the two Churches and that there will be no question as to who is
> the predominant partner. . . . One practical result I see—it will prevent
> overlapping of forces. Take Shettleston alone. Up to the time of this
> Union, we had four Free churches and two United Presbyterians, and
> now there are six United Free churches. Their forces can now be more
> practically distributed. We shall be sorry to lose any of them, but a
> few strong, healthy, well-supported churches are better than many

struggling and impoverished ones. Yet I say that this Union lacks one thing—*you and I of the Established Church are not in it*. I am in favour of a larger Union, so that we can unite forces to face social problems like temperance and the housing of the poor, to say nothing of ending the present wasteful rivalry and denominational jealousy in the foreign mission field."

III

In spite of these jealousies and asperities, the work of devoted men was bearing fruit. Gradually but surely, a change in the ecclesiastical atmosphere of Scotland was taking place. Before the twentieth century was five years old, the time had become more propitious for a union of the leading Presbyterian bodies than it had been since the Disruption. During those sixty years, many a move towards union had been made; indeed, not a single decade had passed without an earnest plea for unity by leaders of the Established Church. Within ten years of the Disruption, and again in 1859, Dr. James Robertson (the Robertson of Ellon who was appointed to the Chair of Church History in Edinburgh University) was urging the Churches to come together; that far-seeing and great-hearted man directed his words to the United Presbyterians as well as to the Free Church. In 1867, the year of John White's birth, Professor T. J. Crawford, also of the Divinity Faculty of Edinburgh University, in a memorable address as Moderator, entreated all Presbyterians to close their ranks and compose their differences. Dr. Charteris was appointed to approach the Free Church informally, and in 1869 he wrote to Dr. Taylor Innes, a prominent advocate who was one of her leading laymen, to make it quite clear that there was a strong and growing desire in the Established Church to unite all branches of Scottish Presbyterianism on equal terms. The phrase *on equal terms* was significant: "It is the desire of my innermost heart, my prayer and my hope," he wrote, "that this will be brought about, for without it I foresee nothing but anarchy and ruin twenty years hence, and for ever, in Scotland." No man of his time was more completely dedicated to the cause of Union than Charteris[1]; and he confessed his heart had been nearly broken by the way the Free Church was treating this great and urgent problem. "What do you propose—what do you want?" he asked Taylor Innes. "I shall do everything in my power to gratify you and yours. But you must meet us half-way." It was plain that there could be no half-way meeting-place; the Free Church reasserted that she could never

[1] He offered to give up half the emoluments of his Chair to help the cause of Union.

consider reunion with the Church of Scotland because of "that Church's spiritual subjection to the State, which had been the cause of the Disruption".[1] But this rejection of the Charteris appeal did not prevent union overtures from coming up next year to the General Assembly of the Church of Scotland: the nation-wide need was apparent to many. The Assembly of 1870 recorded

"their deep sense of the manifold evils arising from the ecclesiastical divisions of Scotland; and, considering the great impiety and abounding wickedness in the land which the divided Churches have not succeeded in removing, the Assembly record their hearty willingness and desire to take all possible steps, consistent with the principles on which this Church is founded, to promote the reunion of Churches having a common origin, adhering to the same Confession of Faith and the same system of government and worship."

All the ministers were called upon to cultivate the spirit of unity and to co-operate with the ministers of the other evangelical Churches; and the first Union Committee was formed with Professor Crawford and Lord Polwarth as joint conveners. Subsequent Assemblies repeated their willingness to join with other Presbyterian Churches. The General Assembly of 1875 recorded their deep anxiety that dissensions among the divided Churches in Scotland were becoming worse, and the Union Committee was reappointed with instructions "to consider any suggestion made by other Presbyterian Churches to remove what they may feel to be obstacles in the way of Reunion".

The Assembly might well express concern. Dissension was becoming more acute with the passing of each month. To a great extent the worsening of relations was the result of a step taken by the Church of Scotland which a quite unbiassed outsider might have reckoned to be one that would have brought the Established and Free Churches more closely together. This was the successful effort of the Church of Scotland in 1874 to persuade Parliament to repeal the Patronage Act, that old and too-familiar trouble-maker of 1712. With Erastian doggedness, the Government had refused to remove it from the Statute Book in spite of continual

---

[1] What was called "the *raison d'être* of the Free Church" was thus described at that time by Dr. Rainy: "In certain circumstances, the civil courts, on the part of the State and acting by its authority, may prescribe to the courts of the Established Church, as statutory duty, the performance of spiritual functions—the ordination of ministers and other functions of the same class; and not only proscribe but forbid to a very large extent spiritual functions being exercised, forbid the ordination of ministers, forbid the receiving of men to sit in Church courts, forbid the dispensation of ordinances."

appeals for redress. To be sure, some ministers who held their benefices under the shelter of influential patrons were glad of it, for they had the comfortable feeling that they could snap their fingers at kirk sessions and congregations, and in 1841 they had petitioned Parliament to pay no attention to the cries of the Church for relief. But the scandals to which the 1712 Act had left the door ajar were too many for the Church in general to tolerate. One of its more preposterous terms was that a Heritor who was a Roman Catholic could not appoint a minister to a church; if he were a Jew or a Hindu or a Hottentot there was no legal bar to his making the presentation. The Benefices Act, passed just after the Disruption, was intended to adjust some of the harsher provisions of the Patronage Act, but it had so little good effect that in the next twenty-six years there were sixty-one cases of disputed settlements, which ran up thousands of pounds in legal costs and had the effect of "exasperating the people, engendering bad blood, tearing parishes asunder, bitterly dividing the Courts of the Church, and inflicting grave spiritual injury". A notorious case had been one in the parish of South Leith, where a disputed settlement had wasted the time of the Presbytery of Edinburgh for no less than twenty-four days.

IV

The leaders of the Church of Scotland had hoped that this removal of patronage would open the way for reunion, but the Free Church asserted that mere repeal of the pernicious 1712 Act was no answer to the Disruption.[1] Something very much wider would be required before they could contemplate reunion with what Dr. Chalmers had called "a purified Establishment" to which they all hoped one day to return. Although he knew well the harm patronage had caused, Dr. Rainy did all he could privately to keep the Act in force: he went to London and at Westminster used his persuasive powers on Mr. Gladstone, who subsequently rose in the House of Commons to denounce the Patronage Abolition Bill while it was being discussed. He declared that the intention of those who sponsored the Bill was that, when patronage was cleared out of the way, many ministers and members would desert the Free Church and go over man by man to the Church of Scotland. Dr. James MacGregor of St. Cuthbert's,

---

[1] The attitude of the United Presbyterian Church can be found in the Pastoral Address of Synod, 1874: "The abolition of Patronage by the Government has not affected our main grounds of objection to the Establishment. . . . We claim our freedom, not as a boon from the British Parliament, however obedient we are to it in civil duties, but as an inalienable part of our Christian heritage. What Caesar has withheld and gives as a favour, he could again withdraw. . . ."

Edinburgh, declared that if Gladstone's implication was that the repeal of patronage would benefit the Established Church at the expense of the Free, and that a dissenting Church had therefore a vested interest in maintaining the defects of an Established Church, then it was the "most repulsive doctrine ever fashioned in the brain of Christian men". The trouble which had been brewing over this Act turned out to be of a particularly odious kind. Some Old Kirk ministers were denounced as sheep-stealers and were accused of visiting members of the Free Church— visiting with much greater zeal than they had ever shown in their own pastoral visitation—and trying to cajole them back into the fold because "the wiping out of patronage had removed the only serious difference between them". In an article published in an important newspaper, the Act repealing patronage was described as "a mouse-trap to catch the more easily lured members of the Free Church". A pamphlet war began, and gibes like poisoned darts were flung to and fro between brethren who could see no hope of their ever worshipping together.

The Free Church leaders had good cause for anxiety. Their Church had, a few years before, been passing through the most troubled period of her history. There had been a split in her ranks which might have developed into a disruption from the Disruption Church. The rift had been largely the work of the famous Dr. Begg of Newington, a man fervently dedicated to the old Disruption belief in an ultimate return to a purified Establishment. With prodigious skill, and the use of costly propaganda financed by those he had infected with his ardour, Begg had managed to wreck the union negotiations between the Free and United Presbyterian Churches which had begun so hopefully in 1863. He had not only set the heather on fire—most of his supporters were in the Highlands—but he had taken legal advice and made no secret of the fact that he believed a union with the United Presbyterians would leave himself and his followers in possession of the whole of the property and endowments and monies of the Free Church. This drastic possibility shook the nerve of many. If Dr. Begg's legal position was sound—and its soundness was to be tested a quarter of a century later—Dr. Rainy would have led a paupered Free Church into a corporate union with the United Presby-terians. In backing out, Rainy was accused of acting from motives of expediency and of placing the dictates of worldly wisdom above the spiritual needs of the time—an accusation which his friends indignantly repudiated. His own declaration was that he had at least preserved the unity of the Free Church: but it was a unity in name only. The passions of those whom the perfervid Dr. Begg had rallied to his standard were so inflamed that from many a Highland glen epithets were hurled at the United Presbyterian Church—largely a Lowland body—which exceeded in acrimony anything ever uttered in the white heat of Church controversy since the Reformation. Dr. J. R. Fleming, the Church historian, describes the Free Church as having then "launched upon an angry sea of strife that in one form or another troubled her for the rest of her separate existence". And so sharp was the bitterness engendered by the propaganda campaign that many of Dr. Begg's colleagues denounced his methods as unscrupulous, and Dr. Rainy called him "the evil genius of the Free Church". It was in the midst of these troubles that the Church of Scotland took a bold step. Most of the older ministers who had remained in the Established Church at the time of the Disruption had passed away. Their places were filled by a generation of enthusiastic men who had learned many lessons from the débâcle of 1843, and their zeal had raised the stricken Church of Scotland to a state of spiritual and material prosperity. It was the voices of this new generation that were now heard in the Church courts; and in an atmosphere of goodwill, the General Assembly of 1878 decided to draft a Minute asking the Free, the United Presbyterian, the Reformed Presbyterian, and the Original Secession bodies "to come into frank and friendly conference in the hope of cementing a union" between them all. Here at last was something more than a mere waving of an olive branch: here was a forthright request, sent by the Established Church to these sister Churches in the land, which said in effect, "In the name of God, and for the sake of His Kingdom, are you prepared to unite?" And it called for an answer from each.

V

A glance through John White's papers makes it clear how carefully he studied the reaction of the other Churches to this Minute from the Assembly. The Free Church gladly acknowledged the "courteous and considerate manner in which, after such a long estrangement, the Established Church had made an approach . . .," and the reply signed by Sir Henry Wellwood Moncreiff, Bt., D.D., emphasised yet again that they held strongly to the principles which had forced them to leave the Established Church at the Disruption. The United Presbyterian Church declared that it was utterly impossible to "contemplate sharing with the Established Church the trust reposed in it by the State," but the hope was expressed that there would be wide co-operation, particularly in the choosing of sites of new churches to be built in large cities, in weighing up the religious wants of country districts, and in unity of discipline and action in the foreign mission field. The Original Seceders were equally emphatic that union was impossible; and the Reformed Presbyterians, nine ministers in all, grasped the opportunity to remind the Church of Scotland that they were not in a state of secession from the Established Church—on the contrary, it was the Established Church that was in a state of secession from them!

In a note which must have been made in his early years on the subject of these replies, John White wrote:

> "The evils which followed from the ecclesiastical divisions of Presbyterians in Scotland were deplored by all the Churches. And in proportion as attention is fixed on those evils, there will grow up in men's hearts a desire for union and a greater unwillingness to be satisfied with any ground for remaining divided short of over-mastering necessity."

If the Church of Scotland made no further approach to the other Churches until 1886, there was good reason for her reticence. A new cause of dispeace had come to add to the clamour of dissentient voices. This was the Disestablishment campaign, the results of which, as we have seen, had so seriously affected the relations between John White and the heritors of Shettleston. Dr. P. Carnegie Simpson stated in his Life of Dr. Rainy that the repeal of the Patronage Act "challenged the principles and even the existence of the Free Church". That was the attitude of the majority; and Dr. Rainy, before even the Free Church had officially declared her mind on the matter, was taking part in a drive for the disestablishment and disendowment of the Church of Scotland. His hand was strengthened when he was joined on public platforms by Dr. John Cairns, Principal of the United Presbyterian Church College, "than whom there was not a nobler Christian man in the Scottish ministry of his time". Both men believed that a union with the Church of Scotland could be brought about only after that Church had been legally wrenched apart from the State. They spoke at meetings held in support of Liberal Party principles. In vain, Lord Rosebery, himself a Liberal and a future Prime Minister, tried to prevent Disestablishment from becoming a political issue. The words of Dr. Horatius Bonar, "When politics come in, religion goes out", were often to be recalled in later years. The Shettleston

Church Case is but one of many quarrels that reveal the blighting influence party politics were to have on matters spiritual. A Scottish branch of the English Liberation Society ("liberation of the Church from State patronage and control") was composed largely of "rabid political dissenters of the narrowest and most aggressive type".[1] The Scottish Disestablishment Association came into being and issued propaganda material which the author of the Life of Dr. Charteris describes as "screaming misrepresentation". As a body, the Church of Scotland was seriously perturbed, and a Church Interests Committee was formed, with Lord Balfour of Burleigh as joint convener, to direct what was known as Church Defence.

The object of the campaign was to use "all prudent means to keep the people of Scotland duly informed on the national position and principles of the Church". Many mourned the fact that she was obliged to descend into the political arena and defend herself there. To counter the action of those who were pulling political wires and those who were using Disestablishment as a pawn on the political chessboard, members of the Church of Scotland were told it was their duty to cast their votes in such a way as "to prevent the return of all Parliamentary candidates pledged to Disestablishment". To a large extent, it was the Church Interests Committee that blocked the passing of the Peddie Bill. Only four weeks' notice had been given of it, and resistance had to be quickly organised. Petitions against it, carrying nearly seven hundred thousand signatures, were presented to Parliament. (The supporters of the Bill succeeded in obtaining less than three thousand signatures.) If the Bill had become an Act, the Church of Scotland would have been deprived of her whole revenues and properties, her buildings, manses, glebes, *quoad sacra* churches and the monies privately donated for their endowment. Of the property to be thus wrested from the Church, some was to be used for secular purposes, but the church buildings might be rented, if desired, by the congregations who had worshipped in them. Behind this Bill was the principle, alleged by the Liberation Society to be logically defensible, that all of the property of the Church of Scotland, whether it had been

---

[1] In a speech, which was to become famous, enjoining the Church of Scotland to be on its guard, Principal Tulloch of St. Andrews University said: "Let no one steal your Christian patrimony under the guise of big phrases, which, speaking of equality, mean robbery and the abstraction of the greatest national blessing you have ever had or ever will have. Make your Church all you would wish it to be. Reform and improve it. Remove any barrier which may still prevent other Presbyterians from uniting with it on the widest possible basis. Reorganise it—but do not overturn it. *It will be a dark day for Scotland if you yield to the claim of English secularism and sectarian rivalry.*"

the gift of individual members or not, belonged to the State and should be seized by the State. "No disestablishment principle ever propounded was so well-fitted and more purposely intended to destroy the Church of Scotland": these words were underlined in red by John White. Nearly fifteen hundred ministers who called themselves "the Liberal Clergy of Scotland" sent a petition to Mr. Gladstone asking him to take steps to put an end to Establishment, which they called "this religious scandal and political injustice". Yet, with no "establishment" bar to union, the Churches to which those clerical signatories belonged chose to remain in a state of disunion: and the incongruity of the situation did not pass unnoted by their brethren in the Established Church. Many of the younger signatories cannot have dreamt that the time would come when they would find themselves members of a united Church of Scotland. Certainly there were some who, when they dipped the pen and signed with such youthful zeal, would have marvelled greatly if they could have foreseen that they would one day proudly officiate in scarlet cassock as chaplains to the Sovereign: for among the signatories on the petitition were those of George Adam Smith, Alexander Martin, and R. J. Drummond. But there were wiser heads than theirs in the dissenting Churches at that time: Dr. Ross Taylor said "it was a monstrous thing to apply the phrase 'religious scandal' to the Church of Scotland", and he added that the petition was but a "loosely worded screed that bore signs of impulsive haste". Prominent men in both the United Presbyterian and the Free Churches were so disgusted with this politico-religious move on the part of the "Liberal Clergy" of Scotland that they betook themselves forthwith out of the Liberal Party and left it and its Clergy to their own political devices.

VI

Year after year the Disestablishment campaign went grinding on. The Church Defenders not only defended their own Church, they attacked that of their dissenting adversaries. Pamphlets tumbled from the presses of both parties. Some newspapers of influence supported the battle for Disestablishment, and counter-attacks against them were launched. Christopher Johnston (later Lord Sands) felt constrained to join in the mêlée and published a small book on Church Defence which some called a book of "Church offence", for the eminent advocate thought fit to indulge in a gentle sneer at the social status of dissenting ministers, their lack of *savoir faire* and cultured manners. Clergymen and laymen, who could have occupied their time and energies to better purpose, kept up the fight, and all they accomplished was to lower the three great Presbyterian Churches in the eyes of irreligious cynics. In the midst of all this dust, the Church of Scotland again held out the hand of friendship, and the General Assembly in May 1886 renewed an expression of "its sense of the evils of disunion", and proposed a talk round a conference table "to promote the co-operation in good works and the reunion of Churches having a common origin, adhering to the same Confession of Faith and the same system of government and worship". A solemn warning was given to all its members to maintain a spirit of Christian charity and "to abstain from all such expressions as irritate or estrange members of other Churches".

Two days later, a reply was handed in from the Assembly of the Free Church then in session. That which separated the two was as narrow as the street which separated their Assembly Halls. Could it be still further narrowed? Would the Established Church be prepared to regard her relation to the State as a matter open to discussion? This was the question the Free Church asked in her reply of 28th May. The Established Church felt obliged to make her position clear beyond any doubt: "The Church of Scotland would be false to her trust if she accepted a proposal that would even seem to imperil the religious advantages secured to the people of Scotland by the Revolution Settlement and the Treaty of Union, and she cannot do anything which might be construed into willingness to throw away the heritage of the Scottish people." An unrestricted conference was therefore out of the question. The words of Principal Tulloch in the last great speech he was to deliver in the General Assembly were to be often repeated: "Because the Church of Scotland is an Establishment, it is a witness to the great principle of a Christian state and of the maintenance of national religion, and it cannot forego that principle. It would forego its very existence if it did. . . . We must stand somewhere. *We stand here.*"

As for the United Presbyterians, their reply to this invitation was the same as that of 1879. Since they believed "the existence of an Established Church to be inequitable and inconsistent with the duty of self-support and with the entire independence of the Church", how could unity be achieved in the face of opposing views on this vital matter? One might gather from the Synod's Deliverance that the Constitution of the United Presbyterian Church must have contained a repudiation of Establishment. In fact, it contained no such thing. That "the State should have nothing to do with religion" was the belief of the extreme "Voluntaries", but a repudiation of Establishment was not a test of United Presbyterian communion, nor was it a test for ministers or office-bearers: "If in maintaining the practice of the Church according to ordination vows, anyone is disposed to believe that he yet holds the Establishment principle, he may be left to enjoy his opinion." Many United Presbyterians held the view that a Christian State ought certainly to acknowledge, honour, and give its support to the Christian faith, but emphatically they did not believe in the State Establishment of a Church: and although it was not part of their Church's constitution, a majority of United Presbyterians held that the State should neither support the Church materially nor interfere with her in any way.

The invitation of the Church of Scotland to come together did nothing to abate the Disestablishment campaign in the political field. There were times when one might almost detect a more strident note in the clamour of dissenting clerical and lay voices. Further efforts to bring about Disestablishment were made. The Cameron Bill, already referred to in connection with the Shettleston Church Case, was described by John White as an attempt to bring about disestablishment of the Church of Scotland by bribing the populace. In the Bill, startling promises were made of what would be done with the property and monies of the Church: these would go to provide funds for "artisans' dwellings, old-age pensions, cottage hospitals, harbours, the stocking of crofts and small-holdings, public libraries . . . and any other purposes of public and general utility sanctioned by the Secretary for Scotland". The Bill "proposed to hand over the parish churches to the Parochial Board and to place them on a level with the Poor-houses—a shameful humiliation to the Church of Scotland". In spite of the fact that the astute Mr. Richard Burdon Haldane, Liberal Member for Haddingtonshire, later Lord Haldane, sponsored the Bill in the House of Commons, it did not become law.

It was difficult for men like Dr. Charteris to understand why those who were lifting up their voices to petition God to bring about Church Union should have believed that He could accomplish that union only if they themselves, by political stratagem, managed to strip the Church of Scotland of all she possessed. That a man of the spiritual stature of John Cairns should have mounted the platform with them made the conundrum darker still: and this very conundrum was the greatest impediment to union throughout the last quarter of the nineteenth century. It created a miasma through which the healing rays of loving-kindness could not penetrate. If Charteris, Mair, Cooper, Scott, Wallace Williamson and other leaders could have *understood* why this should be construed as

G   97

helping God to bring union a step nearer, things would have been different; but they did not, they could not understand. In the end, they accepted it as a conundrum and continued to work for union; and although the Disestablishment campaign was still in progress, some leaders of the Church of Scotland gladly entered into a private conference with the Free Church and the United Presbyterians. The fact that it was unofficial gave it a special value, for none of those who took part in it were in any way committing their Churches, and they were able to thrash out in friendly debate those matters on which disagreement might have been expected. There were two notable absentees. Since Dr. Rainy had for years taken a leading part in the agitation for the disestablishment and disendowment of the Church of Scotland, he had set his face against any talk of union in which disestablishment was not regarded as an open question: so he stayed away. Dr. Hutton, a minister high in the councils of the United Presbyterian Church, had decided to absent himself because he too had been heavily committed in the Disestablishment campaign. The meetings went forward in an atmosphere of harmony, and no better exposition of the beliefs of the three Churches on the relations between Church and State at that time can be found than in the representatives' report of 1895.

They agreed that religion ought to be acknowledged by the State in its institutions, its legislation, its conduct. They agreed that the State should promote righteousness and Godliness, and should seek Divine guidance and blessing in its representative acts and public functions. They agreed that the State should recognise the Church of Christ as a Divine Institution, and should acknowledge her spiritual independence. Although there had been many a rumpus in past days about religious education, all three Churches were now in favour of religion being taught in State schools. They agreed that religious ordinances should be provided for the Armed Services of the Crown. As for that vexed question of Spiritual Independence, all agreed that Christ had appointed for His Church a government quite distinct from State government. But they admitted that any member of the Church could apply to the civil law for redress if he believed that some action of the Church had caused him civil injury.[1]

---

[1] This was a reversal of the old principle of the United Presbyterian Church by which a minister agreed contractually that he had "no right to prosecute for stipend in the civil courts, it being a principle recognised in the Church that the high and sacred claim which Christ has given ministers on the consciences of their people for suitable maintenance is a security perfectly adequate, and excludes any appeal to a civil court for enforcement". (Rules and Forms of Procedure, c. ii, sect. ix. 2.)

Where the conference broke up, as from the explosion of a shell (to use the words of Dr. David S. Cairns), was on Establishment. The Old Kirk members held that the non-established Churches were in the precarious position of being liable to find themselves in conflict with the law of the land because they did not have a contract with the State that recognised the precise range of their jurisdiction: and those non-established members who pooh-poohed this suggestion were to be grimly reminded of its truth before many years had passed. Definitions of Establishment have been legion; that of Charteris and his colleagues was notable for its clarity:

> "Establishment is reasonable and at the same time complete when a State approves of the creed and constitution which a Church submits to it, guarantees the independence of the regular judicatories of that Church, and accepts their legislation (so long as duly pronounced in accordance with that creed and constitution approved) as equally binding with that of the civil courts."

The United Presbyterians had not changed their view on Establishment, and they could see no hope of finding common ground. Nor could the Free Church: for by this time she had travelled far from the stand which had been taken up in the years after the Disruption when she had hoped to return to an Establishment freed from the impositions of an Erastian Parliament. The leaders of the Established Church, including Charteris, Flint, Gordon, Archibald Scott, and Lord Polwarth, hoped that by patient discussion some common ground might yet be found. But the Free Church men, Ross Taylor, J. S. Candlish (son of Dr. Candlish of the Disruption), Taylor Innes, and others, could see no prospect of this, nor could the United Presbyterian group, which included MacEwen and Calderwood. In the words of Calderwood's son-in-law, Dr. David Woodside, "this conference also ended in failure. They agreed to separate with the warmest expressions of mutual regard, with a true and deep respect for one another, and at the same time with the hope that some way out of the tangle might yet be found." How near they were to finding a way out of the tangle few of them could have realised. In the view of Lord Sands, "the only concrete result of the conference was a pamphlet bristling with unreconciled controversial positions"; but few among the fifty-four members of the conference would have approved of this curt summing-up. Among the wise and penetrating statements made by those who agreed to differ was that of Professor Henry Calderwood, whose "high-minded, equitable, and most tactful leadership in the conference was beyond all praise". On the question of Establishment and Presbyterian reunion, he said:

"In the event of the reunion of the Presbyterians of Scotland, the British Legislature, on memorial from the Established Church, and on concurrence of the sister Presbyterian Churches, may recognise the reconstituted Presbyterian Church as *de facto* the 'National Church', thereby acknowledging that the Scottish nation is Protestant in faith and Presbyterian in Church government, and that the reconstituted Church stands in historic continuity with the Church of the Reformation, whose position and interests were provided for in the Treaty of Union between Scotland and England."

That these words of a United Presbyterian were prophetic the future was to show. They made an indelible impress on the mind of John White, who first read them when he was a young minister of two years' standing in Shettleston and on the point of beginning in Church and civil courts the struggle which would never have taken place in a United *de facto* National Church. The words of one whom he regarded as a "great moral philosopher and great churchman" were to be like a signpost pointing him and his brethren along the path they were to take before a dozen years had passed.

Chapter VII

BEGINNING THE CRUSADE

I

AT the time when John White first began his constructive work on union, he recorded these words:

"In entering on conference to achieve Reunion, we ought to ask ourselves seriously and humbly—

Are we fit instruments for God to use by his Holy Spirit to bring about so great a result?

Are we sure that our patience, our loyalty to the faith, our willingness to give up our own way, our love for God and for the spiritual welfare of Scotland, are sufficient?

We dare not attempt anything for Reunion save in the deepest patience and humility. Who are we that we should succeed where our ancestors have failed? We can only hope to succeed because it is God's work, not ours, and that He is graciously pleased to use us."

John White's study of movements and motives had shown him how real had been the desire, not only in the Church of Scotland but in almost all Presbyterian denominations, to break down the walls that separated them. He had perceived how often, with sadness in many hearts, men had left the conference chamber with the knowledge that there could be no reconciling of views on the Church and State relation—no drawing together even, no consent that there might perhaps be a path, precarious and ill-defined, that could lead them to agreement: nothing but a locking of the door and a silent departure. It seemed almost as if God's final blessing had again and again been withheld because men had been so proud of their strength in upholding their own traditions that they could not bow their heads in humble assent that mankind's supreme act on earth is to glorify Him in one great brotherhood. Humility and patience—and to these John White added *loving-kindness*—were requisite in the slow work of preparing a union of Churches: and there were moments when, as he contemplated past failures, he would place loving-kindness in the forefront. There had been men, deeply dedicated to the cause they had made their own, who had spent some of their finest hours trying to smooth away the harshness of disagreement and had died before they could witness the triumph they had dreamed of. These were among the unsung heroes of the Kirk and he felt they should be remembered.

"The most powerful causes of continued separation," he once wrote, "are to be found in misunderstanding and irritated feelings. In all ages, these have done more than intellectual conviction to create and continue the divisions in the Church of Christ. The chief evils of separation in Scotland arise from these very causes rather than an attitude of independence in the different Christian denominations."

Nevertheless, a "union atmosphere" was being created. The churches of the small Evangelical Union had already joined with the Congregationalist federation; another union took place in the first decade of the new century, when three separate Methodist bodies came together to form the United Methodist Church. There were unions in South Africa, in Australia, in New Zealand, in the United States; and there was "an ever growing consciousness of the leadership of the Holy Spirit that was to bring about a union of the Congregational churches of Canada, the Methodist churches of Canada and Newfoundland, and the Presbyterian Church of the Dominion". In India, new ground was broken: there was a remarkable joining up in the Calcutta colleges, as well as in their mission work, of the Established and the United Free Churches. Here was a prick to the conscience of those who thought it a strange anomaly that these two Churches could work together in union abroad but at home should remain divided.

And yet they were not completely divided. The Edinburgh Presbyteries of the Established and the United Free Churches conferred in an unmarred harmony for greater efficiency in the parochial work of ministers in the city. If any straws at that time showed the way the wind was blowing, here was one. Dr. Archibald Scott, leader of the Established Church Assembly, came away from the first of these joint presbytery meetings in a state of elation at the fraternal spirit shown by everybody: "We must get alongside these fellows," he said of the ministers of the other Church. Soon there were conferences at Assembly level on problems of national import. Among the congregations there were signs of a new friendliness, not yet strong but clearly discernible. A stranger would indeed have found it difficult to say whether he was worshipping in an Established or a United Free church: for the form of service was almost identical, and both now used the same Hymnary, which had been compiled by a joint committee of Presbyterians.

II

Another event, or sequence of events, helped to incline men's thoughts towards Union. The first day of August 1904 had been a fateful one for thousands of Scots churchfolk. The announcement of the House of Lords' decision in the Free Church case had been received with consternation. The legal advice given to Dr. Begg thirty years before was waved in the face of Dr. Rainy, who stood with courage and faith in the midst of disaster. Although the nine ministers and eleven elders who declared themselves to be the "legal" Free Church had lost their case in Scotland's Court of Session, they had taken it to the House of Lords; and they had won since (by the casting vote of the Lord Chancellor) it was decided that, by becoming a "voluntary" Church because of her union with the United Presbyterian body, the Free Church had departed from her avowed constitutional position at the Disruption.[1] And so the nine ministers and eleven elders were triumphant—rich beyond their dreams. The Wee Frees, as they were called, met in the Assembly Hall on the Mound, and spread themselves among the empty seats of that great meeting-place, while the members of the United Free Church Assembly crowded as best they could into the old United Presbyterian Synod Hall, which had become the property of the City Corporation. Mr. Hay Thorburn, the astute layman who had regarded himself as the guiding star of the Wee Frees, installed himself in a large room in the United Free Church offices on the Mound and got ready to administer on behalf of his followers, whose numbers by some odd miracle began to increase, the monies and property which had by law come within his control. To the United Free Church, the judgment of the Lords brought much humiliation and tribulation. In some corners of Scotland there were scenes that recalled the darkest days of the Disruption, when ministers and families had been ousted from manses, and when churches had been barred against congregations who were forced to worship God by the dyke-side. The Church of Scotland showed warm sympathy with those

---

[1] The judgment was criticised by lawyers, and is criticised to this day. The fact that the case had to be heard for a second time because one of the law lords died before his written judgment was delivered, and the knowledge that this judgment was against the fragment or residue of the "legal" Free Church and would in consequence have meant a majority in favour of the other side, made the controversy more acute.

who had been deprived of so much by this judgment at law. Officially, the Old Kirk might have been expected to "join with the Wee Frees in a war dance over the discomfiture of Dr. Rainy" because their appeal to the House of Lords had turned upon their passionate assertion that they approved of Establishment. But this did not weigh with the Old Kirk; nor did any rankling memories of the Disestablishment campaign. Since the Wee Frees had hustled the headquarters staff of the United Free Church out of their offices and told them to fend for themselves, the Established Church came forward with an offer of accommodation in their own premises in Queen Street. The fact that it would have crowded these offices to the point of acute discomfort was counted a mere bagatelle, and this offer was but one of many expressions of kindness. Such sympathy, shown at all levels, evoked a quick response among United Free ministers, elders and members, and caused many to wonder whether the two Churches could not come closer together, in one way or another, in spite of constitutional differences.

III

One must not forget the warm personal friendships between certain men which did so much to prepare the way for Union. On a voyage to South Africa there were two who met and talked away the days in a happy companionship. Dr. Archibald Scott of St. George's, Edinburgh (for many years leader, as we have noted, of the General Assembly of the Established Church) and Dr. Ross Taylor (Moderator of the last Free Church Assembly before the 1900 union) were carrying greetings of goodwill from their Churches to the Presbyterian and Dutch Reformed Churches of South Africa, and the friendship of these two men was "one of the seeds of a better understanding between the United Free and the Established Churches". Important too was the old friendship between Lord Balfour of Burleigh and Dr. Archibald Henderson, the one a prominent layman in the Church of Scotland, the other the clerk of the United Free Church Assembly. Theirs was a unity based both on mutual respect and family ties: in the words of Lord Balfour, "my mother came out at the Disruption and was a great friend of Dr. Candlish, and Henderson's wife is a daughter of Candlish; we have always kept in touch". Another of Henderson's friends among the leaders of the Established Church was Dr. William Mair. "Mair of Earlston": here was a name to conjure with. He had been inducted to his Lauderdale parish as far back as 1869 and had ministered there until he retired in 1903 to devote his remaining years to Church union. Born in 1830, he had felt at the age of seventy-three that his time was short, and in his impatience he dug the rowels of his spur into the flanks of those who, as he thought, merely talked of union. He was in fact to live until he was ninety, a patriarch and a prophet, an unforgettable Edinburgh figure to the end, with his white beard and glittering eye, his voice that rang out with a precise and masterful articulation. The Church of Scotland was deeply in his debt for his *Digest of Church Laws*, and every time he got to his feet to pontificate on that subject he was listened to with deference. In spite of the wide disparity in their ages, Mair and John White were to become good friends, and there was to be much plain speaking between them. White said he found the old man "touchy about criticism"; and Mair, for his part, thought John White sometimes deserved reproof and he gave it with vigour. During all the long Disestablishment campaign, Mair of Earlston had been one of the stoutest fighters for Church Defence and was the author of a series of pamphlets in which he parried many a shrewd blow and then went in himself to belabour his opponents. He was now using voice and pen to fight for Church union in Scotland, and a pungent article in *Blackwood's Magazine* deploring continued separation induced the editor of *The Scotsman* to publish a leader under the title, "The Lamentations of Dr. Mair." This was too much for the patriarch of Mayfield Road; he stumped up to *The Scotsman* offices on a November day and insisted on seeing the proprietor. He spoke with such force that the interview set in motion a train of events which greatly helped forward the cause. Thanks to Mair's recommendation, the editor commissioned the Rev. Norman Maclean, then minister at Colinton, to write his leading articles on Church affairs—and strongly to support union. This was an injunction that found a quick response in Maclean's Highland heart.

IV

Although Dr. Archibald Scott was a devoted supporter of union, he had thought it wise to let opinion in the Churches grow before taking any definite step: and now, at the beginning of 1907, he reckoned that the time was ripe for him to make his voice heard as leader of the Assembly. The number of church members who were giving it serious thought was on the increase; even at kirk socials, a quick burst of applause was usually the response to any speaker who mentioned it. There was another reason why the leader of the Assembly decided to move. He knew that Dr. Mair had been planning to hold at his house in Mayfield Road a private conference between prominent men from both Churches; because this would be strictly unofficial, Mair felt they could talk about union without restraint. Dr. Scott had been invited; but he felt it was a matter which should be discussed officially and he had refused. Meeting Dr. Scott by chance, John White told him that he had been bidden to Mayfield Road. Scott urgently advised him to stay away, assuring him that he himself was about to take official action. This he did at a meeting of the Edinburgh Presbytery on 27th March 1907, when he brought forward an overture suggesting a conference with the United Free Church

> "upon the present religious condition of Scotland in the hope that a way may be found of utilising to the utmost the resources at the disposal of each of the Churches in a more harmonious and effective ministration to the spiritual and social necessities of the country, and of laying a foundation, at least, upon which a solid superstructure of Presbyterian Reunion might afterwards be built".

At once, John White got to his feet. In the first place, he said, co-operation was not enough. A full corporate union must be their immediate goal. In the second place, the net must be thrown much wider than Dr. Scott had suggested, and all the Reformed Churches in Scotland must be approached. A week later, at a private meeting of the Presbytery, Dr. Scott again brought forward his overture in exactly the same form. John White stuck to his guns. With his intimate knowledge of the long and tortuous history of Church union and disunion in Scotland, and with his acute perception of the views of the generality of kirk folk, he went into the affray with the zeal of a crusader. His speech at the Edinburgh Presbytery on 3rd April was a vehement exposition of what he had briefly said at the previous meeting.

"An overture on union," he declared, "was inevitable. We are all heartily in favour of some steps being taken by the Church of Scotland that will show our readiness to consider or devise a possible solution of the present unfortunate and unedifying ecclesiastical problem. But the question before us is whether this overture will meet the needs of the case." He repeated that

> "an offer should be made to enter into conference with *all* branches of the Reformed Church in Scotland. Why are we to ignore the

Free Church, which has been loyal to the principles of the Church of Scotland, when some of those who compose the U.F. Church today are bitterly hostile? Are we going to leave them alone to guard the principles which we probably shall be asked to forsake? And why are we not going to offer to enter into conference with our Episcopal friends?"

He reminded his hearers that for a number of years the Episcopal Church had been seeking a basis of union with the Church of Scotland. To exclude the Episcopal Church, he said, would certainly lead to some members of the Church of Scotland refusing to come into such a union.

"It is not an impossible thing, a union between presbytery and episcopacy. Why should we not ask the General Assembly for power to confer with them too? The Assembly has already looked with favour on the Christian Unity Association, which is composed of ministers and laymen of the Church of Scotland, the United Free and the Episcopal Church."

In thus referring to the Christian Unity Association, he was boldly grasping a nettle: for it had been an action of Dr. Scott's which was largely responsible for the vitality draining out of that Association. The Scottish bishops, conferring on the general subject of Church union, had invited Dr. Scott to join in the talks. Then had come an event known as "the Perth incident". Dr. Wilkinson, Bishop of St. Andrews, had declined an invitation for himself and his clergy to attend at St. John's (East) Parish Church, Perth, a service of intercession for the success of the next Unity Conference. Upon hearing of this refusal to pray together, Dr. Scott had promptly resigned from the Association, and his example was followed by many. But the Perth incident, which was still fermenting in the minds of many Presbyterians, did not deter John White from going boldly forward with his plea that the Episcopal Church should be included in the invitation.

"At the last General Assembly," he continued, "we invited the co-operation of all the other branches of the Reformed Church in Scotland to consider the question of religious instruction in schools. Ten Churches accepted that invitation—the United Free, the Free, Free Presbyterian, Episcopal, Wesleyan Methodist, Synod of United Secession, English Episcopal, the Congregational Union, Reformed Presbyterians and the Baptists. I do not say *all* the other Churches would now accept our offer to confer on Union; but the responsibility of refusing should be laid on their shoulders. . . .

"Our overture should ask for power to confer with all our separated brethren, to see if we could not devise amongst us a comprehensive plan to lay before Parliament and ask a new ecclesiastical settlement for the nation."

John White then set forth his second objection to Dr. Scott's overture:

"It does not sufficiently protect the vital principles of our Church. I do not speak of our privileges—for I should be ready to sacrifice these for union. Nor do I speak of many little peculiarities, many little prejudices, that we all cling to, but are not essential to the principles of our Church. The overture endeavours to conserve endowments, and I am glad of that; but it is much more important that we should protect Establishment, so far as it stands for a National Recognition of Religion."

He stressed this particularly because Establishment had not been mentioned in the overture, and he reminded his hearers that, at the last Assembly of the United Free Church, a large majority had commanded the committee on Church and State to watch for every possible chance to bring about the disestablishment of the Church of Scotland.

He ended his speech thus:

"I very humbly ask Dr. Scott to take back his overture and to bring it up again in a form that would widen the reference to Churches and clearly lay down our aims. If he does not, I shall move the Disapproval of the overture."

Dr. Scott saw that he had an intrepid opponent, and he decided to come to terms with him. He wrote at once asking John White to "post-card those who were particularly interested in the matter" and to invite them to attend a private meeting at the Church Offices in Queen Street, where they could thrash things out. At this meeting Dr. Scott expressed his doubts about the wisdom of approaching the "legal" Free Church, for he had learned that it would cause distress to his friend Dr. Ross Taylor and many other United Free ministers. Dr. Taylor was then in correspondence with him about the attitude of the Wee Frees: "They are absolutely uncompromising: they will have nothing to say to joint-occupation of churches, or even to using vacant manses at a rent. Their present bitterness is so well known that any proposal to confer with them would not be taken seriously." The very thought of union would be anathema to them, he continued, for they objected to hymns and organs in public worship and held firmly to the letter of the Westminster Confession: "The true blue Godly will scout the idea of conference. *They* are the people of God, not to be drawn into any alliance with latitudinarians or ritualists." It was not that John White himself had any doubt about the response of the Wee Frees; but he felt, as he had stated clearly to the Edinburgh Presbytery, that the responsibility of refusing to confer should be theirs.

V

Before an organic union with the United Free Church could be completed, John White realised that the Church of Scotland would have to take legal steps to modify her constitution in order to find common ground with the other partner in union: and this change in constitution could not fail to be along the lines laid down in the Claim of Right which the Church of Scotland, spurred by the zeal of her Evangelicals, had addressed to Parliament in 1842. It was this Claim of Right, and the Protest against Parliament's abrupt rejection of it, on which the historic Free Church had taken her stand; and it was the Claim of Right which the Wee Frees now exalted as their own inviolate Urim and Thummim. White saw that if they did not hold out an offer to the Free Church they would be giving that small but vocal sect the best possible excuse to declare in harsh terms that the Old Kirk leaders were going with blandishments to the United Free Church, which was doing everything in her power to destroy Establishment and divert endowments to secular purposes, while they insultingly ignored the Free Church which stood fast by Establishment and the glorious Claim of Right: and this fusillade of criticism might well damp the enthusiasm of the more traditionalist element in the Church of Scotland and infect them with the fear that their leaders might even betray their ancient principles in order to hurry through an act of union. So deeply did Dr. Scott sympathise with the United Free Church, beset by the troubles that had followed the House of Lords' decision in 1904, that John White found it difficult to convince him. But convince him he did, and Scott agreed to alter his overture to include an immediate approach to the Free as well as to the United Free Church.

There remained another point of resistance that John White was eager to break down. He was convinced that the whole union movement would be destroyed by the officially forced system of co-operation which Dr.

Scott wanted to see at work between the Churches before they entered into negotiations for a full union. To friendly co-operation in evangelical work John White had given his whole-hearted support from the beginning of his ministry: but he was convinced that official co-operation would lead to nothing but an *impasse*. It was no new thing. History, he knew, had revealed its futility. Dr. Chalmers, a few years after the Disruption, had been eager for "co-operation with a view to incorporation with the newly formed United Presbyterian Church", and it had come to nothing. Again, in 1863, there had been a proposal "to promote present co-operation with a view to ultimate Union"—a proposal which had petered out long before the two Churches found themselves overwhelmed, as they would have been, by difficulties over the training of ministers, work in the mission-field, the redundancy of churches, and other causes of contention. When the Free Church had suggested co-operation with the United Presbyterians in 1895, the latter had come out into the open and replied that the goal must be Union—and the result had been in the Union of 1900.[1] John White brushed aside co-operation as a foolish lure: it had a fine friendly sound—but was it, to use one of his favourite words, *practical*? Only Dr. Scott's instinctive caution had made him suggest it. But now, assailed by John White's cogent arguments, he agreed to alter his overture.[2] Unfortunately John White was out of Edinburgh at the sick-bed of a friend on the day of the Presbytery meeting, and was unable to deliver the speech he had promised to make. Some of those unspoken words stand forth from his vigorously written manuscript to point the way he was himself to take in his long fight for union:

"It will be for the Church of Scotland to go forward in a broad sympathetic spirit; not to insist on any insignificant privilege attached to what is called the Establishment principle, or to enter into theoretic quibbles over this, so long as the *National Recognition of Religion* is

[1] In his book *The Soul of a Scottish Church*, the Rev. David Woodside, D.D., wrote of the attempts at co-operation made by the United Presbyterian and Free Churches during the three years prior to that Union: "No really new or vital combination of Home Mission and evangelical effort was undertaken; and anything that was done in common for Church Extension was a hindrance rather than a help. The period of co-operation was the hey-day of those who wanted nothing done."

[2] In a short Life of Dr. John White published during his lifetime, the facts are inaccurately stated. In Dr. Scott's original overture the plea was that common ground should be sought with a view to co-operation in the hope that eventual union might be possible. The overture as it was finally presented to the Assembly, under the weight mainly of John White's influence, had been altered, and the plea was that agreement might be sought as to how the existing relations of the two Churches could be "so adjusted as to provide a foundation upon which they can begin to build a satisfactory structure of comprehensive Presbyterian reunion. . . ."

safeguarded, the endowments conserved for religious purposes, and some precaution taken against being tied to a dead orthodoxy on the one hand or against the danger of a vague, misty, indefinite religious teaching on the other. For nothing is more powerless than a dead orthodoxy unless it be a New Theology. . . . Nothing but good can come from conference. We have an instance of a conference at work just now. Seven years ago the South African War began—and today we see Dr. Jameson and General Botha sitting side by side in conference, while Mr. Winston Churchill does the honour of host to his former captor. . . . They propose to do nothing that will endanger the autonomy of individual colonies. Their aim is unity with the utmost diversity. If the Churches' Conference keep this aim in view, it may achieve something."

VI

One event greatly distressed John White. A few weeks before the Assembly of 1907, the Church and State Committee of the United Free Church sent a manifesto to the Prime Minister, Sir Henry Campbell-Bannerman, urging the Liberal Government to disestablish the Church of Scotland and deprive her of all endowments. When the Assembly was asked to approve of this drastic action of its Committee, there were protests, particularly from elders, who objected to such a step being taken in the name of the U.F. Church before the Assembly had been consulted. That the Committee had full power to act there could be no doubt. In the first Assembly meeting after the formation of the United Free Church, Sheriff Jamieson (later Lord Ardwall), one of the wisest counsellors which any Church could ever hope to have, had done his utmost to prevent the old cry of disestablishment from ever being raised in the new Church courts. Let us keep that outside the door, he had begged; leave it for politicians to handle if they want to. Everybody knew it would perpetuate some of the bitterness of the Disestablishment campaign. But Principal Rainy had repudiated Sheriff Jamieson's suggestion and declared that "the world must know where the new United Free Church stood in regard to the objectionable matter of Establishment". Every year thereafter, the Church and State Committee had been given a mandate to keep its weather-eye open for any chance to bring about disestablishment and disendowment. Intolerable, reprehensible, flagrantly unjust: the words of the old campaign were revived by zealots to denounce Establishment. There was regret among Church of Scotland leaders that so thoughtful and able a man as Professor Martin of New College should, at this juncture, be supporting the use of a political weapon. In an astute piece of apologetics, embedded in a newspaper article, Martin demonstrated the logic of his position:

"The view that civil and ecclesiastical interests alike are injured grievously by the existing connection between the State and one section of our Scottish Christianity is, with us, no matter of spleen or prejudice to melt in the sunshine of the kindlier denominational atmosphere for which we are all so grateful. It is a case of deliberate conviction being rendered inevitable both by considerations of principle and by the teachings of history. Is it conceivable that at this time of day it is to go whistling down the wind? It is an intolerable thing that an alien institution like the State should be suffered permanently to disrupt and keep asunder two great bodies of Scottish Christians, comprising between them the vast bulk of the population."

And he declared that only by political action could "the sore scandal and mischief of our present divisions be made to cease".

When John White and others in the Established Church read these words from the pen of one of the ablest men in the United Free Church they realised how formidable was to be the task of reconciliation. Those on the one side were convinced that to further God's kingdom it was a righteous thing to use political force to wrest from the Established Church that which she valued as her traditional patrimony. But many in the Established Church considered the action to be simply a stab in the back, and the fact that it had been delivered at this particular time—a time which Professor Martin himself had described as having a "kindlier denominational atmosphere"—left them bewildered and saddened. Dr. Ross Taylor was one of those in the United Free Church who deplored what their Committee had done. He wrote to Dr. Scott saying that he and many others "deprecated the action". But for this friendly letter, and the words of others in the United Free Church, there might well have been serious doubts in the minds of the Established Church leaders of the wisdom of going any further forward with proposals for Presbyterian reunion.

VII

Dr. Scott's Union overture from the Edinburgh Presbytery was duly brought up at the Assembly in May. Overtures in similar terms from two other presbyteries and seven synods were placed beside it, and action might have been taken had not Dr. Scott warned the Assembly of the tense relations between the Wee Frees and the United Free Churches, with half a million of the old Free Church money hanging in the balance between them. In view of this, it was thought expedient to take no step during the ensuing year. The furthest the Assembly could go was to form a committee and instruct it to consider what could be done to heal the ecclesiastical divisions throughout the British Empire and to consider under what terms the Church could enter into talks with other Reformed Churches of Scotland. The convener was Dr. Norman MacLeod, a veteran living in retirement in Edinburgh and the deeply respected Senior Clerk of the Assembly. It was not long before he had invited John White to become a member of the committee.

When the Assemblies met in 1908, a rearrangement of the business of the United Free Church caused some surprise. The Report of the Church and State Committee was brought forward to an earlier date than usual. Word went round that it was thought to be shrewd tactics for the Assembly to be given a chance to declare that Disestablishment and Disendowment was still the avowed policy of the United Free Church, and the Church of Scotland, if she wished to make an approach, should have no illusions about any weakening in the United Free Church's determination to use a political weapon to separate the Established Church from the State.

In spite of some ruffled feelings, this did not deter the Established Church Assembly from making their approach on the very next day and seeking to confer "in a friendly and generous spirit on the present ecclesiastical situation in Scotland" and on how a larger measure of Christian fellowship and co-operation could be brought about and thus prepare the way for the "union for which many hearts long and pray".

John White found himself once again forced to protest against any proposal for co-operation. Their ideal, he repeated, should be reunion—and as soon as possible. The previous year he had swung round Dr. Scott and the majority of the Edinburgh Presbytery; and now he was faced with the much harder task of trying to swing round the General Assembly. In committee he had done all he could to persuade Dr. Norman MacLeod that the cautious line of co-operation was not good enough, but he had failed, and he warned Dr. MacLeod that he would fight against it in open debate. His plea to the Assembly was supported by two of the most distinguished men in the Church of Scotland, both of whom recognised in him a future leader. Dr. William Mair, his eagle eye flashing, backed him with all his force, and Professor James Cooper of the Chair of Ecclesiastical History in Glasgow University spoke with deep sincerity. But the Assembly preferred to follow Dr. Norman MacLeod's less adventurous line, and it was in his words that the message was transmitted. In spite of the trumpet-call for Disestablishment, the echoes of which had hardly died away, the United Free Church Assembly asserted that it was with pleasure that they received the message, and they at once formed a committee to consider it. The Free Church, on the contrary, rejected it out of hand: in the words of John White, "The Wee Frees sent us a post-card to say NO."

In the nature of things, it was not until the following year that the proposal could be considered by the United Free Church Assembly. Their answer was momentous. Nobody was more delighted with it than John White, and for a good reason. Not co-operation, said the United Free Church: we want *unrestricted* conference on union. Dr. Archibald Henderson, their Moderator, compared notes later on with John White, and both were pleased to discover that each in his own Assembly had used the self-same arguments in favour of union talks.

The special committee of the Established Church went into session without delay. Here was an opening for John White. It could hardly be said that he lacked confidence in himself as a fighter, and this was a matter on which he was passionately stirred. The reply of the United Free Church had given him a chance greater than he had ever dreamed of, and the urgency of his plea for unrestricted union talks began to break down the caution of many who, like Norman MacLeod, had thought co-operation should come first and union grow naturally out of it. Dr. MacLeod found that his own views were being overwhelmed by this new surge of feeling. When the matter went before the General Assembly there was the same swing round to what John White had stormily advocated. It was clear that there could be only one answer now to the message from the other Assembly.

The door was at last open. For the first time in the long history of ecclesiastical schism in Scotland, the Established Church agreed to enter upon union negotiations, with Establishment being accepted as a matter for discussion. The ancient State relationship had always been regarded as something that was sacrosanct, but now it was being offered for criticism around a conference table; and not only criticism but almost certain modification. The paramount problem was whether this relation to the

State could be changed in such a way as to make it acceptable to both Churches.

The first reaction surprised few of the leaders of either body. John White anticipated that many in the Old Kirk would recoil in dismay, as thousands of good folk did, from the idea that the ancient State ties should be loosened. And in the United Free Church there was a breathless incredulity that the Church of Scotland could seriously think of leaving her strong entrenchments of privilege and power.

In both camps, work was begun. The United Free Church chose a committee of about a hundred members under the joint convenership of Dr. Archibald Henderson and Dr. George Robson. When Professor Alexander Martin of New College agreed to become clerk, one of the keenest ecclesiastical minds in Scotland was brought into the storm centre of union negotiations. The joint conveners of the Church of Scotland committee, also of about a hundred members, were Dr. Norman MacLeod and Lord Balfour of Burleigh. The latter, with a magnificent record of service, had great breadth of vision; his guidance and advice were to be a major asset to the Established Church in the forthcoming negotiations. As soon as he was informed that so vital and astute a man had been appointed clerk on the other side, he cast about him for someone of quite outstanding personality "who could," as he said, "hold his own with Professor Martin. The obvious choice was John White of South Leith, and he was appointed without delay."

VIII

The two committees first conferred on 9th November 1909 in the Goold Hall, part of the Bible Society's premises at St. Andrew Square. Twenty years were to pass before Union was to be completed, and many in that hall did not live to see it, but to everyone present this was to remain one of the most memorable meetings of their lives. The reactions of different men were widely at variance. One might have imagined that Norman Maclean of Colinton, with his sensitive Celtic temperament, would have been deeply stirred: yet he said afterwards he had felt no sense of excitement at all. On the other hand, Dr. Wallace Williamson of St. Giles' Cathedral said that "it was the queerest meeting I ever attended and the air was electric". A sketch from White's pen would have been of interest, but he left no record of that first conference except a note to say how deeply he had been impressed by the prayer of the veteran Principal

Alexander Whyte of New College, whose long ministry at Free St. George's had been one of the outstanding features of religious life in Edinburgh. John White preserved the words of that prayer with the comment that "they voiced the hopes of all", and he marked one passage in it:

"Our eyes are filled with a great vision. We pray that it may come and come soon; and if the vision tarry, we will wait for it; and when it cometh we will say, *This is the Lord, we have waited for Him and we will be glad in His salvation.*"

Dr. Norman MacLeod presided; on his right was Lord Balfour of Burleigh, on his left Dr. Henderson and Dr. Robson. A prominent United Presbyterian minister, George Robson was now editor of the United Free Church magazine, *The Record*, and was already organising the great International Missionary Conference to be held in Edinburgh the following June—the Conference which was deeply to stir the minds and hearts of men so that a new splendour was to shine around their ideal of Church unity. The conveners of the committees were supported by the two clerks, Alexander Martin and John White. All of these were to make a unique contribution to the cause of Union. The intense spirituality and missionary fervour of Dr. Robson impressed his friends during the months that preceded his untimely death; Dr. Henderson, with gentle patience and understanding, gave of his great knowledge of Church history and law; Professor Martin, who seemed to some a shade rigid and academic in his opinions, often uttered the keen relevant word that gave point to a straggling argument; Norman MacLeod, while sometimes he seemed a little detached, was unfailing in friendliness; Lord Balfour of Burleigh, far-seeing and statesmanlike, was ready at every check to get things going again; and there was John White himself, quick to lay down the law, impatient, sometimes too impatient, curbing himself with difficulty when things did not go the way he thought they should, afire at all times with a zeal for union, a vital figure in every debate. Thirty from each side were chosen as sub-committees. These were to meet separately or jointly, as it seemed expedient, and to consider the remit of the Assemblies: *To enter into unrestricted conference on the existing ecclesiastical situation and on the main causes which keep the Churches apart.* The lines of procedure had already been suggested by discussions in the two Assemblies of the previous year. The Church of Scotland had stressed the importance of the continuance of the National Recognition of Religion, while Spiritual Freedom had been the dominating thought on the other side. The seven meetings held between December and the following April were a testing time for everybody.

"We looked into each other's faces," said Dr. Wallace Williamson, "strangers many of us, and our looks were suspicious. From the state of suspicion we passed into the state of watchfulness—we were bound to beware of subtle factions which creep in everywhere and have a special faculty of creeping into ecclesiastical gatherings." Lord Balfour of Burleigh put it in another way: "We were shy of one another in those days, we did not quite understand one another." John White spoke plainly: "Not only were we cautious, but we paced round and round in a circle, coming back again to the point from which we started, not making any headway. The greatest difficulties we faced were psychological and temperamental—but these are never insuperable, they go out by conference and by prayer."

In moments of contemplation, after days when his patience had been tried, John White realised that he had sometimes gone further than he should have done in the heat of discussion. He often felt that old prejudice had such a grip on the minds of some men on the other side that they could apprehend the validity of no point of view but their own.

He knew he had been appointed clerk because of his fitness to maintain a dialectical balance with Professor Martin, who might have been reckoned to dominate the proceedings by his swift intellect, and sometimes the talk resolved itself into a quick-fire argument between the two. On 22nd January 1910, after the fourth meeting of the joint subcommittees, Dr. Mair felt sorrowfully constrained to write to his friend:

My dear White,

You did *surprise* me and cause me unhappiness on Thursday. A learned member has said, "We have now two new obstacles to union—our two secretaries"!

Still yours,
Wm. Mair.

But sometimes the boot was on the other foot and John White was trying to restrain William Mair. He has told of a meeting at the Church Offices in Queen Street between Norman MacLeod, Mair, the Procurator, and himself.

"Dr. Mair was going to extremes, and I had to oppose him. It was a heated interview. MacLeod strongly supported me. After a while

MacLeod said, 'I think we should go.' He took my arm, and as we walked along the corridor Mair drew up with us. 'I've been reading your autobiography, Mair,' said MacLeod, 'and it explains a great many things to me.'

"Mair was obviously delighted and said, 'Oh, I am pleased.'

" 'Yes,' said Norman MacLeod, 'I see you were born on the first of April!' "

As the months went by, Dr. MacLeod and John White drew closer together. "He was always phoning me," said White, "and I had to go along to the University Club and discuss things." The older man began to open his heart, and he confessed that he was far from optimistic over the outcome of the conferences. One day he said: "I am sorry this thing has commenced in my lifetime." John White realised that Dr. MacLeod's health was beginning to fail and it was only by an effort of will that he was carrying out what he regarded as his duty. It was not always easy to comfort and sustain one who was so often despondent.

"I don't know what you felt about yesterday's meeting," MacLeod wrote. "To my mind it seemed very hopeless. I am wondering whether we might not have a short meeting of our own committee. I don't like the look of things at all, and I fear some of our friends are a bit weak-kneed about the matter and may commit themselves to courses which the General Assembly will never agree to—a most disastrous result."

Dr. MacLeod was indeed touching on a sore point. John White saw that, however difficult it might be to find agreement with those on the United Free Church side, it might be fully as hard to reconcile the sharply contrasting views of some of his own committee. In particular, there was a divergence on spiritual freedom: some held that a Church should have complete freedom to change her own creed when she chose to do so, while others maintained that the strongest sheet-anchor against rash credal changes was a Church's constitutional tie with the State. White tried to inspire Dr. MacLeod with the belief that these differences were not insuperable and that all but the most fiery zealots would in the end be brought together. But MacLeod became more and more depressed:

"The attitude of some of the extremists at our last meeting was somewhat ominous. My only fear is that some of our men may represent our present 'bondage' as much greater than it is. However I hope not. That would certainly be turned against us afterwards.

Personally I do not believe that we could agree to *unlimited* freedom as to Creed, and I think that this is the general view on our side."

As the committees continued to meet, there emerged one clear fact which encouraged everybody. Between the two Churches there was little or no difference on any fundamental point of doctrine. Minor differences there were, indeed, between individuals, and more often than not these were of the same Church. Gradually members of the committees were beginning to know each other better. "We got to recognise the good that was in each other," said Lord Balfour of Burleigh, "and whatever happens over Union, I believe a firm and lasting friendship has been formed."

John White's comment was: "Personal acquaintance destroyed many a prejudice."

IX

As the months passed and the time of the Assemblies drew near, it became evident that only an Interim Report could be presented. On National Recognition of Religion, the great difficulty lay in the special relation between the State and the Church of Scotland. The committees had given serious attention to the recognition of one branch of a Church as a "national institution" and to the limits on the freedom of the Church of Scotland in her constitution and Confession of Faith. While the United Free Church committee admitted that the Established Church courts had full jurisdiction, whereas their own courts possessed none, they held that the Established Church had no power at all over the membership of these courts since a *quoad sacra* minister was not even entitled to be a member of a presybtery. The Church of Scotland committee agreed that their Church had no control over the rearrangement of parishes, for Parliament regarded this as a civil matter; and although the election and settlement of ministers was now completely in the hands of the Church, the procedure which they were bound to follow had been laid down by Statute Law, not by a decision of their Assembly. In addition to these matters over which they had but limited control, or no control at all, they agreed that they had no power, without explicit Parliamentary sanction, to unite with another Church. Endowments, on which most people anticipated that the conferences would break up in confusion, were not discussed, and the decision to defer this matter proved to have been incomparably wise. The one solid contribution in the Report was provided by Dr. Henderson. In his summary of the state of the Churches in Scotland, he placed before the Assemblies, and indeed before all who were interested, many things which John White had himself been trying to drive home from pulpit and platform: the wasteful and inadequate distribution of churches in a rapidly growing population and the need to unify and concentrate their work. The number of parish churches in Scotland at the Disruption had been about a thousand; and although kirks had been more than trebled by the freewill offerings of the Church of Scotland and by the constituent bodies of the United Free Church, many had been so located as to make for rivalry between denominations. The depressing fact was that, far from having made headway, the membership of the two great Presbyterian Churches had not been keeping pace with the increase in population. Communicants in the United Free Church at 31st December 1908 had been a little over half a million, that of the Church of Scotland slightly over seven hundred thousand. Dr. Henderson gave the figures of the increase in Church membership during 1908: for the Church of Scotland a trifle over four thousand five hundred, for the United Free Church actually less than five hundred. For the Churches to have held their own, the increase would have had to be twelve thousand. Multitudes of people had no church connection whatever, and the number of churchless folk was steadily increasing every month. Bound up with the Report presented to the two Assemblies was a map showing the density of the population in Scotland: and to everyone who had eyes to see, this "visual aid" brought home the truth.

The passage dealing with Spiritual Freedom was but fifteen lines in length. While there was "a large measure of agreement on the nature of such freedom inherently belonging to the Church, and on the matters to which it applied", the committee could say nothing final about a Church's control over her own creed and the means of securing this control. Here indeed was a problem that was to tax the energies and the forbearance of the committees in many meetings and in earnest private talks. It lay deep at the roots of those matters which had separated the Established from the dissenting Churches of Scotland: and the fact that there were divided views within the two great Churches themselves gave the problem an even more formidable aspect.

Chapter VIII

A MOMENTOUS OFFER

I

JOHN WHITE and his friends had good reason to recall the United Free Church's Declaration of Spiritual Liberty of 1906. She had claimed "independent and exclusive jurisdiction and power of legislating in all matters of doctrine, worship, discipline, and government of the Church, including therein the right, from time to time, to alter, change, add to, or modify her constitution and laws, subordinate standards, and Church formulae and to determine and declare what these are".

To John White and his colleagues on the union committee, this began to look like a Halt sign on the road before them. For the Church of Scotland had no such liberty as this. Ministers of the Establishment were still obliged by law to accept the Westminster Confession in its entirety, and the fact that no other Presbyterian Church in Scotland was still shackled in this way seemed to aggravate their hardship. A clause in the Churches (Scotland) Act of 1905 had, for the first time, given the Church of Scotland power to alter her Formula of Subscription to the Confession. But the condition had been laid down that the old Formula must be used until such time as the Church herself could agree upon a new one. Here was the rub. Because the General Assembly had not been able to agree on a new Formula, her ministers were still obliged unreservedly to accept every one of the thirty-three chapters of the Confession, as their forefathers had done since 1693.

In Scotland, the Westminster Confession of Faith embodied rigid beliefs of the sixteenth and seventeenth centuries that were no longer part of what was counted the necessary credo of a Christian. It was as if a prism had slowly turned round so that facets which had once been to the fore were no longer in the eye of the beholder, while others now reflected the light of a newer revelation. During the passing of the centuries, the idea of God as the stern judge of His creatures had to a great extent been replaced by that of God as a loving Father of all mankind. And with the change in theological thought, ministers found parts of the Westminster Confession hard to accept without a good deal of qualification. There

121

were some who suffered real distress of mind as they uttered within the portals of God's House the words of a solemn oath which conscience rejected. The day came when Dr. Archibald Scott spoke out in the General Assembly and said that the legal obligation to accept unreservedly the Confession of Faith was "the cause of a great deal of dispeace, and the expansion and progress of theology during the nineteenth century had made that dispeace so acutely felt that it seemed, at one time, as if it would rend the Church asunder".

II

The Confession, it must be remembered, had been compiled at a time of turmoil: and as an interpretation of the Word of God, it had a special relevance to that time. The defence and expansion of the Church had dominated the thought of Presbyterian leaders; thus it was inevitable that the Confession should have been framed with this thought implicit in its very texture. The National Covenant of 1638, a declaration of the spiritual liberty of the Scottish Church, was a warning to an Erastian Stuart king that his hope of bludgeoning the Scots into a docile acceptance of episcopacy was a fool's dream. The laity of the Kirk were virtually the leaders of the Scottish Parliament; and if King Charles was determined to impose an episcopalian uniformity on England, Scotland, and Ireland, the Scots were no less determined to impose Presbyterianism on his three kingdoms. To this end, another declaration was drawn up; and in 1643 when the English Parliament begged for military help against Charles, the Scots seized the chance to present their new Solemn League and Covenant. It was ratified at Westminster in exchange for a promise of twenty thousand troops. The document was very different from the National Covenant. The religious aggression and intolerance of these times may perhaps be better understood if we recall that it was believed by many pious people to be a Christian virtue to try to suppress all forms of religion save their own: a belief which was not, to be sure, a novel thing in the history of the Christian Church. It was a task which Kirk leaders verily believed they had been given from On High. Their efforts brought dire trouble to Scotland, but one good thing emerged—the Westminster Confession of Faith. It was the work of some of the keenest minds of that time; and the kindred documents, the Larger and Shorter Catechisms, the Directory for the Public Worship of God, and the Form of Presbyterial Church Government, all bear the enduring patina of genius. But fully to comprehend the aims of their makers, and assess the value of the works, one must replace them carefully in the historical context of those events which gave them birth.

When the Westminster divines at last rose from their deliberations, they were far from being a unanimous body. But in spite of the fact that they themselves did not claim infallibility for their Confession of Faith, it was accepted in Scotland by many folk as a true, flawless, and complete interpretation of the Word of God. For the majority of Presbyterians, to permit themselves to have reservations about any line or phrase of it would have been to condemn themselves to dishonour and wrath for their sin.

After decades of persecution under four Stuart kings, who were implacable enemies of presbyterianism, the Scottish Church in 1690 was glad to have her doctrines legally protected by the placing of the Confession of Faith on the Statute Book. It thus became, for the first time, the legal Testimony of the Church of Scotland. Although ministers and elders had not previously been obliged to take an oath that they accepted the Confession and would adhere to it, the Assembly now devised a Formula for their subscription. Three years later, Parliament cancelled this Formula by prescribing a new and stricter form of oath for ministers, and so by Statute Law it was established that:

"*No person should be admitted or continued as a minister unless that he*

"*do also subscribe the Confession of Faith ratified in the aforesaid 5th Act of the Second Session of this Parliament, declaring the same to be the Confession of his Faith, and that he owns the doctrine therein contained to be the true doctrine which he will constantly adhere to.*"

Like the Scots Confession of 1560, it followed the teaching of St. Augustine and Calvin on the subject of predestination, and in Chapter III it was stated that "By the decree of God, for the manifestation of his Glory, some men and angels are predestinated unto everlasting life, and others foreordained to everlasting death." In a cool and ruthless elaboration of this doctrine, the Confession continued:

"God hath appointed the elect unto glory. . . . The rest of mankind, God was pleased, according to the unsearchable counsel of his own will, whereby he extendeth or withholdeth mercy as he pleaseth, for the glory of his sovereign power over his creatures, to pass by and to ordain them to dishonour and wrath for their sin, to the praise of his glorious justice." [1]

These were not the only passages which, taken at their face value, seemed to be out of tune with theological teaching and preaching of later generations, and even before the Disruption there had been trouble over the Formula of Subscription. On 2nd July 1839, John Stuart Blackie, who was to become one of the great figures of Scottish University life, was appointed to the Chair of Humanity in Marischal College, Aberdeen, and he duly signed the Formula, which was then required of all University professors; but as he laid down the pen he declared in a firm voice that he had signed it only as a public action in a purely professional capacity, not as his private confession of faith—for, he said, "I am not sufficiently learned in theology to be able to decide many articles of the Westminster Confession." The Senatus refused Blackie admission to the Chair, whereupon he went to law about it and won his case—a case in which Lord Cunningham decided that nobody could read a single page of the Westminster Confession without clearly perceiving that "there is much in it that most men are not qualified to judge of".

To have a new Formula which expressed a less rigid acceptance of the Westminster Confession was described in 1877 by Dr. Milligan as "a matter of momentous import". No ministers, whatever their private thoughts, had spoken up as Blackie had done, and they continued to take the 1693 oath of adherence. One plan after another was brought forward. Both in and out of the Assembly, the Formula problem was argued. The press declared that the Established Church was out of touch with the times. Many scoffed at the anomaly in a Church that preached salvation for all but subscribed to a Confession that set forth God's plan, formulated before the world was created, of dividing mankind into two groups, the one bound for Heaven and the other for Hell. Some there were, particularly in the Highlands, who preached this doctrine with threats and warnings not unmixed with despair: but they formed a small minority.

In both the Free and the United Presbyterian Churches there had been much dispeace over their relation to the Westminster Confession of Faith. All who had hived off from the Established Church had continued

---

[1] Bishop Usher, one of the leading Westminster divines, put this later into words of his own: "Did God then, before he made man, determine to save some and reject others? Yes, surely, before they had done either good or evill, God in his eternall counsel set some apart, upon whom he would in time shew the riches of his mercy, and determined to withhold the same from others, on whom he would shew the severity of his wrath." *Brief Method of Christian Religion by Archbishop Usher*, 1650.

for a long time to use the old Formula on which they had been brought up. In new Churches overseas, however, the shackles of old beliefs were quickly broken. When the first Council of Presbyterian Churches throughout the world met in Edinburgh in 1877, there was a good deal of surprise at the diversity of creeds then in use by Presbyterians. All had been based on the Westminster Confession. But some Churches accepted only its "system of doctrine"; some had taken from it those passages that contained what was thought to be the essence of Christian truth; some used a creed that was similar to the Confession only in substance. There were more than twenty different varieties. The United Presbyterian Church was the first in Scotland to loosen the trammels that had bound her to the Westminster document, and in 1879 she led the way by passing a Declaratory Act. This required acceptance of the Confession only as "an exhibition of the sense in which the Scriptures are understood". As for the Free Church, it was not until 1892 that Principal Rainy agreed to place before the Assembly a proposal for a new Formula; and he did so with great reluctance because his Church was split into two strong and intractable parties. A committee appointed to consider the matter argued for two years before a draft Formula could be offered to the Assembly; and when it was passed, two ministers and some four thousand members left the Free Church denouncing Rainy for having thrown open the door to apostasy.

III

Meanwhile, in the Established Church, the Confession problem was becoming more and more urgent. Since it was the Church herself and not Parliament which had enacted that elders must subscribe to the Westminster Confession, the General Assembly had the power to revoke, and it passed an Act in 1889 permitting them to take a more flexible oath than the Formula prescribed by Statute for ministers. Overtures were coming up from presbyteries urging the Assembly to tackle the whole question of the Confession and settle it resolutely once and for all. Since an overwhelming majority in the Church of Scotland regarded the Act of 1693 as a gross intrusion upon the Church's spiritual liberty, why could not the Church pass an Act of her own prescribing a less rigid adherence to the Westminster Confession? This question was often asked in these days. A committee was appointed "to consider the powers which the Church possesses of modifying the terms of the minister's Formula of adherence to the Confession of Faith", and after consulting with high legal authority the committee in 1900 declared itself to be "wholly opposed to the view that the Church had power to deviate from the Formula of 1693". This verdict was repeated the following year by a still larger committee, although its convener, Principal Story, vigorously disagreed with the report. He declared that in matters of doctrine the Church had an interpretative power; but others, including Dr. Mair, protested that the powers were in discipline only—in other words, if a minister preached doctrines that were not in conformity with the Westminster Confession, the General Assembly could make the ecclesiastical censure as mild as it chose. That the Assembly would find itself virtually in the position of condoning a breach of law on a point of doctrine was not merely unsatisfactory: it was declared to be preposterous, and Principal Story's party continued to declare that they could change the Westminster Confession without going to Parliament. Dr. Mair, whose knowledge of Scottish Church law was unrivalled, repeated that they had no such power—the Church of Scotland did not possess the spiritual liberty to do any such thing.

"If that be so, we pay too dear for our relation to the State," declared Principal Story.

"This was a view," Dr. Mair said afterwards, "which I did not dispute."

An overture from the Presbytery of Greenock in 1903 fanned the flames of this old and troublous controversy. The General Assembly was urged to "declare the Westminster Confession to be valid only in so far as it accords with Scripture interpreted by the Holy Spirit". Dr. Archibald Scott's words on this might have been an echo of those uttered by the Moderator in the Assembly of 1866: "The Confession stands as the concordat of the Church with the State, and without the consent of the State it cannot be abridged or modified." He further argued that if the Assembly, after these many long years of travail, decided to take the matter to Parliament, it could not have chosen a less opportune moment: "We will be opposed by our own people in multitudes, by the whole of the voluntaries in Scotland and by their friends in Parliament." It was with sorrow that Dr. Scott admitted that political expediency would determine whether the Church would be granted or refused redress on a matter which had for so long been of grave spiritual concern. This hesitation in making an approach to Parliament on the relation of the Church to the Westminster Confession appeared to many dissenters to be a virtual refutation of any claim the Established Church might make to spiritual independence. The Church Interests Committee took the matter up, and the Legislation Committee was asked to formulate proposals for an approach to Parliament. It was fortunate that the Prime Minister, Mr. A. J. Balfour, was deeply interested; and since the Churches (Scotland) Bill 1905 was being introduced into Parliament to rectify the situation created by the 1904 decision of the House of Lords in the Free Church case, a clause was added to the effect that the Formula of Subscription to the Confession of Faith for the Church of Scotland would be in such terms as were prescribed by Act of her General Assembly.[1] But to reach agreement on such terms proved to be no easy process. Controversy not only in the Assembly but in the presbyteries throughout Scotland was as warm as it had ever been. One new Formula after another was put forward and condemned.

John White had studied the controversy from its beginnings; and throughout his ministry at Shettleston and South Leith he had supported those who had raised their voices to bring about a change. Among his papers is a letter from a young minister, who had obviously been deeply troubled, asking him to express his personal views about this matter which had chafed the spirit of Scottish churchmen for so long. "I am sorry to call on such a busy man as you," he wrote, "but I know of nobody who can so easily blow away the fog which envelops the whole question." Judging from the young minister's letter of thanks, the reply was fully satisfactory. John White's opinions about this question can best be set forth in his own words:

> "Regarded historically, the Westminster Confession of Faith is an important document, although it did not achieve its original object of uniting the Churches in the British Isles.

> "It is not easy to exaggerate its influence in our own and other lands where Presbyterianism is strong. It contains a clear and complete utterance of the theological beliefs of the time when it was drawn up.

> "Very few today accept the doctrinal definitions as contained in the Confession. On the other hand, very few will deny the *fundamental* doctrines which it sets forth.

> "No doctrinal statement is final and exhaustive. It is only an approximate expression of truth. It is said that a great change has taken place in the intellectual outlook of men. The social mind or conscious-

[1] In speaking for the Churches (Scotland) Bill in the House of Commons, the Lord Advocate pointed out that the freedom claimed by the United Free Church "would handicap the Church of Scotland. . . . Younger men desiring to enter the ministry would enter the wider portals of the United Free Church, and the Church of Scotland would not get the more tender consciences."

ness has assumed a new viewpoint. As a consequence, a new and richer statement of religious truth, relevant to present-day thought and life, is essential. The argument appeals; but is there any agreement amongst our leading thinkers—scientists, theologians, philosophers—as to what this new intellectual outlook is, or any concurrence in defining the new viewpoint which the social consciousness has assumed?"

Confronted by the fact that Union negotiations could never be consummated by two Churches that had a radically different relation to the Westminster Confession, the General Assembly of the Established Church in 1910 gave its final approval to a new Formula:

I hereby subscribe the Confession of Faith, declaring that I accept it as the Confession of this Church, and that I believe the fundamental doctrines of the Christian Faith therein.

And so, on 30th May 1910, the Formula which had been imposed by Parliament on the Church of Scotland, and which had been in force for two hundred and sixteen years, was laid to rest. Many members, leaving that Assembly with relief in their hearts, could now look forward to the two Union Committees reporting fruitful results of their conferences to the Assemblies in the following year.

IV

That winter of 1910 was the busiest John White had spent since his ministry had begun. More and more were the two joint conveners of the Church of Scotland's Hundred relying upon him. As Dr. Norman MacLeod's health declined, their consultations became more frequent. The other convener, Lord Balfour of Burleigh, was heavily engaged in London and had often to put in letters to John White the opinions he was anxious to place before the Committee.

At the end of the year, John White had the task of summarising the many and diverse views and of making a concise report which embodied the salient features. He had to stress those points that were essential to her historical position as the direct heir of the Church of the Reformation; but he had also to state those concessions made on matters not counted fundamental, and therein a devil lurked. At every move towards common ground, one or other of the High Church party declared that relaxation of the ancient bonds that tied the Church to the State was a throwing away of the safeguards of religion which had sustained their forebears. This party was making its influence felt with increasing power. John White's avowed aim was to go as far as he dare in the wording of his Report to conciliate these zealous men of whose sincerity and piety there could be no question. Professor Cooper, the leader of this party, had been persuaded that it would be inexpedient at this critical stage to make public the fact that there was a serious split in the ranks of the Church of Scotland Committee, and it was agreed that the protests of Cooper and his friends would not take the form of a Minority Report. John White had to keep in mind not only the fact that his summary would be submitted for amendment to those on the Church of Scotland side but would also go to those of the other committee for the unofficial scrutiny of such men as Dr. Henderson and Professor Martin. The Report being drawn up by the United Free Church was going through a similar process of scrutiny and comment. Both sides were anxious that the differences between the two Churches should not appear in the final Report as greater than they were in fact.

By February 1911, John White's draft Report was being discussed at a meeting of the two Hundreds, and on the 23rd of that month he went home and recorded his impressions of the United Free churchmen who had commented upon his words. He put in a category by themselves those whom he described as "Pure Voluntaries". These were the men to whom any State connection was anathema. They recoiled from any suggestion that they might be asked to accept State recognition after a union. They believed passionately that they had a Divine mission to wreck the whole union movement unless the Church of Scotland could be brought to believe that her duty was to disestablish herself and become a Voluntary Church. In a very different category John White placed Professor Denney. Denney, he said, was a party in himself. His was one of the most brilliant minds in the United Free Church, and fortunate were those students who had sat under him. Denney was a master of dazzling paradox, and he was a good deal more. He was quite unpredictable. From some unusual angle of his own, he would focus his eye upon a problem and illumine it in a way that suddenly revealed and interpreted the truth; and there was one memorable occasion when he saved a committee meeting from disaster. The third category, into which John White placed the rest of the United Free members, consisted of those "who recognised that the Church of Scotland had placed on the table a POLICY", and he noticed with satisfaction that these formed a solid majority.

V

When the Joint Report was placed before the Assembly, John White made a speech that raised him to a stronger position than he had ever held. So sharply defined and compelling were his directives that, when he rose to his feet in subsequent Assemblies, he found himself receiving an ovation before he had uttered a word. He had previously spoken on Union, but his speech on the Report of 1911 was his first comprehensive survey of the subject in the highest court of the Church, and thereafter no debate on Union was felt to be complete without the vigorous contribution which his brethren soon learned to expect from him.

"It is a significant fact in the history of the two Churches," he declared, "that there *is* a Joint Report at all! For this we are thankful to God. It is even more significant that there has been revealed so much that is common to both Churches. But the most significant fact of all is the growing spirit of hopefulness and the eagerness frankly to face the situation—*which could not be tabulated in the Report.*

"I venture to affirm, as my personal impression of the meetings of the Conference, that this Joint Report shows the *minimum* and not the maximum of agreement. But it is the most that could be done with unanimity, and it was unanimity we aimed at. If personally I am more hopeful of the ultimate issue than some who have only this Joint Report to found upon, it is because of that untabulated sentiment of sympathy and that desire for Union which characterised very many —if not all—of our brethren of the United Free Church."

Before he went further, he spoke to the Assembly with regret of the sharp difference in interpreting the instructions given to the Union committees of the two Churches. By arrangement, the identical words had been used:

To enter into unrestricted conference on the existing ecclesiastical situation and on the main causes which keep the Churches apart.

"Unfortunately," said John White, "our friends in the U.F. Church placed a somewhat narrow construction on the terms of their remit. They did not regard themselves as authorised in going beyond diagnosis of the present ecclesiastical situation." The Established Church committee, he explained, had been convinced from the beginning that to adhere rigidly to the letter of the remit would bring forth nothing but a cold analysis of the causes of separation—an old, old story which had been told almost *ad nauseam* in past years. Their committee, therefore, had taken it to be their duty to suggest ways in which these causes of separation could be overcome.[1]

> "It is here," said John White, "that the people of Scotland will find cause for regret—if not for just complaint—that our brethren of the United Free Church did not go further and consider the practical question of a prescription that would heal the wounds of the patient Churches. Their *diagnostic* should have been supplemented by a *therapeutic*.
>
> "One consequence of the limited interpretation they have placed on their remit was that they have devoted their time to a criticism of the present constitution of the Church of Scotland. They sum up this criticism by saying that they regard the present constitution of the Church of Scotland as inconsistent with the principle of spiritual freedom."

John White went on to repeat with emphasis that the Church of Scotland held as strongly as any other to the principle of spiritual freedom. It was not necessary for him to proclaim what everybody acknowledged to be the truth—that the Church of Scotland did not, in fact, *possess* spiritual freedom. Her only degree of freedom in matters spiritual was the recent relaxation in a minister's oath of adherence to the Westminster Confession. The Established Church had not the power to alter any of her subordinate standards—to delete, for example, one word from the Westminster Confession—without asking leave of Parliament to do so. The United Free Church, on the other hand, possessed complete spiritual independence and she maintained that no Church, bound to obey in all things the will of her Divine Head, should be fettered in the exercise of spiritual functions by connection with the State; even a voluntary compact with the State might be fraught with peril to spiritual liberty.

John White went on to say that there was also a sharp difference between the legal powers of the courts of the two Churches. Those of the Establishment were legally acknowledged to have full jurisdiction: so that if a minister, deposed by the Assembly, sought redress in a civil court on the grounds that he had suffered materially, the civil court would

---

[1] It happened that Professor Denney was talking on this matter in the United Free Church Assembly across the street: "Our straightforward course would have been to show what was really in our minds on the various points concerned. This was not the course we took. Rightly or wrongly, we held that the remit under which we were acting did not empower us to discuss such proposals as tentative steps towards agreement. . . ."

refuse to reconsider the verdict because it was within the jurisdiction of the Established Church courts to pass final judgment on all such matters. The courts of the United Free Church, on the contrary, possessed no such power: a deposed minister might have his case thrashed out afresh in a civil court and obtain damages if it was considered that he had suffered because he had been wrongfully deposed. That the findings of an ecclesiastical court upon a spiritual matter could be examined by a civil court was abhorrent to those in the Established Church.[1]

Continuing, John White said he was "not conscious of any real hardship or practical limitation arising from the Church's present relation to the State in the fulfilment of the whole commands of her Divine Lord and Head". He did not attempt to maintain that this could always have been said: but since it could truthfully be said in 1911, he said it. And then he went on:

> "But, sir, the Church of Scotland is not asking the United Free Church to unite with her *on the present constitution without alteration and adjustment*. Hence I say this criticism of our brethren is not only erroneous in fact—it is beside the point! What I should like to know is the opinion of our friends in the United Free Church on the constructive policy which we have outlined in our Report. It is a policy that recognises and, as it seems to me, satisfies their conception of spiritual freedom. At the same time, it continues and secures the advantages to the people of Scotland of an effective recognition of religion in a Protestant and Presbyterian Church which would be representative of the religious life of the nation. We have given a restatement of our own position that removes misunderstandings, and we have placed before them a policy we would be willing to promote in the cause of reunion. . . . Sir, I hold that the question of spiritual freedom does not present any insuperable obstacle to Union."

VI

It was John White's wish to drive home in the minds of all Scottish churchmen, both in that Assembly and outside, a full comprehension of

---

[1] This was sometimes abhorrent also to those in the Free Church. When the General Assembly, under the guidance of Principal Rainy, removed Professor W. Robertson Smith from a Free Church chair at Aberdeen University on the grounds that his views were not orthodox, it was feared that he might appeal for redress to a civil court, where the case could be reviewed. To debar him from doing this, Robertson Smith was informed that he could continue to draw his salary. That he would proudly refuse the offer had been almost a foregone conclusion, and the offer was described at the time as a piece of deplorable chicanery.

the step which the Church of Scotland was now preparing to take. To describe it as the most dramatic step she had taken since the Presbyterian Church of Scotland had been established by Act of Parliament in 1592 would not be overstressing the significance of so momentous a measure. The Church was, in effect, drawing up a new Constitution which was to be placed before Parliament for ratification. There would be no question of Parliament *conferring* upon the Church any powers which she had not hitherto possessed: on the contrary, there was to be a statutory acknowledgment that these powers were *inherent* to the Church as a Church of Christ. Nor was there to be any question of the Established Church disestablishing herself: she was to remain the National Church of Scotland in historic continuity with the Protestant Church of the Reformation. The drama of the step to be taken was intensified by the fact that, if Parliament now acknowledged that these powers were inherent to the Church, it was tacitly acknowledging that they had always been inherent. John White emphasised that there was a good reason why the Church had been tied so closely to the State. After the Reformation, it was the Church herself, not Parliament, that had drawn up her Confession and Constitution. To quote John White's explanatory words in the Report,

> "the State came in afterwards, at the urgent request of the Church, and approved of what the Church had done. The object of this ratification by the State was not to fetter the Church, to protect the State against the Church, or to protect the Church against herself, *but to protect the Church's freedom against the Crown and external interference. . . .* The establishment of the Church in Scotland is based upon a series of Statutes of the Scottish Parliament. These Statutes the Church regards with satisfaction in so far as they secure the recognition of the Reformation by the State, the acceptance by the State of the Presbyterian Constitution which the Church had shaped for herself, the recognition of a Spiritual Freedom larger and in a more satisfactory form than is enjoyed by any other Established Church in Protestant Christendom, and the advantages of orderly and friendly relations with the State."

In the section of the Report where the National Recognition of Religion was dealt with, the United Free Church committee agreed that it was the duty of the Nation to render homage to God and to promote the interests of His Kingdom. While the State should not intrude into the sphere of personal religion, it was "bound to give protection in the free exercise thereof to all its faithful citizens". But the committee objected to the expression of a national recognition of religion as it was embodied in the constitution of the Established Church. In particular, the members felt that the recognition of one Church in the land denied to all others "any recognition as Churches possessed of inherent spiritual authority". They declared that they could accept no arrangement which "would involve the denial to other Churches of their proper character and rights".

To this, John White replied in his speech to the Assembly:

"We claim no exclusive privilege. But we do claim the full privilege of performing a national service to the people of Scotland with national protection and with our full and unimpaired resources. As to the disability under which our brethren of the United Free Church labour, I think the attitude of the Church of Scotland should be kept in mind. Our proposed legislation will give an improved legal status, should they desire, to those branches of the Christian Church which are at present only voluntary associations in the eyes of the law. Such legislation would not be inconsistent with, but would indeed be in harmony with, that principle of national homage to Christ upon which the Church of Scotland founds her own claim. . . .

"What I regard as of great moment is that the United Free Church recognises that, as a voluntary association in the eyes of the law, her proper character and rights as a Church are not recognised by the State. She holds that 'such denial of the spiritual rights of the Churches is inconsistent with the duty of the State and with the honour it owes to the Church of Christ'."

And then John White clinched the matter by saying: "The United Free Church representatives, in using these words, admit that their Church is not on the right footing with the State in the eyes of the law. *Our constructive policy will put this right for them in a United National Church.*"

It was plain, he said, that the conditions of the modern world called for the concentration of the forces of Scottish Presbyterianism in a National Church:

"The newer conception of the State as charged with an ethical and humanitarian mission suggests the importance of its continuing to maintain direct relations with a reunited Church which would stand out, not only as an impressive household of faith, but also as the great national school of moral culture, and as the best accredited exponent of the Christian ideals of the Scottish people."

John White briefly went over the four points which the Church of Scotland regarded as of great importance to a National Church:

Firstly, a reunited Church should be recognised by the State as *National*.

Secondly, she must be regarded as the Church with a territorial duty of providing the "means of grace" in every parish in the land.

Thirdly, the courts of the Church must have a separate and exclusive jurisdiction in matters spiritual.

Lastly, the ancient endowments must be preserved for the use of the united Church in her duty of providing religious ordinances throughout the land.

The intention of the Church of Scotland was to go to Parliament and ask that, in all the Acts anent that Church on the statute books, everything inconsistent with full spiritual liberty would be repealed. The Acts themselves would not be repealed: the anullment would be solely of those words or phrases or clauses which in any way restricted the spiritual freedom of the Church. The enactment would secure the State recognition which the Established Church so greatly valued.

"We must go forward, not backward, to this settlement," John White continued. "It is not by way of the present Establishment, unaltered or unalterable, or by way of disestablishment and the squandering of our forces and resources, that this Reunion will be accomplished. It is by going forward and taking with us those principles, and those experiences sacrificially achieved in past years by both Churches: principles that may not be renounced in order that the Churches may be one: principles about which there can and need be no concession, for they are principles common to us both—and we must take with us, too, those valuable elements of Christian experience which cannot be repudiated without disloyalty to historic causes. The United Church of the future—which God hasten!—must embrace all that the Spirit has brought to pass in both branches of the Church in Scotland."

John White was anxious to underline the fact that they respected the ideals of the United Free Church in spiritual freedom: and, he said, to meet them "the Church of Scotland is prepared to go as far as she may without sacrificing her principles". And then he added with special emphasis:

"But the thinking people of Scotland will recognise that she has been generous in her proposals—and that she has given a full and practical expression to her desire for Union. She has indeed gone a generous length. I think she has gone as far as she need go. She must take her stand where she now is."

VII

"She must stand where she now is!"

Those words with their strong Lutheran echo, uttered by Principal Tulloch, spoken again by John White in that General Assembly of 1911, called forth a cheer. He decided to devote part of his Farewell Sermon at South Leith, preached on 4th June, to this subject. Since he might not have another chance for some time to speak to his people there, he was anxious to imprint upon their minds a clear picture of what had been done to further Union and what remained still to be done. He took as part of his text those words from the second chapter of the second epistle to the Thessalonians: "Therefore, brethren, stand fast, and hold the traditions which ye have been taught." His words rang out in the nave and aisles of South Leith Kirk: "The Church of Scotland has given a full and practical expression to her desire for Union. She has indeed gone a generous length." He was repeating the words he had used in the Assembly. "I think she has gone as far as she need go. She must take her stand where she now is!"

On the next day, part of that sermon was printed in the press, and one evening newspaper headlined it: ESTABLISHED CHURCH ULTIMATUM. Here was a journalistic opportunity too good to be missed. One of the leading Church of Scotland Union men was throwing down the gauntlet with a gesture of defiance in front of the United Free Church. Here we stand: from here we shall not move one foot.

It looked as if John White had made a first-class blunder. To speak thus amid the thrust and parry of Assembly debate was one thing. To thunder the words from the pulpit to a large congregation was another. As soon as he read the report with its heading in the evening paper, Dr. William Mair wrote to White a strong letter of reproof.

> "I don't think anyone is entitled to say, *She must take her stand where she now is*. In my opinion, none of us should say this till she has said it herself. Not only this, but it cannot be told *where* she is. Of four matters she has only said they are 'very important'. In short, if what you are reported to have said is a correct report, and if it were the mind of the Church, there is no use of the conference meeting again—Yrs, Wm. Mair."

136

The sermon certainly had repercussions in the United Free Church. We find Dr. Henderson writing about it to Professor Martin. "There will be many voices as antagonistic as the Leith utterance for a little; but by and by the weightiest issues will assert themselves. White may have to fire another shot. . . . Whether real progress will be made will depend on how seriously the *nation* takes up the matter and *resolves* to have a settlement."

Almost invariably there has been presented a picture of the two Churches moving gradually closer and closer together, each conceding a little, until at last they found themselves on common ground, and then the Union was consummated. This is an unreal picture. It may well be that, in uttering the words which he did in his Farewell Sermon at South Leith, John White committed a major indiscretion; and he may have deserved censure. But in this record of his life, it is necessary to state that his words were prophetic. He saw precisely how far it was necessary for his own Church to go, without a sacrifice of principle, to meet the wishes and ideals of the other Church; and he believed that on the basis of the 1911 Report, which he had written with care, there could be a union of the two Churches.

The salient fact in the history of this great union is that, although negotiations were to continue for many years, the Church of Scotland did not move one inch on any fundamental matter from the position she took up in 1911. In all subsequent negotiations, it was the United Free Church that moved step by step nearer to this position until at last the two Churches stood steadfastly together.

Chapter IX

THE RENAISSANCE OF HOPE

I

IT had been agreed once again in 1911 that the remits of the two Assemblies to the union committees should be set forth in the same words. Dr. Henderson suggested them; and he deliberately took a cautious line, for nobody knew better than he that there would be strong dissent by many in the United Free Church if he gave the impression that they were being hustled into a union without having had the chance fully to deliberate upon all that was involved. The gist of the remit was that the reports of the conferences during the past two years be "commended to the serious and prayerful consideration of church members" and that the committees be "continued with instructions to watch over the matter and to report". It was not the remit which the committee of the Church of Scotland would have liked to recommend to their Assembly; but in the absence of both conveners, John White had wisely persuaded the members to agree, and he felt obliged to give an explanation to the Assembly.

> "There is a possible cause of complaint that the Joint Report has a lame and impotent conclusion in the instructions merely 'to watch over the matter and report'. But, sir, the members of the two Churches must have an opportunity to consider the situation as revealed by the report of the committee. With this report before them they can consider it intelligently—and not be simply impelled by heroics. There is one great danger that we must try to avoid—that of going faster than the country will allow."

John White had for some time been troubled by the feeling that, even in his own Church, folk in distant shires might have the impression that the union movement was being forced forward by a few Church leaders in Edinburgh. Complaining voices had already been raised, and to show to church members in general that the two negotiating committees—the Hundreds—had been chosen from parishes all over Scotland, he had had printed at the end of the Joint Report a full list of the members of the committees of both Churches, and had been careful to append to each name the parish or location of ministers and laymen.

The other danger to be avoided, he said, was that of leading people to think there could be no further progress:

> "It is for us to proceed with caution—and under a deep sense of responsibility. But proceed we must. I say, we must go forward with faith in Him who has led us thus far. And is this conclusion *to watch over the matter and to report*, a lame and impotent conclusion? It is both active and passive watchfulness. That I know is the interpretation put on the words by Dr. Henderson, who says it 'would warrant further action if occasion arose, while it would justify no conference if it was not found advisable or needful to meet'."

In putting forward this point of view, John White was clearly sub-jugating his own impulses. He was not the man to use pliant phrases which could be bent to mean this or that or something else. But although it went against the grain for him to sit quiescent while opinion was given time to crystallise, he felt he could not but approve of the caution Dr. Henderson was using with his own people. But he saw nothing to prevent the Church of Scotland committee from beginning to build upon the foundations already laid down in the Report he had made to the Assembly, and an enlarged Business Committee was instructed to "draft a series of Propositions on the leading points dealt with in the Report to the last General Assembly".

How long opinion in the United Free Church might take to form it was impossible to say. Quite clearly there must be no sign of impatience among the leaders of the Church of Scotland. Nevertheless, John White knew that unless they again came to friendly grips, the gap between them might widen. Lord Balfour of Burleigh wrote to Dr. Henderson urging that "action should be taken for formulating, if possible, some definite constructive policy". Three months were to pass before he received a reply, and even then it was far from satisfactory. Henderson spoke about the indefiniteness of the proposals made by the Church of Scotland committee in their Report. He brought forward yet again that hoary cause of separation—the "Parliamentary definition or regulation of the Constitution of the Church". At the same time he freely admitted, since he could not very well do otherwise, that the Established Church did hope to obtain "a recognition of the Church by the State which would not in any way involve the fettering of the Church in her own spiritual legislation and administration. . . . We are most willing," he added, "to consider any suggested scheme to secure this."

It was a fortunate thing that Dr. Henderson and Lord Balfour of Burleigh were old friends, for they were able without giving offence to speak plainly. Balfour of Burleigh wrote back demanding to know what was "indefinite" about the proposals, and he said that they had better meet in Edinburgh and talk things over. But before a meeting could take place, something happened which gave a new impetus to the whole movement.

II

The Church of Scotland Business Committee had lost no time in drafting a series of Propositions based on the proposals in the Report, and had asked the Procurator (C. N. Johnston, K.C.) to draw up the Preamble of the projected Bill for Parliament and provide notes which would give a clear picture of the machinery the Church would use to carry out her proposals. This the Procurator had done. It was discussed and amended, and it became familiarly known as the Memorandum. Essentially it was but an elaboration of what had been set forth in the 1911 Report; but the Draft Preamble to a Bill gave the impression, in a way which nothing else could, that the Church of Scotland was firm in her intention to seek from Parliament an acknowledgment of the liberty which she claimed to be her inherent right. Immediately after the Church of Scotland Hundred had approved of it, the document was sent to Dr. Henderson.

"It is hardly possible to over-estimate the importance of the communication from your Committee." This was Henderson's answer by return of post. The feeling among some of the most discerning minds in the United Free Church had been that the proposals in the 1911 Report would never be more than proposals because, when it came to the test, the majority of those in the Church of Scotland would not be prepared to approve of an approach being made to Parliament. To have a clause slipped in at the tail end of their own Bill of 1905 asking that the oath of adherence to the Westminster Confession might be relaxed—that was one thing: but to go to Parliament and demand that a modified relation to the State be expressed in a statute—this had seemed but a pipe dream of John White's. Not only that: they had been convinced that the Liberal Party then in power was so strongly in favour of the principle of disestablishment that the Church of Scotland leaders were being wildly optimistic if they imagined they would have their way at Westminster. But now, with the Memorandum in front of them, there was a quick change of opinion. Many a difficulty fell away. With the actual terms of a portion of a Draft Bill set out before their eyes, it was plain to the United Free Church leaders that the Old Kirk was really determined to carry out the intentions expressed in John White's Report of 1911.

III

During the early part of the winter, Dr. Norman MacLeod was forced to rely on John White to transmit his views to the Committee. He was too ill to attend any of the meetings, and he died early in December, lamented by his many friends.[1] Since the other joint convener, Lord Balfour of Burleigh, had urgent Parliamentary duties in London, the work that fell to John White became still heavier. The two were in constant correspondence all that winter. They agreed that the Memorandum should not be regarded as being in its final form until Dr. Henderson and his friends had privately suggested amendments which would make it even more acceptable to their own committee. But in the initial stages the main criticism came from within the Church of Scotland. Some members of the Committee, led by Professor Cooper, strongly objected to it, and the Rev. A. W. Wotherspoon wrote to John White: "I can't understand the courage of you men. It seems to me that you are giving away the case of the Church of Scotland with both hands." A parish minister wrote that feeling had risen so high in some parts of the country that

> "there will be a determined attempt made at the Assembly to dismiss the Committee and wreck the whole Union movement. . . . The real enemies of the Church of Scotland for the moment are, however unconsciously, the section of ministers and members who are saying 'The Church Union Committee has betrayed us—they have given away everything!' "

Since he was now a member of the Presbytery of Glasgow, John White caught the often repeated phrase: "What is happening in Edinburgh— how many more concessions are they planning, and how long will our Church remain Established?" It was to meet hostile criticism of this kind

[1] Dr. MacLeod was the second of the Church of Scotland leaders to die since Union negotiations had begun: Dr. Archibald Scott's death had taken place in 1909.

that he addressed a meeting of the Glasgow Presbytery several weeks before the Assembly of 1912.

His object was to drive home in the minds of his brethren, both clerical and lay, that the Memorandum was not a document to cause alarm and despondency.

"The lines of the policy of reunion," he said, "which were intimated in last year's Assembly Report, have been closely followed in the Memorandum. Some necessary details have been filled in. There is nothing new, no fresh concessions. I do claim for our constructive policy that it conserves *all* that is best and vital in the Church of Scotland and in the United Free Church. I am well aware that this Memorandum will excite sharp criticism on the part of some of our own people. That was to be expected. I do not regret it, for it needs criticism to elucidate many points. I have asked our critics to mention any one thing of importance that has been sacrificed, and nothing has been advanced. One man to whom I spoke was in agony of mind lest we should have sacrificed the Lord High Commissioner. I should be sorry to see that picturesque figure removed from Assembly week. But I do not regard the religious welfare of Scotland as inseparably blended with his presence at the General Assembly. Have there not been General Assemblies which did good work in his absence? The Memorandum is not his death-sentence. . . .

"While some tell us 'We have given *everything* away', there is the old Disestablishment Council rising from the dead to protest against our proposal. Why? Because 'we have given *nothing* away!' . . . I venture to say to those on the Disestablishment Council that, if they achieved their object tomorrow, the union of the Churches would not be realised for generations. I think Disestablishment is a dead cry in Scotland—and a rotten plank in the political platform. Union will not come by way of Disestablishment."

John White told his hearers that a fresh declaration of her spiritual freedom by the Church of Scotland would include a statement that the Church had power to modify her Constitution under the conditions laid down in the Constitution itself. And he warned the Presbytery that the United Free Church's claim to complete spiritual freedom contained an element of danger that must be guarded against:

"That Church claimed an *unlimited* liberty in her Act of 1906. Let us appreciate the position. They did so in the hope of protecting themselves against such judgments as that of the House of Lords in 1904. They did this, not with a view to changing their Creed and Constitution, but to *reserve their right* to make any modification on them, without having that right challenged and denied by the Courts of Law. They are prepared to admit that that is not the right relation of Church and State.[1] The right relation is that which the Church of Scotland Committee seek to embody in their proposals whereby *the State would recognise the inherent right of the Church* to order all such matters, subject only to the authority she has from her Divine Head."

IV

The Memorandum was presented to the 1912 General Assemblies of both Churches, and it was received and commended to the careful consideration of everyone. Time was given for discussion at all levels throughout the Churches, and a Conference between the two Hundreds was held on 3rd October. There had been no joint meeting for eighteen months— the last one had been held immediately prior to the Assemblies of 1911— but the conferences were now to meet regularly once a month, and the Memorandum was the subject of discussion. Every suggestion, claim, promise, statement of intention, was torn apart, probed, held up to the light; and a fusillade of questions was aimed at the Church of Scotland men:

"Is it possible that the intention of your Church has been accurately interpreted in the Memorandum?

"Would the State recognition of the freedom which is to be part of your revised Constitution give your Church full liberty in matters spiritual?

---

[1] John White knew that the Rev. A. N. Bogle, who was to become one of the leaders of the United Free Church and, later, of the Church of Scotland, was expressing the view of many of his own colleagues when he said in the General Assembly of 1912: "We have been told that statutory connection with the State has always been a very dangerous thing. All I have to say is that non-statutory connection with the State is a very dangerous thing, as we know from our own experience. The Free Church had no statutory connection with the State, and it exercised its right to join with another Church. The result was that, in the matter of property, we were taken to the House of Lords. Did we find that our position was a very safe one? The mere fact of freedom is surely not enough. The Church may have a recognition which shall be, not the citadel of its freedom, but an outlying buttress of its freedom that shall be all for its advantage."

There were jurists who expressed the opinion that since the United Free Church had considered it unnecessary to have her Declaration ratified by Parliament, the protection was of a dubious kind and gave grounds in certain circumstances for a minority to claim the property of the Church, as had been done in 1904.

"Do you really believe that Parliament will be prepared to give up its right to legislate in the affairs of your Church and, in this respect, treat her as if she were a voluntary Church?

"If a Church were to unite with your Church, would she then come under no Parliamentary control whatever?

"What further elements in the State relationship does your Church value, apart from her consuetudinary recognition?"

These were not a tithe of the questions posed to the Church of Scotland committee, and John White's voice was often heard in reply. Professor MacEwen wanted to know what precisely was meant when the united Church was described as "national, preserving her continuity with the Church of the Reformation". Professor Martin wanted to know what was "involved in the claim to Nationality which the united Church is to make". Professor Orr wanted to know "what the State relationship would be if legislation, on the basis of the Memorandum, were carried out". Yet another questioner wanted to know if, with the Church possessing freedom in matters spiritual, there would be any room left afterwards for interference by the State. To this last query John White replied that, if the United Free Church committee thought there was any danger of it, they might perhaps put forward "constructive proposals showing how spiritual freedom could be obtained without incurring any such danger". There was no response. "They were not ready for this!" John White wrote to Lord Balfour of Burleigh.

There was some talk about endowments. The United Free Church committee held that they did not think their people could become a party to the proposal that the whole of these should be conserved for the united Church: yet they admitted that there was wide sympathy in their Church with the view that these funds should not be diverted to non-sacred uses. The matter was shelved by the United Free committee when they said that they did not consider the question one to be settled between the two Churches: it was for Parliament to decide upon it. But outside the committee it remained a lively topic of dispute, and many said they would not enter a union if the teinds of the Old Kirk were to go into the coffers of a united Church. Others, like Professor Denney and Professor MacEwen, held a very different view. Said Denney in a sweeping repudiation of the whole of the embittered Disendowment campaign: "I would not lift a finger to see the endowments taken from the Church of Scotland—even if it remained in its present relation to the State! The

Church has had them long and is entitled to count on them." He declared
that he would not like to see them "handed over to some Government
department to squander", and since he could never resist a little jest, he
added:

> "I have often been amused at the inconsistent way in which
> Established churchmen talked about them in the committee. In one
> breath they would have it that they belonged to the Church, not the
> State, and that for the State to touch them was sacrilege; in the next,
> they were the State's gift to the Church, and the most important part
> of the national recognition of religion."

The United Free Church committee drew up a preliminary series of
notes on the Memorandum. Because they seemed to break no fresh
ground, Lord Balfour of Burleigh wrote impatiently to John White from
London:

> "I do not understand what their precise object is. To what are
> these notes intended to lead? Surely the time has come when we should
> be given something constructive from their side, in the form of
> definite proposals for the emendation of our Memorandum, Preamble
> and Bill, so as to let us see where we stand."

V

Lord Balfour was not the only one in the Established Church who was
disappointed over the lack of any official constructive criticism from the
other side. In the Conferences towards the end of 1912 and in the early
part of 1913, the leaders of both committees had come to understand each
other's points of view. On all that was fundamental, Dr. Henderson and
his associates now accepted and approved of the Church of Scotland's
proposals. But the agreement among the leaders was in striking contrast
to the growing disagreement in each camp throughout the country, and
some dissentients were deliberately doing all they could to hamper the
union movement. Pains were being taken at every turn to avoid friction.
We find the Procurator writing to a leader of the United Free Church
committee:

> "We all appreciate how desirable it is to avoid expressions that
> may be misunderstood or cause irritation or alarm. *We* are in a better
> position to judge of this in regard to our own people just as *you* would
> be in regard to yours. We must avoid giving shocks to those to whom

certain phrases, which they probably have never analysed, have a controversial connotation which identifies them either with the Ark of the Covenant or a device of the Devil."

John White's comment was: "Sometimes the most bitter partisans are people who could not give a clear or correct explanation of the point at issue."

There was another cause of trouble at this time and later. Those who wanted to put an end to the union movement did not hesitate to make use of the press. A number of periodicals vied with each other to publish the latest news of what was happening at union committee meetings, and the more sensational the report the better for sales. The conveners and clerks of both committees took care to see that their official communiques were issued simultaneously, and all members knew that a breach of confidence might have an unfortunate result. From time to time, it was clear that some news had been allowed to leak out—or, more probably, had deliberately been communicated through some private channel—and since much of it had been inaccurate, it had been a source of embarrassment to John White and his colleagues. A letter to him from the editor of *The Glasgow Herald* dated 28th March 1912 runs: "Somebody has been talking—see the enclosed cutting. I should say a U.F. man from the look of it."

Some newspapers had a high sense of their responsibilities. The Rev. Norman Maclean continued to contribute to *The Scotsman*, and the editor of the *Herald* had actually submitted to John White his editorial on the Memorandum to make certain that a true picture was being presented. Lord Balfour of Burleigh had made a point of asking John White if he would take all possible care to see that no embarrassment to Dr. Henderson should be caused by any indiscreet news items in the press:

> "Dr. Henderson is nervous lest it should be thought in his own Church that he and his friends who are supposed to be favourable to Union have been unduly trafficking with us about the form of the Memorandum. He is anxious that it should be clearly known that this is our document and that the phraseology of it is our responsibility. . . . He is most anxious that those in his own Church with whom he expects to have difficulty should not be able to throw in his teeth that he has been working with us behind their backs."

In spite of all precautions, the two committees found themselves from time to time in a perplexing position. The following letter from Lord

Balfour to John White, written on 10th May 1912, refers to the Memorandum: "Those with whom we were conferring wanted to see our proposals in a more definite form, and when we sent them in that form they could not keep them secret, but allowed garbled and unfair accounts to appear in their organs of the press, which are hostile to us." In that letter he was writing to approve of an unconstitutional step John White had been obliged to take. The garbled accounts of the Memorandum had to be condemned and corrected, and the most effective way of doing so had been to issue the document in its entirety to the press. Since the normal course would have been to keep it private until the Assembly, more than a month later, it was foreseen that the hasty publication of it was bound to be criticised in both Churches.

Unfortunately, the disloyalty of some member or members had continued, and Dr. Henderson felt obliged to write to John White in these terms:

"We have been exceedingly vexed. . . . Someone in our Committee is giving extracts of our Report to the press to serve a purpose of mischief-making in our Church. The accounts in that paper are altogether wrong."

So serious did the risk of irreparable harm become that John White found himself frustrated in a course of action he was anxious to take in the interests of both Churches. He had ready an early draft of a paper which was to become the most important document in all the union negotiations. Since it would be of benefit to disclose this to the Hundred of the United Free Church, he wrote to the conveners and Procurator to ask what they thought of this course. Lord Balfour of Burleigh was adamant in his refusal to allow a copy of the draft to be communicated: "Do you dare to take the risk of showing any draft to their Hundred? They will not preserve confidence. They—or some of them—will let it leak out to their Press hostile to us and our folk will see it garbled, distorted and abused. Is this what you want?"

Yet another cause of anxiety was the revival of the old political source of strife. John White received warning of it in a letter Dr. Henderson wrote to him on 6th May, shortly before the Assemblies of 1913 opened: "We must expect some trouble especially on the part of those who have for long been pressing for political action and are rather chagrined at the probability of its not coming into their hands for settlement. If we can keep it out of the paws of politicians, it will be well for the best interests of Presbyterianism in Scotland."

It was by no means in a mood of serenity that the leaders on both sides mounted the steep causeway that led up to the open doors of their respective Assembly halls.

VI

As we look back over those early years of union talks, we can discern two periods, each a few months in duration, in which it can be said that the two Churches took a decisive step forward. It was as if those who had spent a multitude of days in preparation and prayer had suddenly found their reward in a new revelation, and the way seemed to lie open before them.

The first of these two periods was that in which the Established Church committee, inspired by the splendour of a great ideal, had made the offer to the other Church which John White had put into words in the Report to the Assembly of 1911. The Church of Scotland was ready, in the interests of union, to put her fortune to the touch by going to Parliament and asking for a new Constitution in which her ties with the State were to be adjusted. There was never any move either back or forward from this epoch-making proposal. The Church stood firmly by it, sustained by a conviction that she had God's blessing. And in the second critical period, which fell in the spring of 1913, the leaders of the United Free Church, stirred by the faith in Divine guidance so clearly manifested in the proposal, and inspired by the way in which their own ideals had been respected and cherished, moved forward to accept. But although they themselves had now full confidence in the unequivocal desire of the Established Church leaders and the majority of their committee to do everything proposed in the Memorandum, they had not the power to speak on behalf of the United Free Church. To win the approval of their Church was now the task to which they bent themselves, and nothing could have been more heartening to John White and his colleagues than to read Dr. Henderson's speech to the United Free Assembly of 1913. It was one of the most persuasive and sweetly reasonable of all that prodigality of speeches on Church Union delivered in the twenty years of striving between 1909 and 1929. With compelling power, Henderson put to his own people the historical position of the Church of Scotland in her relation to the State:

"You cannot wonder that the Church of Scotland have said that nothing is to be put into the new Constitution that would be inconsistent with their claim to be identical with the Church of the Reformation. They will surely be entitled to come into Union, if they desire,

148

on a basis of practical freedom and say, 'We unite in present circumstances as our duty, but we do not renounce our ideals of Church and
State.' There are men in *this* Church already who hold their view.
It is an open question among us now. We are not going to create, as a
cause of disunion with them, what is not a cause of disunion among
ourselves. All they ask is that their view shall have free utterance in a
united Church. Are we going to ask them, before they come in, to
take up some humiliating position, saying that *their* fathers were all
wrong and that *our* fathers were all right? I ask brethren straightly if
that would be a just and fair question to be put by men with whom
such views are open questions already."

Dr. Henderson received with obvious pleasure the proposal of the
Established Church that, in the new Constitution, she would have
power to decide upon the membership of her own courts: "There will
be no going to the Court of Teinds before ordained ministers can be
made members of presbyteries." The Church would have power "to
legislate and judge in all matters of doctrine, government, worship and
discipline, membership and office". Dr. Henderson said he hoped the day
would come when an enlightened State would make a declaration for
itself of the spiritual sphere of the Church of Christ as one into which it
had no right to intrude: but meantime the law was such that it was
necessary to write all that she claimed into her Constitution. He described
the attitude of the two Churches to each other. The Church of Scotland
had said, "We wish to make this Constitution such as will satisfy *your*
conception of spiritual freedom; therefore we shall expect your help in
doing so." Dr. Henderson added a powerful appeal:

> "Moderator, I cannot conceive our Church refusing to give that
> help. . . . Are we to say to our friends, 'Draw up your Constitution
> and bring it to us to sit in judgment on it'? Moderator, I decline
> altogether to be thrust into such an offensive attitude. We are not
> going to obtrude ourselves as dictators. If our brethren of the Church
> of Scotland will set down what might be embodied in a Constitution,
> we will give them all such information and assistance as they desire.
> Is there any Christian man who would refuse to help his brother in a
> like case?"

Meanwhile, in the Established Church Assembly, John White's
Report on Union was received with general approval. He had taken

pains to correct a number of minor misconceptions which still seemed to linger among some members of the United Free Church. But it was on something more important than trivial misconceptions that he wished the Assembly's attention to be focused. What excited the interest of everyone was the great hope implicit in a sentence at the end of the United Free Church's Statement on the Memorandum. Could "the extent and reality of agreement" be tested by the drafting of a new Constitution by the Church of Scotland? For if this could be done, a "way might, by God's blessing, be found to remove the main causes which keep the Churches apart and to advance the reunion of Scottish Presbyterianism".

VII

Since the Disruption period, there had been no deliverance of the General Assembly of the Church of Scotland more important than that of the year 1913, when it instructed the union committee to draft a Constitution and place it before the next Assembly. Although an Assembly does not have the power to dictate a course of action to any subsequent one, the remit stated that the draft should be prepared "with a view to its transmission, if approved, as a basis of Union, to the General Assembly of the United Free Church".

Thereupon, John White called together a meeting of the Hundred, and the Business Committee was asked to carry out the Assembly's remit. The members met on 22nd July, and they were surprised when John White laid a document before them. He had been privately working on this for many weeks, drawing deeply on his knowledge of Church history and politics and law. What he now presented to the Business Committee was a draft of the first Constitution covering the spiritualities of the Church of Scotland to have been submitted to a Church court, or a committee thereof, since the Westminster Confession of Faith was laid before the General Assembly on 27th August 1647.[1]

He had never imagined that there would be anything final about it. He had been working on the document while others had talked; he had heard this talk and knew some of it to be timid, cloudy, and indeterminate. He was now offering his draft Constitution with a diffidence that was not always his most salient characteristic when presenting his own point of view; he hoped it might prove useful merely as a basis for discussion— something upon which his colleagues could whet their minds.

[1] See Appendix.

They took full opportunity to do so. The draft was discussed, criticised, altered; parts of it were deleted and then restored; and in the end, it was so changed that its author could not recognise it. Spurred by John White's example, other members of the Hundred came to subsequent meetings with new drafts of their own, and these went through the same process of ripping and shredding. Dr. Mair and the Procurator collaborated in one, and Professor Cooper was another of the eager authors of a new Constitution. These differed greatly. What is interesting about John White's version is that everything in it which he regarded as fundamental was to find a place in the "Articles Declaratory of the Church of Scotland in Matters Spiritual" when they assumed their final shape and were embodied in an Act of Parliament eight years later.

In the Preamble, he referred to the statutory Constitution of the Church and her relation to the State as regulated by the Act of 1592 and others. All such statutes were to remain in force, but anything in them which was inconsistent with the freedom in matters spiritual that was now claimed would be repealed. In the first Article, there was a reaffirmation that the Lord Jesus was King and Head of the Church and that from Him all the Church's powers were derived, such powers not being controlled in any way by the civil government. The Westminster Confession of Faith was accepted afresh as the Church's subordinate standard and she affirmed her inherent right to declare the sense in which she understood that Confession and her right to formulate other subordinate standards. The powers of the courts of the Church were described, and so comprehensive were these powers that volumes of ancient controversy on matters such as the election of ministers were swept into the dust in a few phrases. The powers of those Lords of Council and Session, who acted as Commissioners for the plantation of Kirks and the valuation of Teinds, were transferred to the courts of the Church. There was an affirmation of the Church's power to hold conference with any Church of Christ in matters affecting the religious state of the people. And the Church claimed the inherent right to determine and regulate her own Constitution so long as she retained her identity as Presbyterian, Reformed, Evangelical, National.

During his work on the Articles, John White had come to some conclusions which, he hoped, would be a guide to the committee:

"The most hopeful if not the only practicable way to carry this matter to a successful issue is to seek the line of least resistance in all points which are not vital. . . . We must guard against the danger involved in putting special emphasis upon any one point or another in which any of us may be specially interested and of attempting to deal specifically with it. . . . Our government, our doctrine and our discipline are contained in our historical standard. Our laws are in our Acts of Assembly. Our practice is in our text-books. The wise course is to leave these where they are and to secure that the Constitution, on the one point which makes it necessary (spiritual autonomy in relation to the State), will be as short and as lucid as possible."

By December 1913, a sequence of Articles had been put together and the work of the Business Committee now came under the critical review of the Hundred.

John White reminded members of the agreement to discuss the temporalities at a later stage, and consequently there was no reference in the Articles to teinds and endowments. But there was one other thing which some might have expected to see in the document now before them. There had been no attempt to define the relation between their Church and the State: for he held that to try to define comprehensively that relation—no official definition of which had ever been made before—would be to raise a controversy that might have dangerous consequences.

He explained to the Hundred that he had also been careful to omit any definition of the jurisdiction of their Church courts. In the earlier days of the union movement, Dr. George Robson of the United Free Church had raised this matter in a flurry of anxiety: if there were to be recognition by the State of the jurisdiction of the Church, he had said, then quite clearly the matters coming under the Church's jurisdiction must be defined. John White's reply had been decisive.

"You will be bringing in a new danger," he had said, "and probably a greater danger than any we are now facing. The respective spheres of civil and ecclesiastical courts have never been defined. We do not wish jurisdiction in anything but the spiritual matters that can be dealt with by spiritual courts. We must avoid all approach to Ultramontanism in our efforts to avoid the taint of Erastianism."

Against every appeal to include definitions on these two matters in the new Constitution he remained adamant, and he had his way.

VIII

The goal to which John White and his colleagues were now striving was to win from Parliament an acknowledgment of the inherent rights of the Church, many of which had been set forth in the Act of 1592. These rights the Church had claimed as her own throughout the centuries of storm and sunshine, during periods when prelacy was in the ascendant, in the blood and fury of the Killing Time: and these rights, by words deliberately spoken in Scotland's own Court of Session, during the ten years of conflict before the Disruption, had been filched from the Church. Senators of the College of Justice had degraded her legal status by a misinterpretation of Acts of the old Scottish Parliament. A Lord President of the Court of Session had used phrases which had burned themselves into the memories of Scots folk for generations when he had declared that the Temporal Head of the Church of Scotland was Parliament itself— "Parliament *from whose Acts alone* the Church exists as a National Church and *from whom it derives all its powers.*" He had further made the statement, considered outrageous at the time, and seeming none the less outrageous in retrospect, that although a civil court could not ordain a minister it could *order* a presbytery to ordain him. Another judge, whose misreading of the *raison d'être* of the Church's Charter of 1592 was no less heinous than the Lord President's, had declared that "the Church of Scotland, as an Establishment, is the mere creation of the Legislature and *every* power which it possesses it derives from the Law".

In the years that followed the Disruption, there was in the Court of Session much more sanity in matters ecclesiastical than in that decade of angry conflict before it. It was as if the splitting of the Church in two (the direct result of the approval at Westminster of these preposterous Edinburgh judgments) had so horrified Scotland that a new conception of the spiritual liberty of the Church began to grow. Certain it is that thereafter in the Court of Session a series of declarations re-established without any doubt the jurisdiction of the Church courts as acknowledged in the Act of 1592; and the very certitude and candour of these declarations was an avowal that in the years immediately before the Disruption this Act had been grossly misinterpreted by Scots judges. Not once after the Disruption was a judgment of any court of the Church of Scotland to be challenged in a civil court: and the Church could with validity claim that, from the day when Royal Assent had been given in 1905 to an Act which allowed the Church to define her attitude to the Westminster Confession, she had secured spiritual freedom greater than that of any other Protestant State Church.[1]

In the new Constitution, the Church was indeed claiming even more freedom than she had ever possessed in her history. She was going beyond anything in the Claim of Right, beyond even what the Scots Parliament had acknowledged in the Act of 1592. She was proposing to cancel by a stroke of the pen the statute which had imposed upon her a particular method of electing and placing ministers. She was claiming full control over the membership of her own courts. She was proposing that Parliament should acknowledge her right to modify the Westminster Confession itself, and to create, if she chose to do so, other subordinate standards. And she was at the same time retaining her position as the National Church. Both in John White's original draft of the Articles and in the changes that were made as argument swayed this way and that in the councils of the Committee, the claim was made, and Parliament was to be asked to acknowledge, that the Church of Scotland possessed an autonomy and a status which was unique in Christendom.

[1] After the United Methodist Church Act of 1907 had become law, the United Methodists had claimed that they had "a degree of freedom in the management of their own affairs not possessed by any other Church in Great Britain and Ireland". Although they were then in a more secure position of freedom than the United Free Church of Scotland (because Parliament had ratified their Constitution, whereas the Constitution of the United Free Church remained no more than a declaration of liberty), the United Methodist courts did not have the jurisdictional power of the courts of the Church of Scotland: in consequence, the decisions of their courts were liable to be overthrown in civil courts of law.

Chapter X

AUTOCRAT AND DIPLOMATIST

I

IT was a rough road John White had to travel, as clerk of the committee, before he could see the reformed Constitution take shape. From each meeting he went home to Glasgow with a sheaf of notes and amendments. The conferences with the other Church had for the time being come to an end, but this did not mean any lessening of differences within the Church of Scotland committee: indeed, these grew sharper with each meeting. As far back as the days when the 1911 Report was being prepared, a minority group had made its influence felt. The objectors had been allowed full scope to present their views, and they had taken up the time of the committee even to the point where the patience of some men had been sorely tested. Members had written to John White reproaching him for the amount of toleration shown to dissentients. One minister said: "Could that interminable talk about the Creed of the Church not be ruled irrelevant? You may be having a talk with whoever is to be in the chair. A preliminary *caveat* from him might do good. The dog-days are past, but muzzling would be good for some folks."

Professor James Cooper of Glasgow University stood forth as the leader of a minority whose insignificance in numbers was in an inverse ratio to its passionate sincerity and its determination to convince the majority of the serious error of their ways. Lord Balfour had felt compelled to write to Professor Cooper:

"I have received many communications both written and verbal, and I assure you most positively that there is a considerable feeling of resentment growing up amongst those whom I would describe as moderate, sensible, old-fashioned people, at the sort of assumption, may I say even on your part, but certainly on the part of some others, that your school are the only guardians of the 'Faith' and that we are going forward to organise a Creedless Church. It is not true. It is unfair that it should be alleged, and, if it is continued, will do harm even to those very interests of which you and others are constituting

155

yourselves the sole guardians. Only this morning I have received a letter from a life-long personal friend, senior to both of us in the councils of the Church, and one whose name would carry great weight with you if I were at liberty to mention it. The words he used are these—'I resent more than I can say, the posing of Cooper and Wotherspoon as guardians of the "Faith once delivered" as if we are all indifferent about it'. . . .

"I am quite aware that in writing this I run the risk of your misunderstanding my object. If you will believe me, it is done out of friendship and out of regard, and may I add only under a strong sense of duty to those who have given me a larger share of trust and confidence than I myself feel I altogether deserve."

The charge that the reformed Constitution would turn the Church of Scotland into "a creedless Church" was yet to be the source of much vexation. John White told the committee that he had little hope of gaining unanimity on any statement of leading doctrines. As for the Church at large, agreement would be impossible. Moreover, a credal statement seemed to be unnecessary. That was why, in his draft, he had simply reaffirmed the salient principle that the Head of the Church was the Lord Jesus Christ, from Whom all the Church's power was derived, and her doctrines were contained in the Westminster Confession.

When it was urged that the opening Article should state the relation of the Church of Scotland to the Church Universal, John White agreed, but a group of men rose in protest. The Articles must open with a statement of *all* that was fundamental in the Faith of the Church. From this they would not be moved. In confusion, members went from the committee wondering how harmony could be achieved: it seemed they must give up all hope of that. What John White had feared was coming to pass.

One morning when he was a guest at Kennet, Lord Balfour of Burleigh handed him a letter he had just received from Professor Cooper.

"Had we not been confident," wrote Cooper, "that this open Confession would be granted, we would never have begun negotiations. . . . If we are to be left with the first Article in its present meagre, dangerous and (as I still think) deceptive form, I must tell you that I cannot answer for any consequences that may follow, and that I hold myself free to take whatever steps may seem right and advisable, not simply for keeping myself clear of complicity in the course that is being pursued, but for maintaining and defending the capital interests of the Church in which I am a minister."

After consultation with John White, Lord Balfour replied:

"I read your letter with pain, because it appears to me that the latter part of it seems to amount to the suggestion of a breach of faith on my part. For this I venture to say there is not a particle of foundation, and it is a suggestion which ought not to be made as between friends like you and me without something very definite to go on. . . . I have always argued against loosening our tie with the 'Fundamentals', and the preliminary draft *does keep us as a Church in the same position as that in which we now stand*. . . . That has been my position in the past; that is my position now; and under the circumstances, as I have said, I think it unreasonable and even unfair that you should seem to imply that I personally have changed my ground or abandoned my testimony."

Professor Cooper refused to give way. Some in the committee admired his tenacity; others deplored it. In the end, a majority agreed that a statement of doctrine should be set forth in the opening Article. But many objected to the concession, and said so. The Very Rev. Dr. Mitford Mitchell wrote to John White: "I entirely dissent from the enumeration of fundamental doctrines—it seems to me to show *a want of faith in Divine Guidance of the Church*."

No sooner had Professor Cooper and his associates gained this point than they claimed another. At the end of the statement of fundamental doctrines in the first Article, they said, there must be an explicit declaration that the Church had no power to alter it at any future time. This opened up a new source of conflict. It was a conflict which took the participants deeply into Church history and law. On the one side was the majority, who wondered how far they might dare to go in conciliation: on the other, there was a minority—a very small minority—who were convinced beyond any doubt that they were in the right and the others in the wrong.

II

The dispute, which was to be carried beyond the committee, may be reduced to a simple question. Was the Church in future to be debarred from revising the words she had herself used in setting forth the doctrines or from altering their sequence and the emphasis placed upon them?

To some of the committee, an affirmative to this suggested a despairing disbelief in the possibility of the Church receiving from the Holy Spirit any fresh revelation in the enrichment of these doctrines. It seemed to them wrong that, although the Church might win the assent of Parliament that she possessed the inherent power to modify her own Constitution, she must deny to herself the power ever to alter her own epitome of the Faith. How absurd, they said, that the Church should have been struggling for years to relax her ties with the Westminster Confession, so that newly ordained ministers should have some freedom of conscience in signing it, and that she should now draw up a special credal statement and bind future generations to it by statute law. Why should she be denied the power to modify or add to her own words in the beneficent light of new revelation?

For the best of all reasons: so claimed the minority. The Rev. A. W. Wotherspoon maintained that no branch of the Christian Church could exercise any power over the Faith. Even the Church Universal did not possess such power: she had not created the Faith; she had received it of the Lord. Wotherspoon pointed out the distinction between a Church's Confession and her Creed. In her Confession is embodied the Creed, which is the unalterable basis of all doctrine. A Confession, a comparatively recent thing in the Church's history, contains much that is deduced from the Creed and depends upon racial or national environment; it is a declaration for the times; it distinguishes one branch of the Universal Church from another. A Church has—or ought to have—power to alter her own Confession, since she created it for the guidance of her own people. But not even the Church Universal dared to tamper with the common inheritance of Christendom. The suggestion that a branch of the Christian Church could be mistress of her own Creed evoked from Mr. Wotherspoon a *cri du cœur*: "Here is the doctrine of infallibility run mad. Rome has not approached this pretension. Rome assumes to go on defining; but Rome has never professed to deny the past, never claimed authority to alter or change or modify what Christendom believes."

III

Strong counter-arguments were brought forward. Had John Knox not promised that if anything "repugnant to God's Holy Word" could be found in any part of his Confession he would correct it? In the Westminster Confession it had been admitted that "all Synods or Councils since the Apostles' time, whether general or particular, may err and many have erred, therefore they are not to be made the rule of faith or practice, *but to be used as an help in both*". Nobody could pretend, said Dr. Mair, that the formal expression of the great creeds of the past had *never* been altered by the Church, for the Creed compiled by the Fathers at Nicea had been revised by the second Ecumenical Council at Constantinople: therefore, from the early days of the Christian Church, while the Faith itself was unalterable, in the expression of that Faith there had been alteration in phrasing, lengthening or shortening, adding or subtracting. While it was clear that a Church must have marks of identity and hold certain doctrines as a fundamental basis of communion, it was recalled that the Church of Scotland had never drawn up a statement of those doctrines that must be accepted as essential. In her Act Anent Spiritual Independence of 1906, the United Free Church had made no such attempt, and indeed no Presbyterian Church in Scotland had ever done so at any time. Therefore, to place together those doctrines which, by a majority in the Church, might be counted fundamental, and then to declare the compilation to be unalterable, would constitute a revolution in the history of the Church of Scotland. "That would be to assume," said Dr. Mair, "that in this matter at least we have attained to perfection in our knowledge of truth and in our expression of it." He had the support of John White and others in his denunciation of what he called "this vain attempt to impose our opinions on those who come after us". John White urged that the Church had the right and the responsible duty "to exercise its living powers of adaptiveness, to review its Standards in the light which has broken forth from the Word of God since they were first framed, and to interpret theological truths in terms of present methods of thought and of present need". As for the contention that it was a strong bulwark against the encroaching tides of heterodoxy for a Church to draw up a credal statement and have it ratified by law—this was simply brushed aside by a reminder that every Church which in the past had apostasised had done so in spite of her spiritual declarations.

These and other arguments were arrayed against Cooper, Wotherspoon, and those of a like mind. Not one of them wavered. The doctrinal statement in the first Article must be unalterable. And so the majority of the committee made their second concession. In the eighth Article, the following words were inserted: "The Church, as a branch of the Catholic Church, unalterably adhering to the declaration of faith and duty set forth in the first Article hereof . . ."

It was hoped that this would satisfy Professor Cooper and his friends, but they announced that it did not. At the end of the first Article, after the statement of doctrines, there must follow these words: "*This Article is unalterable.*" Having given way so much, the committee refused to go further. The breach deepened. And the statement of essential doctrines had still to be agreed upon.

"I have the utmost sympathy with those who wish to safeguard the Catholic faith," wrote John White, "and in all the meetings of our committee there has been one mind on the subject that fidelity to the fundamental Christian truths must be secured." But he held that the best way of so doing was to state that the faith of the Church was contained in the Church's principal subordinate standard, the Westminster Confession, within which was embodied the whole of the Nicene Creed. In some doubt, at a later committee meeting, he read aloud a draft of the first Article which had with great difficulty been hammered out:

"*The Church of Scotland is a branch of the Holy Catholic or Universal Church, believing in one God the Father Almighty, and in Jesus Christ His only Begotten Son Incarnate for our salvation, and in the Holy Ghost, three persons in the unity of the Godhead; owning obedience to its once crucified, now risen and glorified Lord, as the sole King and Head of His Church; proclaiming the forgiveness of sins and acceptance with God through faith in Christ, the renewing of the Holy Spirit, and eternal life; and labouring for the advancement of the Kingdom of God throughout the world.*"

Professor Cooper and A. W. Wotherspoon again protested: this did not contain the deposit, the delivered Faith, properly expressed. Where were the Catholic doctrine of the Trinity, of the Person and Nature of our Saviour, of the Incarnation and Atonement, of the Person and Mission of the Holy Ghost? They admitted that the statement contained *a* doctrine of the Trinity—but not the catholic and orthodox one. And there was a mere mention of the Incarnation. Neither doctrine was set forth in any known shape or form, certainly not in the form in which the Church of Scotland knew them. From the doctrines of the Trinity and the Incarnation, declared Mr. Wotherspoon, all others, even that of the Atonement, were derived. He maintained that the committee's doctrine of the Trinity was something new in Christian theology. Professor Cooper vigorously supported him when he declared that the statement of essential truths which the committee proposed to put before the Assembly would, if approved, cut off the Church of Scotland from doctrinal unity with the Church Universal.

IV

These were strong words. John White fought back, and there were some sharp exchanges. But nothing altered the respect which Cooper and White had for each other. Their friendship dated from the time when Cooper had captured the Chair of Church History at Glasgow to which White had aspired. In the early days of the union movement, they had supported each other whole-heartedly. "That most lovable and unique personality," as White called Cooper, was now the leader of the Scoto-Catholic school which strove to revive orthodox symbolism in the Church. The forms of service used in the years that followed the Reformation were closely studied, and the Scottish Church Society which had been established in 1892 carried out work of this kind. The Scoto-Catholics deplored the bleak Puritanism that had been imported from England, and they shrank from what they considered modern laxities in belief and worship. Their attitude to the Covenanting struggles was very different from that of the majority in the Church of Scotland. Principal Story had described the Covenanters as "the traducers of Mother Church", and Cooper himself spoke of "those powerful men of 1637 who persecuted their king and their bishops rather than were persecuted by them". John White appreciated to the full the intentions of the Scoto-Catholics, who counted themselves the spiritual bodyguard of the Church against heterodoxy: but he was certainly not one of them.

"Cooper, the dear man," he wrote, "was always on the look-out lest we should do hurt to the 'Catholic faith' in our statement. The Articles, the first chiefly, were a nightmare to him. That first article did not embody the Nicene Creed in the form he loved. (The Athanasian he would, I am sure, have put in as well.) One phrase was on his mind—*the same in substance, equal in power and glory*—and he pled for it. If we gave him this, we wondered, would he promise not to ask for more? He was very angry because I tried to tie his hands in this way, but I knew that if I didn't we should never finish the Articles. They had taken far too much of our time. They had aroused unnecessary debate. And that first Article was *not* really necessary to the Articles Declaratory of our freedom in spiritual things. . . . But Cooper would not be satisfied."

John White recalled how dismayed Cooper had been when Denney had said that "the symbol of the Church's unity might be expressed thus: 'I believe in God through Jesus Christ, His only Son, our Saviour.'" Cooper could never forget that. "Here comes Professor Denney," he had said, "one of the foremost theologians in the United Free Church, dismissing as the doctrinal basis of reunion not only the Nicene Creed but even that core of all the creeds, the Threefold Name in which we were baptised."

Although they vehemently opposed him, John White also remained on friendly terms with the two brothers Wotherspoon. These High churchmen were the main support of Professor Cooper. Dr. H. J. Wotherspoon of Edinburgh was not on the union committee, and John White greatly wished that he had been—and would indeed have had him in place of his brother from Glasgow. The charm and courtesy of the former sweetened all of John White's association with him. But he found Arthur Wotherspoon "most obstinate in Committee and a wee bit of a bother in asking for his views to be embodied in the Articles—in fact he and Cooper would have pushed their views until Union became impossible." John White told of an occasion when

> "Arthur Wotherspoon had been very argumentative and had held up our business all afternoon; it was time to adjourn, and I suggested that the matter under discussion should be remitted to a sub-committee of eight men to report at our next meeting. The Rev. Arthur W. was dis-satisfied because nobody from his school of thought was on the chosen eight. As time for our trains was short I suggested that we make it ten men and so 'put on the whole school'."

John White summed up Cooper and Arthur Wotherspoon in these words: "They were both *keen* men and, apart from theological controversy, splendid fellows."

It was a fortunate thing that John White bore them the affection he did, for their tenaciously held views were yet to exasperate him greatly. There were eight other Articles to be drawn up and approved, and there was another point on which the minority protested as strongly as they had done over the doctrinal testimony. They held that the phrase "National Recognition of Religion", which had been so much bandied about in the committee, was loose and indeterminate. National Religion, they maintained, was much more important than the mere recognition of religion by a State. In the Articles, no protection was given to this vital

principle of National Religion: and if there was no principle in Establishment that was worthy to be held by a spiritual Society, and was fit to be
embodied in its religious constitution, then the Church ought not to
accept Establishment. They demanded that an addition be inserted
declaring that the Church held it to be her duty to seek the support and
aid of the State and that she maintained the ancient statutory connection
with it. On this, blunt words were spoken. Professor Cooper and his
friends were told that, if they had their way, it would put an abrupt end
to union negotiations.

The committee met on 16th April to approve its Report to the General
Assembly. Realising at last that they had failed to have their way, the
dissentients now settled down to draft a Minority Report on Doctrinal
Testimony and National Religion to present to the General Assembly.

V

While these problems had been engaging the attention of the committee, there was a matter of some delicacy that had been giving a good
deal of concern to John White and the Procurator as well as to the joint
conveners. Since the revised Constitution, if approved by the Assembly,
would be transmitted to the United Free Church, it would clearly be an
advantage to find out beforehand what Dr. Henderson and his friends
thought about it. The best course would have been to have had a joint
conference of the two committees to discuss the Articles in detail.
Unfortunately, such a discussion was out of the question. The remit of
the Assembly of 1913 did not go further than to permit the committee
to draft the Articles and submit them to the next General Assembly.
Indeed, a proposal that they should be drawn up jointly by the two
committees had been decisively rejected. It would have been going beyond
the remit even to hand the Articles to Dr. Henderson and ask him to
discuss them with a few friends and return them with comments.

The Procurator suggested a way out of the difficulty. They could have
a meeting with the Hundred of the United Free Church and, although
the Articles would not be laid on the table, "the general scheme of them
could be explained and the views of the other side could be ascertained".
He thought that a "narrative outline of our document" could be used:
thus they would be obeying the letter of the law. He thought that the
Established Church spokesman could keep within the bounds if he were
to say that "we propose a clause to do this and a clause to do that, some-

times perhaps even quoting a little but without showing that it was a quotation".

Being aware of the difficulty, Dr. Henderson was anxious to help. He wondered if he could not be invited to answer questions privately about the Articles without actual quotations being made from them. But since no joint conference had been held for many months, it was thought better to avoid giving anyone cause to suspect that the leaders were "unduly trafficking" together. With John White this timidity went against the grain. Without consulting anyone, he did a thing which might have called down on him a serious and to some extent a deserved reproof. He sent a copy of the Articles to a layman in the United Free Church and asked for a frank opinion.

Sir Andrew Fraser, a member of the union committee, was one of the most prominent and highly respected members of that Church. He wielded great influence in an unobtrusive way on every occasion when his advice was sought. John White made it plain in his letter why he was approaching him in such strict confidence. It was necessary to have a judgment on the acceptability of the Articles to the majority of broadminded United Free churchmen. Fraser, who might have felt justified in returning the draft, saw how genuine was John White's desire for enlightenment. He studied the Articles with care and sent back a detailed report. To White's relief, there was not a fundamental point to which Sir Andrew Fraser had any objection, and he proposed only one or two minor amendments. As a United Free churchman, he naturally disliked the claim of the Church of Scotland to be *the* National Church; he preferred the indefinite article. His notes showed his confidence that all would be well, and this was reassuring to John White as clerk of the Church of Scotland committee.

Meanwhile, the state of inaction was greatly troubling Dr. Henderson. Understanding so fully what was holding back the leaders of the Established Church committee, he nevertheless felt it would be a mistake if some kind of contract were not made before the Articles were sent to the Assembly. He urged that there should be a private talk between three or four members from both committees, with the Procurator's house as a convenient *venue*. No record seems to have been made of any such talk, but there is a significant note in the diary of John White under the date 20th February 1914: "Special meeting with Dr. Henderson and Co." In speculating upon what happened that Friday afternoon, we can be sure that the Articles were not ostensibly shown to the United Free churchmen, but we can also be sure that many questions were asked and answered. And since only insignificant changes were made on the Articles at the next committee meeting, we can safely deduce that the result of the discussion at the Procurator's house was as agreeable to them all as Sir Andrew Fraser's private report had been to John White. That the fundamental points in the reformed Constitution were acceptable to the leaders of the United Free Church was now assured.

The warmth of understanding which John White and his colleagues found among the leaders of the United Free Church was in sharp contrast to the spirit that was now becoming more manifest every day throughout the Church of Scotland.

VI

As John White, in his many journeys, met ministers and elders and listened to their talk, he became appalled at the wrong-headed views on union he found on all sides. Some men were prepared to argue about it without having studied with sufficient care the committee's Report to the 1911 Assembly on which he had spent such pains and upon which the whole structure of union was built. The Memorandum of 1912 could be read by anyone who was interested—as most Old Kirk folk were—but a good many even of those who had read the documents were looking at them with prejudiced eyes. As John White often said at this time, the more that certain words and phrases were hurled back and forward, the more meaningless they became—and the more terribly important they seemed. Dr. W. S. Provand, a Glasgow minister who was a strong opponent of John White's, stated publicly that he did not blame people for being led astray by these Church documents, and added that the United Free Church's Comments on the Memorandum, which had been circulated in the Established Church, were liable to increase their doubts.[1] Provand said that many people honestly believed that if the new Constitution should be adopted by the Assembly of 1914, it would be hustled down to presbyteries under the Barrier Act—and then, if approved, would be rushed through as an Act of Assembly in 1915, with the certain result that a protesting Minority would become the legal Church of Scotland (as the Wee Frees had become the "legal" Free Church) with power to claim all her property. It was a formidable prospect. Another fear was that the ancient statutes that guaranteed the Church's powers and liberties

---

[1] Dr. W. S. Provand, minister of St. Ninian's, Glasgow, clerk of the Presbytery of Glasgow, and author of *Puritanism in the Scottish Church*, was a notable figure in the Church life of his day, and by none more esteemed for his qualities of mind and character—despite their not infrequent differences of opinion—than by John White.

were to be repealed: which meant that the Church would be virtually disestablishing herself. John White was perplexed to find so much of what he called "unrest and shaken confidence". Since Dr. Wallace Williamson was Moderator that year, and had perforce to move about in the shires, he too had discerned the doubt in folks' minds, but he took a more lenient view and pointed out to John White that "we in the Hundred have had the benefit of all the Conferences and have been compelled to look at all the difficulties from every side; but our men in the Church as a whole have not had this experience and, even when well-disposed towards a settlement, feel uncertain".

The matter became more urgent when John White received a letter from the Dumbarton Presbytery. While its members were in favour of union, they felt it must be "honourably secured"; it must "conserve the principle of Establishment"; it must not involve concessions that would mean "a surrender of the ancient historical alliance of Church and State". In such terms the Rev. Morison Bryce put to John White the suspicions of the Presbytery. "It would be better," he said, "to face the contingency of disestablishment by an Act of Parliament." Into such straits had the majority of the Dumbarton Presbytery drifted in their uncertainty. If this could be taken as representative of the views of many other presbyteries, it was clear to John White that something would have to be done quickly to dissipate the cloud that was settling upon the Church of Scotland.

Without delay, he drew up an "Explanatory Statement" of the work the committee had accomplished, and this was distributed to presbyteries throughout the land. Although it was a clear and matter-of-fact document, it did not by any means allay the doubts of all: there were some who even suggested that it made matters worse.

VII

That was indeed a winter of discontent in the Church of Scotland. At a meeting of the Synod of Glasgow and Ayr in the middle of November 1913, a storm broke. Members spoke vehemently about their misgivings. One speaker declared that the Memorandum of 1912 "bristled with dangers and was full of pitfalls—pits as numerous as those that had strewn the field of Bannockburn". In the whole of that document, he said, the expression "the Church as by law established" had not been used once. With the rescinding of a large body of legislation, said another speaker, "the effect would not be a statutory connection between Church and

State but a vague, indefinite, incohate, nebulous recognition"—and if that did not spell disestablishment, he added, he would like to know what it did.

John White found it difficult to listen to these and other attacks without getting to his feet. Referring to what was taking place behind the closed doors of the committee room, one minister remarked that they had been asked to trust their leaders. He spoke of Dr. Norman MacLeod (a predecessor of John White's at The Barony) having written the hymn, *Courage, brother, do not stumble*—and he added ironically, amid laughter, that a line of that hymn was, "Trust no leaders in the fight". There were principles in Establishment to which they were sworn, and the committee should realise that a large body of ministers and laymen in the Church would carry their opposition from court to court if these principles were not preserved. One speaker referred with bitterness to the duty which the Church had to the people of Scotland. They had a larger membership, while the United Frees had a larger income. The others had the money, while the Established Church had the poor. Warm approval greeted his statement that the union movement was one on which they would forsake poverty and ally themselves with wealth—and how could they expect the blessing of God?

At last John White rose. He pointed out the errors into which previous speakers had fallen—errors of fact and errors of judgment. "It was one thing to have the Reports of the Church," he said, "Reports which were full and held back nothing—but it was evidently quite another thing to understand the salient features of these documents and to appreciate their intention." And he answered the main accusations in a series of swift, cool arguments. Afterwards he was congratulated on "his gallant and statesmanlike stand," as one man described it, and on the way he had kept his temper. "You did noble service alone," wrote Norman Maclean to him; "your very calmness was reassuring."

A fortnight later he was at a meeting of the Glasgow Presbytery called to deal mainly with union problems. He had been given beforehand a long list of the questions that were troubling ministers and elders. In these questions there was a probing into the very core of the union movement. John White answered them, one by one, in detail. He asserted that he and his colleagues were safeguarding all that was valued in the Church's heritage. Presbytery members were impressed by the exposition. It was as if new light had been allowed to shine into dark corners. And then John White looked around him, and confronted them with that daunting glare of severity which he could assume at a moment's notice. His chin jutted out aggressively as he informed the members of Presbytery that he had given them *not one single answer which they could not have read for themselves* if they had taken the trouble to study with a little intelligence the printed documents sent to every one of them. Then he sat down. It is on record that his words had a powerful effect in "bringing many round to consider union in a more favourable light".

It followed naturally that he was asked to speak to other presbyteries. He went to Perth. Twice he spoke to the Presbytery of Lorne. He addressed meetings of church members. On 16th December 1913, he spoke in Bridgend Church to what he described as a "unique gathering of the seven Presbyterian churches of Dumbarton". At that meeting he was in his element, for his hearers were from both the Established and the United Free Church, and he could direct his blows at each side with a satisfying impartiality and good humour. He spoke of the sin of schism, and exploded some of the sincere nonsense that was being talked about it. Even if it were possible, he said, he did not think it desirable now to unite all the Christian Churches of the British Empire. Not even all the denominations in Scotland could now be united.

> "A chain-gang at lock-step," he declared, "was not God's ideal of the Communion of the Saints! Christian diversities were an enrichment of the life and thought of the Church so long as they remained diversities in unity. It would be unfair—historically unfair—to condemn denominational groupings as an unmixed evil. Once upon a time, there was one Church organisation and no other—the Roman Church—and by exaggerating its authority it brought on the darkest days of Christian history. But Presbyterian Churches in Scotland are now in one denomination: for they are alike in worship, discipline, doctrine, government. Many of the issues that divided the sects are today obsolete. Three and a half centuries ago, sectarianism was the high road to freedom. The rise of denominations, after the Reformation, was an indication of progress—not of deterioration. They were historically necessary to save religion from corruption—and to bring to light neglected essentials of Christian truth."

Whether his Old Kirk hearers liked it or not, he went on: "In Presbyterian Scotland, the divisions of the Church laid emphasis on spiritual freedom. They laid emphasis on the duty of the nation to recognise the Church of Christ as something more than a voluntary association." He promised his hearers that the amended Constitution would preserve the vital principles of both Churches. There was talk on both sides, he said, about each giving away too much to conciliate the other; but while both were making concessions these were far outweighed by what each Church would gain if they united with the reformed Constitution as a common basis. He said that the practical need for union throughout the country was increasing with every day that passed. "For Scotland's sake, don't let punctilio ruin all," he urged, quoting the plea made by Professor Charteris more than forty years before. And he recalled too the wise words of Bishop Creighton: "With the cry, '*Arise, Shine!*' sounding in our ears, how can we waste time disputing about the shape of our lanterns?"

VIII

Within four days of his speech to the seven churches of Dumbarton, John White was writing to Dr. Wallace Williamson in terms that reveal his concern about the weight of adverse opinion in the Church. He realised how widely it was feared that the terms of the revised Constitution were being virtually dictated by the United Free Church. There was no news of any meetings of the two committees: but what was going on behind the scenes? Dr. Henderson and his friends had many times in the past said that they would enter upon a union only if certain demands were met. These had been discussed throughout the Established Church, and heads had been shaken. Nor had there passed from memory the words of United Free churchmen like Professor Martin on the need for the disestablishment of the Church of Scotland—words deliberately spoken and written even after union talks had begun. How much was now being surrendered to placate the United Frees? John White heard this question asked almost every day.

That vital document, the draft of the Articles, was on the secret list and could not be published until it was officially released before the General Assembly. It looked as if suspicion would increase rather than fade until folk could read the reformed Constitution for themselves. And after they had read it, what would be the thoughts of those who took pride in the Old Kirk and all she stood for? If they were given time to think and talk about it, to grow accustomed to it, to appreciate the spiritual liberty that was claimed in it, John White was convinced that it would win wide approval. No hasty judgment must be passed on it: that would be disastrous. He left Lord Balfour of Burleigh and Dr.

Wallace Williamson in no doubt about his views on this. If the consequences of every step they took were not carefully considered, he foresaw that the whole union movement might be wrecked. The most pressing concern was the fate of the Articles: and this would be in the balance at the forthcoming Assembly.

Of one thing he was certain. There would be a proposal to send the Articles down to presbyteries for consideration before they were transmitted to the United Free Church. Knowing what he did of the temper of many of their own ministers and elders at that time, he estimated that the Articles would not be approved by a majority of the presbyteries. And so, after all their years of struggle, the union movement would be killed by a rash presbyterial *coup de grâce*.

To avoid such a disaster, some means must be devised. John White calmly decided to forestall any suggestion in the Assembly that the Articles should be sent to presbyteries for outright acceptance or rejection. He proposed that they should be sent down *informally* with the request that the presbyteries make any comments they wished by a certain date so that the document could be amended. In this way, he hoped that confidence would be to some extent established in the presbyteries. Shrewdly he anticipated that "after all the criticisms had been drawn out they would not be so very serious when reduced to writing".

IX

At the General Assembly of May 1914, when John White rose to speak on union he was greeted in a way that showed how his reputation had grown. A writer in *The British Weekly* spoke of it as "White's Assembly", and described his personal triumph. "The Church has learned to trust and rely upon him," wrote the correspondent of *The Scotsman*. "In Mr. White the Assembly recognised a man who is destined to wield a great influence in the councils of the Church of Scotland. A great cause ever provides a leader."

In the opening of his first speech, John White said: "The Church is glad to leave the atmosphere of ecclesiastical littleness and rise to the height of Christian statesmanship." Having travelled so far with them on the road to union, their friends in the other Church had a right to know the result of their committee's work during the past year—a period when there had been no joint meetings. "To be quite realistic," he said, "it would be folly and poor strategy to send the Articles to presbyteries and not to the United Free Church committee. If we did not, we should have the sorry spectacle of the Church of Scotland drawing up a Constitution and then proceeding, by its presbyteries, to fire shot into it, while the United Free Church, without responsibility, stood apart watching our domestic dispeace." He added that both Churches were now in exactly the same position in one very important respect. Neither was being asked to pass judgment on the reformed Constitution. That would follow in due time.

The minority group, now led by Mr. James Clark, K.C., presented their Report to the Assembly. To his disgust, John White discerned that they would do their best to obtain what amounted to a rejection of the union committee's Report. In fact, they proposed that both Reports should be remitted back to the committee for drastic alterations to be made in the Articles. When they were defeated on this, they demanded that their Minority Report be sent down to presbyteries along with the committee's Report, so that they would know what alterations the minority had been fighting for. In agreeing to this, John White insisted that he explain in his covering letter how the Minority Report had been made. He did not wish presbytery members to be bemused: "It would be folly to send down both Reports as they stand, without some guidance, for this might simply divide the Church into factions." [1]

The Assembly followed John White and empowered the committee to resume conferences with the United Free Church committee and discuss the Articles. He did not want the committees to redraft the Articles together: it would be sufficient for their own committee to learn the views of the other. Besides, he said, there was a weighty political reason why they should resume joint conferences:

> "So long as the conferences are being held, it is believed that politicians refuse to deal with the question of the disestablishment of the Church of Scotland. But if we stop conferences for another year, and a General Election takes place within that time, as is now certain, then we may expect the question to be raised on many platforms. . . . The very fact that we are empowered to confer with the United Free Church committee would in itself be some safeguard against adverse political action."

[1] In his speech John White dealt with the Minority Report in carefully measured terms. In private, among the leaders of the Established Church, the matter was discussed with a good deal more frankness. Lord Balfour of Burleigh wrote to John White that "the way in which it was published" was the most deplorable thing he had known in a long public life.

He had his way on every point. Afterwards, Dr. Wallace Williamson wrote to him: "Amongst the pleasantest recollections I have of the Assembly, if I may say so, is the fact that something like due meed of recognition was given you for your splendid service, alike in the committee and in the Assembly itself—not to speak of the tumultuous West."

But the burden of the clerkship had become increasingly heavy, the more so because he had become almost indispensable. Dr. Wallace Williamson's reference to him as "a living encyclopaedia" gives a hint of the way questions were fired at him and his answers were accepted as *ex cathedra*. In spite of the arrangement he had made with his people at The Barony, that much of his time would be taken up with union affairs, he felt impelled to tell the committee that more of his energies must be deflected to his Glasgow parish. When he proposed that he should be relieved of the clerkship, nobody would listen to him, and he was launched upon a further period of effort to bring the day of Church reunion nearer.

X

From the General Assembly he had received what had been, in effect, a vote of confidence in him as a leader in the union movement. None had seen in him any hesitation. He had given directions as clear as those of a commander briefing his officers. His confidence had comforted many doubting ones. We can form the picture of a man who was becoming aware of the influence he was able to wield among his fellows. The Shettleston Church Case, in which he had triumphed over those who had skilfully resisted him, had to some extent shown to him his own strength. But whatever its wider implications may have been, that case had been a parochial matter, whereas he was now handling affairs that involved the whole of Scotland's parochial Church life. A new chapter in the history of the Kirk was in the making, and his part in it was becoming greater as those he worked with saw his stature; and he knew they were counting on his giving of himself to the cause.

A great audience was always a spur to John White. If he knew that among his hearers there were those who would fain have risen to rend his arguments, the effect on him was one of high stimulation. But that confident figure, erect in a packed and applauding Assembly, was very different from the one that can be clearly discerned for many days afterwards in the privacy of his study. Quietly he looked back at recent trends in the union movement. He tried to assess the strength of the opposition to it in both Churches, how far it could be reduced by the written and spoken word, how prejudices could be broken down, fears allayed. In looking into the future, even the immediate future, he knew he was but trying to weigh the imponderable. It could be said that, in spite of checks, things had gone well. But as he thought over some recent actions of the minority, now better organised and growing in number, he was by no means certain that they might not divide the Church. Their influence had been working like a ferment in the committee. At one meeting before the Assembly, the vote in their favour was nearly a third of the members present, and they might win further support among those who were not strongly inclined either way. In a letter to the Procurator, John White described the committee as "sheep without a shepherd who may bolt through any opening in the hedge". As for presbyteries, he felt they should be guided as soon as possible: "If Dundee or Glasgow or Dumbarton should take up the question of the Articles before we approach them officially, a wrong direction might be given to the discussions in other presbyteries."

There was another matter that troubled him sorely. He had spoken in the Assembly about the urgency of resuming conferences with the United Free Church committee in order to impel politicians to keep silent on disestablishment. The editor of *The Church Times* had reported privately that an active member of the Church Liberation Society (already noted as an association pledged to bring about disestablishment both in England and Scotland) had expressed the hope that "the minority in the United Free Church would be able to wreck the union". From what he had learned from other sources he now began to see that some dissenters, particularly in England, might persuade politicians in the Liberal Party that the union negotiations in progress must be no bar to political action, and Disestablishment and Disendowment might well be a lively topic at the next General Election. Not long after the close of the Assembly, John White was writing to the Procurator: "Are we not to be allowed to show to politicians a more excellent way than disestablishment, which would not only retard union for a generation, but would weaken Presbyterianism in Scotland for all time?" Driven by these thoughts, he took it upon himself to do everything he could to suppress those dissenting voices. He asked Sir Arthur Steel-Maitland, M.P., to use his influence among Radicals, and he pointed out that the English dissenter looked upon the disestablishing of the Church of Scotland as a useful lever to bring about the much more difficult task of disestablishing the English

Church. To John White it was a matter of chagrin that the hoary head of that old enemy, which had caused so much dispeace, should show itself again at this time.

To make fine speeches in the General Assembly was one thing: to keep a tight grip on the reins in the midst of hard realities was another. Lord Balfour of Burleigh continued to have many commitments in Parliament and elsewhere south of the Border. His joint convener, Dr. Wallace Williamson, with a sweetness of disposition, a gift of calling out the best in a man, and an ability to stir emotion by holding aloft high ideals, had a place all his own in the Church life of Scotland; but it is doing his memory no disservice to say that he was only too glad to rely on John White as a man better equipped than he was to cut a pathway through an entangled mass of complexities and obstructions. John White gloried in the hours he took from sleep to complete his union work; it was only by night that he could hope to complete committee tasks piled on top of his work as a parish minister. Inaccuracy, the slip-shod handling of detail, called down his wrath. In glee Lord Balfour of Burleigh twitted him on a mistake he had made in a date and admitted that "it was the first and only error I have known you make". More than one minister whom he found to be accurate he referred to as "indeed a Clerk in Holy Orders"; it was easy to deal with such men; he was such a one himself. But his mind's eye was fixed on things far beyond the papers in the pool of light cast by his desk lamp. He worked for the distant tomorrow. And then, of a sudden, all that he had put of himself into the drive for union became as ashes blown by the wind, and all dreams were broken by one word that seemed to flare in letters of fire from newspaper posters in the street—WAR.

XI

For a time, nothing seemed to matter but the great catastrophe. Britain must gather her armed strength; a ruthless enemy must be beaten. But the day came when "Business as Usual" was a slogan sponsored by the Government: the wheels must be kept turning. People grew accustomed to the idea of being at war; many things that had been hastily dropped were taken up again—and one of these was Church union. By the end of 1914, Professor Alexander MacEwen of New College, Edinburgh, was writing to John White:

"I agree with you as to the prospects for union. In this shaking of all things, that which decayeth and waxeth old must vanish and the things which cannot be shaken will remain to draw us together, if we maintain our faith, hope and charity."

In the New Year, John White and Professor Martin were making arrangements for a conference to be held between the two committees. After it was over, Dr. Henderson wrote to John White:

> "I cannot close my letter without saying how greatly we appreciated your patience with us on Tuesday. You were patient because you believed we were sincerely labouring for unity, and we were and felt *you* were also. The delay which is neither your seeking nor ours will, I feel sure, be yet seen to be for the good of the Churches and their ultimate oneness."

It was a comfort to feel that union was still a living thing. But as the weeks passed and news from the battle fronts became more grave, and the war spread itself over the seven seas, the magnitude of the struggle took on a more grim aspect. Union was still alive, but there could be little forward movement in those distressful days. Some presbyteries had indeed considered the Articles and sent comments to the committee, but the Report to the Assembly of 1915 could be only an interim one. Discussion on union had previously occupied many hours; in that year of 1915, the total time was thirty-seven minutes. On Friday, 28th May, John White dined as a guest of the Lord High Commissioner at Holyroodhouse. Before a month had passed, he had said good-bye to wife and family, good-bye to his congregation from the pulpit of The Barony, and was on duty on the Fife coast as a chaplain in His Majesty's Forces. By August he was at the front in France.

Chapter XI

CHAPLAIN AND REFORMER

I

AT the age of twenty John White had joined the Cameronians. As he said proudly afterwards, "I well remember standing on guard, a full-fledged private in the Cameronians, when Queen Victoria came to open the Glasgow Exhibition." The 5th Battalion of this famous old regiment had been raised about thirty years before and had then been known as the Glasgow 1st Western Rifle Volunteers, and later as the 1st Lanarkshire Volunteer Corps. He was qualified to join any one of three companies, the University, the Grain Merchants, or the Partick Citizens, and he enlisted with the first. At South Leith, his allegiance had of course been to The Royal Scots, for it was the home church of the 7th Battalion of The Royal Regiment, but his return to The Barony meant a renewal of his association with the Cameronians. The founder of the regiment, Richard Cameron, had been a boyhood hero of his, and so had his associate, Donald Cargill, minister of The Barony. In John White's own words, these resolute men

> "had, on 22nd June, 1680, entered the burgh of Sanquhar, marched up its streets with drawn swords, and, halting at the Market Cross, read and then posted up a declaration in which they renounced allegiance to Charles Stuart on account of his perjury, breaches of covenant, and tyranny in civil matters; and they declared war against him as a tyrant and usurper and an enemy of the Lord Jesus Christ and His Cause and Covenant."

Cameron was killed one month later, and troops scoured the country for the minister of The Barony who continued to preach on the moors and in the fastnesses of the hills. But his life as a wandering preacher was not to last long. When he climbed the ladder to his execution on the gallows, he said to his friends below that he did so "with less fear and perturbation of mind than ever he entered a pulpit to preach". John White spoke often of his great predecessor in The Barony pulpit and the regiment he had helped to found. "The Cameronians," he said, "stipulated that

176

the officers should be men of conscience, honour, and fidelity, and it was laid down that every man must carry in his haversack a Bible." During the First World War, it was in the Cameronians that John White was to serve.

As a minister of the gospel, he might have held back from active participation in that war. He might have devoted himself to his congregation, to good works within his parish, to the service of the Church in Greater Glasgow, to comforting the bereaved who had lost relatives on the field of battle, to visiting military hospitals and speaking an encouraging word to the wounded. But he deeply believed that it was a righteous war; a war in which the Kingdom of God was being challenged by the forces of evil aggression. Soon he was in demand at recruiting meetings and patriotic rallies. After service with the troops on the east coast of Scotland, he went to France to become chaplain there of the 5th Battalion of the regiment he had first joined as an undergraduate.

The impressions left upon him by his experiences at the front remained with him to the end of his days. The German leaders—who could tear treaties into shreds, break conventions, order poison gas to be used—he regarded as among the foulest of human kind, and he never minced words about Britain's enemies. The pleading post-war call that "we mustn't really be nasty to the Germans" he regarded as a sentimental whine, and he had an even ampler opportunity to expound his views when a second European conflagration had its source in the same trouble-spot. He gathered together his impressions of the First World War in a book entitled *With The Cameronians in France*. Because the military censors had their own peculiar ideas on what was suitable for publication in the midst of a war, they not only deleted the names of officers and places in France, but blue-pencilled quotations from Shakespeare and the Poet Laureate in case they should give valuable information to the enemy. John White dedicated the book to *The mothers and wives of the brave sons and husbands who have shown the greater love.* His own son Matthew was a subaltern in the 5th Battalion of the Cameronians; later, this officer was wounded and mentioned in despatches. Another of his sons, John, joined the 5th Cameronians straight from Edinburgh Academy; thus, for a period, three of the family were connected with the Regiment. Among the officers who went out to France with the 5th Battalion was Second-Lieut. J. C. W. Reith, who was the pioneer of Broadcasting in Britain, and who in 1940 became Lord Reith of Stonehaven.

In August 1915, five days after leaving the Waverley Station, Edinburgh, John White went with the battalion into the trenches, where the men were to spend the next ten months without respite. He wrote home telling of the first church parade he held, and since the rifle companies were in the front trenches he could muster only those behind the reserve line:

"But a service does not depend on numbers, and they enjoyed their little church under the pear and apple trees, with the boom of the guns not far distant. The Old Hundred and the second Paraphrase went all right; and I told the men they were never forgotten by the folks at home, who were thinking of them, praying for them, working for them. We then united our intercessions with those that would, in Glasgow, at that same hour, be rising to the Throne of Grace, for those who had gone forth to fight."

He wrote of another church parade:

"Sunday was a lovely Summer's day, and at an early hour the 5th Scottish Rifles paraded for service. I had chosen a field with refreshing green turf; on two sides were high trees like the pillars of a cathedral; and here, with sentries placed like the Cameronians of old, we worshipped the God of our fathers. . . . The boom of the big guns was not disturbing."

It was one of his great delights to meet his own kirk laddies from Glasgow. He spoke of six of them in the Glasgow Highlanders, "fine young men looking the picture of health". He had a chat with them about The Barony. "Don't forget them," he wrote, "and the others scattered over the far-flung battle line. . . . A handsome young kilty came up and spoke to me today; he was from Crosshouse (near Shettleston)." A letter written by a young man to Glasgow friends ran: "If I am spared to come home again I am going to join The Barony and sit under one of the best and truest men I ever met." He rode on horseback visiting the men under his spiritual care. He was glad to note that the men of his own battalion treasured their home ties: "the 5th Scottish Rifles send out and receive more letters than all the rest of the brigade". He himself kept in continual touch with his people at The Barony, and he was tireless in writing letters home to the relatives of the wounded, the sick, and those who had died in battle.

One picture of John White at the front can be seen in these words written by his own batman:

"I remember him particularly at Doullens where he held a church parade on the top of a small hill just outside the town. The battalion didn't altogether appreciate marching up the hill, but it was a wonderful site for such a parade, just the sort of place to appeal to old John's sense of beauty and the dramatic. We had the usual armed sentries in keeping with our old Covenanters' tradition, and I can still remember parts of his sermon given in that rather harsh penetrating voice of his. He always called a spade a spade. On this occasion he was telling the men quite frankly that their morals required a lot of cleaning up. His expression was, I think, 'imperilling their immortal souls'. The men certainly listened, and I'm quite sure his words had some effect. . . .

"He never went to rest at night when the battalion was in the trenches until the ration parties returned to B-Echelon bringing the men's letters to him for censoring. Then he went through them all so that there would be no delay in getting them off. If a man was killed in the line and the body could not be brought down, he went up the line and gave it *decent* Christian burial. I say decent advisedly, for he would not cut his service short, no matter how hot the area became. I remember once at Crucifix Corner on the Somme, where he was burying some few men. It was being heavily shelled, but he carried through his usual service, although the C.O. wished to dismiss the parade. Old John never allowed fear, or discomfort, or disinclination, to interfere with what he felt was his duty.

"In spite of a rather forbidding exterior, he was most kindly. As soon as word of a casualty reached him, he wrote at once to the parents or wife giving details, and in the case of fatal casualties he sent on a badge or button or something personal.

"The Padre had a small portable harmonium which he used at all Church parades and also at sing-songs, and once we used it for a Burns' supper when the Padre took the chair and proposed the Immortal Memory."

It was John White's own idea to hold that Burns Supper, and he kept the letter he had written asking permission to hold it in a room above an estaminet owned by Mariette Bonquet, Rue de l'Eglise, Beuvry. The Assistant Provost-Marshall wrote back, "Authorised, and I look to you to see that no irregularities occur." John White used to say later that, although he had delivered Burns orations at many suppers, he never thought any one was quite as enjoyable as this. But the harmonium nearly came to grief. "It was being carried home by two men who had been rather enthusiastic in toasting the Bard. It was a night of hard frost, and perhaps it would be more charitable to blame the icy roads for the mishap—but the harmonium reached home *under its own steam—downhill!*"

One of the wounded wrote home:

"You never saw a man getting through so much work in a day as our Chaplain did on 20th July, when we were in the big advance. He was here, there, everywhere, regardless of danger, thinking only of what he would do for us. With tunic off and sleeves rolled up, he moved about bandaging an arm or a leg or a head, cheering everyone with his jokes. When he had placed a wounded man on a stretcher he would put a cigarette in his mouth, light it for him, and see him safely off. Yon's the kind of man we need out here, and the 5th S.R. are lucky to have him."

Another man wrote: "After I was wounded, he carried me on his back more than a mile to the dressing station, only stopping twice on the way, and that was to supply me with a new cigarette."

As the months passed, John White was becoming more and more concerned over the welfare of his congregation at home. When he got leave, The Barony was his first thought. By September 1916, his appointment as chaplain should already have been officially terminated; but the military authorities were disinclined to lose him. He was offered the high post of Assistant Chaplain General; but this he refused, saying that he would either serve at the front as an ordinary chaplain, in touch with the men, or return to Scotland to be a parish minister. During his active service, he had undergone a strain which would have undermined the constitution of many a younger man. His friends saw how greatly the needs of his congregation were pressing on him, and his anxiety was deepened by the knowledge that the burden was resting heavily on the shoulders of other ministers who had tasks of their own. Of his return to Glasgow he wrote from France on 11th September 1916:

"I know it is my duty to be in The Barony this coming winter. The congregation have been very patient, and have kindly allowed me to undertake this work on which my heart was set; but I realise it would be wrong to remain any longer absent from the parish when so many homes are passing through times of intense anxiety and through days of deep sorrow."

And so it was that he left younger men to carry on, and returned to his duties at The Barony, where he was at once immersed not only in the affairs of his parish, but in those of the Glasgow Presbytery and of the Church of Scotland.

II

During the First World War, the shafts of sorrow struck again and again at the manse of The Barony. Five months after its outbreak, the youngest child, Margaret, died as the result of scarlet fever. To John White, his little daughter had seemed to embody the very spirit of youth. Sometimes she would come dancing into his study to put a question to him, little regarding the solemn men who sat there in conference. It has been told how her father would break off and take her upon his knee, to the surprise of some of the clergymen who, from their looks, expected John White to banish the intruder with a reproof. Dr. David Scott, the senior assistant at the time of Margaret's death, wrote:

"John White never rose higher than when tragedy struck him. Little Margaret died on a Saturday, and I took upon myself the task of arranging the Sunday work so that he would be free of all duty. At first he demurred. He was heart-broken, but his feet were on firm rock. In our preaching, he said, we urge steadiness in the face of personal disaster. He wanted to take the morning service as usual. But I would have none of it. I got him to say that I might ask Dr. Norman Maclean to take his place in The Barony, and I hurried off to arrange it. Maclean and he were great friends. Each knew the other's quality, and Maclean had a great spirit which John White appreciated. Years afterwards, people still spoke of the wonderful talk Norman Maclean gave to the children in the Cunliffe Chapel that day. After it was all over, we settled down to life and work, with John perhaps a little softer and mellower and more wistful than he had been. Certainly he was never soured, and you would never find him throwing a shadow of gloom over any company he was in."

Towards the end of August 1917, his son John wrote home from the Royal Flying Corps in France: "I shall not be long now before I get my fourteen days leave. Probably the end of September or the beginning of October ... the Boche is nowhere in the skies. We haven't seen him for days." That was John's last letter. At half-past five on the morning after he wrote it, he had been in a dog-fight and was taking a vertical turn to fly back to his aerodrome when the last shot from an enemy plane got him. "But for Jock's good work that morning," wrote a fellow officer, "the operation would not have been the success it was." The fight had taken place over enemy territory, and for a long time the family hoped that although John's plane had crashed he might have escaped and been taken prisoner. The session clerk wrote in October: "Our hearts go out at this time to our beloved minister and his wife and family who are suffering intense anxiety about their son who has been missing for some time." It was learned later that he had been killed and was buried in a German cemetery. In his father's handwriting a verse by Owen Seaman had been slipped into a copy of the church magazine where John's exploit and fate had been recorded:

> You that have faith to look with fearless eyes
> Beyond the tragedy of a world at strife
> And trust that out of night and death shall rise
> The dawn of ampler life.

III

In 1916, the Church of Scotland had appointed a Commission to consider the Spiritual and Moral Issues of the War, and on his return home John White was made a member. He took a vigorous part in its proceedings, and this work led to the creation of a new and important committee of the General Assembly. One of the tasks of the Commission was to make a report to the Assembly on the Life and Efficiency of the Church. Nobody could have been deaf to the criticism levelled at the Church during the war years; and while some of this had been as slipshod and baseless as it had been virulent, John White and his colleagues on the Commission recognised that a good deal of what had been said was "the outpouring of hearts warmly sympathetic and of minds actively interested in the Church's welfare". They decided to make a list of pointed questions and send them to a large number of laymen throughout Scotland. It was felt that sincere and unprejudiced answers from them might well be of high value in the days immediately ahead. How deep was the need for the Church to put her house in order?

The answers were synthesised and printed in an appendix to the Report of the Commission to the Assembly of May 1919. That appendix remains today one of the most devastating pieces of self-criticism in the history of the Christian Church since the Reformation. The consensus of opinion was that the preaching of the Word of God in Scottish pulpits was "too little of a Christian Message, too much of a Literary Essay. . . . The craving of the people is for the bringing home to them, with burning enthusiasm and absolute conviction, the one and only Salvation. . . ." Instead of preaching the Word with enthusiasm and conviction, some ministers were even "whittling down the authority of the Bible—not bringing their hearers into real and living relationship with the living God. . . . There is vagueness and mystification about the very foundations of the Christian Church. . . ." Work in Sabbath School and Bible Class was criticised; minister, elder, and member must enter more fully into the life of the young. "If there was too great a distance between the pulpit and the pew, there was an even greater distance between the pew and the pew. . . . Christ died for *me*, and every man I meet is a brother for whom Christ died." As to industrial relations, the Church "should be a con- science to the nation—yet she has taken little or no part in social and industrial questions. . . . The Church certainly gets no credit from the working class for ever having taken their part." On drink and bad housing she must take a decisive stand; "over one hundred thousand children die every year through the effects of bad housing". The representative laymen criticised the elders of the Church, twelve thousand strong: "They do *not* perform their whole duty by ringing the door bell and handing in communion cards. . . . Too often they are simply a committee of manage- ment instead of active assistants to the minister." In the opinion of a group of working men, a great number of people stood apart from the Church because of the failure of many Church members to live consistently Christian lives, because the thought of the Church was not progressive, and because of the prevalent idea that the Church existed for the well-to- do—not for the poor. Summing up, the Commission stated that the central defect found by the representative laymen was "a lack of reality in the Message—a grave defect wherever it exists. *The hungry sheep look up and are not fed.*" In her methods, the Church was "too much fettered by the traditions of the past". The old saying that "a house-going minister means a church-going people" was a reproof to those whose pastoral visitation was lackadaisical. "To the elders of the Church no less than to the ministers, the call to Readjustment and Rededication of themselves comes today with great clearness." As for members, it must be brought before them that "membership means not merely a *getting* of spiritual help, but a *giving* of help to the Church, a giving of one's self in thought and prayer and means and service".

IV

In this Report, one can see the hand of John White. Again and again many of his own declarations from pulpit and platform were included in it, and he reinforced it by word of mouth whenever the chance came.

So vigorous and pointed were his speeches and sermons at this time that they received prominence in the press. He got many letters that told of the stimulation he was giving wherever he went. Back in his old pulpit at South Leith, he preached morning and evening, and a member wrote to him about the "trumpet blasts that had visibly stirred the huge congregation. How can we thank you sufficiently for the tremendous uplift you gave in our town? It was just what was wanted." Another letter runs: "*We* know that John White of Shettleston, South Leith, and The Barony is one of the Strong-Hearts; and *he* knows the source of his strength." In the Autumn of 1917, the Synod of Glasgow and Ayr appointed him chairman of its Committee on the Moral Issues of the War, and he became chief spokesman. The General Assembly Commission had already launched throughout Scotland an appeal for National Rededication, and John White now proceeded to bring this, in his usual way, to a practical issue. He urged that there should be meetings of the members of all kirk sessions to consider how best to direct the workers in this National Mission. For his own congregation he prepared what he called the Resolution Card which all were asked to sign:

As a baptized member of Christ, I desire and purpose, God helping me—

To rule my life by the Will of God, in my home, at my work, in the Church.

To let myself be known as a servant of Christ in whatever company I am; and to make no secret of the help He gives me.

To unite with others in making the Church an effective witness for Christ, and a true minister to the highest life of the people.

To commence this by doing something in The Barony Church and Parish, and by seeking to influence those whom I meet in my daily avocations.

For the Synod, he prepared a leaflet setting forth the principles at stake in that time of national crisis. German Kultur, he said, omitted the Christ, and the British people were called upon to reaffirm the authority of the moral law in international relations and the supreme authority of Christ Jesus. The war was a challenge to the nation to repent, to reform social evils, to confess God in all its relations. He spoke of the weakening of home religion, of the unsatisfactory religious education of the young, of slack ideals among both members and office-bearers of the Church. He concluded:

"The opportunity is great. The Divine call is clear. We are asking God to work a miracle of mercy. We must put ourselves in such a posture to Him as shall not obstruct His doing this mighty work for Scotland. To call on God for a day of salvation within the Church and Nation, and to hinder its dawn, would surely bring grievous spiritual loss upon us. If we are ready, God is willing."

Complaints about some of the literature of the Commission had been made; but this leaflet of John White's was so arresting that a large number of copies were printed, and it was sent into every parish in Scotland. Meanwhile, he intensified his efforts on behalf of the Mission. Norman Maclean declared that he was "gripping the situation in the West country". An Army chaplain wrote about the realities in a speech he had made: "It is *reality* the Church lacks—and this is what our men will look for when they return from the front." A Glasgow minister took courage and wrote to him:

"Scarcely a presbytery meeting passes but I feel prompted to write to you in appreciation of your services in the cause nearest to the hearts of us all. I have refrained hitherto partly because I thought you were as insensitive to praise or blame as a rock—especially when it comes from the small fry. For this I envy you, having myself a Hielandman's thin skin. . . . But alas I fear you must go on with your work expecting little from us and saying with Abraham Lincoln, *You must do everything for the people but expect nothing done by them.*"

It gave John White pleasure to receive a letter from a United Free Church minister in Inverness: "There are those in the sister Church who watch with interest and gratitude the leadership you bring us all in the present situation. Your utterances, as reported in the press, offer as wise leading as comes from any part of the Church." The acting Primus of the Scottish Episcopal Church wrote soon after the Armistice to thank him for inviting his people to take part in a united effort on behalf of National Rededication: "You have our deepest sympathy and our prayers. God bless you."

The Mission continued for some little time after the war. But as John White looked around him and candidly considered the results of it, he felt it was not the success it should have been. He had done his best; so had many another.

"The message was the right message, but it lacked a telling force," he declared. "There was not enough heart-stir about it. For its failure we must look to the Church itself. The Mission and its results certainly made clear the *inadequate spirituality of the Church*. The message has still to reach many who are not even curious about it—many who had no idea of its meaning. The Church of Scotland has always been proud that it has held the loyalty of the educated laity. Has the Mission made no appeal to them? So long as we are content to leave our theological ideas unrelated to the thought of today, they will prove ineffective—and thinking men will not be touched by the message. . . . Among the working classes, there were Church members who took some interest in the *social* side of the Mission, but the Church cannot thirl itself to the economic creed or political theories of one section of the community."

V

For some time, John White had been carefully studying the fundamental causes of labour unrest.

"These are not primarily to be found in any special grievance that may come to the surface at any particular time," he decided. "Rather, it is in the growing determination of Labour to challenge the whole existing structure of capitalist industry. . . . The working class is now firmly convinced that production for private profit is not an adequate basis on which to build; it now demands a vast extension of public ownership. The workers can see no indication that either the Government or the employers have realised the need for any fundamental change—or that they are prepared even to make a start to reorganise on more democratic lines."

In a speech he made to the Synod of Glasgow and Ayr, he said:

"Hundreds of thousands of able bodied men, at the beginning of August 1914, were labouring hard for wages that were a disgrace to the flag they went to fight for. Today, Labour has captured a more advanced position than it has ever had. Indeed, a rising flood of democracy is sweeping over the whole Western world. In the present industrial revolution, here is a new opportunity for the Church to take its stand on the side of social justice. There must be no more tinkering with the old system. That will not suffice. The men who invest their lives should have as definite a partnership in an undertaking as the men who invest their money. On the other hand, among the workers, we see slackness all around us. You will hear Labour representatives say—*The less you work, the more work there will be for others*. That is a fatal fallacy. Reduction in the hours of work is depriving people of employment. The price of food is going up. Only by increased production can we hold our own. An appeal must be made to the public on the vital importance of increased production. This fatal lethargy must be shaken off."

In the same speech to the Synod, he spoke about the schemes of reconstruction which were so rife at that time. Many institutions were seeking to put their affairs in order for the future.

"Has the Church no contribution to make?" he demanded. "Is the new structure of our country to be built up again on the old material basis, which has already cracked with the crack of doom? Is the Church to be cold-shouldered, as if it had no contribution of value to make? Is the Church to be shunted into a side track, as has happened over the Education Bill? Is there no place for it in these post-war deliberations?

"It is of supreme importance that the Church should come to an understanding with Labour. The claims of Labour must be examined. Grievances must be considered not in a spirit of resentment but in one of justice and comradeship. Britain has the traditional power of reaching a solution of her most baffling problems without resort to anarchy, for always she has appealed to commonsense and the spirit of fair play. Organised Christianity must be brought into sympathetic contact with organised Labour. The great mass of the members of the Church are from the Labour ranks. While many leaders of Labour are in sympathy with Christianity, there yet remains a hostility to the Church—not because it is Christian but because it is said to be not Christian enough! Many of these Labour leaders have declared that the Church is allied with caste despotism. This is not true. But in its teaching it has not explained either to the few or to the masses the urgency of social justice and Christian brotherhood. If the Church is to reach the wage earners, it must fill its members with the spirit of Christ. And it must preach the same message to the Labour Unions with all their new and intoxicating sense of power."

So convinced was John White of the gravity of the industrial crisis that he urged the Synod of Glasgow and Ayr to make an overture to the General Assembly. "There must be a manifesto from the Church of Scotland to the whole of the Labour ranks," he said. "It must be made clear to them that the Church has sympathy with their desire for justice in a reconstituted society."

John White saw that there were other aspects of post-war life in which the Church could give light and guidance. It seemed to him that there was a practical way in which this help could be given, and he persuaded the Commission on the Moral and Spiritual Issues of the War to ask the General Assembly to create a new body under the title of the Church and Nation Committee.

VI

His advice was taken. The Committee was instituted on Wednesday, 28th May 1919.

"We have arrived at a creative moment," he said to the Assembly. "It is an age that shall have in it more of the ideals of Jesus Christ than any age has yet seen. The duties of this committee are to watch over those developments of the nation's life in which moral and spiritual considerations especially arise. It must consider what action the Church, from time to time, should take to further the highest interests of the people."

The whole conception of the Committee was thought to be daring. People said it might well stir up a lot of trouble for the Church if she made pronouncements on controversial matters. In his Assembly speech, John White had given some of his views on industrial relations, and this in itself was reckoned to be a dangerous topic for the Church to touch even in the most delicate way. He was asked to become convener, and Lord Sands was proposed as his colleague.

"I was never asked to be joint convener of this new committee," Lord Sands wrote to him in great good humour when he heard of the appointment. "I take this as an indication that I am not expected to be obtrusive, and have been conjoined with you merely to give an air of respectability to the convenership!" And as they had always done, and were so to do for many years in the service of the Church, the two men worked together in a fruitful friendship.

The subjects dealt with in the early life of this important committee proved to be many and diverse. The training for the ministry was one; the position of women in Church work was another; there followed housing, the position of children and adolescents, international relations, and these were but a few of the subjects on which the attitude of the Church was defined. The Committee carefully considered the position of the League of Nations, which had greatly changed since its formation, and the 1920 Lambeth Appeal for unity. Indeed, within the scope of the Committee there came any problem of the hour on which it was felt that a helpful pronouncement could be made. It was generally recognised that the main driving force behind it was John White himself, and the reports of the Committee stimulated some of the most lively and valuable debates in the General Assembly.

"In dealing with the many questions before us," said John White, "I have sometimes quoted the words of John Stuart Mill in his essay on Coleridge, 'When society requires to be rebuilt, there is no use in attempting to rebuild it on the old plan.' I added the warning that we must not lay down our plans for tomorrow and then call on God to make tomorrow to our designs. As we adventure into the future, there is need for caution; our experiments may be more noted for their daring than their wisdom. We are all fallible seekers after the wisest policy; and a narrow and obstinate dogmatist is a very troublesome member of a committee."

VII

In all that he had undertaken since he had returned from the battle-fields, John White had been more deeply conscious than ever he had been of the grievous disadvantages in the separation that still existed between the two great Presbyterian Churches. How much more successful, he often said, their efforts would have been if there had been a reunion before the outbreak of war. It was a strange paradox that the war itself had been the means of bringing the two Churches closer together. There had been a time when chaplains of the Army and Navy had been commissioned only from among the ministers of the Church of Scotland, but this was no longer the case. Both at home and overseas, the ministers of both Churches worked together in a close comradeship. Together, the Church of Scotland and the United Free Church established and maintained huts for the troops and supported the work of the Y.M.C.A. Throughout the country, many congregations of both Churches worshipped together if the minister of one of them was serving in the Forces. The two Churches agreed on religious instruction in schools. While there was still a difference of view on the use of alcohol, both Churches now agreed in denouncing the enormous increase in its consumption which was impeding the war effort. The Churches joined in holding intercessory services. The Theological Halls of the Church of Scotland, which were departments of the four Scottish Universities, planned a curriculum with the United Free Church for the training of ministers. A school for postgraduate study was established which later became "practically a Union Faculty of Divinity destined to establish a new fellowship with America and the British Dominions, as well as with the continent of Europe, in the interests of a higher and broader religious scholarship".

Talking at this time on the need for the reunion of the Churches, John White often reminded his hearers that when men faced death on the battlefield they did not stop to ask the denomination of the padre who administered to them the Last Sacrament. Union was a task which could not be delayed.

Chapter XII

SPIRITUAL FREEDOM REGAINED

I

JOHN WHITE tried to revive public interest in Church union, but this was not easy. Did Church union matter at such a time of crisis? He strove to show that at least it must not be forgotten. After making a speech at a Church Congress, he received a letter from a minister that carried a message of hope: "On no subject did you so *enthuse* your audience as that of taking Union negotiations a stage further." He managed to organise a meeting of the union committee, and it was held on 12th April 1917. Only twenty members of the Hundred could attend. Two of the old minority, A. W. Wotherspoon and W. S. Provand, failed to convince the others that it would be well if the Assembly brought the union movement to a halt. But as the months passed and the war news became more and more depressing, it was not easy to keep thoughts of union from utterly fading in the smoke of battle that seemed in some transcendental way to drift across from Flanders fields. To many, it was the darkest winter of the war. With little hope of making progress, John White planned a meeting of the Hundred for the first week in March 1918. As it turned out, this was one of the liveliest gatherings the Church of Scotland Hundred had ever held.

Professor Cooper arrived, charged with zeal for his own case. More strongly than ever he pressed for alterations in the draft Articles. The Minority Report of 1914 was to him the very hinge upon which the union movement should turn. So strong were his feelings that he would rather it be deferred, or given up altogether, than carried through in the way the committee wanted. On this meeting, John White made a note: "It seemed that there was to be no end to Cooper's proposals. At our meeting of 5th March I moved that we drop all of the first Article which dealt with doctrine. This was carried. It worked a cure."

It certainly silenced Professor Cooper for the time being: but the cure took a more drastic form than John White anticipated. He received a letter from a minister who travelled home with Cooper from that meeting: "He is furiously angry over the exclusion of the doctrinal statement, and if the majority insist on the position now arrived at, *he will certainly secede from the Church and carry all of like mind with him.*" The minister added that, in his opinion, "the majority should complete their labours without trying even to conciliate the minority—we may safely leave our vindication to the country".

With regret, John White learned that his old and valued friend had thoughts of leaving the Church. Although he had made the proposal, as he admitted, "with the simple object of ending an interminable discussion", he had not thought that Professor Cooper would take the matter so grievously to heart. He still believed it to be unnecessary to give a list of the fundamental doctrines held by the Church, for "the selection may be said to be arbitrary and incomplete, and the task was undertaken only under the compulsion of a strong demand". He would have been prepared to stick to his guns over the omission of the doctrinal statement and try to make his peace with Cooper, but Lord Balfour of Burleigh asked him privately if he would do what he could to have it restored. A note from John White's pen runs: "Lord B. of B. thought that Cooper might say we had jeopardised the Faith. . . . I agreed to have it restored if it was to be accepted now as 'the finished Article'." And so yet another doctrinal statement was drawn up and presented to Professor Cooper, and was accepted by him as providing "the essential thing for which I and others have been contending, viz., an explicit confession of the Catholic Faith on those two great fundamental doctrines of the Trinity and the Incarnation". The seventh Article (on the relation with other Churches) was emended and accepted. But however anxious Lord Balfour of Burleigh was to avoid repetition of old conflicts, there was still the committee to be faced. The majority were in no mood to rewrite the first Article which, after so much labour, had been agreed upon and presented to the Assembly of 1914, but they gave way to Cooper so far as to adopt some of his modes of expression, particularly about the Trinity, "the same in substance equal in power and glory". The result was a compromise. Professor Cooper said that he would have preferred to see a full use made of the strictly orthodox words he had set down in the Minority Report, but he was ready to accept the new amalgam and voted for its adoption. Some little imp of mischief made John White point out that Cooper's "strictly orthodox and Catholic mode of expression" almost exactly coincided with that used in the Shorter Catechism which had been prepared by the Westminster Divines specially "for those of weaker capacity".

John White's final comments on the matter were these:

"The doctrinal statement is not fully satisfactory to anyone. But it was the very best settlement that could be arrived at, and it was only reached in a spirit of concession and brotherhood. . . . To satisfy everybody, the Westminster Confession of Faith would have had to be rewritten—and the New Confession would have been dotted with asterisks because of a multitude of qualifying footnotes."

His own 1913 draft of the Articles, the first to have been prepared, had stated that the "Westminster Confession of Faith shall be the public and avowed Confession of the Church". These simple words, he had said, were sufficient; and these he preferred to the end.

"But without some such statement as the First Article contains," he admitted ruefully, "it would have been impossible for the Church of Scotland to go forward with Union negotiations without the prospect of *a protracted and bitter domestic conflict.*"

II

John White's union speech in the Assembly of 1918 was given a good deal of publicity. He made his points with such effect that criticism was heavily discounted before it was uttered. One member went so far as to ask the Assembly to discharge the union committee and appoint a better one—"a truly national committee, not one composed largely of Edinburgh lawyers". But the Assembly was of a different mind. John White described the steps they would now take. At the next Assembly, he said, the finally adjusted Articles would be sent down to presbyteries under the Barrier Act; at the Assembly of 1920, if all went well, "they would become the declared constitution of the Church in matters spiritual"; Parliament would then be asked to ackowledge them, and that would leave only the question of endowments to be settled before organic union could be completed. Meanwhile, in the year ahead, the United Free Church would advise on the Articles to make certain of a full agreement on the two all-important principles, National Recognition of Religion and Spiritual Freedom.

John White told of men who had come to him with a warning: "Don't hurry; you're going too fast; wait till you have the people of Scotland behind you." To this he had replied: "The people of Scotland—why, they're away ahead of us, almost out of sight!"

The value of his unceasing work was acknowledged throughout the Church. The clerk to the Edinburgh Presbytery was referring to him as "the guide and adviser of the Union Committee". When any enlightenment on union was sought, more than likely the question would arrive on his desk. At the root of most of the difficulties lay the old doubt about the Churches' new relation to the State. In spite of all that had been spoken and written, some men in the Old Kirk were still dubious about the loosening of the ancient ties, and as many in the United Free Church were afraid that for them the bond would be so tight that their spiritual liberty would be strangled. The gist of what John White told those in both Churches who appealed to him can be found in words he must have written scores of times:

"Anything in the existing relation of the Church to the State that limits the spiritual freedom of the Church is rendered inoperative by the Articles."

And the minority group would not be stilled. Almost single-handed John White had to cope with questions raised in the Synod of Glasgow and Ayr, and criticism of the Articles became more and more aggressive. Ministers tried to create a storm about the change the committee had made in the eighth Article. In the 1914 draft, the Church had been bound to "adhere unalterably" to the declaration of faith and duty set forth in the doctrinal statement, but in the 1918 draft this was qualified by the phrase "as interpreted by the Church". Here was a selling of the pass to heterodoxy! Here was an invitation for those infected with New Thought to bedevil the ancient Faith! John White replied:

"While the creeds are true, they cannot always be accepted in the minute technical detail that was in men's minds at the time they were composed. . . . We have a right from the Head of the Church to adjudicate in matters of doctrine: therefore, the Church has the right to interpret the credal statement in the first Article."

Some ministers pressed for *legal* safeguards that would prevent the Church from destroying her presbyterian identity and from being carried away by unorthodox beliefs that were tainting the air of Christendom. One of John White's stoutest opponents, W. S. Provand, tried to persuade the union committee that the Articles should inhibit the Church from making any change in her constitution without the ratification of Parliament. He held that the State itself was the "best safeguard against the Church wandering into by-lanes". In any case, without this governing condition, he was certain that Parliament would reject the Articles with contumely. Dr. Macmillan of Glasgow helped him to press his case.

"It is of course evident," said John White, "that this would destroy
—and is indeed intended to destroy—the whole value of the Articles.
For what is claimed would not then be claimed as the inherent right
of the Church. It would become the constitution of the Church *by
permission of the State*. . . . Obviously, if it were thought that the Church
had strayed, it would fall to the Civil authorities to decide upon the
matter. . . . There is a stronger, more realistic, more *practical* safeguard
than any legal enactment," he went on. "Embodied in the constitution
is the proviso that the General Assembly cannot tamper with the
Articles before the change has been approved by two-thirds of the
presbyteries of the Church in two successive years: and in presbyteries,
the ministers and elders are numerically equal, so the laity will have as
big a say as the clergy. Thus, the Church of Scotland cannot cease to
be presbyterian until Scotland herself ceases to be presbyterian, or
unorthodox until Scotland has deflected from the ancient verities."

Worse storms than these roared round John White's head. Some
ministers told him they foresaw the utter ruination of the Church. They
repeated the old charge that there had been "an abject surrender to the
demands of the United Frees". For a Church to have the right to alter her
constitution as she thought fit seemed as preposterous as to declare that one
believed in the Apostles' Creed with the proviso that one could alter it
according to one's fancy. Critics attacked the "insidious fallacy" in the
third Article, the real intention of which, they said, was "to conceal the
disestablishment of the Church under the word 'national' ". The fourth
and fifth Articles were denounced as going "a very long way towards the
severance of the connection between Church and State". And because the
adoption of the Articles would be "tantamount to self-disestablishment",
how could the Lord High Commissioner be retained? And how could the
King's Chaplaincies be reserved exclusively for ministers of the Church
of Scotland? How could the Moderator of the General Assembly continue
to be placed in rank and precedence in Scotland next to the Lord Chancellor of Great Britain and before the Dukes? "In fact, the policy of the
Church of Scotland committee has been one of surrender all along," wrote
the Rev. J. M. Finlayson. "It has surrendered the principles of Establishment in the Draft Articles, and it will go on surrendering, if necessary,
though there is little left to surrender." Yet another criticism was: "Union
upon the basis of these Articles would result not in a reconstructed Church
of Scotland but simply a voluntary Sect on a national scale with the fluid

constitution and an indeterminate creed." Even the doctrinal statement itself was still the target for a fusillade:

"We should have expected to find the guarantee of Catholic faith set forth with the utmost plainness. *We look for it in vain.* In its stead, nothing appears but a catena of participial clauses—clauses of a quasi credal character, but clauses wholly destitute of categorical authority; theologically inaccurate, confused, defective; and so loosely attached to their proper subject that it remains debatable (the insertion of a semi-colon notwithstanding) whether they are meant to qualify 'the Church of Scotland' or 'the Holy Catholic Church'. Catholicity is not accustomed to display its banners in this oblique and hesitating way."

Never a month passed without squalls blowing up from some quarter. John White had long ago learned how to stride through them. He came almost to welcome criticism. Crass stupidity and inexcusable ignorance raised his ire: but he was ready to meet and join issue on equal terms with the man who was moved to protest because of deep conviction and had the courage to hit hard in the sight of all.

III

To everyone, the end of the war brought a great lightening of the spirit. It now seemed that the union of the two great Presbyterian bodies would become possible. One of John White's friends, John M. MacLeod (later Sir John MacLeod, Bt.), a chartered accountant of Glasgow, took an increasing part in the movement, and to further it he got together a committee of laymen drawn from both Churches.[1] As a Member of Parliament, he was to give valued help at Westminster. Within a few months of the Armistice, joint conferences were again being held. The Business Committee met, and groups of two or three from each side had informal talks. Cordiality was spiced with frankness. The day was long past when the two parties weighed each other up with suspicion. They could look back on times of despair when, as one minister put it, "we thought that God had left us and that nothing was to come out of all this labour—but still God led us on and cleared the way for us". In the clearing of that way John White had taken a share that was now acknowledged by those in the United Free Church. It had once seemed that his tussles with

[1] One of his sons, George F. MacLeod, was to enter the ministry, found the Iona community, and was to be elected Moderator of the General Assembly of 1957.

Principal Martin, the man whose influence in joint conferences he had been chosen to counteract, had revealed a cleavage of opinion and so different an approach to union that harmony had seemed unlikely: but now they were on the best of terms. On 23rd January, Martin wrote to him:

"Good man! I was just about to sit down and draft a minute when yours came in. I haven't a comma to change. I went home somewhat depressed yesterday (having been myself, perhaps, the cause of some depression!) but after a night's sleep am cheerfuller again. These legal differences between us should and *must* evaporate.—Yours, A. M."

That all differences should evaporate at the earliest possible moment was John White's highest hope, and he did everything in his power to quicken the process. He launched a vehement appeal to his colleagues to join hands and go forward together:

"It is eleven years since the Church of Scotland sent their invitation to the United Free Church to enter into conference. It is nearly ten years since the two Committees were appointed. We have done something; and yet that something is so little, where so much has to be done—and must be done with haste if it is to be done at all. . . . If one lives in a centre of great massed populations, restless with the stirrings of a great movement, one realises what the need is. How trifling are the questions we are discussing when we place them against the primary and urgent need of contributing *our* factor—the spiritual factor—to the new settlement of the people.

"We are in a new world from that in which we lived when these negotiations commenced. We are face to face with tremendous responsibilities and unparalleled opportunities. I should not feel happy if, in Assembly or in the country, I were called on to justify another year's Report of nothing but kindly and brotherly conferences that had no practical settlement to offer.

"There have been earlier negotiations for Union, prior to the successful Union of 1900, which had to be given up. On the day one of these attempts was abandoned, Dr. Candlish was heard to say that he felt like a man holding the plough when the plough had come to a stand in the frozen furrow. . . . It was not then the will of God that the furrow should be completed.

"In 1900 the springtime had come, and with its softening influence the furrow was drawn to the end of the field. And we have reason to thank God that He has led us thus far on our way to heal our divisions.

"Further delay would be disastrous. Failure to proceed now would be the cruellest blow the Church has had dealt to it for many generations. It would be more disastrous than the Disruption."

His appeal was not made in vain. Differences began to evaporate. Dr. Henderson said that his committee were particularly pleased that the Church was claiming the power to interpret her statement of fundamental doctrines. He suggested some minor changes in word and phrase—and one change of immense magnitude. He startled John White and his colleagues by pointing out that, in their anxiety to conciliate their minority group by using ancient credal phraseology, they had made no mention whatever of that which "lay at the very basis of the evangel—*that God was a God of Love*". In any definition of the Godhead, however elliptic, was it not vital to state that He was all-loving? Here surely was an example of how the stress laid upon theological truths may change as the centuries pass. The all-powerful, all-just, and all-wise God of the Westminster Confession—was He not today also the All-loving One? Frankly did John White acknowledge the fault in their statement, redolent as it was of the seventeenth century. And without a murmur of dissent the committee approved of the United Free Church addition.

In the confidence, which was justified, that the majority of the United Free Church would follow the lead of Dr. Henderson in his pronouncement on the declaratory Articles, John White said to his committee:

"There will be general satisfaction that Dr. Henderson considers the Articles to be the best statement of the Claim of Spiritual Freedom to be found anywhere in the entire Church of Christ. It would have gladdened the heart of many who are no longer with us to have heard the announcement today that a solution of the vexed question of Spiritual Freedom had been reached, and that it had been reached consistently with the principle of a national recognition of religion."

IV

The Assembly of 1919 gave instructions that the Articles should be sent down to presbyteries for approval or rejection. A joint statement was issued by both Churches. In subscribing to this, the United Free Church was deemed to have committed herself to the acceptance of the Articles, thus in the eyes of the world taking her stand beside her sister Church. The following words from the last paragraph are significant:

> "On the terms now proposed . . . the continuity and identity of the Church of Scotland would be maintained, while at the same time the Church would bear the character of a purely spiritual institution, in no sense deriving powers from or controlled by the State, nor enjoying any privilege to the prejudice of other Churches. In this way, the respective principles which the negotiating Churches were charged to safeguard in entering into conference may be harmonised."

Significant, too, is this passage in the joint report which was quoted from the General Assembly's Report of 1919:

> "The Joint Conference is in agreement that the endowments are not to be secularised. . . . When the time comes to arrange the terms of union all the endowments of the Church of Scotland must be vested in it under a tenure which is consistent with the freedom which is set forth in the draft Articles."

Many men in the United Free Church had travelled a long way since the days when they had condemned the Church of Scotland for receiving "State aid" in the form of what they called a "tax on the land imposed by the State".

In that General Assembly of the Church of Scotland there was a good deal of confusion in the minds of ministers and elders because no mention was made of the Barrier Act. On this, John White became the focus of critical questions. He was reminded of how, in the previous Assembly, he had stated that in the following year the Articles would be sent down to presbyteries under this Act. He had made this announcement with the authority of the union committee, which had been advised by Lord Sands. But between the Assemblies of 1918 and 1919, Sands had changed his mind. He had now come to the conclusion that such a procedure would be unconstitutional, and he wrote to John White:

> "The Articles cannot go down at present under the Barrier Act for the purpose of adoption by the Assembly, for they are *ultra vires* of the Church in relation to the Civil Law. It would be the Veto Act over again. . . . The Church would put itself in the worst possible position if it provisionally adopted them subject to State sanction."

Since he was now a judge of the Court of Session, Lord Sands was forbidden to give an opinion on a legal matter, so John White became the official expositor, and to one puzzled elder he wrote:

"Before we go to Parliament, we must be assured of the goodwill of the Government—we must be assured that the Articles will be made a government measure—but it would of course be idle for us to go to the Government without first knowing whether they have the approval of the presbyteries."

That approval was duly sought, and when the Church of Scotland Commission of Assembly met on 17th December to receive the results, Dr. Wallace Williamson announced:

"No more decided vote of presbyteries in a matter of high consequence is on record in the history of the Church. Ninety-eight per cent of the constituency has approved. In the face of that fact, it is not possible for this Commission of Assembly to refuse to go forward—or even to hesitate."

The Commission did not hesitate. By an overwhelming majority, it authorised the committee to ask Parliament to embody the Articles in an Act which would be the first great span in the union bridge. John White was appointed one of the delegates to wait upon the Prime Minister.

V

The interview at 10 Downing Street was planned to take place on 19th March. By this time, all was not well with John White. The strain of the war years had been undermining his health. Family sorrow had left scars, and his August holiday in the first year of peace, which might have been a time of great happiness in the family reunion, served to remind him of his loss and had not refreshed him as holidays of old had done. He had faced the winter's work with a full engagement book: in addition to parish duties, which he organised with care, he had given of his best to the Mission of National Rededication, and at the Assembly following the Armistice the Church and Nation Committee had been created. This child of his own making had been much in his thoughts and needed nurturing. Social problems perturbed him. National reconstruction was being trumpeted from platforms and headlined in the press: but where were the fruits of it? And continually in his thoughts and prayers was the Church union movement . . . a delicate plant in the frosts of spring. He looked ill, but stuck doggedly to his oar: he must pull his weight, he said. Then in March he was found to be seriously ill with pneumonia, and there followed a week of suspense from which he emerged with the prospect of a long, slow convalescence. He was given five months leave of absence, and indeed it was not until the fall of the year that he was back in his pulpit.

The deputation to the Prime Minister had gone south without him. There had been a breakfast at Downing Street with Mr. Lloyd George, who had talked with that pervasive charm that was one of the most lethal weapons in his armoury. One of the delegates who returned and went straight to John White said it had been an extremely pleasant breakfast, indeed a delightful breakfast, but Lloyd George had seemed more interested in the recent international Rugby match, in which Wales had been beaten by Scotland, than in the object of their visit. There was a certain amount of Celtic mist about the promise that legislation would be introduced at one time or another, and no member of the Welsh Rugby team could have been more adroit in avoiding a tackle on the subject of a date for the Bill. Firm news of it might have helped John White's recovery; but it was not until May that Bonar Law, Leader of the House of Commons, made an announcement that was definite: "The Government were prepared to introduce, or to give facilities for, a Bill to enable the Church of Scotland to adopt the Draft Articles." So far as it went, this was good. But no date had been given; mist was still on the road. A few weeks later, John White was reading the Assembly speeches in the newspapers, and he learned how movingly Wallace Williamson had referred to his illness and his work for union:

> "To John White, the Assembly owes a very deep debt of gratitude for all his services during their long years of conference on union. No man knows this subject better. There is no man with a better head among the ministers of this Church—no man with better business capacity or greater loyalty to the highest interests of the Church of Scotland. I am proud to have the opportunity of paying this tribute to him."

That was pleasant, but it was no salve to the fret of waiting for word from Westminster about the date of the projected Bill.

During that autumn session, it was true, the Government were struggling with urgent national and international matters: but as John White put it, "there is deep regret in Scotland over the Union Bill, for delay is likely to weaken enthusiasm". New Year came and went, and there was still no news. John White could bear the delay no longer. To him, there seemed to be only one thing to be done. Another personal approach must be made to Downing Street, and on 9th February 1921 he was on his way south to London.

He stayed that night with Dr. Archibald Fleming of St. Columba's, and at half-past three the next afternoon was talking to Bonar Law at 11 Downing Street. With him were one or two of his colleagues, and the Chancellor of the Exchequer was supported by Robert Munro, Secretary of State for Scotland, and others. Bonar Law was a Scot who took a cautious view of any project of which the end was doubtful, and he said frankly he was depressed about the difficulties that the Scottish churchmen would yet have to overcome: indeed, if the proposed Bill became an Act, he said, their troubles had only started. John White snapped his fingers at the talk of difficulties. Let the Enabling Act be put on the Statute Book, he retorted, and the Church of Scotland's spiritual freedom was assured. That was the important thing. The only remaining barrier between them and the United Free Church would be the Teinds—and among theologians, financial matters could be more easily arranged than spiritual ones. He pointed out that in the Joint Statement of the two Churches, the United Free Church had committed herself to a general agreement on what the Church of Scotland proposed to do over Teinds and Endowments. But Bonar Law did not seem to be moved. And he had good reason to dwell on the problems ahead of the kirkmen. He recalled the attempt already made to bring about "commutation and redemption of Teind Stipends". A committee of the General Assembly had tried to thrash the matter out with representatives of some of the chief heritors in Scotland. This had actually got the length of a Bill which Robert Munro had presented to Parliament in November 1920. This ill-timed measure had been put before a Commission of Assembly; and because the members had been sharply divided, and proposals in the Bill had been turned down by a small majority, the whole thing had been hastily dropped. To avoid another fiasco of this kind, Bonar Law maintained, would be far from easy. The two Churches might agree: but what of the heritors? John White replied that they would be faced in due course. Meanwhile, the Church of Scotland union committee was at a standstill until the declaratory Articles were on the Statute Book. Bonar Law refused to do more than repeat the promise already made: "the Government would either introduce or give

facilities for a Bill to enable the Church of Scotland to adopt the Articles".
It was a very short conference at No. 11 Downing Street on that February
afternoon, and John White spent the next day in Cambridge, where he
had the pleasure of watching his son, "J. B.", lead the Corpus team on the
Rugby field. A football match, if it were a hard-fought game, was always
a cure for a bout of depression engendered by an interview that had not
gone his own way.

A pity, they said afterwards, that pneumonia had stopped John White
from going to Downing Street the previous year—if his voice had been
heard then, the delay might not have been so long. It remains to be put
on record that five days after his voice *was* heard in Downing Street, the
King's Speech to Parliament gave assurance that the Government programme did include "a Bill for facilitating the Church Union in Scotland",
and it was presented to the House of Commons in April.

John White had always urged that a measure of such importance
should not be sponsored by a private member and was glad to hear the
announcement that it was indeed to be a Government Bill.

VI

Without delay, he sent to all Scottish members of Parliament and
others a Memorandum he quickly prepared with a colleague's help. He
wanted to drive home some things that might easily have been overlooked.
To show the magnitude of the union, for example, he pointed out that
no less than ninety-five per cent of Presbyterian congregations of Scotland
were either in the Established or the United Free Church. The other five
per cent contained the Wee Frees, the Original Secession Church, and all
others. The doctrine, worship, and government of the two great Churches
were the same; a minister of the one could be elected to a pulpit of the
other; there was no conflict in their ideals: indeed, the only differences
were due to what John White described as "an historical accident". And
that accident had been the bane of the Church of Scotland. For her own
protection, in the sixteenth century, she had asked the State for certain
statutory provisions which in after years had been so interpreted as to
limit her liberty of action in a way foreseen by nobody when these
statutory provisions had been made. They were obstacles to union, and
they must be removed.

On 22nd June, John White was given a special seat in the House of
Commons (the galleries were closed in those troublous days of Irish

rebellion) and he heard the Secretary of State for Scotland move the second reading of the Church of Scotland Bill. He had been in close conference with Robert Munro and had set before him every relevant point in the entire history of the union movement. He had supplied him with documentary evidence and had underlined the important points. In the speech that followed, he was to hear many of his own phrases repeated, many of his own arguments laid before the members of the House. It was an exhilarating experience to listen to his own contentions being used as ammunition.

The Secretary for Scotland said that he submitted his motion with a deep sense of responsibility:

"No one will deny that the present schisms are wholly deplorable. The Church will in vain urge the world to set its house in order until the Church has set its own house in order, and the world today is bemused and shocked by all the ecclesiastical rivalry and strife. The Churches themselves," he went on, "are grieved by it and even ashamed of it, but they are powerless under existing conditions to remedy it. It is practical considerations of that kind which have given driving force to the union movement in Scotland."

The constitution of the Church of Scotland, declared Mr. Munro, was a statutory constitution, and the Church was precluded by constitutional law from adopting the Articles: "Parliamentary sanction must be given—that is the necessity of this Bill."

Mr. Munro pointed out that the United Free Church and the Church of Scotland were now agreed upon certain points:

"They are agreed that the new Church must hold the Teinds and Endowments as fully and as freely as the United Free Church holds her property today—and that the State shall exercise no control over the Church as a *quid pro quo* for the enjoyment of those Endowments. . . . The Churches will not enter into any union until the question of endowments, as well as the question of Articles, has been duly dealt with. This Bill is thus the forerunner of a further Bill dealing with endowments. . . . And the Churches feel that they cannot properly tackle the subject of 'temporalities' until this preliminary question of spiritual freedom has been settled and cleared out of the way."

In his concluding words he spoke with gravity:
"If this Bill passes, I believe in my soul it will make for the healing and

the appeasing of ecclesiastical rivalry and strife. If it does not pass, then I do not believe a similar opportunity will recur during our generation." He appealed to the House of Commons to rise to the full height of its privileges and opportunities and give authoritative sanction to what he called "an epoch-making and sacred compact, and thus pave the way for the advent of a Church that would be both national and free".

Robert Munro had already said he was aware that some members were opposed to the Bill: "And I know quite well," he added, "that the House will listen with respect and interest, as it always does, to the views of the minority."

Looking around, John White could have pointed out all the Scottish members who made up that minority. He knew some of them were "bonny fechters", and he awaited their onslaught. The first to attack was MacCallum Scott, who began by saying he was a strong advocate of union and was in fact a member of the United Free Church. He objected to the Bill because it was only half a Bill—it ignored the Teinds. The leaders of his own Church had said they would not negotiate until the Church of Scotland had secured freedom from all restraint—both on spiritualities and temporalities. This Bill dealt only with matters spiritual. "And we are asked to take a leap in the dark, hand in hand, with a blindfolded Secretary for Scotland!" He held that in the uncertain political future there might never be a Bill dealing with the Teinds—"and in that case," he added, "the present bill will be known to future generations as Munro's Folly." [1]

MacCallum Scott struck a blow at the Bill from another angle. Since the Church was to have complete spiritual freedom, he held that she had the power even to become Episcopal if she wanted:

"Why should it not? Episcopacy is an admirable form of religion—for those who like it. But why should the Church be given the power to divert the whole of the national endowments of religion in Scotland from presbyterianism to the support of another system—without the consent of the Scottish people? . . . If this Bill is passed into law," he said, "the Church of Scotland will cease to be a national Church. It will become merely an endowed sect. . . . The ecclesiastics who framed this Bill wanted to have absolute independence in spiritual

[1] The name might well have been more suitably tagged to the abortive Teinds Bill Robert Munro had sponsored in the previous session.

matters. They also wanted an absolute monopoly of national funds. They cannot have it both ways."

Thomas Johnston rose to support MacCallum Scott. Johnston was himself to become one of the greatest of all Secretaries of State for Scotland, and by 1921 he was already making his mark in Parliament. He had attended many General Assemblies as an elder of the United Free Church, and he spoke as a member of that Church. He thought the Old Kirk had been consistent all through. It was the position of his own Church which was most extraordinary:

> "After long years of agitation for the State Church to be disestablished and disendowed, the great democratic United Free Church is now abandoning that position and preparing to become part and parcel of the Establishment! The House must not be under any false impression. . . . All Churches should have the right to adopt any form of government or any creed they like—but they cannot then be a State Church. It is the duty of the State to compel the State Church to observe the form of Church government, doctrine, and worship upon which it has been established and for which State funds have been provided. In its policy on worship, if State funds are provided, it is essential that she should obey the State. . . . *I believe the leaders of the Scottish Church have in view the possibility of union with Episcopacy.* . . . The people of Scotland should not be humbugged."

And he hammered home the point MacCallum Scott had made: if the Bill became law, the ecclesiastics could change the form of Church government and adopt Episcopalianism. . . . After the Reformation, he said, it was a question long in the balance whether the Reformed Church in Scotland was to be Episcopalian or Presbyterian. . . . It would be very easy for clever State lawyers to argue that Presbyterianism was no necessary part of the Reformation in Scotland. As for endowments and properties, these belonged to the State for the benefit of the Church.

> "The Teinds," he said, "were intended not only for the supply of religious sustenance, but were also meant for the maintenance of the poor and the education of the young. In any union of the two Churches, whatever wangling there may be over the State Endowments, the interest of the whole of Scotland, and not merely a section, must be taken into account. The United Free Church is going to cease to be a free Church. She is going to abandon her policy of religious

equality. In entering into a union with a State Church *she will bring about another Disruption in Scotland.*"

He urged that the Bill should be dropped until the Government showed its hand over what would be done with the Teinds and Endowments.

J. M. Hogge was another of those who raised strong objections, and the Hon. Alexander Shaw struck a warning note. "To believe that when we have passed this present Bill we have got over the whole difficulty— that is to live in a world of unreality. . . . If you are going to have union, let it be on a real basis. . . . This Bill has been presented in one way to the Church of Scotland and in another to the United Free Church." He declared that one Church had been told she would be Established more firmly than ever—with added freedom and privileges—while the other had been fervently assured that this Bill "is really equivalent to disestablishing the Church of Scotland". He said he had just asked the Principal of a Church College whether the united Church would be established or disestablished. The only reply he could get was that it would be neither one nor the other. "Is it, then, to be some entirely novel intermediate state," demanded Shaw, "a state which cannot be precisely explained but must be accepted as an article of faith? It is unfortunate," he added pointedly, "that a Bill intended to promote Church union should depend upon exhibitions of casuistry which would have been a credit to the Middle Ages."

Robert McLaren, a distinguished mining engineer, and for many years a member of the General Assembly of the Church of Scotland, also struck a note of warning. Although he supported the Bill, he felt that if union took place a great many in the United Free Church would be bound to come out on a matter of principle. There would be another Disruption. Men like Thomas Johnston, keen supporters of Disestablishment, would certainly come out. Where would they go?

"They cannot go back to the old United Presbyterian Church," said Robert McLaren, "for it does not now exist. Nor could they go back to the Free Church, for the Wee Frees believe in Establishment. They cannot join the Free Presbyterians—they do not believe in either side and would not take them in. They cannot join the Baptists, for the Baptists are too wet. The Congregationalists would not have them, for the Congregationalists do not believe in presbyteries. They will have to go out into the wilderness. They will find no water there. No manna will be sent from Heaven. In the Exodus, the Children of Israel were led by God. In this case, I am afraid they will be led by men like the Rev. James Barr."

A. J. Balfour was another speaker to whom John White listened intently. The elder statesman, as he was then called, always attracted an interested audience in the House. He said that he had watched with deep sympathy the growth of the union movement: "In the first year I entered Parliament, 1874, I supported a Bill which abolished lay patronage." The relation between Church and State, he said, had in every country in Europe proved itself a stumbling-block during the whole period of ecclesiastical history.

> "In the drafting of the Articles, I think an admirable work has been performed by the leaders of religious thought in Scotland. The events that have divided the two Churches in the past may be regarded as only the preface to that profounder unity which I hope will make them one great religious body for the infinite benefit of the country to which they belong."

Afternoon merged into evening as the speeches continued. John White's interest quickened as the critics of the Bill marshalled their arguments. Of the seventy-four members for Scotland, more than three-quarters had said beforehand that they would support the Bill, and Sir John M. MacLeod had approached members of the Church of England party and had asked them "not to intervene for their own ulterior purposes, as their action might arouse Church faction peculiar to England". From the English non-conformists, MacLeod had told John White privately, there had not been a "sough" of opposition. But in spite of this assurance, there was no guarantee of the way the English vote might go, and Scots members were a small minority in the Commons. John White's order paper of that 22nd June 1921 is a revealing document: he made notes on every speech; to the nearest minute he recorded when every member rose to take part in the debate; he noted that A. J. Balfour spoke for exactly forty minutes; and that James Brown rose at 7.20—"a plain Christian man; said great Christian Churches were never more active than today; none of the Secessionists ever went out against presbyterianism; strong Doric—grand to hear Labour speak". This was the James Brown who three years later was to be appointed Lord High Commissioner to the General Assembly, and was to become a good friend of John White's. The Bill was passed without a division. John White's note is: "8.30 *Ayes have it.*"

VII

A dark cloud was unexpectedly cast over the passage of the Bill by the announcement of the death of Lord Balfour of Burleigh.

A few days before, the deliberations of a House of Lords Committee had been interrupted by his advent to the Committee Room. In the words of Lady Frances Balfour, "his face was aglow with a great joy; and he told the surprised peers, many of whom were not conversant with Scotland or its Church, how the Church Bill in the Upstairs Committee Room of the House of Commons had passed one stage in as many minutes as it had taken years to bring together the fruits of conciliation in Scotland". B. of B., as many of his friends called him, died on 6th July; and from the Memorial Service in St. Columba's, many Scottish members of Parliament went back to St. Stephen's to record their vote on the third reading of the Bill.

John White suffered the loss of a friend to whom he had become deeply attached. His admiration and respect for the older man (Lord Balfour of Burleigh was the elder by more than twenty years) had increased as they had shared with growing intimacy that long trek over shifting sands towards Presbyterian union.

"In his passing," he wrote, "the Church has been bereft of one of its foremost elders, most sagacious counsellors, and safest leaders. When the broken fragments of Scottish presbyterianism are pieced together, not a little of the credit will be gratefully ascribed to his perseverance and wisdom and faith."

Much of the work Lord Balfour of Burleigh would have carried out while the Bill was passing through the House of Lords now fell upon the shoulders of John White. It was a task he took up with sorrow and with pride as he recalled the words Lord Balfour of Burleigh had written to him not long after they had begun their work on union together: "I know no man I would trust further than you."

On the day before the Bill was to be debated in the Lords, John White was invited by Lord Finlay to visit him at his London home. Finlay said he would support the Bill and would be glad to have some enlightenment from the man best equipped to give it.

"It was a hot summer day," wrote John White, "and Lord Finlay discussed the Church question with his jacket off. I explained the whole situation to him, and he said to me—'But back in 1886 I gave you all this in my own Bill.' [1]

" 'Yes,' I replied, 'it was a great effort of yours to prepare the way for union, but the other Churches did not approve of your Bill, for its terms were that the State was *giving* the Church of Scotland the right to exercise spiritual freedom. The point is that the presbyterian Churches of Scotland always held that *spiritual freedom belonged to them as their inherent possession.* Had your Bill passed and been accepted by the Churches, they would have had a State-conferred freedom. In our Articles we declare that we *possess* spiritual freedom as a Church of Christ. We are asking the State to acknowledge it, and by so doing we are safeguarding it.' "

On that visit to London, John White spent much time with the Lord Chancellor, Viscount Birkenhead. Birkenhead was to introduce the Bill in the Lords, and his knowledge of the Scottish Church question was sketchy. John White was astounded at the rapidity with which he took every point that was put to him. "Birkenhead's assimilation of facts was remarkable," he said afterwards. "He arranged them logically in his mind, and he would suddenly pull out of his memory some relevant fact from the history of another country. 'F. E.' has a prehensile grip on everything he touches—a jurist of rare ability." It was with acute anticipation that he awaited Birkenhead's speech from the Woolsack.

Since he had become Chancellor, Lord Birkenhead began, he had not had placed in his hands a task over which he had felt so great a responsibility: "It involves an area into which politicians should intrude only with the greatest self-distrust—and then only with the complete assurance that the spiritual interests involved need the intervention of Parliament." It was his considered opinion as a lawyer that the four clauses of the Bill, apart from the Articles, contained "every safeguard that prudent care would suggest". He pointed out that the ecclesiastical history of Scotland was in contrast with that of any European country known to him in the same period. While the other countries of Christendom had been divided by differences in dogmatic opinion, it was peculiar to Scotland that the two Churches now proposing to form a corporate union had been divided

---

[1] In the year after he had entered Parliament as member for Inverness, Robert Bannatyne Finlay had thought fit to present a Bill to Parliament in the interest of Church union. The Church of Scotland had not suggested it and considered most of it unnecessary. It had aroused some intense opposition. Dr. Rainy had violently opposed it, saying that it would "efface the non-Established churches in Scotland". It was dropped for lack of support.

only by historical causes which had long since passed away. He noted the surprising agreement, almost amounting to unanimity, between them, and he informed the noble Lords that of the three hundred and sixty votes cast in the General Assembly of the Church of Scotland, only fourteen had been against the introduction of the Bill into Parliament. He gave a detailed survey of what the passing of the Bill would mean, and turned to the Articles: "I recommend them to this House with the remark that the learned and devoted men who have agreed upon these precise and scholarly formulae claim to have embodied in them the ancient view upon these sacred matters held by the Scottish nation through the centuries with a rugged and vigorous independence."

When Lord Haldane rose to support the Bill, he said: "I do not speak as an Established churchman or as a Free churchman, or even as a Presbyterian; I am not connected with any particular Church." But he did of course speaks as a Liberal politician, although he was shortly afterwards to change his political colour and sit upon the Woolsack as the first Socialist Lord Chancellor in British history. In a speech by no means free from error of fact, he glanced at the history of the relations between the two Churches and said: "The success of the appeal which the U.F. Church made to Parliament to pass the Bill of 1905 was largely due to the generous support given by the Established Church of Scotland to her sister Church in its dire necessity. The Established Church came forward and fought for that Bill as if it had concerned itself." Haldane's memory must have failed him badly, for the statement is entirely erroneous. To the indignation of many in the United Free Church, the Church of Scotland had been allowed to add a fifth clause to the four clauses of a Bill that concerned the United Free Church alone. Permission had been granted largely because of the sympathetic attitude of A. J. Balfour, the Prime Minister, who realised the need for a new formula of subscription for the Church of Scotland. Lord Haldane was on firmer ground when he spoke of his own participation in the notorious Church case of 1904: he was aware, he said, of some "apprehension among people in Scotland as to whether, even by the constitution given by the Bill now before the House, there will not be some power on the part of civil courts to interfere with the Church of Scotland". In view of past history, he admitted that this apprehension was most understandable, and he recalled the time when he had stood at the Bar of the House of Lords, seventeen years before, to plead on behalf of the newly formed United Free Church of Scotland: "I was then convinced, as an advocate is rarely convinced, of the justice of my cause. I fought for what I believed to be its just title of spiritual liberty on the part of the United Free Church."

These words awakened memories in the mind of John White, who had followed the 1904 case with close interest. Principal Rainy had then sought Haldane's advice on the legality of a Free Church fusion with the United Presbyterians. In spite of the fact that Alexander Asher, Solicitor-General for Scotland, had warned him that union would bring a grave risk of the Free Church forfeiting her property if a minority refused to enter the union, Rainy had accepted Haldane's opinion that all would be well. Even if a judgment should go against them in the Court of Session, Haldane's view was that it would certainly be rectified by the House of Lords. Haldane now admitted that his confidence had been unjustified. "We turned out to be wrong in our contentions," he said, and he proceeded to lay the blame upon Dr. Chalmers for having taken the skeleton constitution made by legal advisers at the Disruption and "filled it up with magnificent theological phrases" which had pinned down the Free Church to certain doctrines—doctrines from which the Church had moved away as the years had gone by. And to deviate from these doctrines, he added, "meant the forfeiture of over two million pounds' worth of property". He compared the position of the Free Church in 1904 with that of the Church of Scotland in 1921. He declared that it would depend upon the title which the Church of Scotland could make out to her identity and continuity whether she could retain her property if challenged, for the civil courts had the right to ask whether there was continuity with those who had hitherto enjoyed the title to that property. Speaking purely as a lawyer—for he was no churchman, as he had emphasised—Lord Haldane gave his opinion that "the Church of Scotland will have under this constitution (as set forth in the Articles) the most unlimited power of determining, in her own courts, the doctrine which would be followed. No civil court can intrude." He showed the same confidence as he had done in expressing his opinion to Principal Rainy; but John White reflected with comfort that it had now a more substantial basis in law than the unfortunate advice he had given more than twenty years before.

Lord Finlay supported the measure, as he had promised, and made some comparisons with his own Bill of 1886 which were as obscure as they were irrelevant. The contribution to the debate of Lord Parmoor (father of Sir Stafford Cripps) contained praise of the courageous way in which the Church of Scotland had claimed the right to interpret the Articles, a right acknowledged in the Bill. That is a matter of first importance, he declared. "If you allow the interpretation of the Articles to be carried out in a civil court, it is quite clear that the so-called independence of the Church of Scotland would not be a real independence but would be subject to superior authority." And he added with wistful expectation: "It is a freedom and liberty which *I hope we may sometime attain ourselves in the Anglican Church.*" In giving the Bill his blessing, the Archbishop of Canterbury refrained from touching on this delicate point of disputation about the Church of England's lack of power over her own Faith.

The Lords had their say and the proceedings closed. At five minutes to eight that evening, a telegram was handed in at the Post Office at the House of Commons. It was addressed to Mrs. White, 15 Dundonald Rd., Glasgow, and it ran:

"BILL THROUGH HOUSE OF LORDS 7.45 WHITE."

Chapter XIII

THE ANCIENT PATRIMONY

I

FROM the day when the Act acknowledging the Church's spiritual freedom had been passed, the thought uppermost in John White's mind was the speedy creation and passing of a Bill which would give the Church power over her endowments. Most people assumed that the Articles would be at once sent down to presbyteries under the Barrier Act and at the next meeting of Assembly become an Act of the Church: thereafter, it would "come into operation on such date as His Majesty would fix by Order in Council". It would indeed be a blessed day for many when the Church's freedom would be acknowledged by the State, and there seemed no reason for delay until it occurred to Lord Sands that it would be better to hold this up until the Church were "vested with the administration and enjoyment of her temporalities in such a manner as to enable her freely to exercise the powers contained in the Declaratory Articles". He pointed out that the Act which had just been passed gave the Church power to change the boundaries of ecclesiastical parishes and to raise *quoad sacra* churches to the status of a parish church; and since this was so closely tied up with teinds and endowments, he thought it better to refrain from embodying the Articles in an Act of Assembly. And by this wise afterthought the Church's charter of spiritual freedom, the most momentous piece of legislation passed for the Church of Scotland since 1592, was left suspended in the air until such time as the problem of teinds and endowments had been settled. The drafting of a Teinds Bill was obviously the task of the Government, and the sooner this was begun the better.

To John White's disgust, he found that speed appeared to be the last thing in the thoughts of those in Whitehall. Months later, in a speech to Glasgow elders, he denounced the "inexplicable and inexcusable delay", and he added in exasperation: "The union movement—if one can call it a movement when it is held up in a side-room of the Secretary for Scotland —has been suffering severely." Although the Act on spiritualities had been passed in July 1921, it was not until 19th April of the following year that Robert Munro signed the minute appointing and briefing the

Departmental Committee which the Government had agreed to set up. The terms of its remit were:

"To enquire and report as to the existing law as affected by the Church of Scotland Act 1921, and as to what further legislative amendments or readjustments—particularly in relation to the tenure and enjoyment of the property and endowments of the Church of Scotland —are necessary or expedient in view of the coming into force of the said Act, in order to facilitate Church Union as contemplated therein."

Lord Haldane, chairman of the committee, being both a lawyer and a politician, was accustomed to groping for facts that lay hidden behind a mist of ambiguous verbiage, and he perceived that his task was to recommend the most equitable and practical way of abolishing the teinds and giving the Church unrestricted control of the income she had been deriving from them. It was as simple as that. But Haldane knew that his mission would take him into a dark thorny jungle. A man of immense industry, he had never in a long and distinguished career drawn back from a task because the way seemed rough. He had known what it was to suffer misfortune and unpopularity, even to have his loyalty to his country unfairly questioned. In dolorous days, he had carried himself with dignity and philosophic calm. And in accepting the chairmanship of this Departmental Committee, he knew he was undertaking a work which would make him the target of yet more of the criticism to which he had become accustomed. He was in fact criticised before he had summoned the first meeting. It was recalled that he had fought for the disestablishment and the disendowment of the Church of Scotland: and those who reminded the public of this asked how he could be expected to bring an impartial mind to bear upon the emoluments he had once been so eager to wrest from the Church. As to the four other members of his committee, it was conceded that the balance was fair since two of them (the Very Rev. Sir George Adam Smith of Aberdeen University and John Prosser, Crown Agent) were of the United Free Church, while the other two (Sir Joseph Maclay, Bt., and Sir James M. Dodds) were Old Kirk men. Throughout twelve more months, John White was to wait impatiently for the result of their deliberations.

II

"In actual working it may be questioned whether any mode of payment could be invented more uncertain in results, more antiquated in principle, and in operation more troublesome to all concerned."

This comment on teinds had been made in a report by a committee of the Church on fiars prices in 1895. It applied with equal force in 1922.

Teinds have been called the lawyer's nightmare and other names a good deal more opprobrious. Many, if not most, parish ministers had suffered, in this way or that, over the time or method of collecting stipends. An example can be taken from some draft suggestions for a report on property and endowments made by members of the Church:

"A minister who has settled in a parish, say in November, has to work for about a year and a quarter before it is possible for him to collect a single penny of victual stipend. On the other hand, if a minister is settled in a parish a single day before either the 15th May or 29th September he becomes, after one day of holding the office, entitled to six months' stipend—which, however, he cannot collect until the fiars prices are struck. Further anomalies sometimes arise in consequence of the law of Ann which gives to the next of kin of a deceased minister half a year's stipend of the parish. Thus, if a minister dies, say after 29th September 1920, his executors become entitled to the whole of the stipend for that crop and year, which would be payable in March 1921 on the fiars prices being struck, and his next of kin would also become entitled to one half of the stipend for the crop and year following, so that assuming a new minister had been appointed five months after the vacancy by death, that minister had to serve the cure for a whole year and at the end of it there would be only half a year's stipend available for him, since the other half had gone, as already explained, to the next of kin of the late minister as Ann."

This perhaps shows the system at its worst, but it is little wonder that young ministers were bemused by such quirks and quiddities. When they grew older, they became wearily resigned. As prices rose and fell, their stipends fluctuated. Nor was there even a uniformity of prices in the different counties. Most ministers envied the method by which United Free churchmen received stipends that did not go up and down like mercury in a thermometer and were paid by cheque drawn regularly by a Church treasurer. Many United Free Church ministers had scant pity for their Old Kirk brethren: since the antiquated system of teinds was part of that grand old tradition of which the Old Kirk was so proud, let her ministers suffer blithely the irritation of collecting stipend from heritors who in some parishes were numbered in hundreds and even in thousands.

JOHN WHITE

In the disestablishment and disendowment campaign, there had been more battles over teinds than any other matter. Their origin, their validity, their being or not being a State bounty, their being or not being a tax on the land, their control by a civil Court of Teinds in which the Church could plead but could not adjudicate—these had been attacked and defended.[1] An Old Kirk minister, asked to define teinds, would have replied that they were the religious patrimony of the people of Scotland, held in trust by the National Church, the only Church with an organised ministry in every Scottish parish. A refutation would quickly have been made by ministers of non-established Churches, and it might even have been backed by a quotation from jurists like Sir John Campbell and Lord Shaw of Dunfermline.

In 1835 Campbell (who afterwards became Lord Chancellor) stated:

> "While the property of the Church ought not to be touched while it could be beneficially employed by the Church, it is the property of the State. The State conferred it. The State might take it away when it could be of no further use to the Church. Tithes were *not* a voluntary donation of the patron. They were imposed by the legislature. It is a remnant of paganism. It is the pagan doctrine that what was once appropriated for religious purposes should never be diverted to any secular use. . . . In origin, tithes were a property tax."

And Lord Shaw of Dunfermline stated:

> "Every temporal right possessed by the Church of Scotland dates from *after* the Reformation and was created by the State. For over half a century after the Reformation, teinds were levied and enjoyed by the Crown, the nobles, and others to whom the right had been transferred —and that without any reference whatever to the salaries of the Protestant clergy. The year 1560 begins the series of Acts of Parliament which constitute the present Church of Scotland clergy as a body of men paid, at the option of the State, out of funds which it chooses to allocate for the purpose."

All of which has been described as preposterous nonsense by Old Kirk lawyers. Said Lord Sands:

> "Had there been no Church, teinds would not have existed. For any rights the nation has in the teinds, the nation has to thank the

[1] This Court of Teinds, in which Senators of the Court of Justice sat, controlled not only the teinds but supervised, among other things, the endowments of *quoad sacra* parishes provided by the voluntary subscriptions of members of the Church of Scotland.

Church. Teinds are in no sense a tax upon the land. They are a separate estate based upon as solid a title as private property in land itself. The State may deprive the Church of her estate in teinds just as the State may confiscate the property of a private citizen, but the justice and morality of the two proceedings are quite on the same footing."

So different were these points of view that John White and his friends had wisely put the matter on one side until the two Churches had found and ratified their agreement on spiritual matters. The Church of Scotland had said in no uncertain terms that she would not give up the teinds and permit them to be put to secular uses. The United Free Church had said, in terms equally unmistakable, that she would not unite with any Church part of whose income was derived from teinds. However, the majority in that Church now admitted that if the teinds system could be converted into some different system, over which the Church had complete control, they would be satisfied. To devise such a system was the task to which Lord Haldane and his committee had put their hand. One condition dominated all others. No acceptable Act of Parliament could go on the Statute Book unless there was fundamental agreement on teinds between the heritors who paid and the Church of Scotland who received.

III

The plan suggested by Lord Haldane was that, since the teinds must be abolished, the heritors should be compelled to redeem them by paying an agreed sum, and the fruits of the land would then be freed from their ancient burden. The heritors should hand over the redemption money in the form of Consols, the interest on which would yield an annual sum equal to the stipend. The stipend in each parish was of course to be fixed in perpetuity. Any heritor who did not wish to redeem his teinds in one payment could pay in instalments until his obligation was cleared. To many folk this seemed simple enough. If the heritors were to be relieved of paying teinds, they must pay in some other way. They, or their ancestors, had not bought the land without knowing that there was the burden of a teind on its fruits; if there had been no teind, the cost of purchase would have been greater than it was. The important thing was that the Court of Teinds, with Court of Session judges sitting therein, would be abolished, and the Church would be the possessor of Government securities over which she had full control. The Haldane committee had of course a good many other problems to consider. They made proposals about free teinds held by universities; the handing over to the Church of church buildings, manses, glebes, churchyards; Parliamentary churches and Exchequer grants; ecclesiastical assessments; Burgh churches and other matters. The publication of the Haldane proposals in April 1923 seemed to everyone to be a landmark in the history of the union movement.

They were studied at once by the General Committee of the Church, who worked so speedily that they were able to present a report to the General Assembly in May. They recommended acceptance if the Church could have the opportunity to make amendment in detail. In the Old Kirk it was noted with satisfaction that the United Free Assembly "cordially welcomed" the Haldane Report; and a special committee was formed, with John White and J. A. S. Millar, W.S. (who was later the Law Agent of the Church), as conveners, to protect the interests of the Church in the drafting of a Teinds Bill in Whitehall. And so, for the first time, John White came officially to handle the problem of teinds and endowments. He was determined upon one thing: since the Haldane recommendations were acceptable to the Church, there must be no further delay in Whitehall.

The projected Bill was in the hands of the Secretary of State for Scotland. This post was now held by Lord Novar. Better known as Munro-Ferguson of Raith, he had estates in Fife which, added to his lands in Ross, made him owner of twenty-seven thousand acres. And some felt that, inevitably, the point of view of the heritors would not, to put it mildly, be ignored. Moreover, like Haldane, he had been a Liberal supporter of the disestablishment and disendowment of the Church of Scotland. John White did not feel like giving him a free hand and was determined that the provisions of the Haldane Report, officially backed by the Church of Scotland, should be followed. Together with some of his colleagues he went to see Novar in July, and they came away satisfied that he had promised they would see a draft of the Bill before it was presented to Parliament. The Lord Advocate,[1] who was in touch with the Secretary for Scotland, wrote in October to John White that Lord Novar fully realised the advantages of letting Church of Scotland representatives see the Bill before presentation. But still the Secretary made no move, and towards the end of the year White wrote to the Scottish Office asking Novar if they might meet and talk about the Bill.

"It is important," the letter runs, "that its terms should be informally communicated to us as was suggested at our July interview. If it

---

[1] William Watson, previously Procurator of the Church of Scotland.

219

embodies the Haldane recommendations there will not be any general opposition to it. If there is any serious alteration, it would be well that we should learn what is proposed. One would not like to see our fourteen years' conference-work jeopardised at the last lap. . . . The proposed Bill would not arouse any party opposition, and it would be a great boon to Scotland."

To this, Lord Novar said that he thought he had made it clear at the July interview that there would be no discussion of the terms of the Bill until after he had presented it to Parliament, and that ample time would be allowed for talk before the Second Reading. John White wrote to the Lord Advocate:

"I am getting anxious about the fate of the Bill. I understand it is drafted, and may be introduced at an early date in the new session of Parliament. On 14th October you wrote to me that 'Lord Novar had fully in mind the advantages of letting representatives of the Church see the Bill before it is actually introduced'. On the strength of this I had a committee of five appointed to receive your communication. Do you think we may expect this?"

To this, the Lord Advocate replied that here was an example of how difficult it was "to be precise in language" because a meaning had been read into his words that had not been intended. He had been most anxious, he said, not to prejudge any decision of Lord Novar's as to whether or not a draft of the Bill would be shown to Church representatives. Since he could get no satisfaction from the Lord Advocate, John White wrote yet again to Novar asking for an assurance that the Bill generally followed the terms of the Haldane Report. The reply was that it did, except in the method of redemption of teinds by Consols. It became clear that no chance would be given to see the Bill itself.

A letter from Lord Haldane surprised John White; for Haldane, too, assured him that the recommendations in his Report were "substantially carried out in the Bill", which deviated "only on minor points which may prove to be of little importance". Meanwhile, John White had learned, through a certain channel, that what had been substituted for Consols in the Bill was a fixed money payment. This private information had startled him. He foresaw that the "minor deviation" might well mean a drastic reduction in stipends in the years to come: it favoured the heritors at the expense of the Church. He replied to Haldane that the "minor points" were indeed major points and the change would certainly not be acceptable to the Church of Scotland. "I am primarily concerned about Church union," he wrote, "and I fear that a Bill which offers terms so much less favourable than your Report recommended would arouse strong opposition in the country and jeopardise the Union movement."

John White decided it was high time his committee made formal representation to the Scottish Office. He sent a strong letter reminding Lord Novar that the Haldane Report had been accepted in its entirety on condition that the Government adopted it with changes only in minor details, and he said that "a very different situation would be created if there was a departure that would heavily reduce the future income from which stipend would be paid". He pressed strongly that the teinds should be redeemed by the heritors paying an annual sum over a term of years, the total amount being enough to purchase Consols that would yield interest to cover the fixed stipend.

His worst fears, it seemed, were to be realised. He wrote to Lord Sands:

> "I had a talk today with Lord Maclay,[1] and he is of opinion that we should insist on an interview with Novar as he feels the whole union movement will be defeated if the Bill is contentious. . . . It will be a thousand pities if we do not score a try after our long years of scrummage. Novar is not proving much good behind the scrum—and Watson, his stand-off, is never in his place and doesn't seem to know what to do with the ball when he gets it. He is ignorant of the Union rules."

John White did what he could but (an unusual result for him) achieved nothing. Disgusted by the whole pettifogging business, he and his colleagues waited with what patience they could muster for the day when Lord Novar would present to Parliament his Church of Scotland (Property and Endowments) Bill.

IV

Lord Novar introduced his Bill into the House of Lords on 15th January 1924. In spite of all that had been said about the opposition it would provoke in Scotland, he had made no attempt to bring it into line with the Haldane recommendations. There had been a General Election

---

[1] A member of the Haldane committee.

in December, and the Tory Party under Stanley Baldwin (Bonar Law had left politics, a sick man, the previous May) had a working majority in the House of Commons only so long as Asquith gave it Liberal support. Before Baldwin had been Premier for many weeks, that support was abruptly withdrawn on the tariff issue, and at the beginning of February Ramsay MacDonald became the first Socialist Prime Minister, with a tenure of office also precariously depending upon Liberal votes in the House of Commons. This, then, was the situation soon after Novar had introduced the Church Bill. Nobody now knew what its fate would be. It would almost certainly have been dropped if it had not been for the labours of John White.

In March, Lady Frances Balfour was writing anxiously to him and recommending an early conference with the landlords. He replied:

> "Before Lord Novar introduced his hurtful measure (which he kept from our knowledge, despite our repeated requests to see a draft of his proposals) I was in touch with Lord Haldane that he might know we would accept a Bill embodying the recommendations of his committee, but could not possibly accept the crude proposals of Novar. It is astonishing that the Lord Advocate who advised Novar was a former Procurator of the Church and a member of the Union committee."

As to the suggested conference, he was trying to arrange it with the only organised body of heritors that carried any weight—the Scottish Land and Property Federation. "Even the heritors must admit that some of Novar's proposals are based on financial ignorance. That is the most charitable view, otherwise this would be another instance of the Lords of Congregation helping themselves to the patrimony of the Kirk." He said he sincerely hoped pressure could be put on the Cabinet to ensure that the Bill would not be dropped.

"Your letter has been a great relief to me," wrote Lady Frances, "for I see somebody is still at the helm and that the Ark of the Covenant is not foundering on the rocks." She urged him to lose no time in using all the influence he could exert on as many members of both Houses as possible. In this he had some success. He got the support of the young Lord Balfour of Burleigh, whose mother had written: "Nobody has done such work as you, of which I doubt if many can even realise the weight. I think with gratitude of all the help you gave to Balfour, how often he has told me of it and *how* much he valued it. . . . My son will, I am sure, be proud and pleased to do anything that he can." Others who gave active support included the ever-vigilant Sir John MacLeod, Sir Arthur Steel-Maitland, Sir William Lane Mitchell, Lord Younger of Leckie, and Sir William Mitchell-Thomson. To ensure that the Bill would not be dropped, everything that could be done was done in those early weeks of 1924. As a result of John White's efforts, there came the news that it would have its second reading in the House of Lords on the 1st of April.

V

Since Lord Novar was no longer a member of the Government, Lord Haldane (now Socialist Lord Chancellor) sponsored the Bill. While he disagreed with some of its clauses, he said he hoped it would be an acceptable framework. He had taken the helpful and rather unusual course of producing a White Paper containing proposed corrections for use at the Committee stage. The Duke of Buccleuch had put down an amendment to reject the Bill, not because he wished to press it to a division but to make certain that his views would be heard. He objected both to the suggestions of Haldane's committee and some of the provisions of Novar's Bill. In particular, he protested against complete redemption of the teinds, which both of them wanted; for whether this was done by payment of a lump sum or in instalments, it would bear too heavily upon the landowners. "It will mean their final ruin," he declared. "Why should we be asked to pay for Church union, for that is what it amounts to?" He said that neither Lord Haldane nor Lord Novar had given the heritors a proper opportunity to speak their mind. A much better plan would be to wipe out the teinds by placing an annual charge on the land itself—an annuity, with priority over any other charge. This would secure for the Church of Scotland a non-fluctuating income in perpetuity. If any heritor was anxious to redeem, and could afford it, let him arrange terms with the Church. If the Church, on her part, wished to convert the land-charge into a lump sum, she could sell the annuity to the highest bidder. That was his plan, and he "spoke for the heritors of Scotland who had been bled white in the last few years". The gross rental of an estate of his in 1920 had been over forty-two thousand pounds; and although the ministers had received in stipend nearly four thousand, he himself had been left with a net sum of only four hundred and eighty-five pounds. He hastened to assure his peers he was not complaining; the ministers had a legal right to it. But those landowners who depended entirely on their rents were in none too easy circumstances, and both the Novar Bill and the Haldane recommendations would put them in a much worse case. The total cost to the heritors of a compulsory and complete redemption, over and above what they were paying in teinds, had been estimated at two and a half million pounds. "A large number of Church people," he added, "are anxious to come to an agreement, but some on either side are perhaps rather violent and extreme. It would be an unfortunate thing for the Church of Scotland if this Bill left bitterness behind."

Joining in the debate, Lord Novar admitted he had once believed the State should take the teinds from the Church of Scotland and apply them to secular purposes, but he had supported that only because people once thought it was a necessary step to Church union. He disagreed with the Duke of Buccleuch, and still maintained that the complete redemption proposed in his Bill was the best plan. The Church was in no need to drive a hard bargain with the landowners. When united, the two Churches would have an income of over two and a half million pounds. Less than one-tenth of that, he pointed out, would be derived from teinds. Even in asking that churches and manses be handed over in good repair, he declared, the Church was too grasping. And how illogical it was, he said, that any burden of a national Church should rest upon the industry of agriculture alone—an industry struggling with depression and depleted of capital. Many farmers had but recently bought their farms and were now being weighed down with their burdens. "It would be extremely unfortunate if the great achievement of union were marred by any suspicion that the Church was insisting on its pound of flesh 'to the twentieth part of one poor scruple'." It fell to Lord Haldane to round off the debate, and he did so with this comment: "It is a very dry discussion, and requires a very special taste, though perhaps it is not amiss that your lordships should have had, for once, a Scottish afternoon."

It had not been a dry discussion. Certainly John White had not found it so. He could smile gently at the fight the peers were making against the intolerable burden of redeeming the teinds, for he knew what was dominating the minds of most landowners. They feared that if the teinds were removed and no other imposition put upon the land, here would be "an open temptation to any Government on the outlook for a source of revenue". So long as they had the teinds or some similar burden to bear, the heritors felt that they had a compelling argument against any new land tax. It was the old saw that the devil you know is better than the devil you don't know.

In the course of that April, John White exchanged letters with the Duke of Buccleuch. They came to a fair understanding of each other's point of view, but there were things on which they could not agree. John White kept driving home the argument that, if the heritors would accept the complete redemption plan, they would actually be paying in instalments (even including the annual sum for the sinking fund) less than they had paid in 1923 in stipends from the teinds. The reason for this apparent anomaly was that the chalder of 1923 stood at a higher value than the chalder taken at an average over the previous fifty years, which would be the fixed chalder on which the redemption would be calculated. Could a more tempting offer be made to the heritors? Was it not an offer by which the Church, quite obviously, stood to lose, since the taking over of churches and manses would cost her, on the heritors' own estimate, seventy thousand pounds a year to maintain? But still there was no agreement.

Day followed day, and the opening of the Assembly drew nearer. It was essential for John White to reach agreement with the heritors; for if a pact was not announced in the Assembly, it would be known at Westminster that the Church and the heritors were still at loggerheads and the Bill would almost certainly be tossed up on a shelf to gather dust. Ramsay MacDonald, still walking a political tight-rope and liable to fall from the premiership at any moment, had said he would not touch this measure unless the two sides agreed. Shortly before the Assembly was due to open, John White's joint convener, J. A. S. Millar, wrote to him that, in his judgment, unless the Landowners' Federation had its way, "the Bill is, in all reasonable probability, *dead*".

"Everything seemed pretty hopeless," John White recorded afterwards, "and I asked Lord Haldane if he could summon a meeting of heritors and Church representatives in Edinburgh and take the chair. I hoped we might at least reach a basis for negotiation. This he kindly agreed to do. We met at Alan Menzies' room in Rutland Square.[1] All were lawyers except the Duke of Buccleuch and myself.

"After a long and unsatisfactory discussion, Lord Haldane said: 'Dr. White, it is evident we cannot reach agreement. Without agreement there is no hope of the Bill. I am exceedingly sorry to say this after all your endeavours.'

"I told him I was bitterly disappointed. 'The discussions have been

A. L. Menzies, W.S., was then Law Agent of the Church of Scotland.

almost entirely in the hands of lawyers,' I reminded him, 'and if the two members of this conference who are not lawyers—the Duke and myself—were given full powers, I am confident we could settle the main outlines in a very short time. I suggest that the whole business be remitted to three representatives of the heritors and three of the Church under the chairmanship of the Lord Advocate.' [1] This was accepted, but few thought it would bring anything of value.

"At our meetings in the Lord Advocate's rooms in Edinburgh, many were the long, barren and irrelevant arguments. It was a trial of patience. But it had to be endured. I suggested that we argue about the Haldane scheme and see what we could agree to accept. We argued our friends into silence. We won on points, but there was no knock-out. We were no further forward."

And there, it seemed, the matter would have to remain.

VI

To add to John White's anxieties, the leaders in the United Free Church were becoming anxious and restive. They were afraid that the failure of the Church and heritors to reach a settlement would strengthen the hands of their own minority.

"I quite see you are pushing the heritors all you can," Principal Martin wrote to him. "I fear some of them are very dour. . . . I see the exceeding difficulty of your problem. You may perhaps be able to hit off something with the heritors, but what about getting your General Assembly to accept it?"

John White saw that there was no hope whatever of hitting off anything with the heritors so long as *complete redemption of the teinds* was the basis of settlement: "To me it was quite evident that we must consider the scheme put forward by the heritors themselves. There could be no settlement without it."

Outwardly calm and steadfast, John White felt gravely disquieted. The Assembly opened with the annual pageantry that never fails to bring animation to Edinburgh streets. John White had a crowded week ahead of him. There were debates to attend, speeches to make; and judging from entries in his diary, one would imagine he had little time left for thoughts

[1] H. P. Macmillan, K.C., later Lord Macmillan, son of a United Free Church minister, Dr. Hugh Macmillan of Greenock.

of union. He had an important speech to deliver on his "Church and Nation" report. He was due to speak at the United Free Church reception on Tuesday; to attend his own Moderator's At Home on Wednesday evening; to speak to the Elders and Office Bearers on Thursday afternoon; to dine with Sir Harry Hope (a strong union supporter) on Friday and go on to the reception at Holyroodhouse; to put in an appearance at the United Free Church Moderator's At Home on Saturday evening—and besides other duties, he had determined to go out to Balerno to find peace to have a quiet talk with Alan Menzies, whose wise advice and tireless labour had so greatly helped him. But the two most important of all the many entries in his diary were those of the private meeting of the Assembly at nine o'clock on the evening of Monday, 26th, and of the open Assembly meeting at 2 o'clock on the following day.

At both of these he was to speak on union. He was to make his Report not only to the General Assembly but to the whole Church of Scotland, waiting to hear what had been happening behind closed doors. The private meeting of Assembly, to be held on the previous evening, was a comparatively new institution, and it had been of John White's own making. He had felt in past years that it would give an opportunity to ministers and elders to ask questions without the restraining presence of the press and the public. At the meeting on Monday night, informal and utterly frank, he would be bound to confess his failure. There was to be one more meeting with the heritors before the week-end. This was to be held at quarter to eleven on Friday in the Lord Advocate's room. John White went there determined to find agreement if it could be found without a sacrifice that was unjust to the Church.

"I at once anticipated the heritors' argument against compulsory redemption of the teinds," he wrote afterwards; "I said I would advise the Church to give up all thought of it and to agree to *a permanent land charge in the nature of a feu-duty* ranking prior to all other charges on the land."

In saying this, John White knew the risk he was taking. He knew he would have to ask the Assembly to cancel by one stroke of the pen the most important clause of the Haldane Report, which it had formally accepted. And with the United Free Church he was running an even greater risk: for her committee had already frowned upon the heritors' plan of a land tax and had said that, if adopted, it might indeed "prove a hindrance to union". It was only too evident to him that its acceptance would embarrass Dr. Henderson and Principal Martin; but he was buoyed up with the conviction that by God's grace a way of conciliation would be found.

In the Lord Advocate's room on the Friday morning he had hardly made his announcement before the spokesman for the heritors, Sir John Milne Home, was expressing pleasure. But Milne Home was not so pleased when John White said that his agreement would depend on how far the heritors would go to meet him on a number of points. "We had to watch very vigilantly to safeguard the Church's patrimony," he said afterwards. He asked that the value of the chalder be written up. To take an average of fifty years, as Lord Haldane and Lord Novar had suggested, was not good enough in view of the big concession that was being made. He demanded an increase of seven per cent.

"This led to a stiff argument," he recorded. "The heritors pointed out that the land itself was a better security than the fruits of the land. An increase in the valuation of the chalder was out of the question."

John White made a number of other claims, and the battle continued. "Many present simply did not believe that agreement could be reached," he admitted, but he continued to press his demands. On the revaluation of the chalder, Sir John Milne Home eventually asked him how far he was willing to give way. He replied that, as a compromise, he would accept a five per cent increase. That was the critical moment of the interview.

John White's suggestion was accepted. This seemed to break the ice. Other adjustments quickly followed. And then, to the surprise and gratification of everyone, it was realised that, on all fundamental matters, an agreement between the heritors and the Church had been reached. The Lord Advocate rose and clasped John White's hand.

"Do you realise," he said, "that within the last few minutes, you have made Scottish history in this room. . . ."

VII

On Monday evening, at the private meeting of the General Assembly, John White announced the news.

"For weeks on end," he told members, "I have been engaged in negotiation. I was the only clergyman. The others were lawyers. I took courage when I thought of Daniel in a similar plight. Well, I have survived to tell the tale. One or two of the lions were purring behind me. I want to acknowledge the help given me by my joint convener, Mr. Millar, by my financial expert, Mr. Alexander Wallace —and of course the Procurator and the Agent, who attended but were not allowed to growl unless poked up on some question of law. . . .

"I was afraid we were faced with the impossible. But I knew we had to succeed. I knew Church union depended on a right settlement. I asked that only two of us should be allowed to handle the matter— Milne Home for the heritors, I myself for the Church. This was my last resort, and the Lord Advocate agreed. The rest listened and Milne Home and I talked. In a short time we were at one on the main issues. We had found agreement. The lawyers noted our findings. I am grateful to God it was Milne Home I had to deal with. He was as loyal and generous to the Church as I could have wished. He was ready to barter with me. . . ."

John White then told members of the main points on which agreement had been reached, and he added:

"The Lord Advocate was overjoyed. Instead of failure, I can now report to you a success which, if there be no hitch, will carry us forward to union."

It was nearly midnight before the lights were put out in the Hall.

Next afternoon, as two o'clock struck, John White rose to speak at the open meeting of the General Assembly. Every gallery was crowded and excitement ran high, for the news had flashed round Edinburgh that John White had reached agreement with the heritors. Dr. Norman Maclean described the scene in memorable words—the solemnity of it, the tension, the high hopes.

"To those of us who remember the first meeting of the union committees, the atmosphere that afternoon seemed almost incredible. Doubts had vanished; cavilling had ceased. It was to an Assembly already convinced that Dr. White began to speak. Few know the amount of self-sacrificing work he has given to the union movement. In season and out of season he has toiled. No difficulty has daunted him, no opposition discouraged him. And the Assembly showed their appreciation by the warmth of their welcome. . . . His speech was a human utterance. He gave the Assembly a glimpse of the dynamic force behind the union movement."

John White told how, before going to the final meeting with the heritors, he had quietly read the fourteenth chapter of Exodus:

"The words of it came home to my heart," he said. *"Fear ye not, stand still, and see the salvation of the Lord.* And it was as if the exhortation were specially for myself. *Speak unto the children of Israel that they go forward.* I went to the meeting on Friday morning with that message singing in my heart. The conviction possessed me that the way would open up. And at the meeting the way was indeed opened."

Dr. Norman Maclean said that John White's voice was thrilling with emotion as he spoke, and his hearers felt some of those unseen forces that shape the affairs of men. Presently he took his audience back to the day when the committees of the two Churches first met, and he recalled the prayer of the veteran Dr. Alexander Whyte:

"Our eyes are filled with a great vision. We pray that it may come, and come soon, and if the vision tarry we will wait for it, and when it cometh we will say, *This is the Lord, we have waited for Him and we will be glad in His salvation.* . . . The vision has tarried. The War retarded the work while it revealed the growing need. Many of those who that morning joined in Dr. Whyte's prayer have now joined him in the General Assembly of the Church of the First Born."

And he named them lovingly one by one, Balfour of Burleigh, Norman MacLeod, Scott of St. George's, Mair of Earlston, Robson and Denney and Taylor Innes, Fraser and MacEwen and many another—gallant crusaders who had not lived to reach the journey's end.

"The vision is not yet a reality," said John White. "In our waiting, we must not allow our courage and our faith to weaken, for never was a strong Church bearing a united testimony to Our Lord more needed in our beloved land. We must seek union—seek it to a triumphant finish. . . . It will be the fulfilment of the will of the Great Head of the Church Who desired to see His people have fellowship one with another that the world might believe."

And after the report submitted by John White had been unanimously approved, the leader of the Assembly, Dr. Ogilvie, rose and said, "This is the Lord's doing, it is marvellous in our eyes," and he moved that thanks be rendered to God. The Assembly stood in perfect stillness while the Moderator offered up a prayer of gratitude to God for the way by which He had led the Church.

"Never in the Assembly Hall had there been a moment of greater solemnity," said one who was there. When the Amen had been spoken, there was another silence. And then the feelings of all seemed to find sudden release. From the corner long known as Lord Balfour of Burleigh's place, the man who led the cheering that burst forth was the Lord High Commissioner himself. Because James Brown was an elder of the Church and wished to show his joy over the pact John White had made, he had not that afternoon taken his seat on the throne. His face showed the depth of his feelings as the great cheers of the Assembly rose again and again like surging waves. "Verily it was the Lord's doing."

Chapter XIV

"PRIMUS INTER PARES"

I

JOHN WHITE left the Assembly on that Tuesday afternoon with the cheers of his brethren in his ears. Well did he know that his reception might have been a very different one. Critical voices might have been upraised to tell him that his victory had been but a climb-down to the heritors. Had he not accepted their own plan of a land charge, which he had previously refused to consider? As to his persuading them to agree to put all churches and manses in good repair before handing them over to the Church, the heritors were being relieved thereafter of a vast annual burden in maintenance. Although he had won a five per cent increase in the value of the chalder,[1] had the heritors not gained more than they had given? . . . But in the General Assembly, on that Tuesday afternoon, there had been no hint of recriminations. If there were critics, they had been silent. The sign manual of the Assembly had been thankfully placed on the deed he had set before them. Among many letters of congratulation, one was from the Lord Advocate: "We should never have reached our satisfactory conclusion had it not been for your own admirable statesmanship." Lord Haldane wrote to him: "Your effort in the Assembly was a great one, and it was crowned with a great success. I congratulate you warmly. The Church owes much to your statesmanship." The Law Agent for the heritors wrote: "I sat through the debate and was greatly gratified by your masterly speech and by the magnificent result—enthusiastic unanimity. The Church and the Country will, I am sure, recognise that to your untiring efforts this splendid result is largely due. Thanks for your many kindly references to the Heritors' representatives, which we much appreciate, and which we can reciprocate with real good will."

If any churchman at that time could have looked three decades into the future, he would have been in little doubt about who had gained by the institution of a *fixed* stipend derived from the land. Warnings had indeed been given in the committee by those who, from the start, had feared that the Church was running the risk of financial loss in establishing

---

[1] "When I told Lord Sands that I had gained a five per cent increase from the heritors," John White wrote afterwards, "he could not believe his ears. It was estimated to bring in an additional £15,000 a year for the stipend fund."

a stipend that did not rise, as did stipend from teinds, with increases in the cost of living. The value of the chalder in 1919 had been so high that some heritors had protested they were paying three times the old stipend. By 1924 the chalder value was falling; it might fall further still; but might it not one day rise again—might it not rise, in some national crisis, to a height nobody then dreamed of? Would it not therefore be a good thing to create some scheme that linked the stipend with the cost of living, sharp fluctuations being avoided by taking each year an average of the previous decade? Those who uttered warnings were silenced by the reminder that the opinion of a great economic expert had been accepted. And so stipend and the cost of living were divorced; and because of that decree absolute, *the Church of Scotland was later to be deprived each year of a quarter of a million sterling of her ancient patrimony.*

It goes without saying that the heritors had neither intended nor anticipated that their plan would turn out to be so greatly to their advantage. Behind all their bargaining lay the principle they had been determined to maintain—that in place of teinds there should be a tax of some kind upon their land to fend off a worse evil. From the start of their talks, John White saw that the heritors had the Church of Scotland in a cleft stick. Alexander Wallace had said in the Assembly: "Full well they knew that behind everything lay the question of union—and how far they might have pressed that knowledge! We must respect them for having played the game. The historic bond between the heritors and the Church remains untouched."

II

Dr. Henderson received with dismay the news of the agreement John White had made. His union committee, asked to comment on the land-charge plan, had expressed their disapproval; and in the very hour when the Church of Scotland Assembly had been applauding John White for having accepted the plan of the heritors, the United Free Church Assembly had been agreeing that it "would create grave practical difficulties and might prove a hindrance to union".

The situation was one of considerable delicacy. In an effort to meet the objections he expected to be raised by his own people, Dr. Henderson wrote to John White to say that some of the sting might perhaps be taken out of land charges if a civil trust were formed to collect them from land-owners and to sue defaulters in the courts, "so that the Church would not appear as the aggressive creditor". Also, he said, those in the United Free

Church who detested State endowments of any kind and under any name might be a little comforted to know that the money from the landlords would be kept, on behalf of the Church, in a special fund isolated from voluntary contributions. In the same letter he gave John White in confidence a sufficiently broad hint of his personal opinion on the land charge. He did not regard it as a matter of principle. The *practical difficulties*, referred to in his committee's Report and accepted by the Assembly, did not involve any "fundamental difficulties which are matters of conscience". In fact, he personally was prepared to accept land charges in place of teinds, and he added: "I see great advantages in being able to show how 'grave difficulties' may be met without offending those whose desire is for union." But he was sharply aware that much careful, discreet, and persuasive work would have to be done before many in his Church could be reconciled to the step John White had taken.

Principal Martin was in a like frame of mind. To John White he wrote:

"We understand one another fully. You and I, at all events, have no thought on Church union except how it may be carried out effectively and smoothly. . . . The mere possibility of setting up a 'wee' United Free Church in Scotland makes one's heart sick. We must strain every nerve to prevent it. What can be done to placate them? We ourselves are trying our hardest. . . . But it is from your side only that anything can be accomplished."

Knowing the opposition there would be to the land-charge scheme, he too suggested a way by which he thought that many might be pacified. There was an Exchequer grant, made to maintain certain churches, amounting to some seventeen thousand pounds a year, and Martin wondered whether this could not be given up altogether. "A gesture here," he said, "might have a wonderfully mollifying effect. . . . Also, it would look well all round. We ought not to do good works to be seen of men; but if, in carrying this business through, we can do the handsome we shall lose nothing by it." [1]

---

[1] On the proposals of his two friends in the United Free Church, John White has left a memorandum. Of Dr. Henderson's suggestion, he stated that "the points were met but not in the way he suggested; stipends were no longer to be dealt with by the minister of a parish but by the General Trustees". On Principal Martin's proposal he wrote: "I could not agree; it would have made a minority of considerable size in *our* Church. He and others did not realise that the Exchequer Grant did not affect our negotiations with the heritors. These monies, £17,040, do not come from heritors but from ecclesiastical property in the hands of the Crown. Lord Sands and Professor Paterson advised me to give them up, while conserving life-interests. I did not, I could not, and later on I had them redeemed after negotiations with the Treasury, adding to the capital funds of the Church a sum between £130,000 and £150,000."

Very different from the conciliatory mood of these United Free Church leaders was the attitude of the dissentients led by the Rev. James Barr. They conducted their campaign in pulpits, on platforms, and in the press. Some of them confidently believed they would one day bring the union movement to a halt. The resignation of one of the joint conveners of the United Free Church union committee, Dr. John Young, had been a shock to many people. He had been a leader in the movement from the beginning, but he now was advising delay and denouncing State endowments. His action gave support to those already in James Barr's camp, and inclined others to join them. Barr himself was a man of many outstanding qualities. Like Professor Cooper, the good friend of John White's who had striven with him in the union committee, he was passionately sincere, and he felt he had a mission to prevent union with a Church that was determined to maintain the flow into her coffers of State endowments to which she had no moral claim. John White had always liked James Barr and respected him, and now he fought him tooth and nail. They exchanged fiery letters in the press, and neither of them minced words.

"One could not meet a kindlier man than Mr. Barr," wrote John White in *The Glasgow Herald*, "but so far as Church union is concerned his kindliness always leaves one cold. His approach to union irresistibly reminds one of how Joab treated Amasa. 'And Joab said to Amasa, Art thou in health, my brother? And Joab took Amasa by the beard with the right hand to kiss him. But Amasa took no heed to the sword that was in Joab's hand; so he smote him therewith in the fifth rib.' "

James Barr had been "in kindly conference" over union since 1909, and had made no demur to the joint statement subscribed by both Churches; but after thus coming forward to kiss, John White said he was now using the sword. When he had given Barr a trouncing in a column of print twenty inches long, he added the hope that they would both now work together "as fellow-ministers in the United, Free, National Church".

James Barr's determination to wreck the union grew firmer as the months went by. He had formed the United Free Church Association: and since this was an unofficial body, there were protests because its name led people to believe it had been officially instituted by the Church. Although its directors had nothing new to say, and but raised again what John White called "the old battle-cries", it became an effective propaganda machine. James Barr offered himself as a Parliamentary candidate, won a seat at Motherwell for the Socialists, and continued with increasing fervour to urge members of the United Free Church to oppose the union.

Throughout all the years of controversy, John White and he maintained their friendship. Professor Allan Barr (who followed his father in rejecting a union he could not conscientiously approve of) has thrown a ray of sweet and gentle light on that friendship and has shown how it had been cemented in the midst of war-time loss and sorrow:

> "My brother James had been serving in the R.N.V.R., and after an Atlantic crossing had been given leave, and had joined the family on holiday at Grantown-on-Spey. Dr. White and his family were there on holiday also. My brother went down with a sudden illness, contracted on war service, and died. At my father's request, Dr. White at the funeral service read the hymn 'Shall we gather at the river?' which my mother had so often sung to her children. Many years later, recalling past times, my father told Dr. White that at every funeral service since that day at Grantown-on-Spey he had repeated the same hymn. To which Dr. White replied, 'So have I.' In the words of my father, 'Such is the strong chord of tender and mutual sympathy which links us all together, stronger and more enduring than all the discords of ecclesiastical strife.'"

III

The speedy passage of the Bill through Parliament now became John White's chief concern. He wrote to Ramsay MacDonald asking him how quickly it could be put through: "There is a national desire to have this settled. I have had letters of congratulation from all ranks, all Churches,[1] all political parties; they regarded the Assembly of 1924 as the positive and constructive complement of the negative and disruptive 1843." Alan Menzies, the Church's Law Agent, spent much time in London working with the Lord Advocate over the proposed amendments. He found it heavy going, and John White hurried south at the end of June to help him:

> "I remember one very hot Sunday afternoon (I had been at church in the morning) sitting in the Scottish Office, along with Alan Menzies and the officials, all with their jackets off—the Lord Advocate

[1] This was not wholly accurate. The following telegram was later sent to Parliament: "Baptist Union of Scotland hostile meeting to-day earnestly urges that the Church of Scotland Endowments Bill be not passed on the ground of religious equality for all citizens."

and myself with our jackets on. We were working at the Bill that had to be submitted on Tuesday in the House of Lords. It was a Bill that cost much perspiration and a good deal of inspiration, and probably one of the most complicated Bills that passed through the Scottish Office for many years."

John White was present at the uneventful third reading on 1st July. Since it had been first introduced in the House of Lords, it had still to go through the Commons, and its fate there was uncertain. James Brown was worried over "the increasing virulence of certain members of Parliament. . . . There is no question," he warned John White, "that a tremendous effort is being made against us." In September, Lord Balfour of Burleigh was becoming anxious about the Bill:

"Are you satisfied," he wrote to John White, "that room for it has definitely been allotted in the House of Commons this autumn? The Lord Chancellor told me he was afraid there was a very real risk that the Bill would be crowded out. He was keen that there should be a deputation to the Prime Minister. Better not say the stimulus comes from him."

Will Adamson, the miners' leader who had become Secretary of State for Scotland, was pressed to help. John White spoke and wrote to many people who were reckoned to have influence with the Prime Minister, and he led a deputation to meet Will Adamson and made a speech that was widely reported. Then, in the late autumn, there was a political upheaval. The Liberals withdrew their support; Ramsay MacDonald's Government fell; and after a General Election, Stanley Baldwin again became Prime Minister. For John White, there followed many weeks of exhausting activity. He did his best to influence men in all three parties; he saw the Prime Minister at Chequers; he had meetings with Sir John Gilmour, the new Secretary of State for Scotland; he maintained contact with William Watson, now back in the post of Lord Advocate. Because the Bill was everybody's business, John White was afraid it would become nobody's business, particularly since no political capital was to be made out of it. Lord Younger of Leckie cheered him by saying he thought the change of government would be in the Church's favour. Pressure was increased, and with joy John White read in the King's Speech in mid-December that the Scottish Church Bill would come up in the next session. At once Dr. Archibald Fleming of St. Columba's, who had taken a hand in the work behind the political scenes, made his acknowledgment: "I am sure it is due to your diplomacy that the Bill has this excellent place assigned to it."

Those who were with John White constantly at this time have said that he found no period in his work for Church union quite so harassing as the next few months. His eyes were focused on Westminster. He was determined that no impediment which he personally could remove must be allowed to stop, or even slow down, the progress of the Bill. After it had been passed, his final work for the consummation of the union would lie among the churchfolk of Scotland, and he would be in his own element again. He knew where he stood with churchfolk, even though they opposed him: he was never quite sure of the politicians.

IV

The debate on the second reading in the House of Commons took place on 10th February 1925. The whole intention and scope of the Bill was heavily bludgeoned from the opposition benches. That the attack should come from that quarter struck John White and others as odd since the Bill had been steered through the House of Lords by a Socialist Chancellor who was still ready to support it. The debate was much more fiery than the one in the Commons over the 1921 Bill, and there were two outstanding maiden speeches by the Rev. James Barr and Rosslyn Mitchell.

Barr attacked Exchequer Grants, Burgh Grants and teinds, as if he were back in his pulpit attacking the works of the devil. He quoted Winston Churchill, then Chancellor of the Exchequer, as having said that when a Church was freed from the State it became powerful, zealous, and went down into the homes of the people, whereas in the hands of the State it lost its fervour. He declared that the Bill would merely support a disastrous privilege granted to the Church of Scotland— a privilege flagrantly unjust to all other sections of the community. Rosslyn Mitchell, a Glasgow lawyer, was more subtle and picked his points with the forensic skill that was one day to make him the executioner-in-chief of the English Prayer Book Bill. He told of a church in the business heart of Glasgow, St. George's, the property of the Corporation and subsidised by it even to the cost of the bread and wine used at the Communion services. This church was no longer necessary, but its site was valuable. Under the Bill, all churches would be handed over to the Church of Scotland. What would she do with it? Tear it down and sell the site for a quarter of a million! He spoke of two young friends of his, ex-servicemen, who had bought a farm and were struggling to make it pay. Suddenly they were served with a bill of seventy-five pounds, their share of the teinds—more than they had earned in a year. Was it fair? "Let the Church of Scotland have faith in the people!" he cried. "The people of Scotland have never failed the Church yet. If the Church of Scotland had faith in the people, she would never lack voluntary gifts. The day she lacks voluntary gifts, she ought to know her day is done."

After Will Adamson and James Maxton and others had spoken, it was plain that, although they failed to win a majority of votes, there would be fireworks in the Scottish Grand Committee. John White received an anxious letter from Sir John MacLeod: "The Rev. James Barr and his satellites will be indomitable in putting down amendments. He knows the subject and will coach his friends, who will form a debating group in opposition. Unfortunately . . . there will be very few Scottish members able to back up the Lord Advocate in debate. What can we do to overcome that?"

The surest way to overcome it was taken by John White. So that he could be on hand to give an expert answer to every question, he got a seat in the Committee Room at Westminster, with a desk placed for him beyond the bar.[1] "I was constantly referred to," he said, "at times even by those who opposed the Bill." At the first session he felt like knocking together the heads of some Scottish members who hurled about remarks more suitable for a back-street of the Gorbals. He was glad to record that a later discussion on the small heritors was "conducted on a higher level", and the same night he wrote a letter to the Scottish press asking ministers of the Church of Scotland to send him full details about all heritors who paid a shilling or less in teind. The result was that these were relieved of their small burdens. In the final draft of the Bill, heritors in the next group who paid up to one pound were obliged to redeem the teinds on an eighteen years' purchase and with the same length of time to pay: while all who paid more than one pound would come under a perpetual land charge, with the option of making a private redemption bargain with the Church. Between meetings of the Grand Committee, White hurried back to Scotland and came to an agreement with the Edinburgh and the Glasgow corporations on Burgh and City churches. He had previously

---

[1] "I seem to be an expert in teind law," he had written, "and the amazing thing is that the intricacies of teinds know no law. Any knowledge I possess must be judged, not with reference to the thing itself, but by comparison with the ignorance of others."

had to face the Law Agent of the Free Church over a demand for a money grant in northern districts where the Wee Frees claimed that they predominated. Two Church of Scotland ministers in the north had made careful enquiries and reported to John White that the claim of the Wee Free leaders that "their Church was doing the work of the national Church had no foundation in fact—on the contrary, our ministers are in many parishes doing pastoral work for the Free Church which it cannot do owing to an insufficient ministry". The Law Agent of the Wee Frees then bowed his head and withdrew the claim, and so John White spared the Standing Committee from yet another wrangle.[1] The twelfth and last session was held on 7th April, and the Bill successfully passed its third reading in the House of Commons five weeks later. At once John White wrote to Lord Balfour of Burleigh asking how soon it could be put through the House of Lords and receive Royal Assent. It would be a tragedy, he said, if delay at Westminster should hold up the union movement until after the next Assembly. Lord Balfour of Burleigh replied that he would do what he could, but it was touch and go whether the Bill could be passed through the House of Lords in time for the union debate in the Assembly on Tuesday, 26th May. On its second reading on 19th May it was sponsored by Lord Balfour himself, who made a notable contribution to union in a speech that was well-informed and statesmanlike. The Duke of Buccleuch supported it as strongly as he had disapproved of the original Novar Bill; the Archbishop of Canterbury benignly congratulated everyone concerned; and the Bill had its second reading in an atmosphere that was a good deal sweeter than that of the House of Commons. John White heard the news from Westminster with feelings of gratitude to those who that day had shown themselves to be good friends to the Church of Scotland.

V

Many leaders of the Church had hoped that 1925 would be one of the most important years in the history of the union movement. The great

---

[1] "One looks forward to the day," wrote John White, "when the Free Church, which holds in common with the Church of Scotland so much that is essential to the religious welfare of the people, and retains in several parishes the affections of many who, though outwith the pale of the Church of Scotland, are yet faithful to it, will see its way to co-operate, if not indeed to unite, in the same spiritual ministry. . . . After legislation has been passed, one would hope that a conference between the Churches would be possible, and that this would lead to some better and less wasteful methods of supplying religious ordinances in many parishes than are in use at present."

John White in 1925 during his first Moderatorship of the
General Assembly.

things that had been promised in 1911, when the Report drafted by John White had been accepted by the Assembly, were coming to pass. The claim of the Church of Scotland that she possessed spiritual autonomy as an inherent right had been acknowledged by Parliament in its Act of 1921. And now the day was drawing near when another Act would be placed beside it on the Statute Book—an Act that would give the Church of Scotland full control over her "temporalities". She would continue to be the National Church: but now she would also be free, with the jurisdiction of her ecclesiastical courts confirmed by the State. There was to be a new era for the Church of Scotland, and the General Assembly of 1925 would, it was confidently believed, mark the beginning of it. To those who had the task of nominating the Moderator, it seemed that nothing could be more fitting than that the honour should be bestowed upon John White. There seemed to be a grand inevitability about it, and he was duly selected. Three hundred and sixty-five years had passed since the Reformation, and, as John White himself said of 1925, "this is to be the year of years".

The Assembly, with the Earl of Elgin as the Lord High Commissioner, opened on 19th May, the very day when the Property and Endowments Bill was having its second reading in the House of Lords. Until it had successfully passed its third reading, John White could make no announcement to the Assembly that it was through Parliament. It was on the 26th—the following Tuesday—that he was scheduled to make his report to the Assembly on the Bill and propose that the 1921 Articles be sent down to presbyteries under the Barrier Act so that they could become the law of the Church. At the same time, the passage of the Bill through Parliament would clear the way for the United Free Church Assembly to ask presbyteries, kirk sessions, and congregations whether they now considered that all obstacles to union had been removed.

To his dismay, John White learned that, even if the peers reluctantly agreed to put the Bill through with exceptional speed, they would not be meeting on Monday, 25th May, and so Tuesday, the 26th, was the earliest day that the Bill could have its final reading. This would be too late, for that was the day on which he would have to make his report. He asked himself what he could do to prevent the union movement from being held up for a whole year.

Those who knew John White personally have exchanged many stories about him—stories which will keep his legend alive in the Church of Scotland for many a day—and his action at this time has often been recalled:

> "The House of Lords would not sit that Monday. But if the Church Bill were not put through on the Monday, it would be too late for the Assembly. . . . For the life of him, John White couldn't see why the House of Lords shouldn't be made to bestir itself, cut short its week-end and meet on Monday. So he sent a telegram to London to say that the House of Lords *must* sit on Monday. . . . And it did!"

With a thankful heart, John White was able to tell the Assembly on Tuesday that the Bill had passed through Parliament.[1] Save for the adjustment of details, the property and endowments of the Church of Scotland was a subject no longer *sub judice*, and the Bill would in due time be placed upon the Statute Book. John White asked the Assembly to recognise with gratitude the "friendly action of His Majesty's government in introducing and granting facilities for the passing of the Bill". It was agreed at once that the declaratory Articles of 1921 be sent down to presbyteries under the Barrier Act. John White made it clear that it was not until the presbyteries had given their assent, and the Articles had been embodied in an Act by the next Assembly, that the Churches could begin work together on fully detailed plans for the consummation of union.

Throughout that Assembly, John White was accepted as *primus inter pares*. The words of John Prosser, W.S., the Crown Agent, in a letter to him the previous November, have relevance here: "There is clamant occasion for a leader of spiritual fervour, a statesman and tactician, learned in the historical and legal and technical aspects of the complicated matter of union now before the Church, and I am fully persuaded that the Church has found the man to fit the occasion." It was indeed so. John White accepted the position, to which events had elevated him, with no special feelings of pride: rather did he count it a task which he felt, in all humility, he was equipped to carry out. And he accepted the praise of wise and knowledgeable men as confirmation that he had worked hard and well. To the flattery of the many he was impervious.

A contributor to a Scottish newspaper wrote at this time:

> "In his youth the Rev. John White was a prodigy; he is now a portent. . . . For many years past, the Crusader has been a figure

[1] This was largely due to the efforts of Lord Balfour of Burleigh, who explained later to John White that he "managed to demolish the opposition of some sticklers for etiquette among the Liberal peers".

conspicuous by his absence from the Moderatorial Chair. The assiduous, careful, calculating, committee man has been frequently there; also the faithful pastor and the eminent scholar: but Douglas, with the heart of Bruce embalmed in a casket, going to wrest a jewel from the Turk did not happen to arise. Have we got him now? . . . It is said that the need brings forth the man. Certainly the need is national, even imperial. It is held on every side that if Dr. White had chosen to 'carve a career' in politics, he must have been included in any outstanding Cabinet—or that he would have splendidly adorned the highest office in the Law. The tributes are no more than just to his proportions. One likes to think of him not merely or even chiefly as a modern ecclesiastical statesman, but as that gigantic phenomenon— a throw-back to ampler and more heroic times. Irresistibly, there grows upon you the impression of 'a very perfect gentle knight'. The athletic and ascetic stature; the poised head and sculptured brow; those eagle eyes lit with responsive tenderness; that governing nose; those aristocratic lips and the dauntless chin—these do not belong to our modern age. . . . And if one is not mistaken, Dr. John White intends to break the juggernaut which in this scientific age is crushing the souls out of human beings."

VI

Those who had been most closely associated with him have said that the work which had fallen upon his shoulders from the beginning of his ministry, and particularly during the most trying years of the union movement, would never have been done so well if his days had not been deliberately and minutely organised. Early in his life he realised the value of efficiency, and it was this subject that he chose as the theme of his closing address as Moderator. Here was a challenge which he threw down to all churchfolk, clerical and lay. One point he wished specially to make:

"The union of the Churches is not an end in itself: it is for the great purpose—that the world may believe. It may provide us with a more efficient ecclesiastical machine, but that will depend for its movement on the dynamic of God. It is not forces in equilibrium, but forces in motion, that are effective in the world's progress. . . . The Church needs more efficient organisation; not less does it need men and women full of faith and vision if there is to be spiritual efficiency. Within our Church there are many known to God whose faith is

JOHN WHITE

vital and true; but one cannot close one's eyes to the fact that, while many of our three-quarters of a million communicants have some link with the faith of their fathers, their interest in the advance of Christ's Kingdom is languid. A respectable institution of respectable people, whose standards are traditional good form, with small provision for penitence and the heroism of faith, is not the ideal of a Christian Church. . . ."

At the end of his address he spoke these words:

"Another assembly-parliament occupied with things pertaining to the Kingdom of Jesus Christ now draws to a close. Opinions on matters affecting the constitution and the activities of the Church have been expressed with energy and keenness and candour, but no one will return to his parish with wounded feelings, for all have sought the common good of the Church they love and serve. Our prayer and hope is that this Assembly will prove to have done something to deepen and quicken our interest in the work of Christ, and to bring new inspirations to the hearts and minds of all. . . . Ministers will return to their pulpits in time for Whitsunday. It will be a fit occasion to emphasise the brooding, fructifying power of the Holy Spirit. Nothing that this Assembly has done will amount to much until 'the flaming torrent of fire' fall upon the Church throughout the land."

Chapter XV

ARCHITECT OF UNION

I

IMMEDIATELY after the rising of the Assembly of 1925, John White received a letter from his old friend Dr. Henderson, now approaching his ninetieth year. He had come over from the other Assembly and had been given a seat on a front bench so that he could hear the speeches. He wrote:

> "Dear Moderator, Very many thanks for the gift of your closing address. I thank you for it and for the message it carried to the Churches of Scotland. Many incidents of our past years were called to mind, and especially of the early years when there were with us so many now gone. . . . The delays were trying to us both, but we can see now how essential these patient labours were. . . .Whatever occurs to cause a halt—I pray nothing will—do not let go your full assurance of the sincere and devoted purpose of the brethren of the United Free Church to see this through for the blessing of Scotland and the honour of our common Lord. Yours sincerely, Arch. Henderson."

It was with this benediction that John White set out on his moderatorial tour of Scotland. He had said he was anxious that the folk in the more remote parts would not feel neglected by the Moderator, and this guided him in planning what turned out to be an intricate and exhausting itinerary. It had not been the practice of Moderators to make so many long journeys among the outlying presbyteries, and John White left to his successors a legacy of travel that was to take its toll of many a Moderator's strength. People in all parts of the country were eager to hear for themselves what the great protagonist of union had to say about it—and some had questions to put to him. Thus it fell out that his tour became a union tour. The declaratory Articles were before presbyteries under the Barrier Act. John White felt that here was a God-sent chance to speak in distant shires of how the Kirk had won back her spiritual freedom from the State and of the union he hoped would come soon. It was a chance also to confer with ministers—particularly the younger ones who had been schoolboys when the first joint conference had been held and who had followed the union movement only in its later years. From some of these men he had received questioning letters. One wrote to him:

> "My position is this. I feel there are strong reasons why our two Churches should be united. But I would not care to sit an examination on these reasons. In this I am like many others of the younger clergy. We have come into this movement at a time when a great deal we are not familiar with is simply taken for granted. If we had more data to work on when we address our congregations, we could turn their acquiescence into enthusiasm. I would claim that my need of education is representative."

The task of enlightenment was one that went with him everywhere on his journeys.

II

In his personal diary, the entry of Saturday, 11th July 1925, reads: "Travelled off to begin work in Tain—10 days allotted." This took him into the north-east of Scotland, beyond the Moray Firth. On Sunday the 12th he preached both at Tarbat and at Tain, where the service was a joint one with the United Free Church. Next day he travelled to Edderton, then on to Fearn, to Nigg, to Logie Easter, to Kilmuir Easter, to Rosskeen, and on Sunday preached both there and at Ardross. He took a day off to fish on Monday and then went on to Kincardine. On Wednesday he was at Creich, and on Friday attended a conference of the Dornoch presbyteries of both Churches at Golspie on the coast. He conducted three services on Sunday, one at Clyne, another at Loth, and a third at Helmsdale; he pushed on to Lairg, Assynt, Lochinver, Stoer, then from the Atlantic shore he travelled back across Scotland, arriving again at Dornoch, to preach there in the morning and go north to take a service at Golspie in the evening. Still there was no question of his making tracks for home. Westward across Scotland he went again, this time to Oban, toured that part of the country, preaching and speaking, and sailed to Iona to take a service there on the following Sunday. From the port of Mallaig he sailed to the small isles, Canna and Eigg, then took the steamer north to Glenelg, motored to Glenshiel and Lochalsh, went on to Plockton, made the long journey inland to Garve, travelled up into the north-west towards Loch Broom and at last reached Ullapool, where he preached on Sunday, 23rd August. By Tuesday he was back at

Dingwall and spent the night at Inverness. He had resisted the temptation to "travel light". Feeling he had a duty to look the part of a Moderator in the eyes of the folk who dwelt in lonely places, he took his robes with him and stood up in the little Highland churches, a memorable figure panoplied in the splendour of black silk and white lace.

On the last week-end of August, he was a guest of King George V at Balmoral and preached at Crathie kirk on Sunday. Travelling again westward, he addressed the Synod of Argyll at the parish church of Dunoon two days later. His speech there was widely reported in the West country. His theme was that God was moving in their midst, and it was a higher Christian statesmanship to discover a divine direction to remove all hindrances to union. He spoke of the wastage there had been, and told of a young minister who had been called to a kirk in a parish with a total population of six hundred—and to serve them there were four churches. "Did any one of these ministers win over a family from one of the other churches?" he asked. "And was there rejoicing in heaven over the snatching of a brand from the burning? . . . No!—but there was rejoicing in hell over the friction caused in that parish." Before the meeting closed, Sir Norman Lamont of Knockdow recalled John White's speech in the Assembly of 1924: "Until that speech had been delivered, we had questioned union with doubt and even hostility, but from that time there has been no question—all were unanimous. We are convinced that union is for the greater glory of God, and agreement on it is due more to Dr. White than to any living man." On 7th September, after an absence of two months of travel, John White returned home.

Until the beginning of November, he made Glasgow his base. His diary shows the usual round of duties that fall to a Moderator: public meetings, special services, after-dinner speeches, bazaars and sales of work, centenary celebrations. . . . The list could be formidably prolonged. In the five days from the 3rd to the 7th November there is a record of his having visited twenty manses as well as being present at a variety of meetings and receptions in different parts of the county of Angus. Dr. A. W. Fergusson wrote of a presbytery meeting in Dundee:

"It was of course in private, that the discussion might be of the frankest. None of us were hostile but many had real difficulties; and these were fired at him point blank. A dozen bowlers, each with a new ball. All of us were doing our uttermost to break his Church-union wicket. Talk about Hobbs! White was the perfect batsman. He made his century that day, his double century, without a single weak stroke. And revelled in it all the time! Though he was a sorely done man when I proposed that stumps be drawn, the whole presbytery gave him an ovation for his matchlesss exhibition of power and skill.... We had never seen such a brilliant feat. To hear a great oratorical triumph—well, that was rare enough, though we have had his equal these last years in our General Assembly. But to do what White did that day was what we have never seen another man do so supremely well."

The same minister gave his impression of John White, as Moderator, in action: "With a razor-edged hatchet, he cleaves between what really matters and what doesn't matter at all—till all that is subsidiary has been lopped off and cleared away, and only the central and abiding fact remains: so the mind of our new Moderator works."

Because there are few things the Scot enjoys more than a good argument, folk crowded to his meetings to have their doubts and fears demolished; and if some came to catch him out on a point of history, law, or procedure, the others were able to enjoy the deft way he picked off his opponents. Always he seemed to revel in controversy: he would have shone in the disputations held at mediaeval university courts. "Opposition," he said, "has great value if it leads people to reflect on the urgent need—and the great gain—of Church reunion in Scotland. Questions of national magnitude are never settled with unanimity except where there is widespread apathy. An active opposition ensures that nothing is settled without careful scrutiny." That solid serious work was done at these many meetings there can be no doubt; the records are an ample testimony.

Early in the New Year, he was off on his travels again. He visited the Presbytery of Ayr, went south into the Stewartry to take in towns, villages, and landward kirks in the Presbytery of Dumfries; a little later he was back on the east coast visiting St. Andrews and a score of other places. Times innumerable he must have told the same union story, but there was no flagging in his enthusiasm; to the very end of his tour, newspaper correspondents referred to the zest and vitality of his speeches.

When his great task as Moderator had been completed, one of his chaplains, the minister of Langside Parish Church in Glasgow, the Rev. J. McNeill Frazer, sent him a grateful note:

"On getting home, my heart tells me that the first thing to do is to write a few words saying how intensely glad your chaplains are that you have been enabled to complete your year of high office in such a memorable manner and with such benefit to our beloved Church. You have set an example which not all future Moderators may be able to follow, but your journeyings will become a treasured memory in many manses, and they have shown to the Church at large what can be done by one whose soul is on fire to the Glory of God and for the uplifting of Scotland to a still closer witness for Our blessed Lord. . . . It will be a joy to look back upon this past year and watch for the growing fruits of your unwearied labours, which will only deepen our belief that you have been God's Man for this *annus mirabilis*."

III

On 3rd May 1926 there began the calamitous General Strike, which partially paralysed Britain for nine days. The Assembly met as arranged in the week after the strike had been broken, but it was thought well to adjourn until the first day of June to give time for the printers, who had been on strike, to prepare the Assembly reports and other papers. The United Free Church had made a similar decision. The great hour of excitement in both Assemblies was when the vote was taken on union. There had been little doubt about the approval of the declaratory Articles by the Old Kirk presbyteries. The response had been overwhelming, and only a sparse half-dozen members represented the minority which had fought so stoutly in the union committee since 1909. But it was a different story in the United Free Church Assembly. Over a hundred members declared against the motion that the obstacles to union had now been removed. Eighteen per cent against union! To John White, the news of this vote came as a grievous disappointment.

He realised that the so-called United Free Church Association had been more successful than he had thought. "The unceasing flow of literature from anti-unionists," he had written, "has misled a few as to their numerical strength." And he had thrown out a challenge: "It is high time that the Churches, and especially the laity, were making it clear that they not only welcome union but that they demand it." The anti-unionists were still beating the old war-drums. It was an iniquitous thing, they cried, that the United Free Church, a Church which accepted not one penny of State aid, should unite with a Church in which stipends had been paid out of teinds and which was now to receive the support of a permanent charge upon the land. John White took a suitable opportunity to remind them that the United Free Church had, in fact, received benefits from the State in the form of money, property, and privileges. In 1923, for foreign missions, she had received a State grant of nearly a hundred thousand pounds; again, in the foreign mission field, she had received a grant of land in Livingstonia five times the area of Glasgow; she had built the church at Gretna with a grant; she had received State grants for her naval and military chaplains; she had enjoyed the perquisite of complete freedom from national taxation on over ten million pounds' worth of property and investments; and her places of worship were free from local rates, so that taxpayers of all religious denominations (and of none) were providing, as a gift to the United Free Church, police protection, sanitation, drainage, water, and other public services. No shame indeed to the United Free Church for accepting these grants and privileges! But to maintain that she never on principle accepted a penny from the State, and to say in the same breath that the endowments of the Church of Scotland were iniquitous and unjust, was preposterous. John White was careful to add that he had the greatest respect for the Voluntaries of the old days who believed it was a God-imposed duty upon them to pay for their "means of grace".

To counteract the activities of James Barr's anti-union group, the leaders of the United Free Church made plans to lay before all ministers, office-bearers, and members the true story of the union movement. A committee, known as the Publicity Sub-Committee, was formed to prepare and distribute pamphlets throughout the country. One of these was designed to blow sky-high the opinion, once widely accepted in non-established Churches, that teinds were a State bounty that saved all Old Kirk congregations the trouble of dipping very deeply into their pockets. Many folk were surprised to learn that, among the fifteen hundred congregations of the Church of Scotland, less than nine hundred of their ministers drew stipend from teinds—and many of that number drew only part of their stipend. The free-will offerings in the Church of Scotland amounted to considerably more than three times the total amount of the teinds in an average year. These and other facts were plainly set forth by United Free Church ministers and laymen, and gave the pause to many who had been accustomed to say that "Old Kirk folk were never taught to give".

What passed John White's comprehension was the attitude of James Barr and his friends to the Church of Scotland's Declaratory Articles ratified by Parliament in 1921 and now a Church Act. Times without number in recent days they had stated that these did not establish the spiritual freedom of the Old Kirk. The United Free Church was *free*,

James Barr insisted; the Church of Scotland was not. In a public speech in Aberdeen, Principal Martin took up the point with a clarity that was characteristic of the man:

> "There is, let us remind ourselves, no such thing as an absolute or abstract freedom. A Church neither has, nor can be accorded, freedom to be anything but itself, true to its own character, faithful to its Lord. It is no hardship, therefore, to be told that a Church must have a permanent substratum . . . and that the law will not support a Church for objects changeable at will. The United Free Church has its permanent substratum, namely, Trinitarian Protestantism, which it neither desires *nor is at liberty* to alter."

And a few weeks later he publicly threw down the gauntlet to all those who appeared to imagine that, because they claimed to have spiritual freedom, they had the liberty to alter the fundamentals of their creed:

> "Adherence to the catholic and evangelical faith, as interpreted by the Church, is essential to the continuity and corporate life of the Church. . . . On these terms we shall continue to hold our property. If we should desire at any time to change the doctrinal terms of our title, would it be any hardship to have to seek Civil Authority before we would be free to do so?"

These words were, explicitly, an admission that the United Free Church was secure in the tenure of her funds and property *only as long as she adhered to the fundamentals of the doctrines she upheld.* In that respect, she was on precisely the same basis as the Church of Scotland. If any of the substance of the credal statement in the first of the declaratory Articles were altered by the Assembly, the funds and property of the Church of Scotland would at once be in jeopardy.

As John White had pointed out from the start of the disputes in his own union committee, the credal statement, imposed by Professor Cooper and others, would be crystallised as soon as it became law—and only with the sanction of Parliament could it thereafter be altered by an Act of Assembly. And there could be no doubt whatever that this would equally apply, in days to come, to the united Church.

IV

It was inevitable that the torches carried by some of the older leaders in the union movement would have to be taken into the hands of younger men. Not many weeks after the 1926 Assembly rose, Dr. Wallace Williamson was to pass away; with sweetness and devotion, he had given of his best to the cause. Frailty had for some little time prevented that great old leader in the United Free Church, Dr. Archibald Henderson, from taking an active part, although his interest in union was as acute as it had ever been. The end of that richly fruitful life was now to be not long distant, and in the following April he died at his home in Crieff, where at the graveside of his old friend John White was to pronounce the prayer of committal. Dr. Henderson's son, Professor Robert Candlish Henderson, wrote on behalf of the family to John White:

"It is to us a happy remembrance that the last service was by one for whom my father had so deep an admiration and affection. . . . Never did he think it possible that he should be spared to see the union, but he rejoiced that he had lived to see the long train of preparation reach a stage which, in his eyes, made the final completion of the work inevitable."

But although younger men had of necessity to take up the duties of those who could no longer serve, there were still many familiar names left among the members of the new committees appointed by each Church to arrange the details of corporate union. John White and Lord Sands were joint conveners of the Church of Scotland committee; the Rev. J. Hutchison Cockburn of Dunblane Cathedral, later to become an outstanding figure in Scottish Church life, was appointed Secretary, and Mr. E. F. Gibson clerk. The corresponding men in the United Free Church were Principal Martin, Dr. R. J. Drummond, and Dr. A. N. Bogle. Confronting them was a formidable array of tasks. They had to review all the documents, old and new, of the two Churches and to make joint recommendations on the constitution and powers of the Church courts; on the training, election, and appointment of ministers, and on the position of divinity faculties in the universities and United Free Church theological colleges; on property and finance, on Assembly committees, the rules and forms of procedure, on relations with other Churches, and on sundry other matters. Seven sub-committees were formed,[1] and these in their turn had so many satellite committees that at one time there were

---

[1] When Lord Sands heard that, in addition to being joint conveners of the committee, John White and he had been appointed conveners of the sub-committee on the Basis of Union, he sent this *cri du cœur* to his colleague: "I was horrified to learn that they have made us conveners of the sub-committee on the 'Basis'. I had thought we were to be left with a roving commission—and that some younger or less tired man would take this on. Oh dear, am I to be up against Article One again?"

no fewer than thirty-one separate committee meetings held in one week. It was work in which every detail, every turn of phrase, might one day be of critical importance. Dr. Hutchison Cockburn had the task of co-ordination, and his guiding hand was felt everywhere. He has left it on record that John White's driving power had never been so forceful and inspiring: "He was like a man on fire with zeal to bring matters to a successful end." Because of overwork, Cockburn himself became ill, but he set himself grimly to struggle through: "I felt it would have been nothing less than treachery to John White if I had taken even a spell of short leave from the committee at that vital time."

In a spirit of conciliation, the two Churches went forward together. The sharp edges of many a difficulty were thus smoothed down. Because of the long separation, there were minor differences of usage, and every-one was eager to come to an agreement so that nothing likely to cause friction would be bequeathed to the united Church. John White stressed that "the settlement we seek is one in which it should be possible for all to acquiesce, even if some details are not welcome either to one Church or the other. As to those words and phrases which recall long-standing controversies, let us have the widest latitude of interpretation." He tried to keep before his eyes, he said, the guiding rule of St. Augustine: "In essentials UNITY, in unessentials LIBERTY, in all things CHARITY." The enthusiasm with which he pressed forward had an effect upon him which surprised some of his associates who had so often seen him driving through a tangle of difficulties to reach a settlement. He had taken a short holiday at the end of his heavy Moderatorial year and had been so impatient to begin the committee work that one minister had described him as "like a steam-engine drawn up at the station, at a standstill, but blowing off steam, throbbing and snorting to be off". But now, when difficulties cropped up, as they so often did, his approach was one of gentle patience with those who held other views. Again and again, his ameliorating touch was felt. Principal Martin spoke of this spirit: "Our Church of Scotland brethren have shown a magnanimity and a readiness to defer to our wishes which deserve our most public recognition and gratitude." He spoke too of the great joy they had in a work that was going forward: "The ease and smoothness with which it was done was a delightful and exhilarating experience."

To the surprise of all who knew the magnitude of the work, the Basis and Plan of Union was ready for both Assemblies when they met in May 1927. Through the forest of detail the committees had mapped their pathways, with only one or two small corners left by intention unexplored. In that two-fold document, the *Basis* included those fundamental matters on which both Churches already agreed, while the *Plan* covered all important matters on which there had been divergence and on which agreement had been found. As part of the Basis of Union there were six declarations. The chosen documents of both Churches were cited, from the old Westminster Confession of Faith to the recent declaratory Articles of the Church of Scotland. The inherent right of the united Church to control her own constitution was confirmed, as was her obligation to extend the Kingdom of Christ throughout the world. And it was declared that all members of the united Church would have the right to assert and maintain the views of truth and duty which they had had liberty to hold in the Church to which they had previously belonged. Here was freedom of conscience indeed: not the strongest Voluntary nor the most stubborn upholder of State connection could be debarred from full communion nor restrained from expressing his opinions. The united Church was to be large enough to contain all who followed the one Lord.

There was a very simple question that had been discussed from the Solway to the northern isles: simple but charged with explosive possibilities. *What was the united Church to be called?* Amalgams of the two names were argued over in many a kirkyard. Would it be "The Free United Church of Scotland"—or "The United Church of Scotland"? In the Old Kirk, of course, it was the old name they wanted. Over the settlement there arose another of the legends which are repeated by those who knew John White:

> "At last the day came for the committees of both Churches to decide some issues that were still outstanding. The first item on the agenda was the settling of the name of the united Church. Dr. White was in the chair. 'Well, gentlemen', he said, 'in this very difficult matter, those of us in the Church of Scotland have decided that it would be only right to admit a claim that the United Free Church has always made. She has always claimed, has she not, to be the Church of Scotland? Very well. The united Church will be known under that name. Surely nobody could disapprove of our giving way to our brethren! Since that is settled, let us take up the next item on the agenda. . . .'"

If the incident is characteristic, and can be related light-heartedly, one would miss the real point of it if one were to ignore the wisdom which lay behind this piece of gay autocracy. If he had not snatched the question from the grasp of disputants, he knew it might have been made a bone of contention for a long time in the presbyteries and kirk sessions of the United Free Church, and the announcement of the committee's decision put an end to it. Principal Martin was one of those who gratefully approved, and he backed his approval by saying he had never regarded himself as ever having been out of the Church of Scotland. He quoted these words of the great John Cairns:

> "The true Church of Scotland was with John Knox in the galleys, with Melville in exile, with the Covenanters on the mountains, with Erskine and Gillespie in their solitude, with the Great Separation of 1843 that went forth to new conquests—though I grant also, that those who remained in the same spirit partook of the same inheritance."

To this, John White's own words have an apposite ring:

> "It is the Church of Scotland that represents the Presbyterian Tradition which still holds the hearts of the Scottish people. It is the chief symbol of Scottish nationality. It has been the chief factor in moulding the national character. It is the oldest institution in the land. It is rooted in the history, in the life, in the very soil of Scotland. It is the greatest Scottish heritage which the past has bequeathed."

And so the ancient name, The Church of Scotland, did not pass away but was to be graven the more deeply on the tablets of history.

V

On his appointment as convener of the Business Committee in 1926, John White had become the leader of the General Assembly. And now, in 1927, from the seat of honour below the Moderator's chair he saw and heard the Basis and Plan of Union being presented, discussed, and accepted. While some of the Old Guard still felt that "John White had given too much away" and that the old form of Establishment had a more solid foundation than the new constitution with all its liberties, most of them were in no doubt that the Church had been led by God into union and they accepted it as His Will. The Assembly gave instructions that the Basis and Plan be sent to presbyteries and that copies be supplied to all ministers and kirk sessions so that it would be available to every member; and comments were invited. After the Assembly had risen, an observer published his impressions: "The most dominating figure of all had been that of Dr. John White. As he sat in the place of Leader of the House, at the head of the table of the circumtabular oligarchy, his hand was ever on the pulse of the Assembly. His pre-eminence has never been more pronounced."

An unexpected thing had happened to John White. An announcement of importance had been made in the Assembly. Representatives of a number of influential laymen in the Church had consulted with the kirk session of The Barony, and plans were made to relieve John White of his parochial duties for a year so that he could devote his whole time to the cause of union. This was to bring in a rich harvest of enlightenment and agreement within the Church of Scotland. Soon he was off on his travels once more. He made it his special duty to address all the synods, and at his meetings in different parts of the country he was anxious that every elder should be present. It was the *inevitability* of union that now became his theme:

> "We have advanced beyond the hypothetical stage. The movement has acquired such momentum that it is to-day irresistible. It would have been here before this if we had had faith to expect what all true Christians long for. Remember that love, as Latimer said, is 'Christ's livery'. Where love is, outward unity of some kind will soon appear. . . . I hope that a spirit of conciliation, similar to that of our conferences, will be present always at the discussions on the Basis and Plan of Union in presbytery, kirk session, and congregation."

He found that many people looked askance at some of the proposed changes, and he pointed out that those in the other Church had an equal right to dislike changes in what they had been accustomed to. Since both sides must have their say, change was inevitable. In one of his talks to those who did not like the thought of moving from the old ways he said:

> "Change does not necessarily mean a betrayal of fundamental principle. Although a man's countenance changes with his growing character, there yet remains an identity of feature—and Church procedure and discipline may be modified according to time and circumstances. The face of the Church will show the deepening of spiritual character while its leading features remain."

On learning how much he was taking out of himself on these long and frequent journeys, Dr. Norman Maclean wrote to him: "You fill me with admiration and wonder with all you are able to do. But . . . take in some sail!" Principal Martin urged him not to drive his body too hard:

Francis Caird Inglis

AN HISTORIC PHOTOGRAPH

The final meeting of the two Union committees of The Church of Scotland and the United Free Church of Scotland prior to the union in 1929. They met at New College, Edinburgh, in the room which has been named Martin Hall, in memory of Principal Alexander Martin D.D. On John White's right sits Lord Sands, Dr. Robert J. Drummond, and Dr. J. Hutchison Cockburn. Principal Martin is at the head of the table, and to the left are Dr. A. N. Bogle, Dr. Joseph Mitchell (at that time Moderator of The Church of Scotland), Professor Adam Welch, Dr. W. M. Macgregor, Professor W. P. Paterson and Dr. P. D. Thomson.

as he put it with a neat Franciscan touch, "Have pity on Brother Ass." But however tired he was after a long day on the road, the sight of an audience at night aroused him like a trumpet call. At one of those meetings, a shorthand writer took a note of what he called "Dr. White's Aphorisms" and published a list of them in a newspaper. These are a few of the sparks from the anvil:

"Democracy is in danger of septic dissolution, but Church union will prevent that.

"On the one day of the week that is dedicated to Christian unity, you can hear the division bells ringing and can behold the Ayes and Noes going into their separate ecclesiastical lobbies.

"Clergymen sometimes lament our industrial divisions, but the captain of industry and the artisan can both reply: 'Physician, heal thyself.'

"A united Church must face the man in the slum as well as the slum in the man.

"Western civilisation has to cross a dangerous river. The new Church of Scotland will be a national bridge."

The same writer said that John White had

"unrolled for his audience a national film of history, biography, topography, statistics—accompanied by a flashing commentary—all towards one definite end, a united Church for a Greater Scotland. . . . Church union, as handled by this preacher-patriot, ceases to be simply a much needed improvement in ecclesiastical machinery—it becomes a triumphant organisation for the rejuvenating of Scottish national and social life. No clansman ever carried the fiery cross of war with more self-sacrificing energy and passion than Dr. White has carried the gospel of goodwill among the Scottish people. He has challenged the echoes of Woden and Thor in the Orkneys, and gazed upon their modern remembrances sunk in Scapa Flow. Among the Hebrides, in the kingdom of Somerled, he has revived the tradition of Columba. In every town and hamlet, his message has been received with thanksgiving. With his vision and evangel of a united Church, Dr. White is in the line of national liberators and builders."

The writer said he came away from that meeting "with the experience of having been enthralled by a great orator and a much greater patriot, whose prayer was that of John Knox's: *Give me Scotland ere I die.*'"

VI

It distressed John White that the threat of a storm in the other Church was not abating. The United Free Church minority were making their voices heard more loudly than ever. At a meeting of United Free Church office-bearers in Glasgow on 10th December 1927, Principal Martin confessed that he was haunted day and night by the thought of the joining of the two Churches being marred by a split in their own ranks. Indeed, he went a good deal further. He spoke of a threat of some of the minority to appeal to the Courts of Law, with the odious possibility of a fight like that of 1904 when the House of Lords had declared that, by union with the United Presbyterian Church, the Free Church had lost her identity and must give up all her property to a handful of dissentients who claimed to be the sole representatives of the old Free Church of Scotland. Martin and his colleagues had felt obliged to take counsel's opinion, and were advised to declare formally that the constitution and principles of the United Free Church were not inconsistent with the new relations between the Church of Scotland and the State. They hoped in this way to disperse the difficulties of some of the hesitating minority, but there was still a solid core of those who refused to accept it. Dr. George M. Reith, a United Free Church minister and editor of the Assembly's Proceedings, said that "it was simply a putting of obvious things into braille for the benefit of the blind; but since none are so blind as those who will not see, even braille is illegible to those who keep their hands behind their backs".

The minority put out a manifesto in which they proposed that the Church allocate to them a portion of the funds and properties. The press seized upon this and reminded them that their ancestors in the Free Church had gone into the wilderness to fend for themselves, expecting not a halfpenny from anyone, fortified only by their faith in the worthiness of their cause. Principal Martin and his colleagues promised that if the minority did in the end stand out they would be generously treated, but he pleaded with them "to think once, twice, and yet again before they committed themselves to a course so grave—and on grounds which nearly all Protestant Christendom everywhere would deem wholly insufficient".

The promise to treat them generously was to be kept, and was indeed described as one of the most generous gestures ever made in ecclesiastical history. Since it was not within the power of the United Free Church to dip a hand into monies given for specific purposes, a fund that reached twenty-five thousand pounds was raised and presented to the minority.

A final plebiscite showed that, of all the congregations of the Church, only three per cent voted against union. They asked that the Church's offices in Glasgow be handed over to them. This was rejected, but several concessions and privileges were accorded them. For conscience' sake they were going out into the wilderness—but not to fend entirely for themselves.

VII

By the time the adjourned Assemblies met in November 1928, the Basis and Plan of Union had been in the hands of the subordinate courts of both Churches for a year and a half. In his speech, John White described the revised document which was now being sent down formally under the Barrier Act for the acceptance of presbyteries, and explained why there were still "minor problems that can only be unriddled by time and tolerance". The magnificent Assembly Hall of the United Free Church on the Mound was to be their meeting place after the union, and he dwelt on the mixed feelings they would all have when they left for the last time the Tolbooth kirk: "It has been for so long our Assembly hall, and it is laden with memories of great and momentous acts and is for us charged with the continuing spirit of devoted churchmen of the past."

At the May Assembly of 1929, in the presence of the Duke of York, the Lord High Commissioner, and his Duchess, the Basis and the Plan of Union was adopted [1]; and after the last of its business had been completed, the Assembly adjourned until the beginning of October, when the work of twenty years would come to fruition and the two Churches would at last be one. Looking forward to that time, John White said:

"The old walls of partition are down, the former alienations are at an end, the war cries of sectarian jealousy are hushed. We are about to serve in a closer fellowship the One Lord, as we already profess the one faith and worship the One God." The words he spoke with a sonorous solemnity left their impression on the minds of all who heard him: "*Finis coronat opus. Magnum opus. Opera praeclara. . . . Te Deum laudamus. . . .*"

It had been the hope of King George V that he would be present in October at an event so important to Scotland, but ill-health prevented him, and once more the Duke of York came as His Majesty's Commissioner. In view of a piece of drama that was played behind the scenes, it was well that so sympathetic and understanding a man as the Duke was there to represent the King. Many in the United Free Church did not

[1] Every presbytery of *both* Churches had approved of them under the Barrier Act.

greatly relish the prospect of a Lord High Commissioner being present at all at the deliberations of the Assemblies of the united Church; nor did they like his military escort. John White realised that feelings were sensitive on this, and he was determined that nothing should be done to cause needless irritation. He stressed yet again that

> "so far from there being any infringement on spiritual freedom by the presence of a Lord High Commissioner, it should be regarded as a great triumph of religious liberty which the Church has won against stupendous odds. I must repeat that the Commissioner is not even a member of the Assembly. He exercises no restraint on it in any way. The General Assembly could go on quite well in his absence—it has often done so. But his presence we surely welcome, in that it represents the nation's homage to their King of Kings."

John White knew, of course, that the opening words spoken by the Lord High Commissioner could be misconstrued into an admission by the Church of Scotland that the Sovereign had some measure of control: "In the name of His Majesty, I now invite you to proceed to the business for which you are assembled, and I most earnestly commend your labours to the blessing and guidance of Almighty God."

The Lord High Commissioner's words at the end of the Assembly were liable to the same misconstruction, for he dissolved the Assembly in the King's name and officially appointed the next Assembly to meet on a certain date. The fact that always the Assembly had already fixed that date did not meet the objection. In 1927, John White had decided that with union drawing near he would make a change in procedure to meet the wishes of those in the other Church, and an approach had been made to Sir John Gilmour, then Secretary of State for Scotland.

The reply from the Scottish Office had been

> "that His Majesty the King has been graciously pleased to approve of the change in procedure which was proposed in the memorandum which accompanied your letter. . . . The Secretary of State assumes that you will take the steps necessary to secure, as far as the Church is concerned, that the new procedure shall be followed, and he will see that the necessary instructions are given to the Lord High Commissioner."

Unfortunately, by some mischance, the necessary instructions had not been given, and the Lord High Commissioner of that year, the Earl of

Stair, used the old opening formula and in the name of His Majesty invited members of the Assembly to proceed to the business for which they were assembled. John White was distressed. At once he got in touch with the Solicitor-General and said that the strongest possible representations must be made to Lord Stair. If, at the end of the Assembly, he dissolved it in the King's name, and appointed the date of the next meeting, it might disturb many of the brethren in the other Church. Lord Stair naturally protested. He was following tradition. Who was this turbulent cleric who was giving him new orders?

He soon learned. John White had a peremptory message sent to the Scottish Office. The procedure agreed on must be followed. There must be no blunder at the end of the Assembly as there had been at the opening. As soon as Lord Stair knew that John White was only insisting on a formula which His Majesty had approved of, he gave full assurance that he would use it. The Assembly was closed with the words John White and Lord Sands had composed:

> "Right Reverend and well beloved, your labours are now at an end, and I shall inform His Majesty that, having concluded the business for which you were assembled, you have passed an Act appointing the next meeting of the General Assembly to be held upon 22nd May 1928, and now in the King's name I bid you farewell."

Members of the Assembly then bowed to the Lord High Commissioner; and turning to his brethren, the Moderator said: "In the name of the Lord Jesus Christ, sole King and Head of the Church, I now dissolve this General Assembly, and appoint the next General Assembly of this Church to be held at Edinburgh upon 22nd May 1928." Finally, he asked members to line the corridors as the Lord High Commissioner retired from the Assembly Hall.

That had happened in 1927, and the procedure then established was to become the rule in the united Church. But now in October 1929, when the Act of Union was about to be completed, there arose a still greater complication connected with the King's representative. When John White learned that a Royal guard had been rehearsing at the front entrance of the Hall where the first Assembly was to meet, he called for an explanation. The Hall was an immense building in Annandale Street specially prepared for the meetings, and plans had been made for the Lord High Commissioner to enter from a side door and take his seat on the throne, which was shut off by a low partitition from the rest of the

Assembly. In the eyes of the Church of Scotland, the partition indicated symbolically that the King's Commissioner took no part in the proceedings of the Assembly and was merely there as a spectator. To the Church, it was much more than an interesting tradition: it was a matter of deep importance. For her freedom, in the first century of her existence, she had been compelled to fight stoutly against the Stuart kings, whose encroachments form a dark chapter in her history; and the sovereign's coronation oath to defend this hard-won liberty is cherished with loyal respect and gratitude. The fact that the Sovereign's representative is physically shut off from the Assembly is the symbol of this liberty. And so it was that John White was horrified when he learned that Admiral Sir Basil Brooke, who was in attendance on the Duke of York, had announced that His Royal Highness would make his entrance by the front door of the Hall and pass through the Assembly to take his place on the throne. At once a message was sent to Admiral Brooke telling him that this plan must be changed. The Lord High Commissioner must not walk through the midst of the Assembly; he must enter from the side, as had always been done at the Tolbooth Church.

The Convener of the General Committee, Mr. Herdman, who had been in charge of the arrangements, was summoned to the Palace of Holyroodhouse. There, he was told by Admiral Brooke that, in spite of John White's message, in spite of any arrangements which the Church had hoped to make about the entrance of His Royal Highness, His Royal Highness would most certainly enter through the front door, where a military guard of honour would be drawn up and where a military band would be playing. Admiral Brooke added that he had the final say, and these were his instructions. Mr. Herdman protested in vain, then sent a hurried message to John White:

"I am afraid it is useless to argue further, and unless I hear from you to the contrary I shall take it that you acquiesce."

John White had not the least intention of acquiescing. His record of the incident is clear-cut: "I instructed Mr. Herdman to inform the Admiral that *the last word was with the Church of Scotland* and that I, Dr. White, had spoken it."

He further asked Mr. Herdman to arrange that the Purse-Bearer and Admiral Brooke should wait upon him at the Church of Scotland Assembly Hall at the Tolbooth to give him a definite assurance that the Duke of York would not enter by the main door of the Annandale Street Hall and walk through the Assembly. He instructed Mr. Herdman to state in unmistakable terms that, if the Admiral and the Purse-Bearer did not agree, they could have no Lord High Commissioner present.

The *impasse* was explained personally to the Duke of York, and John White's own comments on the outcome are these:

"No one could have been more considerate and sympathetic than the Duke of York the moment it was explained to him what it all meant. We are fortunate in having had, as Lord High Commissioner, a man of that quick intuition and courtesy that the Duke always shows."

And so, by a spontaneous royal gesture, an ancient and valued symbol was maintained.

VIII

Before the two Assemblies came together under the one roof for the act of uniting, they gathered in their own Assembly Halls. That Tuesday, the first day of October 1929, was memorable to thousands. There was bright autumn sunshine, with a touch of chill in the air that speeds the step of folk on Edinburgh pavements. Without any of the usual military display, the Duke of York drove quietly from the Palace of Holyroodhouse to the Tolbooth kirk and took his seat on the throne. After the usual courtesies had been exchanged, the Principal Clerk, for the last time in that place, gave the order "Lock the doors"; and, with members standing, the Assembly was constituted with prayer. The opening psalm fitted the mood of all: *Oh sing a new song to the Lord*. The Moderator, Dr. Joseph Mitchell of Mauchline, for many years one of the leading supporters of union, drew attention to the silver casket on his table, and explained to the Assembly that it contained the Burgess ticket of the City of Edinburgh which had, with due ceremony, been presented on the previous day to Dr. John White. He told the members that Dr. White himself looked upon the granting of the Freedom of the City as being an honour not to himself alone but to the Church of which he was a representative. When John White rose to present the final report of the union committee, he said:

"It is today, as the last word is spoken, that the solemnity of our course is so keenly felt. We are parting with some very sacred associations, dear for our fathers' sakes, and doubly precious from our own experience. But we are giving up nothing they held dear; we take with us, intact, a heritage they left. . . . We cannot but be in reminiscent mood as we step forward into the new path. The occasion brings a pathos with it. Personal memories tend to cross and blur the wider issues we have kept before us. But we have no misgivings. We are taking the treasures of the past with us to enrich our future, and we go forward with full assurance of hope towards the new horizon to which our God of Hope is summoning us."

In the other Assembly on the Mound, Principal Martin was presiding as the last of the Moderators of that Church; appropriately, he too, to the delight of John White, had received the Freedom of Edinburgh on the previous day. Before the session ended, he asked the Assembly to pause for one single and solemn moment.

"The history of our undivided United Free Church is now at an end," he said. "With our historic claims fully met and satisfied, we adjourn to rejoin our brethren from whom we have been separated so long. It is a common sorrow that we do not enter upon it with ranks unbroken. . . . May God over-ride and over-rule that which, in our infirmity, we have been unable to avert."

Next morning after prayers had been said, processions set out from the two Assembly Halls, to meet and mingle at the top of Bank Street and move into the dimness of St. Giles' for the service preparatory to the solemn act of uniting in the afternoon. From the Annandale Street Hall Sir David Cameron had taken all bleakness by wall hangings of red and blue and by draping great billows of white fabric under the glass roof. Representatives from Scottish cities were there in their civic robes, Lords of Session in crimson and white, the Archbishop of Canterbury in purple cassock and scarlet-and-black gown and hood, the Archbishop of Wales, the Primus of the Scottish Episcopal Church, and many another from home and overseas. In the presence of the Duke and Duchess of York,[1] the documents of the uniting act were laid upon the table, and Lord Sands moved their adoption: "It has been given to us," he said, "to close one of the rents in the seamless robe." And then the audience rose, and each Moderator spoke for his own Church. As the senior, Principal Martin

[1] To the great pleasure of Dr. White and his wife, they received a signed photograph of the Duke and Duchess and the child Princess Elizabeth as a "souvenir of that interesting and memorable occasion". In his letter of thanks, John White said that in the photograph "there is an added charm in that it includes the little Princess who holds sway over us all". He spoke of the great pleasure of everyone in having "Their Royal Highnesses to honour and grace our proceedings. . . . What impressed the whole Assembly was the real interest which the Duke and Duchess took in the reunion, and we all felt that their presence was more than an official recognition."

made the official Declaration of Union, left the Chair and, with Dr. Joseph Mitchell, sealed and ratified it, using the quill pen with which the deed of separation at the Disruption of 1843 had been signed.

Then there was the calling of the Moderator of the first Assembly of the united Church. The nomination had been made at a joint meeting of the full union committees of both Churches, which had met in New College, Edinburgh, on 14th June. In the Church of Scotland there was only one man to whom everybody felt the honour should be given, but John White and some of his friends were anxious that the offer should be made to the United Free Church committee that, in the very special circumstances, a break should be made with tradition and a joint Moderator be appointed from their own Church. Principal Martin and his colleagues deeply appreciated this gesture; it was but another of the many examples of the fraternal spirit that had animated all their recent conferences. When the two committees had met to put the business through, Principal Martin had risen and nominated John White as the sole Moderator of the united Assembly, and the proposal had been received with acclamation. Following tradition, the new Moderator had not been present within the Hall but was waiting beyond closed doors for his call if the Assembly should approve of his appointment. In recommending John White, Principal Martin referred to him as "a possession of the whole Church, enjoying not least the confidence and esteem of that section of our now united Church to which he did not himself belong. . . . No one is more deserving of honour at the Church's hands than our able, devoted and trusted brother." There could be no doubt about the reactions of the united Assembly. All the previous Moderators of both Churches at once left the platform, accompanied by the Clerks, and returned to the hall escorting the man who had been unanimously chosen for this unique honour. John White received a full-hearted ovation as he took his place in the Moderator's Chair.

He looked around at his audience of over twelve thousand—the largest indoor audience that had ever gathered together in Edinburgh. Storms of hail beat upon the glass roof and interrupted his speech, but he carried his hearers with him in words that penetrated to the heart of things and brought the Church of Scotland face to face with all that lay ahead.

"Our history is a long one: we go back beyond the Disruption, the Relief, the Secession; back beyond the Revolution Settlement

265

and the Scottish Reformation, in which we are proud to claim our portion; back by way of Iona, guided by the light of St. Kentigern and the Candida Casa of St. Ninian, even unto Jerusalem. And in the forefront of our testimony today we claim our part in the Holy Catholic or Universal Church. . . . Yet great as is our inheritance from the past, we believe that the future holds greater things for us. We lay strong hands of faith on the promise, *Greater works than these shall ye do*. But what we claim we must worthily earn. The first task that faces us is that which was a main motive in the reunion movement— the moral, social, and the religious well-being of the people of Scotland. The Churchless millions is a first challenge to the united Church. In these late years, it has grown complex and intensive—a sphinx-like problem. It touches the slum and the suburb; woe-land and wealth- land. There must be a girding up of the loins. Great things must be done. . . ."

John White spoke of realities. In that hour, flames from the Burning Bush on the Church's banner leapt high. To many who regarded him as a great ecclesiastical statesman, he now stood forth as a man of simple piety—a man who assuredly did not wear his heart upon his sleeve but who could, in his very depths, be powerfully moved. And some of his emotion he communicated to his hearers on that great day of joyful reunion—and to those who, in their homes, listened to his broadcast words on the drawing together of the forces of God's Kingdom on earth.

From the clergy and the laity of the united Church—and from those in many other Churches—letters were soon to pour in upon him: some of them grandiloquent, some simple and direct. He would have been blind indeed if he had not seen that it had been largely through his efforts that union had at last become a fact. But on that night of 2nd October 1929, as he sat in the quietness of his hotel room, he was moved by the splendour of a great and absolute certainty that in anything he had accomplished he had been used of God. And into his heart there poured again the gratitude he had expressed that morning in his first words to the united Assembly:

"We must make our thanksgiving to God, Who has guided the union movement, bringing the Churches in these late years steadily in the direction of this closer fellowship. Very humbly, very reverently, and with deep gratitude we acknowledge and believe that it is He alone Who has brought us to this hour of realised hope, of answered prayer, and of fervent desires fulfilled. And now that the seal has been set to the Solemn Covenant declaring the Churches no longer twain but one, our first act of thanksgiving is to consecrate ourselves anew to the service of our Lord and Saviour, humbly acknowledging our entire dependence on the mercy of God and the leading of His Holy Spirit for all the happy issues we look for in the coming days."

Chapter XVI

PASTOR AND PEOPLE

I

THE eighteen years that had passed since John White became minister at The Barony had seen many changes in the parish. Soon after his coming he had written: "In Dr. Norman MacLeod's time (he died in 1872) the population was sixty-seven thousand. Today there are over three hundred thousand in the area he ministered to. But since then, parish after parish has been carved out of the old Barony, with the consequence that we now have but a small fraction of that population." By the erection of the Buccleuch *quoad sacra* church, which was later united with another to form the present St. Stephen's Buccleuch, the disjunctions numbered over forty. In 1929, all that remained of the ancient and far-flung parish of The Barony was split into two districts, one encircling the church itself, the other composed of the streets round the Mission Institute in Black Street.

Soon after his translation from South Leith, John White had purged the Communion Roll. This had reduced the membership to less than the three thousand which was generally reckoned to be the size of the congregation. Not until 1924 was it above that number again; but with the slow falling away in the next ten years, the Roll now held two thousand three hundred names. Here was a large church in the heart of a great city. From it the tides of population had continued to recede; and office-blocks and shops and warehouses, deserted at night and silent on the Sabbath, gave no nourishment to its life. The old ideal of the Church of Scotland, that she should provide a territorial ministry in all the land, could no longer apply to The Barony of Glasgow. Its territorial ministry, in terms of parochial life and work, had resolved itself into the activities of a mission institute, and three-quarters of the members of its youth organisations were from the nearby mission areas. The Barony stood like an isolated rock; and it continued to stand because there were those who regarded it with affection and, held by an old loyalty, wished their names to remain upon its Communion Roll.

From one depressing fact John White had never been able to escape.

Not for a long time had the finances of The Barony been on a firm basis. All through his ministry there, he was handicapped by lack of funds. There had been a small deficit on the Congregational Account in the year he had come; small deficits were the rule, never the exception. No seat-rents were paid in The Barony, and the minister's stipend came out of teinds. The main source of revenue was the collection taken at Sunday services and the donations gathered by church collectors on their monthly visits; but in 1925 John White pressed for the Free Will offering system to be introduced. Some people adopted it, some did not. At first, this new system cut down the annual deficits, but they began to creep up again and the economic conditions of the late 'twenties and early 'thirties did not improve the financial state. But sympathetic as he was to the difficulties of making ends meet, he never failed to urge his flock to face their responsibilities. "In our giving, many of us are thoughtless, careless, unsystematic," he once said to his people, and he told them how great a difference it would make if they would take thought. "What is the good of the Weekly Free Will offering if it merely becomes a monthly offering at a weekly rate? Because of a deficiency in the treasury, the work of the church is being crippled." He told them of the need to repair the church building and organ, of strengthening many parish activities. He had already made an appeal; but the response, he said, "has not been so great as to encourage me". He reminded them that Dr. Marshall Lang, on a similar occasion, had called upon the folk of The Barony to bestir themselves—to remedy a state of affairs that he had called *tiresome and vexatious*.

"Finance—it is an irksome theme," said John White. "It will never be satisfactory until *all* members of the congregation consider their responsibility, as followers of Jesus Christ, for carrying on His work by giving as God has prospered them. . . . *A church's finance report reveals how much the Holy Spirit is dwelling within that church.*"

II

In spite of the compact between John White and the congregation of The Barony that much of his time would, of necessity, be devoted to the affairs of the Church of Scotland, there were some members who criticised him for his failure to pay them pastoral visits. He deeply desired in those strenuous years of the union movement to be able to give more time than he did to his own people, but there were occasions when he felt obliged to reject the criticism. An inexperienced elder had listened to the plaint of an old woman who declared that the minister had not paid her a visit for years, and he took her story to John White. Out came from his pocket the familiar diary, with a full page to each day of the year. He flicked over the leaves, then fixed the elder with a cold eye: "This old body was visited by me on the 17th, 19th, and 23rd days of last month when she was poorly." He snapped shut the book and added: "Don't you realise that the poor old soul has lost her memory?" Mr. Stewart Brown received several criticisms of a like kind:

"Though I was his assistant, I admit I could not know at that time of the immense commitments he had all over the country. With the heavy strain of the oversight of that huge congregation, I now wonder, as I look back on it, how he was able to do as much pastoral work as he did. Even in the midst of a crisis in Church union or anything else, never was he an indifferent pastor. In front of me now is a bundle of letters from him. On 5th June 1931, he writes of a sick woman he had visited both at her home and in hospital, and of six others he had personally visited in Bishopbriggs and elsewhere. In a letter dated a fortnight later, he writes about a funeral and mentions members of the family by name—how he remembered them I do not know—and suggests a way to bring them back into the church. In another letter about a marriage I had arranged for him to take, he again mentions members of the family by name; he arranges for communion cards for two strangers; he adds a name to the Sick List; then he gives a list of twelve names of people he had visited the previous week in places from Partick to Dennistoun. Another letter encloses a reply from Sir Charles Cleland to whom he had written about a young man seeking a job. A letter dated 19th October of the same year mentions the names of other people he had visited and gives full details of pension, super-annuation, and other income and discharge, in a case I was to put before the Parish Council. Over that period how much more passed to me by telephone and through other channels I cannot recall; the messages and instructions were constant and voluminous. At the very time when a few folk were criticising, I knew him to be a vigilant pastor, ever practical and orderly in all his ways."

III

In the period that followed the union, a good deal of John White's time was taken up with administrative detail. To the General Assembly of

1930, as convener of the Committee on General Administration, he presented a report that covered the ground of eight committees which, before the union, had reported separately to the two Assemblies. Later, he was chairman of the Church of Scotland Trust, which held all invested funds not under the control of the General Trustees. He was on the committee formed to work out a method of nominating Moderators that would be agreeable to both Churches. He was founder member of the Scottish Churches Council and was its president for its first three years. He was on the Pan-Presbyterian Council and on the Church Extension Committee of the Presbytery of Glasgow. In 1930 he was appointed chairman of the Religious Tract Society and went to London to its 131st Annual Meeting to deliver a speech on Christian literature that was widely quoted. On the same visit, he delivered the Burge Memorial lecture at King's College, and addressed the General Assembly of the Presbyterian Church of England.

The widespread suffering that followed the slump in trade caused him deep concern. At the Assembly of May 1931, he proposed that there be a record of their "sympathy with all who are suffering from unemployment through the long-continued trade depression, and their pride in the steadfastness and courage of their faithful people". He pointed out the serious moral and social dangers in the situation, especially to younger folk, and voiced the desire of the Assembly "for the development of schemes to remedy these evils". He told the Assembly of his own people of The Barony: many had been without work for months, some even for years and—as he said—were worrying their hearts out. Young folk were not undergoing the skilled training in trades they had looked for, and some had to give up all hope of fulfilling their aspirations. The Church must do what she could to forward plans to bring employment to Scotland: for, he said, "there is a close and obvious connection between economic sufficiency and spiritual vitality". It had always been a profound conviction of his that until a starving man had been fed it was futile to talk to him about his immortal soul.

The Church and Nation Committee, of which he had been the chief begetter, was now dealing with matters on which it was felt that the Church should make her mind known: the censorship of cinema films, Britain's colonial policy, the drug traffic, gambling, and many another. To gambling, John White had always been vehemently hostile. He was vice-president of the Scottish National League against Betting and

Gambling. In his pastoral letter of 1925 as Moderator, he had hit out fearlessly:

"We run the risk of being called ultra-puritanical, but the Church must assert its strength. There is no room for compromise. We must do all we can to eradicate an evil that is threatening the foundations of society." In the course of a speech at that time, he said: "No nation can prosper that lives on excitement and sensation. There is no increase of wealth to a nation through gambling, but there is a large increase of social weakness. Gambling flourishes best where there is a lowered vitality. In fact, it is a mug's game." In Tasmania, when he was visiting his son, he found that many of the barbers were bookmakers and took bets from their customers. So that this gambling traffic should not be quite so apparent, the bookies were offered offices in back streets. In Hobart, when John White discovered that a larger jail was being completed, he said from the pulpit that he was not surprised to hear this, since the immorality of gambling was now being transferred to the back streets of the town. As a result of his attack, he said afterwards, he found it extremely difficult to get his hair cut!

On the vexed subject of total abstinence from alcoholic liquors (on which the Church of Scotland and the United Free Church had never seen eye to eye), John White's view was that

"we must consider what is immediately possible and seek to get there —but with the resolve to take another step as soon as possible. . . . We have Local Option, so the decision is in the hands of our citizens. As a Church, it is our duty to teach them what is best for them, what is best for society, best for industry, best for the homes of all the people, and what will help most in advancing the Kingdom of God."

When challenged on whether Communion wine should be fermented or unfermented, he said:

"We must not have any divisions at the Table of Fellowship. We must seek to follow closely our Lord's example when He sat at the Last Supper. I cannot be sure what sort of wine was drunk at the Passover Feast. Certain sons of Rechab partook of the Passover and no wrangling took place there. The Church would act wisely if it were to recommend that no wine should be used at the Holy Table that was not of the lightest kind, and even that should be mixed with water. Cyprian's Epistle shows that it was the custom of the Church to mix wine with water, water representing people, wine the blood of Christ, and so Christ and his people are united in the Cup."

IV

That children should be given religious instruction in the day schools had always been one of his firm convictions; and where he saw that there was a danger of its being done away with, he entered the fray. In a sermon preached from the pulpit of The Barony, he had urged his people to bestir themselves and vote in the Local Education Authority elections. He had trounced them for their laxity at the previous one, when seventy-three per cent of the population had not even taken the trouble to go to the voting booths. If this laziness continued, he had said, the Socialists and Roman Catholics would soon be in a dominating position.

"I have no quarrel with the Labour Party; they are entitled to their place in the politics of this nation as much as any other party. But so far as education is concerned, I would rule them out of court with the Independent Liberals, the Coalitionists and the Diehards. I have no quarrel with them as labourists, for it is possible to belong to that party and yet be a good and loyal member of the Church, as some are. But it will be an evil day for the nation when the education of our children becomes the plaything of party politics.

"I have no quarrel with the Roman Catholics," he continued. "They have many children in the city and are entitled to a fair and just representation on the authority that administers the Education Act. But when I see the Roman Catholics holding twelve seats out of forty-five and asking for more, I am forced to ask, Why? Is it that they desire to safeguard the huge revenue they have within these last three years secured from the rates of Glasgow?

"For me, the chief concern of the present election is the right of our children to be trained in the religious faith of the Church to which we belong. Everything depends upon yourselves," he said emphatically. "You will not accomplish much unless you rouse yourselves from the apathy in which you lay at the last election. You are called upon to decide by your votes what is to be the policy for the next three years— whether there is to be a continuance of that customary religious teaching that has distinguished Scottish education since the Reformation, an education that has done much to equip the young for their duties in the world, sending them forth with their young hearts

S   273

enflamed with the love of virtue, inspired with high hopes of living to be brave men, worthy citizens, dear to God and helpful to their brethren."

John White's sermon was reported in the press and widely read. A few days later, when the election results were announced, it was found that the poll had been almost exactly doubled, and any fear that religious education in the schools might be discontinued was for the time being allayed.

It was some six years later, in 1928, that a Government Bill proposed to abolish the Local Authority and set up new Education Committees in the town and county councils. Once again John White feared that there might be a move to abolish religious education in the schools. He took the initiative in forming an association of Protestant Churches. Accompanied by some of his colleagues, he went in October to have a talk with Sir John Gilmour, then Secretary of State for Scotland. He said that there must be included in the new Bill a clause in which it was laid down that there would be Protestant religion in schools and that presbyteries, within the areas of town and county councils, should have the right of nominating two or three extra members of the Education Committee. Sir John Gilmour liked neither suggestion: he did not want too much clerical representation on Education Committees. John White went to the Educational Institute of Scotland; he went also to Sir George Macdonald, then head of the Scottish Education Department; and there followed another argument with the Secretary of State. Sir Robert Horne took up the cudgels on John White's behalf and advised him to come to London before the clauses were debated in Parliament and interview the Secretary of State again and the Lord Advocate. Horne had argued with them both and thought their attitude was now a little more pliable. By the end of January 1929, John White felt that he had made progress:

"The Secretary of State for Scotland has told me he would move an amendment to the Bill requiring a referendum of the electors in the event of any proposal to debar religious instruction from schools. This is a real safeguard." But he was still not satisfied that the Protestant Churches would have proper representation.

In February he was at Westminster and watched the Bill as it went through the committee stage. He talked urgently with members of all parties. He got them to agree in principle that the Evangelical Churches should have two members co-opted on the Education Committee. It was

John White himself who drafted the clause to be inserted in the Bill.[1] He took it to Sir John Gilmour, whom he described as "a bit obstinate". He took it to the Lord Advocate, "who listened to my arguments which were backed by the strong deputation of M.P.s I took with me". He went to the Labour Party and "won them over". He convinced the small body he described as the Liberal Remnant. Then he "gave all parties separately the amendment; and on receiving their Papers next morning they were all amazed to find such great unanimity prevailing". When James Maxton realised what had happened, he shook a minatory finger at John White and exclaimed, "I can see we have had a Cardinal among us!" By the time the Assembly met in May, the Bill had become law. In the General Assembly of the United Free Church, the last Assembly before the union, Dr. Mackintosh Mackay said:

> "For our successful efforts, we are indebted largely to the Very Rev. Dr. John White. Dr. White is a past master in negotiation, Knowing as he does many members of the Government he was peculiarly fitted to this task. He threw himself into it whole-heartedly. And the committee—and indeed the whole Church—is deeply indebted to him for the results obtained. The Assembly can be assured that, under the new Act, religious instruction has been placed upon a foundation as secure as it was under the old Act."

V

It was recognised that the most important committee of the Church in the years ahead would be that of the Home Mission, and the man chosen to take the chair was John White. He accepted the task, and in his place Dr. Hutchison Cockburn was appointed to the convenership of the Church and Nation Committee. Dr. Cockburn said: "This did not mean that there was any fading of John White's interest in our deliberations. Although he was no longer to be the convener, we knew he was in the background always ready with help and advice when we needed it."

With his energies directed into the work of the Home Mission Com-

[1] Dr. White sat up into the "small hours" of the morning trying to devise a clause that would be acceptable to the Government draughtsman of the Bill, who had held that a solution was impossible. John White's solution, ingenious and all-embracing, was thus described in the Memorandum on Religious Instruction in Schools in Scotland: "Provision was made for the appointment of Education Committees, and these Committees must include two persons interested in the promotion of religious instruction to be nominated by a meeting of representatives of the Churches or denominational bodies having duly constituted churches or other regularly appointed places of worship in the area. . . ."

mittee, John White found himself immersed in a multiplicity of affairs. A number of committees whose work was closely affiliated with Home Mission activities had their functions clearly defined; and he became a member of most of them. He was on the Church and Manse Building Committee, which helped congregations that were too poor to keep their buildings in good repair. He was a member of the Highlands and Islands Committee, which helped to care for the spiritual welfare of folk in lonely glens and the Western Islands, poverty-stricken many of them, their lives restricted by the very remoteness of their dwellings and primitive or costly transport. The Highlanders and Islanders had long been a special problem of the Church; and after the union, when the committees of the two uniting Churches were fused, John White made a number of journeys to the north and west country to see things for himself. With Highlanders he had always felt most happily at ease. He had rubbed shoulders with many of them, young and old, in Glasgow and in his holiday haunts; and his admiration for their finer qualities helped quickly to create a bond between them. Dr. Roderick Macleod once wrote to ask him to address a gathering of Highland ministers:

> "You know the Highlands better than most Lowlanders; indeed better than some Highlanders themselves, and you have got the feel of the men in the North. They will be greatly stimulated by a word from you. What is more in a Highlander's esteem than a Lowlander's, they would appreciate the *courtesy* of a visit and talk."

John White was a member of the Women's Home Mission Committee, with its special responsibility for Church Sisters. Well over a hundred of these devoted women were working in industrial areas and the new housing estates; and this carefully trained and dedicated regiment formed a living link between the Church and the non-churchgoing masses.

The Home Mission Committee controlled many mission stations and chaplains in different parts of the country. It arranged the work of those who ministered to the wandering groups, the "gangrel bodies", of Scotland, many of whom had their lairs in the north-west: the folk who, in John White's words, followed the trade of John Bunyan and who sorely needed the pilgrim message of the inspired tinker. The Committee had a mission among the berry-pickers and among those gangs of hardy men who constructed new roads. There were missions to the fisher folk. The Gospel was taken to poorhouses and infirmaries. The very contemplation of this splendid service never failed to warm the heart of John White.

From the earliest days of his ministry, he had been sensitive to the problems of town and country.

"The large towns and cities," he said, "tend to estrange men from what is best in human life—to dwarf the individual and weaken his personal responsibility. In the surge of city life, the individual is of far less account than in the small rural community. In the city there are the residential districts of the wealthy, the zone inhabited by the middle class, and the quarters in which the masses of the population dwell. Between the first and the last there is a great gulf fixed. The House of God is often the sign of the distance by which they are parted. . . . The strong West End churches have done splendid work by conducting missions in poor and densely populated districts. The pastoral ideal of one man visiting a thousand members must give place to the missionary ideals—the ideal of each one of the thousand members visiting someone who was outwith the Church and giving help and counsel. . . . On the other hand, in the country districts, the constant migration of farm workers, the long distance from any centre where social life could be organised—these do not foster a community feeling."

Here was a matter for the Home Mission Committee to ponder; to John White it held problems he had faced before he had been many months in his first charge at Shettleston.

Quietly and realistically, he assessed the nature and scope of the work ahead of him in his new convenership. In presenting his report to the Assembly in May 1930, he said that "the main motive in the union movement has been the more effective working of those projects that come under the wing of the Home Mission Committee; and these are the primary and hard task of the Church at the present time". And among all of that multifarious Home Mission work which he found so fascinating, he counted Church Extension to be the most important. He foresaw that, as the years passed, it would become the one thing that would call for the most active and whole-hearted support of every section of the Church.

From the beginning of his ministry, Church Extension had been in his blood. The two daughter churches of his own he had added at Shettleston had been the start of it. He had been convener of the Church Extension Committee of the Presbytery of Edinburgh while he had been at South Leith; and after the union, his energy and zeal found a deep channel. In vacating his chair in 1930 as the first Moderator of the united Church, he said:

"We must justify what we have done. We must show that union has brought new strength and a radiating influence to the Church of Scotland. We are proud of the Church reunited but we dare not sit quietly expatiating on what has been accomplished while the great world sweeps on into the future without us."

In the sermon he preached at St. Giles' as retiring Moderator, he urged the need for a new evangelism. "We are members of the body of Christ, who came not to be ministered unto *but to minister*."

VI

Before the time was ripe for John White to organise the Church Extension campaign, there came an interlude in his life on which he was to look back with pleasure. In fulfilment of a promise made to his son, James Bishop White, that he would visit him in his new home in Tasmania, he decided to set out for there in the autumn of 1930. His doctor and all who were then working most closely with him urged upon him his need of a long rest. He had undergone a continuous strain in the final phases of the union movement; the ceremonies in which the fusion of the two Presbyterian Churches was completed had been uplifting to the spirit, but they had sapped his strength; and in his Moderatorial tours he had taken a leading part in large Home Mission demonstrations organised by the Presbyteries of Glasgow and Dundee and had journeyed into many parts of Scotland to address meetings of office-bearers. After the Assembly of May 1930, it was hoped that he would be able to relax for a season and allow his life to settle into a slower tempo; but he himself felt that this was a dream that could not be fulfilled for some time to come. He knew the amount of committee work that would inevitably follow the union; he realised that if tact and forbearance and patience had been needed in bringing the union to completion, these would be needed again in full measure if all sections of the two Churches, now one body, were to work together in harmony. Hallowed customs, he knew, were often harder to change than many of the things that had once been looked upon as matters of principle. He was to have his share, and more than his share, in this great transfiguration in the days to come; but soon after the Assembly of May 1930 had been dissolved, his objections were broken down and he was forced to admit that a longer respite than the usual summer holiday in the Highlands was needed to restore him in mind and body. Once the decision was made, it seemed a God-sent chance to keep faith with his son in Tasmania, and plans for the journey to the southern hemisphere were talked over.

John White was troubled about his folk of The Barony. Looking back over the years since he had returned from his duties as chaplain at the front, he thought of the amount of time he had been obliged to give to the wider affairs of the Church of Scotland. The energy he had devoted to these greater tasks had meant an inevitable loss to his congregation. Under his supervision others had given much of the close personal care he himself would have liked to give. Was it quite fair to his people, he wondered in some perplexity, to leave them for as long a period as the projected visit would stretch out to? He decided that the least he could do was to offer to resign so that the congregation could bring in a fresh minister to guide them in the days to come. "I have been so much away from my people," he said, "as Moderator in 1925, in connection with Church Union and in the general work of the Church, and I was Moderator again in 1929 with all that this entailed in a newly united Church."

The answer of the people of The Barony to any talk of resignation was emphatic. They would not hear of it. Their minister must go to Tasmania; it would be an easing of the strain he had undergone and a break that was long overdue; and they would welcome him home on his return. The Presbytery of Glasgow gave him leave of absence, and in the missive were these words: "We commission you to convey our greetings to the Presbytery of Tasmania and any other judicatory authority of the Presbyterian Church of Australia. You have done a big work for the Church here, the effect of which will be permanent, and you deserve a good holiday." John White was touched: "The kind words of the Presbytery made it possible for me to go on a Sabbatic half-year with an easy conscience." The Rev. James M'Cardel of Shettleston agreed to become interim-moderator during his absence; and on Thursday, 18th September, he set out with Mrs. White from Glasgow. The last thing that was thrust into his hand as he leant from the compartment window was Dean Inge's new book on *Ethics* with the request of the editor of the *Scots Observer* that he would review it and post his article from Gibraltar.

There was heavy weather in the Channel and Atlantic rollers in the Bay, but the book was duly read and the article posted when John White went ashore on the Rock to hold a service at St. Andrew's Church there. One of his fellow passengers was E. Phillips Oppenheim, a popular writer of that time who never seemed to tire of depicting in his novels scenes of high life on the Riviera: "Oppenheim spends most of the day in his deck chair writing and browsing," wrote John White. "At such moments he is quite unapproachable and unapproached. Later in the evening he is a gay old spark." But the novelist disembarked at Marseilles and disappeared in dust on the road to Monte Carlo. Another passenger was H. N. Brailsford, a fellow student of Glasgow University. He came on board at Marseilles and was travelling to Bombay "to study the Indian question". Reminiscences were exchanged. At Bombay, John White and his wife were welcomed by Principal John McKenzie of Wilson College, and the Whites paid a short visit there.[1] They met a procession of about forty thousand followers of Ghandi who assembled on the Chowpatty Sands opposite the College. They were harangued by a number of speakers, including H. N. Brailsford. John White's comment was:

> "This is Brailsford's first visit to India. He intends to stay seven weeks, giving one week to Bombay. He will be writing, he told me, to English and American papers. As the Round Table Conference is meeting in London, what he writes will influence British opinion. He had been only a few hours in India at the time of his utterance on that platform."

VII

They reached Australia and disembarked at Fremantle on Tuesday, 21st October. The forthcoming visit of John White had been widely publicised, and many preparations had been made to welcome him. The first greeting he received was that of a Glasgow man who rushed on board to meet him, waving a copy of the Glasgow *Evening Citizen*. Reporters demanded to know what his impressions of Australia were.

"I haven't seen the place yet," he said, looking them over, "but already I have seen its reporters. I'll give you my impressions of them if you don't skedaddle!"

Officials of the Presbyterian Churches of Australia came on board and took the Whites off to a reception at Perth, where the Lord Mayor received them. People spoke to him there of their ties with The Barony,

---

[1] After Dr. White's death, the Very Rev. John McKenzie, C.I.E., D.D., wrote of him: "We met him first when he was off duty in our own house in Bombay, and neither we nor our colleagues shall forget the vivid interest he showed in the work of the Church in India and in the problems we were facing—and in the missionaries themselves. We have been indebted to him since then for much kindness, and we shall continue to remember him as a big-minded and a big-hearted Christian man."

with the Partick district where he had lived as a student, and with his first charge at Shettleston. At Adelaide there was another large reception. John White wrote: "Fortunately it was a Saturday, so it had not been possible to arrange a civic reception for us—*Laus Deo*!" But they did not escape being fêted at Melbourne. The Lord Mayor received them, and the Moderator-General of the Presbyterian Church of Australia was there to offer his salutations. On to Launceston in Tasmania they sailed, but there was to be little rest for him until he had satisfied those who wished to do him honour. On the second day after his arrival he had to open the new Scotch School for Presbyterian boys, where the impression he made was such that he was asked later to return and address the assembled college and distribute prizes. "Everyone has held you in great regard since the day you came," wrote the Headmaster. "I overheard one of our sixth form boys say he 'would walk ten miles to hear that chap speak or preach'." Speaking and preaching, for a man who had come there for a rest, became so frequent that his wife and son had to exert gentle pressure to keep him away from the pulpits and platforms to which he was invited. He made journeys throughout the island and was struck by its likeness to Scotland.

"What a variety there is in the landscape! Travel among those hills and by the loch-sides, and you can almost imagine you are back in Perthshire. As for the towns, Hobart is surely one of the most beautiful in Tasmania, with that mighty Mount Wellington beside it. I motored half-way up its side and had one of the grandest views I had seen anywhere in the world."

He could be counted among the minor connoisseurs of landscape, for his travels had included France, Germany, Greece, Asia Minor, Madeira, the Canary Islands, Canada, and America; and the copious but abbreviated notes he made would suggest that if he had had the patience and the necessary leisure, he might have written a memorable travel book.

The plenitude of Scots place-names in the island gave him pleasure. The names of many of the folk themselves told him that their ancestors had come from Scotland, and they had brought with them a love of the old country and its traditions. John White told them they enjoyed a better climate in Tasmania than their ancestors had done in that other island off the north-west coast of Europe. He found the climate very much to his liking:

"the long hours of sunshine, the dry air, the clean atmosphere, the absence of those extremities of heat and cold that the Scot must thole with as good a grace as possible. I was not surprised," he said, "that these two hundred miles of water between Tasmania and the mainland have not prevented this island from becoming the holiday resort of Australia."

John White specially blessed the Tasmanian climate because it was bringing new health to his wife. She had been so ill before their setting out that the doctor had had some misgivings about allowing her to make the journey. But her mind had been set upon it, and the prospect of the sea voyage and of meeting her son in the home he had made for himself in the Antipodes had kept up her spirits; and as John White saw the continual betterment, he knew that the journey and the happy visitation had been providential. They had now been married for thirty-eight years. To her they had been years of supreme happiness—but also of devoted service to her husband and his work. She had accompanied him on many of his journeys throughout Scotland, including some of his exhausting Moderatorial tours; she had always taken her full share in the women's work in his parishes; but the greatest strain of all had been the period when her husband had served as a chaplain at the front. Then she had acted almost as an organising secretary of The Barony; on four nights a week she had faithfully attended meetings at the church, the vestry, the Mission Institute; and many a problem had been taken to her by the assistants, who knew how greatly John White himself had relied upon her wise guidance and quietening influence in moments of stress. And during those wartime days, in common with other wives and mothers, she had lived with one great fear not far from the fringes of her consciousness—the fear that any moment might bring to her a telegram announcing that something had happened either to her husband or to one of her two sons on active service. In spite of the interval of years that now separated her from those days of tension, she still suffered from their aftermath. "How she has improved in this wonderful climate," wrote John White. "The sunshine and peace are doing her a world of good. She is taking the Tasmanian remedy for rheumatism, honey and sulphur, and her determination to get quite well again is helping to complete the cure."

VIII

John White's love of football never left him, and at York Park in Launceston he watched many an exciting struggle. The addiction of the tall Scots clergyman to the game became known, and he was interviewed on the subject by one of the local papers. He spoke as a critical commentator, and was able to express an expert opinion:

"You allow forward passing in the Australian game, and I'm surprised you don't make more use of what you call hand-ball. When I arrived at the ground and saw a Hundred Points marked up, I began to wonder whether I hadn't come to a cricket match—it looks more like a cricket score to me! I'm impressed with the speed of your playing, the high marking, the long kicking."

That other great pleasure of his, fishing, he was able to indulge to the full on many a happy day by the side of a stream or on "that splendid fishing ground of Lake Leake". It was his considered opinion from all that he had heard and read and experienced that "Tasmania has some of the best trout fishing in the world, Rainbow trout, Loch Leven trout, brown trout". He was to take home with him to Scotland many a memory on which were based the tales he was to recount to friends in the smoking-rooms of Highland hotels.

He was astonished at some of the wild life that throve among the hills of the island. There was the Tasmanian devil, a beast like a badger with a huge head and fierce teeth; there was the Tasmanian wolf, or tiger, as it was sometimes called, with its ferocious muzzle and long tapering tail; above all there were the Tasmanian snakes. Of all moving creatures, they were John White's greatest abhorrence. With a vigour, unaccountable to those who watched him, he helped to clear half an acre of grass near his son's house, and afterwards he kept the lawn-mower going. The reason was not made clear until he admitted that he had been determined to demolish any lurking-place for those loathly reptiles.

The visit was a sequence of surprises. Even the range of Tasmania's minerals—zinc, lead, copper, iron, tin—astonished him. He was impressed by the richness of field and orchard crops, by the quality of cattle and horses, above all by the fine sheep; he found that the stud merinos of Tasmania had a world-wide reputation. This came closely home to him because his son managed the factory of the great British spinning firm, Patons and Baldwins, that used wool as its basic raw material.

Each journey through the island brought fresh interest, and the Tasmanian summer passed in a long tale of pleasant days. Autumn was upon them when they set out for home; they arrived back in London towards the end of March, and he gave a series of sittings to Sir John Lavery, who had been commissioned to paint a portrait that was to hang with the portraits of other Moderators at the Assembly Hall in Edinburgh.

He was glad to be back among his people, to get the reins again into his hand, and to find out for himself the progress made during his absence in the many committees of the Church in which he was interested. He had a lot of hard collar-work to put in before the Assembly opened on Tuesday, 19th May. His long rest had obviously restored his vigour, and he spoke on a wide range of matters: Finance, Relations with other Churches, the Place of Women in the Church, Unemployment, Spiritualism, Religious Education, Church Property, Chaplains, and above all on Home Mission work. In seven days of that Assembly he was on his feet no less than thirty-seven times. In his speech on the main problem facing the Church in large cities—the transfer of population to new areas—he was touching upon a matter to which he had been giving more and more careful thought. Soon his great energies were to be exerted in an enterprise of supreme importance—an enterprise which, it was clear, the Church of Scotland would have to nourish with all her resources if she were not to fail in her duty of providing a territorial ministry throughout the land. Henceforth, John White's own ministry was to a large extent to be that of planting new churches, new congregations, new centres of Christian life and work in communities which a great social revolution was creating. The General Assembly instructed the Home Mission Committee to submit a scheme for the building up of a fund to provide religious ordinances in these districts. And John White's motto was one that was to ring through every presbytery in Scotland: THE CHURCH IN THE MIDST.

Chapter XVII

EXTENDING THE KINGDOM

I

"Dr. Chalmers, in depositing this volume among the other books of the Theological Library, would earnestly recommend the study of Church economics. . . . The Fathers of the Reformed Church in Scotland gave their utmost attention to it, and to this we owe that goodly parochial system which has done so much for the Christianity of our people."

THE goodly parochial system: to establish and maintain it had been the proud endeavour of the Church. Hers had been a ministry that provided both for churchgoers and non-churchgoers. A parishioner was a parishioner, though he were a Moslem or an atheist; he could call at will on the services of the parish minister. And the Church of Scotland, carrying out her duty as the National Church, was to be confronted in this third decade of the twentieth century with the greatest task she had ever known in her Home Mission work.

In the first half of the nineteenth century, during the years covered by the volume of reports in the Theological Library, it had been Dr. Chalmers who had inspired a church-building enterprise that daunted many of his colleagues. The population of Scotland had more than doubled, but the number of churches and parishes had not increased. Chalmers had appealed to the Government of the day for funds to build new churches for the rapidly developing industrial areas. His plea was rejected; and he decided to go ahead alone. He saw that if poor people in crowded cities were to be looked after by the Church, some of the very large parishes would have to be broken up and *quoad sacra* churches established. To finance the first of these Chapels of Ease, he persuaded a number of friends to subscribe one hundred pounds each, and he hoped that a reasonable rate of interest would be paid on the shares. The ill-devised plan failed, but some public-spirited Glasgow men had faith in Chalmers and were infected by his zeal. They organised the Church Building Society, and made plans to erect some twenty parochial churches in and around Glasgow, with the stipulation that the patronage of new churches could not be held by patrons of

mother churches. Parliamentary approval was given; but there was consternation in Whitehall when the General Assembly proposed that the
new chapel ministers should have the right to become members of presbytery and to have separate kirk sessions of their own. That did not deter
the Assembly from passing the Chapel Act, and the new Church Building
Society raised a sum of no less than twenty thousand pounds in a few
months.

This great success in Glasgow proved to be a sharp stimulus to the
Church of Scotland. Dr. Chalmers gripped the reins and drove his team
of helpers with such vigour that a quarter of a million pounds were raised;
and the Central Committee, of which Chalmers was convener, added
another fifty thousand. After the Disruption the energies of Chalmers
found outlet in providing kirks and manses for the homeless Free Church;
but the Church of Scotland, after she had recovered from the shock of
the great secession, continued to build; and the Church Extension Scheme,
founded in 1834, was made fruitful by the Endowment Scheme with
which Dr. James Robertson's name will always be associated. He gave
his life to the task of helping to endow these new churches so that the
work would be carried on in the disjoined parishes in the more densely
populated areas. By the time John White became minister of The
Barony, four hundred and fifty new parishes had been established and
churches built since the day when Dr. Chalmers had begun the great work.

It had been a fine record of fairly steady achievement. But in the years
that followed the end of the First World War, the nation was faced with
the largest housing problem in its history. Wide stretches of countryside
on the outskirts of the larger towns were transformed into new communities. Both the Church of Scotland and the United Free Church tried
to keep pace with the growth of these communities; but they had other
problems in their hands as well, and they lacked the resources to do all
that might have been done. Each year, they fell further behind in the
race to provide "religious ordinances for the people". In the Glasgow area,
new extension charges were established at Gartcosh, Burnside, and elsewhere; others had been established at Rosyth and Kirkcaldy in Fife. At
Kinlochleven in Lochaber, the two Churches had run a joint mission and
a congregation had grown there. The Home Mission Committee had
given grants to build halls as well as stipend grants. By the time John
White presented his Home Mission Report to the General Assembly in
1932, there were nearly twenty new centres of Church life in Scotland
which had been created over the course of about a dozen years.

II

When John White's joint convener, Dr. P. D. Thomson, retired, it was decided that he should be the sole convener of the Home Mission Committee; and he was glad to have, as his vice-convener, Dr. Harry Miller, who had had long and fruitful years of experience in Home Mission work at the New College Settlement in the Pleasance of Edinburgh. He was glad also to have the advice of that great Scottish artist, D. Y. Cameron, who had transformed a commonplace little parish church near his home at Kippen, in Stirlingshire, into a place of singular beauty, with an atmosphere which nobody who had worshipped there would ever be likely to forget. To advise on the beautifying of the sanctuaries throughout the land was to be Sir David Cameron's fine contribution to the Church of Scotland. As a colleague of John White's, he was not only anxious to recreate old churches: he was eager to create new ones. However modest, these could have their own beauty. "We must build," he said; "let our day and generation leave behind it shrines from which prayer and praise may rise, beautiful and chaste in their grave simplicity."

John White laid before the General Assembly of 1932 his plan for the speeding up of the building of churches in the new housing areas. The cost was to be one hundred and eighty thousand pounds. Many people did not consider the times propitious for the launching of a general appeal to the Church at large, but the receiving of private gifts was sanctioned. The great blizzard of trade depression had blown across the Atlantic from America. In many parts of Britain, industry was stagnant; the lists of the unemployed were of a formidable length; but John White felt that an appeal to the members of the Church should not be long delayed, and he was determined that the General Assembly of 1933 should be asked to sanction it. When he put this to his Committee, many members sat silent. One or two were as eager as he was; but the majority merely acquiesced. The secretary of the Committee, the Rev. Arthur H. Dunnett, learned privately that many members doubted the wisdom of making such a large demand in these hard times. Since John White was afire with zeal for the cause, some of them admitted they had not cared to go against him. But the general feeling was that "John had a bee in his bonnet and it had better be left to buzz there until trade picked up and the money could be more easily found". Mr. Dunnett wrote to him in some concern: at the next meeting of the Committee he hoped members would not hesitate to speak out if they still felt doubtful about the wisdom of making an appeal at that time. If they were silent, he added, he felt he ought himself to propose that the whole scheme be laid on the shelf for ten years: this, he hoped, would force them to disclose their position. "In some ways," he said, "I shall be very sorry if this proposal of mine were adopted, but I think it is the only means whereby we can test the weight of opinion for and against our Scheme."

John White appreciated the perplexity of the secretary of the Committee, but he was not deterred. "I am told the time is not opportune," he said. "It is not the time I would have chosen. But it is God's time."

Before the Assembly of 1933 met, he had convinced the majority of the Committee that his own way, which he was persuaded was God's way, was the best and indeed the only way. It was agreed that he would ask the Assembly for permission to make a general appeal throughout the Church of Scotland and for approval to go ahead with the building programme. As he had done so often before, John White was driving himself too hard, and he went down early that spring with a serious attack of pneumonia. He was sent to the warmer climes of the south of England to recuperate. Impatient to be in harness again, he returned and put in a hard week of committee meetings at Edinburgh, only to collapse at his hotel and to be forbidden by his doctor to attend the Assembly in May. They sent him away to one of his favourite spots in the Highlands, Grantown-on-Spey, for a second convalescence. It fell to his vice-convener, Dr. Harry Miller, to ask for the Assembly's approval and for a beginning to be made on the building of new churches. Up on Speyside, John White was none too confident of how the Assembly would react. There was no man he would have trusted more than his friend Harry Miller to take the plan forward—but if only he could have been there himself! It was a happy moment for him when he received news of what had happened. Not only had the General Assembly given approval, but "hoped he would be fit to take up in the Autumn the great task to which he had so generously, so gallantly, and so characteristically put his hand, and sent him a message of affection and good cheer, assuring him of their loyalty in the cause which was so dear to him". George Macfarlane, a Glasgow business man and an old friend, went north to visit him on Speyside and reported that he had found him "fishing and already working out plans to make money for building his new kirks".

III

And so the National Church Extension Fund was opened. George Macfarlane's brother, Sir James, had become joint convener of the sub-committee, and part of his self-appointed duty was to prevent his friend from again over-working. The appeal was launched in a spirit of enthusiasm and confidence. Since the Assembly of 1932 had given permission for the fund to be opened to receive private gifts, a number of John White's friends had already come forward with donations in a spirit of magnanimity that deeply impressed him. His old friend Lord Maclay had headed the list with a gift of ten thousand pounds. Between them, the two Macfarlanes had given five thousand pounds[1]; and it is significant that, among the hundreds of those who subscribed generously were many ministers of the Church of Scotland. In addition to John White himself, the list included Dr. Charles L. Warr, Dr. Harry Miller, Dr. Norman Maclean, Professor H. R. Mackintosh, Professor W. P. Paterson, Principal Cairns of Aberdeen, Principal Macgregor of Glasgow, W. White Anderson, Arthur H. Dunnett, William Jardine, and many another. When he published the list of subscriptions, John White said he was delighted that the response had already overtopped by five hundred pounds the amount collected by Dr. Chalmers in 1834. The editor of one of the great Scottish newspapers told him he had made a blunder in announcing that he hoped to raise the full sum in three years; he ought to have declared that he must have it within a year. "I admit there was a good deal to be said for that criticism," was John White's comment, "but of course the generous churchfolk of Scotland can remedy that for themselves!" He went on to quote a passage in Addison's account of Sir Roger de Coverley's visit to Spring Garden—an answer from the past, he said, to those who thought that an over-abundance of churches in the heart of a city rendered it unnecessary to build any in the suburbs:

> "After some short pause, the old knight turning about his head twice or thrice, to take a survey of this great Metropolis, bid me observe how thick the city was set with churches, and that there was scarce a single steeple on this side Temple Bar. 'A most heathenish sight,' says Sir Roger: 'there is no religion at this end of the town. The fifty new churches will very much mend the Prospect; but Church-work is slow, Church-work is slow.' "

[1] Mr. George Macfarlane proved to be one of the most generous of all the private donors to the fund and added greatly to his original gift.

Nobody knew better than John White how slow Church work could be, and he was determined that there would be no delay in making it known to every congregation that it was their duty as Christians to support the cause. He established his offices at 232 St. Vincent Street, Glasgow, the Church's headquarters in the West country.

"I was working there myself in that year of 1933," Dr. White's widow has recorded. "At that time these offices were not very much used. The Glasgow Presbytery had some of the rooms, and I remember that part of the Foreign Mission work was being organised there.One heard talk of closing the place down because it seemed more efficient to have all branches of Church work under one roof at George Street in Edinburgh. But soon after his return from convalescence at Grantown-on-Spey, John White changed the atmosphere of these silent offices. From there he launched his great National appeal for the Church Extension Fund, and before long the whole place was humming with life."

Thirty churches and twenty church halls were needed—needed with a desperate urgency. That was the hard core of his appeal. From platform and pulpit, from the columns of the press, in every way that lay to his hand, he sent out the fiery cross over all Scotland. In one of these speeches he said:

"St. Paul was the first great Church Builder—the first organiser of Church Extension in Eastern Europe and Asia Minor. He recognised the cities as the strategic points in his campaign and built churches at Corinth, Ephesus, Thessalonica, Rome, and in every big centre of progress. . . . Sometimes you will hear a candid critic argue that the new suburbs ought to build their own churches. He is one of the great tribe of Talkers without knowledge. How can people from a slum clearance area establish a church for themselves? In our new housing areas, many have been uprooted from an environment where they had grown indifferent to religion. In a new home with new surroundings, what a chance there is for the Church to win them! In these communities boys and girls are growing up who will be the men and women that will guide the future of Scotland. Dare we let them grow up estranged from religion? The cynic and the agnostic might ask, Why build churches at all—can a State not get along without them? Remember why King David wanted to build a temple in Jerusalem.

He felt that God must be at the heart of a nation's life—that God must be at the very seat of Government, and he wanted Jerusalem to be the religious as well as the political capital of the land. A State without a Church is not firmly established. That was as true then as it is today. The national recognition of religion is a first principle of the Church of Scotland. It is our duty as the National Church to provide religious ordinances for all the citizens of this country."

The complaints and protests he had expected began to flow in to the St. Vincent Street offices. There were those who said that the scheme was too lavish; some repeated that the time was inopportune; others muttered among themselves that it did not affect their particular area—let the wealthier churches in places near the new housing areas dip into their ample funds and do this work. In no spirit of complaint, but rather in sorrow, one minister wrote that "economic conditions in this north-east corner of Scotland are appalling. In two and a half hours' visiting last night, going from house to house among the congregation, I did not find a single person—I mean the head of a household or a grown-up son or daughter—who was in employment." A number of letters telling a like story reached John White, and he could do no more than send back words of sympathy. But it was stimulating to receive a letter such as this:

"The appeal for £180,000 when depression is at its worst in Lanarkshire, when many churches can hardly meet their ordinary commitments; when Foreign Missions are languishing for lack of support; when the Maintenance of the Ministry is in a parlous condition—it is a most daring action to ask for that sum of money. It is so daring that only a John White would have attempted it. The very boldness of it appeals to the imagination. As a lowly placed country minister, with but a little influence, I shall do my best for the scheme in parish and presbytery."

I shall do my best for the scheme. It was these words, often repeated, that quickened the pulse. Inspiriting too, was a letter from John Moffat,[1] then minister at Alloa: "It has been made emphatically clear to me that something drastic must be done for Church Extension. I have almost exhausted my own resources for work here in Greenside Church—but where there's a will there's a way." And John Moffat's way was to give up the last Sunday of his holiday to provide supply for a vacant pulpit and give the

---

[1] He had been a refugee from the Hitler regime in Germany and had entered the service of the Church of Scotland.

fee to the National Church Extension Fund. "If two thousand ministers did it," he said, "we could build another hall from those fees that would amount to over £4,000. Could one thousand ministers not do so next summer? This is a mere suggestion from a man anxious to do his bit. We ministers must give a lead to the people."

IV

John White's methods of gathering in the money were many and diverse. The campaign was organised under the business-like eye of Sir James Macfarlane. Schemes were sent out to presbyteries for transmission to congregations; and suggestions ranged from sales of work to the delivery of envelopes at the house of every member. John White made plans to capture the imagination of the young folk of the Church. Few knew better how to bring out the finest in boys and girls, and with a child he was at home in a twinkling. He caught the interest of the Youth Organisations, and the One Million Shilling Fund was started. He opened the Children's Million Pennies Fund; and the late King George VI and the present Queen Mother, then the Duke and Duchess of York, wrote to express their interest in it. "From my heart I wish it a full measure of success," the Duke wrote to John White, recalling the occasion when he had been Lord High Commissioner in the year of the union of the two great Presbyterian Churches. The Duchess of York sent a donation of a hundred pennies each on behalf of her children, our present Queen and Princess Margaret.

To the children of the Church of Scotland John White sent a message: "The cost of a *brick* is 3d. and of a *stone* 10d. Many will want to have at least *one* brick or stone in one of our new churches. Those who follow the lead of the little Princesses and send 100 pennies will have 33 bricks." In the same message he told of a boy who had given two sixpences he had received "for his Christmas" and had sent them with a letter: "Dear Dr. White, I hear you are needing money to build new churches. I am sending you Two Sixpences to build one." John White read this to a friend who had already promised a thousand pounds, and the man was so impressed with the little letter that he said he would double his gift. His brother came into the room and was told what had happened. When he read the letter he said that he also would like to double what he had promised. This brought their gift up to four thousand pounds. At once John White intervened: "It takes *five* thousand to build a church." The brothers looked at each other, smiled and said: "All right—we'll make it five thousand between us." John White told this story many times, and he always added—"And that's how twelve pennies built a church!"

In the midst of the campaign, he was told more than once that he was the best beggar in Scotland. He answered this with characteristic vigour:

"I have never in my life *begged* for money for the Kingdom of God. Never! But I do state the need. I state the obligation, I state the privilege of giving. . . . Money is the stored potentiality of life's forces. When placed on God's altar it is laying thereon a part of the very best of one's life. What is money but a contribution of a man's interest and thought and sympathy? If a man earns a thousand a year and gives one-tenth, he has contributed a tenth of his time, of his energy. . . .

"We are not building churches merely; we are building sanctuaries for the spiritual well-being of our brothers and sisters. The problem is not one of stone and mortar only, but of living stones in the Temple of God. . . . We need the consecration of the whole membership to the service of the Church. We need money. I am not begging for it. But I ask you to consider whether you give to the cause of God even one-tenth of what you give for your own pleasure. When you pay for a few gallons of petrol for a pleasure run, do you ever consider whether you have *even once* given as much as that to the cause of Church Extension?"

Sir James Simpson made a tour of the Presbytery of Fordyce in wintry weather to try to interest congregations there. His report was in the hands of John White before the Assembly of 1934. Meetings had been arranged for him in many parishes. One minister promised him an audience of two hundred, but it was no more than twenty-eight. Attendances were poor wherever he went, but again and again he spoke of them as "fine meetings" and said: "I have not been worried by the small numbers, and carried on as if two thousand were present! Those who did attend were undoubtedly interested—and the type who will see that the message gets around. That is what we are aiming at. When I addressed the Presbytery I sensed the atmosphere of a good meeting." John White told Sir James he had done splendid work: "It is easy to address crowded meetings of convinced hearers; it is much more difficult and much more necessary to interest and instruct the indifferent. Your meetings will lead to good results, but they must be followed up. Later, it would be a good plan to remind the ministers of your appeal and ask them what has happened." These letters of reminder John White always counted a vital part of the plan. He left nothing hanging in the air.

V

In a survey of the first few years of the enterprise, one Scottish newspaper spoke of "the initial deadweight of opinion against the scheme". The writer added that the question John White had been compelled to answer was: "Would the Church succumb in the face of the growing indifference of the people and the defection of youth?" John White's answer had been a blunt negative, and the writer concluded: "So urgent did this negative seem that he was constrained to outline a scheme of such boldness that it almost took the breath away." The writer was but echoing the words of the Lanarkshire minister who, at the beginning of the campaign, had said it was so daring a scheme that only a John White would have attempted it—and only a John White could accomplish it.

After two years of effort, he could look back on a considerable achievement. Churches and halls were being built; new sites were being secured; and already young congregations in the housing areas were growing in number—and, by a miracle of grace, some were already financially independent. John White took pleasure in citing the case of the Church Extension charge at King's Park, Glasgow. There, a start had been made with only a few sheets of paper—nothing more tangible than that—but on these had been jotted the names of one hundred and fifty people who might become members of a new church if one were planted there. The decision was made to begin. While a church was being built, a wooden hut was acquired for public worship. A minister was appointed to look after the people which had been gathered together by missionary efforts. Soon the congregation numbered five hundred, and the next report was that this figure had been doubled. Within two years of the opening of the wooden hut for public worship, a new church, costing over ten thousand pounds, was dedicated. Ten months later, the membership had increased by fifty per cent. It was a story of a steadily mounting success. The original wooden hut had been bought from the Presbytery for eight hundred pounds; the minister's manse had cost four hundred. By 1935, the new congregation had paid off both these debts and had also contributed five hundred pounds towards the building of the church. It had agreed to pay a further three thousand six hundred pounds. What specially pleased John White was that the Sunday School of this Church

Extension charge was the largest within the bounds of the Presbytery of Glasgow.

He had allowed himself three years to raise the one hundred and eighty thousand pounds, and by the end of 1934 he had more than half of that sum in hand, with eighteen months left in which to collect the remainder. The country had begun to pull out of the slough of depression, but nobody was thinking in terms of national prosperity. Many people were amazed that the growth of the fund had exceeded the programme which John White had laid down, and he could say that in truth the response had been heartening.

The response of the Church was by no means the only thing that cheered him at that time. He went often into the new housing areas and conducted services in their churches or their wooden huts (he took one in a little shop which they locally called the "shop church") and there he found much to inspire him. A doctor in one of these new areas told him how some children had been a constant worry to himself and other people because of their deliberate destruction of property. There was a wave of what almost could have been called minor hooliganism. And then, to his surprise, he noticed that the cases of wilful destruction were becoming fewer. When they stopped altogether he began to make enquiries and found that the children who had been the ringleaders were still living in the neighbourhood, but instead of amusing themselves by breaking things they were helping bus passengers with their luggage and carrying out many another worthy job. The doctor enquired further. In the new church, a club for boys of eight to twelve had been started. In his wisdom, the superintendent had chosen a dozen of the worst youngsters he could find and had formed them into a committee to lead all the others in a drive to protect property and a help-your-neighbour campaign. That was but one of many stories told him as he went round the country.

The coping stone seemed to be put to the whole enterprise when the news was published that the call for one hundred and eighty thousand pounds had been answered before the end of 1936.

Chapter XVIII

PRESBYTERY AND EPISCOPACY

I

THE Lambeth Appeal to all Christian people had been made by Archbishop Davidson in 1920. It had been a plea to consider whether, by a closer unity, the Churches could help to heal the wounds, spiritual and material, caused by the First World War and prevent the recurrence of a like catastrophe. The Church of Scotland and the United Free Church were approached in May 1921 on the basis of the Lambeth Appeal. At that time, since these two Churches were striving to complete their own union, the Church of Scotland had replied that she would gladly confer at a more convenient season.

When the time for conferring arrived, much of the responsibility fell on John White. To him privately the first letter in a long sequence on unity was addressed by the Archbishop of Canterbury, Dr. Cosmo Gordon Lang. That first letter, in March 1930, contained an invitation to him to be a guest at the palace while the Lambeth Conference was in session. Lang said they might then have a chance of talking over points of difference and agreement between their two Churches. In accepting, John White reminded Lang that he could not represent his Church officially without the sanction of the General Assembly. At his suggestion, Lord Sands was also invited, and from 17th to 19th July the two men were guests at Lambeth Palace. The Assembly had met in the interval, but John White had decided not to ask for a mandate to represent the Church; it would be better at that early stage, he felt, to go to Lambeth as a private guest of Cosmo Lang's. The Archbishop of York, William Temple, presided over a large gathering of bishops; Hensley Henson, who was among them, has recorded his impressions of the meeting:

"Both the Presbyterians made an excellent impression, especially Dr. White. He was straightforward, informing, and humorous. More than one bishop observed what an excellent type of bishop he would have made, had his lot been cast in an Episcopal Church." [1]

[1] *Retrospect of an Unimportant Life—1863-1939*, by Herbert Hensley Henson (Oxford University Press).

John White and Lord Sands expressed sympathetic interest in the closer fellowship of the Churches, but added that it must be recognised that "the Lambeth proposals embody a very different proposition from that which had recently been settled in Scotland. It was not a question of a difference between members of the same family. On the contrary, it concerned two families who differed in some aspects of doctrine and polity." The bishops questioned them about the ordination of ministers in the Church of Scotland, the admission of elders, the office of deacon, how deaconesses were set apart, and in particular about the re-marriage of divorced persons on which there was a cleavage of opinion and practice between the two Churches.

In their replies, John White and Lord Sands laid down with emphasis a number of principles. "There can be little prospect of any advance," John White said, "until we all realise that it will not enrich—rather it will impoverish—the Church to seek unity by elimination or by submission. We must proceed on the principle that there must be included all that we regard as essential. We can allow compromise only in administrative readjustments."

Another of his statements was: "Even if it were desirable, it is premature to seek one organisation of the Church. But in spite of widely different ecclesiastical traditions, it ought to be possible for us to hold a true Catholic unity and communion with one another. This would find expression through fellowship in witness and in social service." Both men stressed that, in structure, the Church of Scotland was Presbyterian; she was Catholic and Evangelical in her foundations; and Presbyterianism was proved to have been best suited to the genius of the Scottish nation.

The Archbishop of York spoke hopefully of the situation; but Bishop Hensley Henson had a private talk immediately afterwards with John White and made a note of the impression left on his mind: "Plainly, Dr. White was not very hopeful of union with Anglicans!"

To everyone, John White made his own position abundantly clear: "Now that the union within Scotland has been accomplished, one of my tasks is the furthering of Christian unity in the United Kingdom—*but not at the sacrifice of the traditions and rich spiritual heritage of our Church of Scotland.*"

II

Cosmo Lang agreed that it would be premature to suggest any conference between the two Churches with organic unity as the object. With his upbringing in a Scottish manse—his father, it will be remembered, had been Dr. John Marshall Lang of The Barony—he knew that many a long year must pass before the gap between the two Churches could be narrowed, far less closed. He had himself been present at the great union ceremony in Edinburgh in the previous October and was fully aware that the Church of Scotland, by Parliamentary ratification of her Declaratory Articles, had obtained recognition by the State that she possessed that spiritual freedom which she had always claimed as her inherent right: a freedom which the Church of England did not possess. Cosmo Lang was fully aware also that, while the Church of Scotland did not regard ordination by a bishop as invalid, many Anglicans believed that no minister of the Church of Scotland had been validly ordained in the Presbyterian ceremony: indeed, by many in the Anglo-Catholic section, Scots Kirk ministers were viewed as heretics. Before union could be contemplated, Lang knew that there was a basis of constitutional difference that required solution. The Church of Scotland had the power, if she so desired, to unite with the Church of England. But the Church of England had no power to unite with another body; the permission of Parliament would first have to be sought; those who held the keys were the members of the House of Commons, without whose consent the Church of England was powerless to complete a union even with another Episcopal Church. As for Church government, Lang knew that to say there had been bishops in the early years of the Reformed Church in Scotland was but to blur the issue, since their status and powers had been very different from those of the bishops of the Anglican Church. The one Church was prelatic, the other democratic. Even the Altar of the Anglicans and the Lord's Table of the Presbyterians had at least one sharply differing tradition, and Cosmo Lang was not unmindful of the fact that the law of the Church of England had debarred Scottish Presbyterians, save in exceptional circumstances and only by permission of a diocesan bishop, from taking Communion in an Anglican church. That in some parts of England the law was broken by clergy who did not approve of the law merely served to show that irregularities were tolerated. The legal bar was prominently in John White's mind when he was a guest at Lambeth Palace in that July of 1930. He has left his own account of an experience there:

"At Lambeth Palace, morning prayers I always attended, but not Communion. On one occasion, when retiring for the night, Lang said to me, 'We are having Communion tomorrow—will you be there?'

"I replied that I would not. 'I should like to communicate,' I said; 'but as I have not been invited it may be better that I should not place you in a difficult position by attending.'

" 'I invite you now,' said Lang, 'and I do trust you will come.'

" 'Thank you, I shall be present.'

"The Archbishop, Alan Don, and Serjeant, officiated. I was the only other person present. But just as I was moving to the rail, Archbishop Temple joined me. Later at breakfast, Lang referred to the historic happening: 'Three Archbishops, two nominal and one real—and he from the Church of my father.' "

John White went to Lambeth again in the following year, and this time he took with him Dr. Archibald Fleming, of St. Columba's, London. They said they wished to "deal direct with the Church of England and not with the Episcopal Church in Scotland"; but Lang stipulated that the Scottish Episcopalians must take part in the talks, and he agreed as a compromise that the English Presbyterians could be included with the Scottish. Later, John White wrote to the Archbishop saying that the General Assembly had entrusted the whole matter to a standing committee and "the way to conference lay open so far as the Church of Scotland was concerned". He suggested that a deputation of three (two others and himself) should have an informal meeting with the Archbishop (and any others he might wish to attend) to settle a number of points of procedure, and his letter concluded: "I need hardly say that it would be a unique privilege and a very great pleasure to me as minister of The Barony, if the first step towards giving fuller expression to the friendly relations existing between the Church of England and the Church of Scotland should be taken when a son of The Barony is Primate."

To this Lang replied cordially and suggested a day for their meeting. He wrote: "I find it very difficult to envisage what the results of the proposed conference between our Churches may be, but to enter upon it must be an act of Faith and we must leave its issue in God's hands. I need not say how greatly I was touched by your recalling my old associations with the Barony church."

John White found the proposed date inconvenient and dropped Lang a note to say so, but suggested that his two colleagues, Principal Martin and Professor Curtis, might travel south without him. A telegram arrived from Lambeth Palace: Lang was dismayed at the thought of having a meeting without John White, and he suggested another date. The meeting duly took place on 29th April, and John White and his two friends spent a couple of nights at the palace as the guests of the Primate. The Lambeth Minute of the meeting covered the points that were talked over. In the Archbishop's view, the primary aim of the conference was not to prepare the way for a union of the Churches under one government: on the contrary, it was to be inter-communion between them. The ultimate consequence, as he called it, was to be "an organic union between the Scottish Episcopal Church and the Church of Scotland".[1] However, he was persuaded to modify his views. Without restriction, there was to be a frank exploration of the questions at issue in the hope that the conferring delegates would be "enabled to reach some useful expression of the measure of unity already existing". The delegates were to discuss ways in which that unity might be manifested, and to consider "how they might most effectively co-operate in the common service of God's Kingdom". It was agreed to recommend that nine delegates be appointed on each side to confer together alternately in London and Edinburgh. Each delegation would have the power to take others into consultation. Since the invitation was to come officially from the Anglican side, the Archbishop thought it would add to its significance if he were invited to be present in person at the General Assembly in May and commend the proposal to the supreme court of the Church. This was approved by the committee; he was duly invited by the Moderator-elect; and he travelled north to speak to the Assembly on 27th May 1932.

III

Before that Assembly had met, there arose some discord (which found its way into the press) over the "unrestricted" nature of the proposed conference with the Anglican Church. In the minds of many ministers, there was a clear memory of how that word had been used and underlined soon after union negotiations had started between the Church of Scotland and the United Free Church. It had been the operative word in the famous report which John White had drawn up for the General Assembly in 1911. For the first time in the history of union, the Church of Scotland had then announced that she was ready to confer on union with her relations to the

---

[1] If any organic union was contemplated, it was widely felt that the first to be considered should be one between the Church of England and the Scottish Episcopal Church, which were in full communion with each other; and it was also felt that union between the Church of Scotland and the English Presbyterian Church should become a matter of practical politics before consideration should be given to the much more complicated question of a union between the Church of England and the Church of Scotland.

State as an open question; the assurance that talks were to be "unrestricted" by any conditions had been a throwing open of the door to union. And now, because the same word was being applied to the projected conferences with the Church of England (it had been used in the Lambeth invitation of 1930), many ministers feared that there was a move on foot to throw Presbyterianism into the melting-pot. On the day before the Assembly met, John White felt obliged to write a letter to the press. He emphasised that the use of the word certainly did not "throw open to debate the whole question of our Presbyterian government". He pointed out that in putting forth the Lambeth Appeal in 1920, the claim had been made that the *Episcopate was the one means of providing a ministry possessing the commission of Christ*, and the following words had been used: "We desire that the office of a Bishop should be everywhere exercised in a representative and constitutional manner. . . . Nay more, we eagerly look forward to the day when, through its acceptance in a united Church, we may all share in that grace which is pledged to the members of the whole body in the apostolic rite of the laying-on of hands."

Quoting these words from the Lambeth Appeal, John White demanded:

> "Was our acceptance of the invitation of Lambeth to be 'restricted' to conference on *that* issue? . . . If so, it serves no useful purpose to go further at this time, for we are not ready to discuss ways of uniting the Church of Scotland and the Church of England under one and the same form of government. Such a 'restricted' conference would be a fruitless conference."

And thus, to the Church of Scotland, and all others who were interested, John White made his own position and that of his colleagues as clear as cold prose could make it.

When the Archbishop of Canterbury rose to speak in the General Assembly a few days later, he explained where he stood on the question of union.

> "There is one point, one misapprehension, which I am anxious at the very outset to remove—I would rather say to dismiss. This conference is not in any way to negotiate terms of union between our respective Churches. I hope it would have no such desire. Certainly, so far as I can speak, it would have no such authority. That stage of negotiation is far distant, if it ever be reached. . . . Need we contemplate any amalgamation of churches under one identical government?" he asked, and added amid applause: "There is no reason why they

should not remain autonomous in their respective areas. *There is no such value in mere identity of government as would make it worth while to face the difficulties of history, of law, of character, of sentiment.* My own hope rather is simply this—though perhaps it may be premature even to express it—that if these conferences reach some agreement on such questions of faith and order as each side might deem to be necessary, they can come into full communion with each other, retaining their own autonomy—that is to say—an unrestricted inter-communion among their members and an unrestricted fellowship of their ministers."

Mr. J. G. Lockhart, in his biography of Cosmo Gordon Lang, said that unfortunately Lang's presence at the Assembly was not the olive branch it was meant to be. "Some of the presbyterians were irritated and suspicious," he wrote, "smelling a backstairs intrigue. While they received their visitor politely and listened to him with deference, among themselves they were asking by whose authority he had been invited." If any of them had indeed imagined they could smell a backstairs intrigue, there can be little doubt that the reason for this fantasy lay in the fact that the Archbishop of Canterbury had been invited to address the General Assembly on a question that deeply concerned the Church in a manner that many regarded as unconstitutional. The approval of the Assembly, which might have been obtained on the opening day, had not been obtained. Who had invited the Archbishop? Since no explanation had been given, this became a question asked in the lobbies and answered with shrugs. Dr. Charles L. Warr in his memorable book, *The Presbyterian Tradition*, published in the year that followed the Archbishop's address to the Assembly, touched upon the appearance of Lang in this way:

> "Considerable dissatisfaction was expressed that the origin of his visit was strangely veiled in mystery. This, to some extent, prejudiced the issue from the start. . . . The Assembly of 1932 was merely informed that on a certain day the Archbishop of Canterbury was coming to address it. Thus, unauthoritatively invited from some quarter which had not yet been revealed, the Archbishop came north and delivered his eirenicon."

Lang himself felt what his biographer describes as "the slight chill in the atmosphere", and as he left the Assembly with Bishop Reid of Edinburgh, the latter remarked ruefully, "Nothing will come of it." What did happen was thus described by Dr. Warr:

"Seriously divided as to the expediency of the whole enterprise and feeling itself to have been stampeded, the Assembly, courteously adverse to showing ungraciousness to the Head of the Sister Church, agreed, though without any unanimous enthusiasm, to appoint representatives to negotiate with representatives of the Anglican Communion."

On the same day as the Archbishop had spoken, the disputable word "unrestricted" came again to the fore. Lord Sands had publicly admitted it was an unfortunate term. Dr. Hector Macpherson said in the General Assembly:

"In unrestricted conference on the basis of the Lambeth Appeal, only *our* principles are to be in the melting-pot. . . . The Revised Prayer Book of the English Church was something of a compromise, but on the whole substantial gains were made by the Anglo-Catholic party. That Prayer Book, as you all remember, was twice thrown out by the House of Commons on the ground that it registered a definite move on the road to Rome. Yet, despite its rejection, the Prayer Book is used in many churches throughout England. To enter into unrestricted conference with a Church rent by controversy and torn by doctrinal strife is calculated to arouse the deepest disquiet throughout the membership of our Church .. . . The question of bishops or no bishops has been settled for us in Scotland long ago," declared Dr. Macpherson amid applause. "Our liberties were secured for us by the blood of the martyrs—those who glorified God in the Grassmarket, endured the rack and the thumbscrew, and languished in the prisons of Dunnottar and Bass. We shall not tear out the brightest pages of our country's story and give up the liberties so dearly bought."

John White listened to these perfervid utterances, and was silent. There was no need for him to add his word to views he had already expressed—or to add to assurances he had already given. There was no need for him to whip up the enthusiasm of the Assembly for "liberties so dearly bought". The temper of the great audience—the Hall was packed on that Tuesday afternoon of May 1932—was plain to see and to hear.

IV

In 1933, his spell of convalescence at Speyside kept John White from the Assembly. Principal Martin presented the report, and told what little there was to tell of the progress they had made at the joint conferences. They had been trying, he said, to lay the foundations for common endeavour and common service.

> "We of the Church of Scotland know our own position clearly as a branch of Christ's Church Catholic. As ministers, we were ordained to the ministry not of the Presbyterian, and still less of a merely Scottish Church, but to the ministry of the Church of our Lord Jesus Christ. Whether we are recognised by others is the affair of those others solely. If the Pope of Rome, for example, denies it, we must wait for his better enlightenment."

He spoke of the points on which agreement had been reached in the two joint conferences held since the last Assembly. These struck many of his hearers as points that could be called fundamental to any Protestant Church in Britain. Where might the next step take them to? The misunderstandings about the "unrestricted" conference still seemed to be disturbing many ministers and elders. They were afraid that, in the minds of at least some of the Anglican delegation, there might lurk the misapprehension that by accepting the invitation to an "unrestricted" conference the Presbyterians were willing to throw into the crucible the validity of their orders and sacraments. After some discussion the Assembly gave an instruction to the committee. The representatives of the Anglican Church must be informed that "any agreement with regard to the Orders and Sacraments of the conferring Churches can be based only on the *recognition of the equal validity of the Orders and Sacraments of both Churches and of the equal standing of the accepted communicants and of ordained ministers* in each".

The sponsor of that proposal was Dr. Archibald Fleming of St. Columba's. He spoke on mutual admission to pulpits and intercommunion. This seemed to him to be fundamental—a prerequisite to any further talks on unity.

> "If we cannot all meet at the Lord's Table," he asked, "where can we meet? At any rate, the next move is not with us. Our pulpits are open to every Anglican divine. The way to the Lord's Table in our churches lies unobstructed to every Anglican communicant. What more can we do? Surrender the validity of our ministry and sacraments? Never! . . . Must we undergo a form of re-ordination that would seem to some of us a farce? Archbishop Leighton, with the noblest intentions, but with disastrous results, tried the experiment

George Outram & Co Ltd

Their Majesties King George V and Queen Mary leaving St. Giles' Cathedral, Edinburgh, after divine service and a visit to the Thistle Chapel, on Sunday, 6th July, 1931. Accompanying the King is Dr. Charles L. Warr, Dean of the Thistle. With Queen Mary is Dr. White, who conducted the service.

George Outram & Co Ltd

The unveiling of the plaque by Mrs. Anne White in the John White Chapel at The Barony Church of Glasgow on 21st April, 1953. In the dedication service, the Memorial Address was delivered by Dr. Charles L. Warr; and among those present were Dr. G. Johnstone Jeffrey, Moderator of the General Assembly, the Lord Provost of Glasgow, the Lord Provost of Aberdeen, and the Rev. W. Roy Sanderson, successor to Dr. White at The Barony.

once and for all. . . . Let us get out of our minds the unscholarly interpretation of the Lord's prayer for unity which implies that unity means
uniformity."

He spoke of the report of the committee, and said there was one phrase in
it that seemed to him most offensive and insulting. The committee had
asked to be continued for another year to consider with the Anglicans the
question of the admission of Presbyterians to Holy Communion in an
Anglican church only "in exceptional circumstances". He repeated the
phrase with scorn. To partake of Communion in a church of the other
denomination only in exceptional circumstances was not true communion.
Amid the loud applause of the Assembly, he demanded: "Since when has
the old Church of Scotland, the old United Free Church, the old Free
Church, and the old United Presbyterian Church developed that new and
wholly uncharacteristic inferiority complex?"

In his speech to the Assembly of 1934, John White recounted those
matters on which agreement had been reached.[1]

Based upon them, the joint conference had recommended six points
for the consideration of the two Churches. The first was mutual admission
to pulpits, the second a welcome to members of either Communion out
of reach of their own accustomed ordinances to the Table of the Lord as
members of the Catholic Church of Christ. Other points for consideration
were: the exchange of official delegations; joint pronouncements on
matters of importance; the formation of a joint advisory council to consider matters affecting the local relations of the two Churches at home and
abroad; and the promotion of a better understanding of each other's
history and genius and of co-operation in public service. It was noted that
one phrase which had given offence in the previous Assembly had now
been dropped: there was no mention of communion only *in exceptional
circumstances*. But another phrase had been substituted which now called
forth even stronger objections. That there should be inter-communion
only when members were "out of reach of their own accustomed ordi-

---

[1] "These included agreement on the Scriptures; on the attitude to Credal statements; on
the Gospel of God's grace as the divine instrument of individual and social regeneration; on
the Sacraments of Baptism and the Lord's Supper; on a recognition of the ministry of the
Lord Jesus Christ to the Church; on the Church as grounded in the will of God; on the
inward unity of believers made visible in a common Church life and fellowship and in the
acknowledgment of the obligation to seek and promote that visible unity; on the continuity
of the Church; and on the sovereign right of the Lord Jesus Christ to govern human life
in every sphere—not only in the ecclesiastical order—but the whole ordered life of mankind."
—Dr. White's summing up of the points of agreement as he explained them to the General
Assembly on Tuesday, 29th May 1934.

nances" brought down the denunciation of Principal W. M. Macgregor of Glasgow, a man of vigorous and incisive speech. The offending words had, in fact, been taken *verbatim* from the rules of the Church of England,[1] and John White had sanctioned their use in the report. Principal Macgregor thought it deplorable that communicants be admitted to the Lord's Table in the other denomination only if they were "out of reach of their own accustomed ordinances" .What did "out of reach" mean—was it ten or twenty or thirty miles? "This is an entirely dishonouring conception of the Holy Sacrament," he declared, and he asked why members of the Catholic Church of Jesus Christ could not be received at the Lord's Table at any time and without a geographical quibble. Nevertheless, he felt it was desirable that the Assembly should, without a division, agree upon the deliverance: and the Assembly did so and approved the six recommendations in the joint statement.

John White told the Assembly he was afraid it was impossible to predict when—if ever—these matters on which the joint conference had agreed would be considered by the Church of England. Clearly, the chief obstacles to their approval by the Anglicans were mutual admission to pulpits and inter-communion. The delegates of both Churches had recognised this; it had been patent to all; and they had been forced to agree that the joint conferences should be suspended for a time. "The grave differences of polity and of doctrine as associated with polity, which divide our Churches, will have to be faced—and faced soon," he said. "That has been brought before us in the mission-fields in South India, in Africa both East and West. What answer are we to give?" He referred to the relations between Britain and Germany, rapidly worsening in 1934. "The world situation," he said, "reveals the urgency of Christian unity. Where Churches can speak unitedly with the authority of Christ's Evangel to the world, they should do so."

V

For a whole year, John White waited in vain for some word of hope from England. Little or nothing seemed to have happened: certainly nothing that brought the unity any nearer. At the General Assembly of 1935, he had nothing to report. He tried to turn it aside with a jest. In

[1] In the Church of England, a diocesan bishop, if an application were made to him by a parish clergyman, was empowered to give permission to admit to Holy Communion members of other Christian denominations for a limited time if they were out of reach of their own accustomed ordinances.

the committee they had argued on whether there should be no report, or whether they should make a report to say that they had no report to make. "It reminds me," he said, "of the old discussions between the Nominalists and the Realists as to how many angels could stand on the point of a needle. . . . Let us report that there is no report, and give the reason why." He blamed what he called the "cumbrous ecclesiastical machinery of the Church of England".[1] In doing so, he had the Archbishop of Canterbury warmly on his side. But the cumbrous ecclesiastical machinery had actually been in motion. The report of the joint conference, which had been so heartily approved by the General Assembly, had come before both Houses of Convocation. The Upper House of Canterbury carried a resolution commending the report to the sympathetic attention of the Church. Some of the bishops thought that the words *sympathetic* and *commend* were much too strong and they pressed for their omission. These bishops held that if the report were commended to the sympathetic attention of the Church, it might give the impression that they agreed "that the Presbyterian Church of Scotland was just as much a branch of the Catholic Church as the Church of England". The very thought of such a thing, wrote John White, appalled the Bishop of St. Albans (Dr. Furse), the Bishop of Ely (Dr. Heywood), and the Bishop of Truro (Dr. Frere). These men were strong Anglo-Catholics and made no bones of their belief that the Church of Scotland was a heretical and "Protestant" Church, not an orthodox branch of the Catholic Church. In the end, the "Broad" Churchmen in the Upper House of Canterbury had their way, and the report was commended to the sympathetic attention of the Church of England. In the Lower House (the Clergy), there was an even more striking division of opinion. By fifty-seven votes to fifty-six, the Clergy decided to delay passing any resolution on the report until the Episcopal Church of Scotland had expressed a corporate opinion on the proposals contained in it. Members of the Lower House seemed to have overlooked the fact that the report had been signed by the Primus of the Episcopal Church of Scotland and also by the Dean of Edinburgh, the two Scottish Episcopal delegates who took part in the conference. The Upper House of York followed the Upper House of Canterbury, but the Lower House rejected the word "sympathetic". The Clergy felt that this was going too far, and they insisted on substituting the slightly cooler term *respectful*.

[1] "You will realise the immense difficulties which are created in this country by dealing with no less than four separate Houses of Convocation—difficulties which have a deep root in past history but from which you in Scotland are happily free."—The Archbishop of Canterbury to Principal W. A. Curtis, 15th February 1935.

At the same time they decided to delay any detailed discussion of the report until a later meeting. As a result of these decisions, the Archbishop of Canterbury wrote to the committee in Edinburgh to say that, since neither Convocation had approved of the report of the joint conference, he might be giving offence if he appointed Anglican representatives to meet the committee which the General Assembly had already elected. He said he was disappointed, but could do nothing until such time as Convocation met again.

The Scottish Episcopal Church, in response to the invitation of the Upper House of Canterbury to give a corporate opinion on the report, responded by sending a memorandum from their bishops. While there was a general welcome for an approach to fuller unity in faith, order, and practice, there was an amendment that insufficient recognition had been paid to "the claim of the Episcopal Church in Scotland to be the historic Church of that country". Another objection was that the report failed to make it clear that "Episcopal and Presbyterian ministers cannot be regarded as of equal standing". A long story of exasperating delays can be read in John White's epitome: "The General Assembly of the Church of Scotland accepted, with thanks to God, the recommendations of the Joint Conference as a step towards a fuller expression of Christian unity. The Church of England held back their approval until the Scottish Episcopalians had expressed their views. *They could not assent.*"

VI

"The General Assembly regret that it has not been found possible to have Anglican representatives appointed to consider, along with the representatives of the Church of Scotland appointed by the Assembly of 1934, how the recommendations of the Joint Report of that year might be carried out, and that the conference initiated in 1932 must be regarded as now closed. The General Assembly . . . renew the expression of their earnest hope that these Churches may be increasingly brought into such relations with one another, both of fellowship and of common service, as shall promote the cause of Christian unity and further the interests of Christ's Kingdom at home and abroad."

That was the Deliverance of the General Assembly of May 1937. It was regarded by some as the swan song of an endeavour that had been hopefully begun. It was in fact but the beginning of a movement which was to prick the consciences of men in the years ahead and is today still exercising the minds of hundreds of thousands of Presbyterians and Anglicans. It is one of the most lively topics in ecclesiastical circles in Great Britain. The failure to find agreement in certain matters was as greatly illuminating as the agreement found on a number of points. In the Assembly that approved the above Deliverance, Dr. C. W. G. Taylor, Secretary of the Inter-Church Relations Committee, made several statements of fact which stand today as the record of what had happened in these talks:

"In appealing to All Christian People in the interests of Unity in 1920 (an appeal which lay behind the recent Conference, and upon which it proceeded) the Anglican Communion put forward the historic episcopate as the only practicable basis of the ministry of a united Church."

That had not been accepted by the Church of Scotland. On the instructions of the Assembly, the Anglican delegates had been informed that there must be recognition of the equal validity of the Orders and Sacraments of both Churches and of the equal standing of accepted communicants and ordained ministers in each Church. They knew that it lay at the very heart's core of the difference between the two Churches, but it was not a thing on which they had any power to decide. Being a shrewd and prescient committee man, John White had foreseen that if the Anglicans wished to break off the conferences, here in this stipulation of equality was an excuse that lay ready to their hands. Dr. Archibald Fleming wrote to John White that the Archbishop of Canterbury had complained to him that the Presbyterian delegates had come to an "unrestricted" conference and then had imposed this "condition" of equality. The excuse that lay ready to their hands was in fact used to throw upon the Church of Scotland the blame for having ended the conferences by her claim of equality for her ministry and communicants.

This grievous misreading of the truth gained ground in the Anglican Church. It has persisted to this day. It can be seen in the biographies of Cosmo Gordon Lang and of William Temple, who succeeded Lang as Archbishop of Canterbury. The biographer of Lang said that a motion introduced by Dr. Fleming, and passed by a narrow majority, declared that before the conferences went any further the Churches must mutually recognise the validity of each other's Ministry, and he added that the motion begged the whole question and so the meetings came abruptly to an end.[1] Here we are confronted with a double error.

That the Churches must "mutually recognise the validity of each

---

[1] *Cosmo Gordon Lang*, by J. G. Lockhart (Hodder and Stoughton).

other's Ministry before the conferences went any further" was a condition that was never put to the Anglican delegates. The General Assembly had not intended that any such condition should be imposed. The absurdity of the statement of Lang's biographer is apparent to anyone who takes the trouble to glance at the carefully worded Deliverance of the General Assembly that eventual agreement must depend on "the recognition of the equal validity of the Orders and Sacraments of both Churches and of the equal standing of the accepted communicants and ordained ministers in each". That this recognition was not a matter which could be decided by a handful of delegates to a conference that had power only to make recommendations was obvious; on the contrary, the question of recognition was of such grave moment that it could be decided only by supreme ecclesiastical courts. On this point, the statement in the biography of Cosmo Gordon Lang is inaccurate, misleading, and unjust.

The second error is in the statement that the motion begged the whole question and so the meetings came abruptly to an end. The meetings did no such thing. Dr. Fleming's *addendum* was passed by the Assembly in May 1933, and the Anglican delegates were officially informed of it. Far from its bringing these meetings to an abrupt end, William Temple, who led the Anglican delegates, wrote in the midst of the next conference that all was going very well, that they had conferred all day and, after a pause for dinner, they intended to go on again. He said they had been "reaching a large measure of agreement" both about what to do and what to leave over at present.[1] After quoting this cheerful letter, the biographer of Archbishop Temple has stated that the conferences came to an abrupt end because the Assembly of the Church of Scotland had passed a wrecking resolution that made "unrestricted" conference impossible. On the contrary, all continued, in Temple's words, to go very well; and yet another conference was held in the spring of the following year. Fortunately, John White has left on record the result of their deliberations then. He wrote that the delegates of all four Churches represented at the meeting were unanimous in the report, drawn up for presentation to the Church of England and the Church of Scotland, in which it was recommended that serious consideration be given to the interchange of pulpits and intercommunion. John White added: "I had the privilege of presiding at the meeting of conference when this unanimous finding was reached, and I was proud to observe the satisfaction with which one and all signed the historic document."

[1] *William Temple Archbishop of Canterbury*, by F. A. Iremonger (Oxford University Press).

In a speech made to the General Assembly on 29th May 1934, John White made a statement which further refutes the claim that Dr. Fleming's *addendum* brought the conferences to an end. His words were:

"The *addendum* is not in any way responsible for the recommendation to suspend conferences meantime. There has been no controversy in the Conference on the point raised by the *addendum*. The conferences have been carried through with goodwill by representatives of the two National Churches—branches of the Church Catholic—who recognise each other as such. Everything has been done in the belief that it is possible for the two Churches to find some way of manifesting a unity of witness and of service, and the joint-statement of Agreements shows that this has been accomplished."

Even when a pause in the conferences was recommended, so that the Church of England could deliberate upon the recommendations, there had been no thought in the minds of the delegates that all was over. In the same General Assembly of May 1934, a committee of seven members was appointed to deliberate with a similar Anglican committee and representatives of the Presbyterian Church of England and the Episcopal Church of Scotland, to consider how the recommendations put forward at the joint conferences could be carried out. But John White knew—and William Temple knew—that before any question of conceding to the Church of Scotland the validity of their ordination ceremony and of their confirmation as members of the Catholic Church could be even whispered, the attitude of the small but powerful Anglo-Catholic section of the Church of England would have to be taken into account.[1]

The words of Bishop Talbot of Winchester spoken to some Presbyterian ministers at the time when conference had been first suggested were quoted by Principal Macgregor in the General Assembly. "Now please," Bishop Talbot had said, "if you ever come into negotiation with the Church of England, don't repeat the blunder of Dr. Carnegie Simpson. As soon as we met, he said—*What about free inter-communion?*" Principal Macgregor had continued:

"That devoted and great-hearted man, Bishop Talbot, confessed that to press such a question would have split his Church from top to bottom.... The Lord's Supper is not a sectarian office; it is not a family

---

[1] Dr. White had always been fully aware of the power of the Anglo-Catholics. "It would be a foolish error," he wrote, "to imagine that the Anglo-Catholics are but a few pallid curates leading a few old women along the road to Rome."

party; it is an office of the Catholic Church. . . . Our friends in the Church of England are not ignorant of that, but they know that, if they abandon their sectarian view of the Sacrament, they would run the risk of splitting their own Church. . . ."

The fundamental question had, in the words of Bishop Talbot, been whether any move towards inter-communion and interchange of pulpits would have split the Church of England. Such a split would have been between the large body of Broad and Evangelical churchmen and the minority section of Anglo-Catholics. Many of that section of the Church professed doctrinal beliefs which, with the exception of one or two points such as the infallibility of the Pope, were in consonance with the beliefs of their brethren in the Roman Church. They dressed like Roman Catholic priests; they expected their parishioners to call them "Father"; their church services, in which incense was used and High Mass celebrated, were almost indistinguishable in many cases from those held in Roman churches: their adoration of the Virgin—"Our Lady"—was similar to that expected of those within the Roman communion; they had their hours for the hearing of confession; they gave instruction in the use of the rosary; they denied that they were part of the "Protestant" Church for the reason that they were members of the Catholic Church; and some of them even held that Anglican bishops were in grievous error when they took part in that portion of the Coronation service in which the Sovereign takes an oath to defend the "Protestant" faith. The doctrines taught by many of them diverged so far from the orthodox doctrines of the Church of England that many members of the Anglican communion were gravely puzzled. A friend of John White's, Dr. Spens, later Sir Will Spens, Master of Corpus Christi College, Cambridge, had told Dr. H. M. Burge, Bishop of Oxford, that he was heartily sick of the wide differences in doctrinal belief currently tolerated in the Church of England. Pressed by Dr. Burge, the Archbishops of Canterbury and York (then Davidson and Lang) had in 1922 established a commission "to consider the nature and grounds of Christian doctrine with a view to demonstrating the extent of existing agreement within the Church of England and with a view to investigating how far it is possible to remove or diminish existing differences." The terms of reference of that commission indicated the extent of the lack of discipline maintained over that section of the clergy who openly claimed that their doctrinal views coincided largely with those of the Church of Rome and that they even regarded the Thirty-nine Articles as a document not free from heresy. The Archbishop of Canterbury did not like the idea of establishing such a commission; he feared it might bring forth into too penetrating a light some matters that meantime were better left quietly in the shadows; but he knew that many men besides Sir Will Spens of Corpus were dismayed by the lack of doctrinal uniformity in the National Church. And this commission was still in session at the time when the report of the joint conference on a closer unity with the Church of Scotland was drawn up in April 1934, and it was to continue to sit for a long time. Indeed, fourteen years passed from the date of its inception before a report was produced. This dealt with the doctrines of God and Redemption, with the Church and Sacraments, and with Eschatology; and it was as vague on many matters as expediency required. The Dean of Lichfield was forced to admit that those who most needed the reassurance of certainty on a number of points of belief considered that the report "displayed the irritating inconclusiveness of Anglican compromise, while others felt that it was a triumph for toleration and for the comprehensiveness of the National Church".

The efforts of the commission failed. It had been impossible to suggest any way "to remove or diminish existing differences in doctrine within the Church of England" without the danger of a rupture in the Church. But the commission did put on record the fact that serious differences existed between the Anglo-Catholic body and the massive majority of Anglican churchmen. And in the opinion of most of that majority, the great weakness of the National Church lay in her "toleration and comprehensiveness". With the Anglo-Catholic minority were associated many in the Episcopal Church of Scotland, and it had been the weight of their combined opinion in 1935—not the respectful message sent by the Assembly in 1933 to the Anglican delegates—that had finally brought the joint conferences to an end. There had, in plain words, been a refusal to acknowledge that the ministers of the Church of Scotland had received ordination as valid as ordination by a bishop, or that her communicants had equal status with communicants whom a bishop had confirmed.

In the General Assembly of 1937, Dr. C. W. G. Taylor said:

"We of the Church of Scotland may be permitted, I hope without offence, to be thankful that it is not our Church principles which prevent the sister National Churches from standing together openly for the defence of the Gospel—above all in days like these! Nor do we see anything in scripture, or in right reason, to justify any Reformed Church in the *intransigence* which has been shown."

In the same Assembly John White said:

"Our aim is Christian unity. There can be no effective Evangelisation of the nations until that great task of expressing Christian unity has been further advanced. *As Thou, Father, art in Me and I in Thee, that they also may be one in Us, that the world may believe that Thou hast sent Me.* The Church of Christ is at sixes and sevens," he declared, "and THE WORLD DOES NOT BELIEVE."

In that Assembly of 1937, there was many a sad heart because of the final rupture in the talks between their Church and the Church of England. It was felt that something more should be expressed than had been covered in the Deliverance. One member said he would be sorry to think that their great historic national Church should rest content with a condition of permanent alienation from the great national Church of England. He said he would be sorry also to stand aloof from the Scottish Episcopal Church: those old Scots Episcopalians with such honoured names as Dean Ramsay and "Tullochgorum" Skinner were as Scottish as they themselves. The way might not be open at the moment, but some day it would open. John White sympathised full-heartedly with their wishes, but pointed out that the Deliverance had expressed their hopes. "That is as far as we can go. Our report emphasised that for two years we have been waiting, ready to enter into conference, not only with representatives of the Anglican Church, but likewise with those of the Scottish Episcopal Church, and it is they who have refused at the present time to proceed further." Then he repeated these words from the report:

"The issue is in God's hands. The future, it may be confidently hoped, will yet retrieve the past, and then the present will seem not to have been in vain."

Chapter XIX

"SCOTLAND HIS PARISH"

I

IN December 1934, there was placed before the Presbytery of Glasgow an application from John White for an assistant and successor. Since this was the first time there had been any mention of a successor to him at The Barony, folk wondered whether it was his intention to retire within the next year or two. The immediate cause of his request was the invitation to Dr. A. Boyd Scott, his co-adjutor at The Barony since 1932, to minister for a period to a church in Melbourne, New South Wales. But there was a significant reason why a more permanent arrangement should be made. To those who were associated with John White in the wider affairs of the Church of Scotland, it seemed that the time had come when he should be relieved of most, if not all, of his parochial duties, so that he could conserve his energies for the larger tasks. The most onerous of these was of course Church Extension, and his friend Dr. MacLean Watt had summed up what was in the minds of many when he wrote: "This job of yours is heavy and I don't want to see the new churches built on your grave." As to his severing his ties with The Barony, this was the last thought in his mind: he intended to continue his interest in all its work; and he wished the pulpit to be always open to him. In short, to the relief of everyone concerned, he was still to be John White of The Barony: and that title was to be his until the end.

Dr. Charles L. Warr wrote to him:

> "I read with thankfulness in this morning's paper that you had at last decided to apply for an assistant and successor and that thus some of the great burden you have so gallantly carried all these years will be lifted from your shoulders. I only hope that whatever freedom you will achieve by your deliverance from parochial responsibility will not be wholly absorbed by your activities in other directions. You really do need to ease the strain, and you are of too supreme a value to the Church to risk impairing your health. . . .
>
> "Presbyterianism is a rigid and inelastic system and through its

315

rigidity no one has suffered more than yourself. It has taken us four centuries to realise this; and perhaps in another four, our succeeding race may have managed to evolve some system whereby it can utilise the aptitudes and gifts of its outstanding Leaders by liberating them from parochial charges."

The Presbytery unanimously granted John White's request; and the choice of the congregation fell upon the Rev. R. F. V. Scott. This young minister had served as a combatant with The Royal Scots in France, and after his ministry in the village of Strathmiglo he had gone to the populous parish of St. Andrew's in Dundee. He was not inducted to The Barony until October 1935; and by then John White was on a second visit in the southern hemisphere. A rest and a change of scene that winter had been demanded by his doctor, and he was asked to represent the Church of Scotland at the centenary celebrations of the Presbytery of Tasmania and to carry also the greetings of the Home Church to the Presbyterian Church of Australia. He accepted the mission; he knew he had again been driving the human machine too hard.

Shortly before he sailed, the Church of Scotland held a luncheon in Edinburgh to celebrate his having become a Companion of Honour: it was the first time a Scottish clergyman had received this mark of distinction. Principal Martin, recently resigned as head of New College, was in the chair; and although the two did not see each other as often as in the years of the union parleys, their friendship was as warm as ever. In his speech, John White referred to that affection. The administration of New College might now have been lifted from the shoulders of Martin, he said, and he himself might have been relieved of parochial duties at The Barony, but they both seemed to be busier than ever. He spoke of modern youth, how impatient it was to undertake leadership: "We must find a fuller scope for their vitality and their buoyancy, but there will always be need for the wisdom of experience of their elders— and even for men of the age of Martin and myself so long as we retain touch with the forces of the hour—so long as we avoid the closed mind that sees only the past and lives in an atmosphere of old-fogeyism."

He gave thanks for congratulations on his having become a Companion of Honour. He said he was pleased to think it had been conferred upon him at the King's Silver Jubilee, and he had accepted it as a mark of His Majesty's personal recognition of the Church of Scotland: "The King, with a genius for doing the right thing, has bestowed no title on the Church but has declared it to be a Companion of Honour to the Throne 'in action faithful, in honour clear'."

This was his last public appearance before he sailed.

II

With Mrs. White he arrived in Australia towards the end of September, and his reception was even warmer than on his first visit. Somebody said he had been welcomed in 1930 as the great architect of Church union in Scotland; but now, because everybody knew him, he was welcomed for himself. His heart was gladdened by many things within the family circle. As on the first visit, his wife's health improved in the gentle spring weather of those October days. He was continually elated by the companionship of the children of the house. They were with him for as many hours each day as he could contrive. If his own children had sometimes found him a little distrait before a big Assembly speech or a little remote when he was trying to solve an uncommonly hard problem, his grandchildren found him always an eager and high-spirited companion. "I am a slave to my grandchildren," he confessed, and no state of bondage was ever entered into more gladly. With fatherly pride he recorded his satisfaction at what he could see of the developments his son had carried out in the wool-spinning factory.[1] By carefully planned adjustments, a full storey had been added to the building without any unit of the vast battery of machines stopping for a single day. Under the roof of that factory there were now a thousand workers, and John White was not slow to perceive that his son had created a team spirit which would have been a good thing to see in many a factory in Britain. One Socialist leader of a trades union told John White that his job was practically a nominal one. When asked for the reason, he said that if any worker had a grumble he went straight to young Mr. White, who gave ear to the complaint and settled the matter with a minimum of fuss—so men would rather go to him than to a trades union boss. The renewal of friendships John White had previously made was a continual delight, and many people called in person or sent a kindly message to him. It seemed indeed that everything was working together for good on that visit.

With memories of how difficult it had been to persuade his father to avoid pulpit and platform engagements, his son did his best to protect him

[1] "I still find it difficult to understand," said John White, "that my son has grown up and is able to do all this without asking his father's advice!"

317

from being overloaded with public work. But there were centenary functions that could not be avoided. John White counted it his duty as a delegate from the Church at home to address many gatherings. In particular, there was the great Communion service at St. Andrew's Church in Hobart, attended by members from five different congregations—"one of the heartiest services I have ever conducted" was his description of it. The Lord Mayor of Hobart gave him a civic reception; there was the garden-party at Royal Park; there was the spectacular pageant in the Albert Hall which featured the history of the Scots Kirk since the days of John Knox; and at the cemetery where the early pioneers had been buried, the address he delivered among the tombstones enkindled the great gathering of people who had come to pay tribute to their sturdy forebears. In his speech at another meeting, John White recalled that it was on 30th May 1836 that the Colonial Committee of the General Assembly of the Church of Scotland had made its report on the churches in Van Diemen's Land, as Tasmania had then been called, and the Assembly had instructed it to "provide a suitable pastor for the church in Hobart Town and to take other steps in the interest of Scots folk who were settled, and to settle, in the distant Colony". Largely by the efforts of Dr. John Lang, who bore a name that was to become famous to later generations in the religious annals of both Scotland and England, and who was described as "clergyman, statesman, editor, historian, orator, colony-maker", a presybtery had been established in Tasmania as part of the Presbyterian Church of Australia.

John White's journeying in Australia itself was full of interest. It had always been his habit to make a careful study of the lands he travelled in, and he would return home not only with sharp impressions of places and people he had seen but with a knowledge of their social and industrial history. Australia, he said, was crying out for a heavy immigration of stout-hearted men. With its two inhabitants to the square mile, it made a poor showing compared with Britain's four hundred and sixty-eight; and to John White there was dismal reading in the report of the Overseas Settlement Committee which disclosed that the backward flow to Britain was greater than the outward flow of emigrants, and those returning from Empire countries outnumbered by over eleven thousand those who went out to settle in the dominions and colonies. On his return home, John White never tired of telling stories he had heard of the old pioneers who had "fought their way through a land inhabited by the toughest blacks in Australia, forded rivers, fought flood and bog and fire and their own isolation, penetrated a thousand miles of country upon which the foot of no white man had ever trodden. And," he would say significantly, "they made no noise about it, these men of British stock, fresh from the Old Country, with the blood of a race of battlers in them."

Among the happiest of his contacts with old and new friends in Australia was his meeting with Dr. A. Boyd Scott, who was ministering with great success to a large congregation in Melbourne, where he was establishing for himself a unique position in the life of the city. John White was invited by the Archbishop of Sydney and his clergy to address them, and his impression of Archbishop Mowll was that of "an ambassador of reconciliation and a uniting force among the Churches of the Dominion". He spoke to them of the great union of the Presbyterian Churches of Scotland in 1929, and he made a suggestion he had already made to the Churches of Britain. In the Presbyterian union, he said, they had found a governing principle in the Articles and had not wasted time discussing Orders; so, in a future union with an episcopal Church, if ordination could be shared by both Churches, the certain result would be that, after twenty-five years had passed, the validity of ordination would not be questioned by either Church. Pained by the number of the divisions between the Churches in Australia, as in the mother country, he asked: "Why should every little village have so many churches, Congregational and Baptist and so on?" And the answer was the same as the answer at home: and it was no less unsatisfactory. He upset the equanimity of some people by his hard hitting on public platforms. He said he would have liked to shoot down from the sky some of the advertising kites that were being flown over public places. He condemned what he called the "silly vices of gambling and betting—a fool's idea of a sport that is threatening to change Tasmania into Tattersal-mania!" He told them flatly in Australia that he considered them to be "numerically over-weighted with legislators and public servants—all of them riding on the backs of the merino sheep, plucking the golden fleece".

High summer came and went: too soon February arrived, and friends were gathering to see them off on the homeward journey. Foremost among John White's memories of Australia and Tasmania was their good fellowship and hospitality, and after that there was the loyalty to the Crown which he found on all sides, a deep and overwhelming loyalty that was shared by a people of whose forebears ninety-seven per cent had been British. He had been glad to note the close connection between the

Churches and the Municipalities. He had been impressed by the irrigation systems that covered nearly a million acres. Among the visual memories, there was that of Sydney Harbour, impressive in size and beauty and in the scientific achievement of its world-famous bridge. Then there was the beauty of Adelaide, that great garden city, with its university and art-gallery and museum—and what he called "the American ugliness in the skyscrapers of William Street"—and he could not forget its railway station, "large enough to serve a continent", or Mount Lofty with its panoramic views of sea and mountain and plain. Among the memories ecclesiastical, there stood out the service he had taken in a Melbourne church with Dr. Boyd Scott, and he recalled that the last time they had worshipped together had been at a service they had shared at The Barony.[1] Dr. Boyd Scott wrote afterwards:

"How profound was the impression Dr. John White made in Tasmania! I meet Tasmanians from time to time, and they declare that his vigorous and statesmanlike intervention in their Church courts, centenaries, and their social life in the Church, has had a result in the way of quickening and encouraging them which cannot be over-estimated. I know at first hand the power of good he was during his all too brief visit to Sydney. There he moved naturally like a great prelate among Moderators and Archbishops. But the memory of him which is most affectionately cherished is that of his simple Gospel addresses to people and ministers. To me personally his stay there was a joy indeed."

"The whole cause of Presbyterianism," wrote the Clerk of Presbytery in Tasmania, "seems to have gained a new footing, the message of the Church has made a new appeal, and the whole State, including every religious denomination, has gained a fresh vision and impetus from his statesmanlike Christian outlook."

John White returned home to his tasks refreshed in mind and body. One of his first places of call on his arrival in Glasgow was 232 St. Vincent Street, where he studied the latest reports of the Church Extension campaign and met the Rev. William Jardine and the Rev. Arthur H. Dunnett, who had kept the flag bravely flying in his absence.

[1] In Melbourne it gave Dr. White pleasure to recall that his own predecessor in the pulpit of The Barony, Dr. Marshall Lang, had visited Australia at the time when The Barony church was being rebuilt. Dr. Lang had spoken to the Presbyterians there of his great task at home, and they had collected sufficient money to build a church hall, which was named appropriately the Melbourne Hall.

A snapshot taken in the sunshine of Tasmania.

III

In one of his speeches, John White described how Lloyd George's Budget of 1909-10 had imposed land taxes which had slowed down the building of houses in Scotland. After the First World War, government subsidies had helped those who desired to build; and later some steps were taken to clear away the overcrowded tenements in the cities. The big drive for slum clearance did not come until after the Housing Act of 1935, which foreshadowed a national effort to lift people out of the dense, dark back-streets and alleys and take them into the air and light of new houses and fresh surroundings. One-sixth of the total population of Scotland was to be rehoused: "and most of these new homes," said John White, "are to be built for the poorest and the most needy of our people. They are, in fact, the very people who are peculiarly the care of the Church."

Here was a task greater than anything he had anticipated in the years immediately ahead. It meant a reorganisation of the plans he had made a few years before; and he saw it would call for another appeal to the generosity of kirk folk throughout Scotland.

In speeches and sermons, he tried to answer some of the questions which, it was inevitable, people would ask about the new plans he had in hand. Where were the new houses to be located? On the outer edge of the existing residential areas, he replied, practically all of them remote from any existing church: "Take Glasgow—North and South Balornock, Blackhill, Nether Pollock. . . . Take Edinburgh—Carrick Knowe, Pilton. . . . Take Dundee—Mid-Craigie. . . . Take Aberdeen—Middlefield. To some who know these cities, the very names of these new areas are unfamiliar, yet each is scheduled to carry a considerable new population." Who chose the sites for these new churches? It was the duty of the presbyteries, he replied, and the greatest vigilance was needed. The new Town and Country Planning Act laid it down that a site for a church must always be reserved, and he urged that presbyteries should quickly confer with local authorities. Where there was to be a population of over ten thousand (roughly the size of a new parish) there must be another site for a satellite hall. Each site must have the approval of the Church Extension Committee, and this committee made all further arrangements, legal and financial. Was it the duty of a municipality, he was asked, to help the Church? His answer to this was that it was certainly the duty of a municipality to do everything in its power to make the way smooth for the planting of these churches in the midst of the new housing areas. John White demolished the assertion that a public authority cannot recognise the Church because it is only a section of the community.

"What about providing bowling greens for the use of a very small number of people? What about subsidising houses for only a section of the population? I say nothing against either of these, but I do say it is a foolish argument to talk about the Church being only a section of the community and must therefore be ignored by public authorities. Neither Edinburgh nor Glasgow have done so—and the same with many another town and city. The Edinburgh Corporation has been exceptionally helpful. To be frank, I think Glasgow could do a little more than it is doing. We ought to have more help in allotting sites for churches if Glasgow is to live up to its own motto and '*flourish by the preaching of the Word*'."

He told how the great Dr. Chalmers had gone to the Government and said it was their duty to pay for churches for the people and endow them.

"Dr. Chalmers was flatly turned down," said John White. "In some ways, I am glad he was. I can tell you now that the Church of Scotland has never, at any time, received one single farthing of money drawn from public revenue collected from the people by taxes. But I do expect all public authorities today, not to give us money, but to work on the kindliest terms with us. I expect them to encourage the Church in the building of the walls of the city and providing a strong citizenship."

IV

On what had been achieved between 1933 and 1936, his helpers could look back with pride that was amply justified. Sixteen churches or church halls had been built or were in the process of erection and sixteen further sites had been secured. Around the fringes of Glasgow, a dozen new communities had been formed with populations that ranged between three and twenty-three thousand, while in Edinburgh there had been a migration to the suburbs of something like thirty thousand people. There had been no increase in the population of either city, no great influx of strangers: the change had been a movement from the central districts. Now John White saw that he would be compelled to ask for another ninety thousand pounds. It was a challenge to the Church of Scotland

and to his helpers in the Church Extension Scheme, and it was a challenge to himself.

On Wednesday, 12th August 1936, a Glasgow evening paper printed these words in a bold headline: DR. JOHN WHITE HITS OUT. The reason for his blows can be found in a survey, made by his staff, of the givings to the Church Extension fund of every presbytery and congregation in the Church of Scotland. There could be no question that "the National Church Extension movement had been one of the most successful in the long history of the Church of Scotland", to quote the words in a report to the General Assembly; but while some congregations had given generously, John White disclosed that many another had given little or nothing. One hundred and seventy churches had failed to give more than one pound as their total contribution over three years. The congregations who had given not one single penny were two hundred and fifty. The scheme had been a success thanks only to the great liberality of a certain number of churches and to the donations of private individuals. But John White stated that one thousand congregations had not taken their fair share. Why had it happened? . . . It was on this point that he hit out at a meeting, and his words were reported:

"I hold," he said, "that this situation is due to the apathy and the timidity of the minister himself—and in many cases it is due to his sheer indolence. Nor am I forgetting the parochial obstinacy of the office bearers in those congregations who have contributed nothing. . . . I say that these non-contributors are nothing less than a spiritual drag upon the life and work of the Church of Scotland."

Within a few weeks of that meeting, he wrote:

"The Church is summoned to a heroic task. With one-sixth of the population of Scotland to be set down in new homes, it is the duty of the Church to be there to welcome them—and to gather them in. A deep moral obligation rests upon every individual member to take a worthy part in our great and noble Christian task."

That one thousand churches should remain apathetic was a state of affairs that John White refused to tolerate. He wrote to every minister in the Church of Scotland. For each congregation a target was set. If any minister left John White's letter to gather dust in a letter-rack, or flung it into his waste-paper basket, as some admitted they did, they were not left in peace. A second letter arrived upon the breakfast table demanding immediate attention. If any flagrant case of neglect were suspected, a third and more trenchant letter was despatched. The needed stimulus was given, sometimes gentle, sometimes barbed, if a congregation fell seriously below its target. The "indolence of ministers" would no longer be accepted as something which verbal dynamite would not dispel. And not by letters only, not by circulars and statistical encouragement, but also by the personal appeals from platform and pulpit of John White and his team of helpers, was the second great demand launched.

V

In the Assembly of 1935, John White spoke of those congregations that had lost heart and had been struggling to avoid debt. It prevented them from sharing in the joy of helping in this splendid missionary effort of the Church. He quoted from one letter: "I am very sorry, we are building halls and require every penny for our own work. If, however, you would make us a generous grant, it would put an end to congregational isolation which we dislike."

A letter he received from the convener of the Home Mission Committee of the Presbytery of Duns ran: "There is very little enthusiasm for the appeal hereabouts. I don't know if we are peculiar, but there is a feeling that Church Extension is *not our business*. Rather sad parochialism, no doubt, but there it is." However, in the end, the Presbytery did resolve that kirk sessions should be supplied with statements of the contributions they had already made, together with a note of the arrears, and it was agreed that each parish should be asked to do what it could to work these off and try to fulfil their new quota.

In a Scots newspaper, a contributor wrote:

"Now that Dr. White is free to devote his great driving power to the National Church Extension campaign, consternation is already apparent among some apathetic souls in pulpit and pew over the untethering of the redoubtable minister of The Barony. For those who had hoped that new kirks would be biggit without their putting a hand upon a hod, there could be no more unfortunate prospect."

The apathetic ones he continued to stir up. Some of them he tried to stimulate by news of a gift he had received from overseas. The churches of the Blantyre Mission in Nyasaland, founded in 1876, had been celebrating their Diamond Jubilee, and they had decided to set apart one Sunday on which they could give what the natives had called a "Thank-you Offering". All the money collected on that day had been sent to John White to help Church Extension in Scotland: for by what "she had done far back in 1876, Church Extension had been made possible for them in Nyasaland".

John White took pleasure in telling of one minister who had sent "a worthy offering" from a small Sabbath School of fifty children. "They handed in their penny each week," he said, "and the minister asked the parents to give their threepennies and sixpences, for he remembered that it was pennies, threepennies and sixpences that had enabled Woolworths to pay dividends of nearly one hundred per cent."

Many small donations reached his hand, donations that had been gathered with care among humble frugal people, and these seemed to come with a special blessing from the givers. When John White told of gifts from folk who could ill afford them, his appeal seemed to glow with added warmth and colour. To those who said they were staggered at the size of the new demands now made upon them after they had given something to the first appeal sent out in 1933, he would quote the story of St. Francis who, while helping to build a new chapel, carried the stones in his fragile hands, all the time singing psalms and breaking into ejaculations of gratitude, while his face was beaming as if he saw visions of an unspeakable splendour. When someone asked him why he had sung he said: "I build for God's praise, and desire that every stone should be laid with joy."

John White never lost an opportunity to bring his Church Extension fund to the fore. Even in the General Assembly, where it was the custom for members to pay a shilling at the clerk's table every time they entered a dissent, he suggested with a twinkle in his eye that the "dissent shillings" could not find a better home than in his fund. Lord Sorn, a well-known Senator of the College of Justice, has told of an incident at the Palace of Holyroodhouse after dinner when the Purse-Bearer went up to a group of men and asked if any of them had lost anything. "Not I," said Lord Sorn. The Purse-Bearer then held out a one-pound note and asked, "This isn't yours?" He added that it had been picked up behind Lord Sorn's chair at the dinner-table. "Now I remember," said Sorn, "I did have a pound note in my cigarette case, and when I looked for it I found it wasn't there. This must be the note." As it was being handed over, his friends made a joke of it: "It's easy to claim lost property when you know what it is!" The Purse-Bearer suggested that the Privy Purse was really the proper place for it, and at that moment John White joined the group. "Money passing, gentlemen?" he said. "This can be nothing but wagering. I must remind you of the Act of 1621." The others agreed that the Act should certainly come into force. Lord Sorn, who afterwards took delight in relating the incident, concluded:

"Realising how impossible it would be to defeat Dr. John White's arguments, I held out the note and said to him, 'It's yours!' For a moment he was taken aback, then with a laugh accepted the note. I said I thought the victim had a right to know to what Church purpose the money would be devoted. At once he replied, 'Why, of course, Church Extension!'"

When it was evident that the Church would have difficulty in keeping pace with the growth of the new housing areas, John White and his committee decided that there must be a change in policy. The cost of building a church was upwards of ten thousand pounds, but a hall-church [1] could be quickly built for very much less than that. To plant one of these hall-churches in the midst of an area where houses were going up and would soon be occupied was to provide at once a nerve-centre for the new community—a place where old and young could be gathered around an altar. Sites for churches were chosen and bought, but the vital thing was to create as soon as possible the nucleus of a congregation and to put up a hall-church quickly. As things turned out, there was some rough criticism of this policy. One correspondent wrote in a newspaper: "Halls are being erected, not churches. The result is not congregations of worshippers, but congregations of whist players, dancers, and people seeking social recreation. Good as this is, it does not give an impetus to people whose common inspiration is found within a sanctuary, however humble the church may be."

John White sent a copy of this letter to a number of those young congregations whose only place of meeting was a hall-church, and his reply to the newspaper critic did not lack pungency.

VI

One of John White's great joys was to lay the foundation stone of a new church or hall-church. The service he held at Craigiebank, in the

---

[1] Hall-churches were so designed that they were appropriate for worship and on week-days could be readily converted into places for the general activities of a congregation.

Presbytery of Dundee, might be taken as typical. His words on laying the foundation stone there were these:

> In the name of the Father, and of the Son, and of the Holy Ghost, we lay this cornerstone of an edifice to be here erected under the name of Craigiebank Church, and to be devoted to the worship of Almighty God.
>
> Behold I lay in Zion a chief cornerstone, elect, precious, and he that believeth on Him shall not be confounded. . . .

He then repeated the Creed, and continued:

> In this place may the faith flourish, the fear of God, the love of the brethren. Here may the voice of prayer continually be heard, the voice of rejoicing and salvation, the voice of praise and invocation of Thy most glorious and honourable name, even the name of the Father, and of the Son, and of the Holy Ghost, henceforth and for ever. . . .
>
> And when this house, built to Thine honour, stands complete in strength and beauty, let Thy glory, we beseech Thee, dwell in it for ever, that by the worship of Thy Name and the comfort of Thy Word and Sacraments, Thy people may be built up for the indwelling of Thy Holy Spirit.
>
> So grant that, being devoted to Thee with their whole heart and united to each other with a pure will, they may ever be found both steadfast in faith and active in work for the honour of Thy Name.

In the course of his address, John White told his hearers what the Home Mission Committee had done for the folk at Craigiebank. A site had been purchased at the cost of nearly five hundred and fifty pounds and a grant of twelve hundred pounds had been made towards the hall itself, which would cost three thousand three hundred pounds. Then there was the new church, which would cost seven thousand pounds, and half of this would be paid by the Home Mission Committee. The new congregation had promised to pay one-fifth of the cost of the church, and they would have fifteen years to do this. John White added that his committee had guaranteed the stipend of the minister, who had been working there among them for a number of years, and would continue this guarantee until at last the church was erected into a parish. He took the opportunity of telling his hearers at Craigiebank that the new migra-

tion of population to housing areas amounted to over one million souls—
six times the number of all the people in Dundee. He added that

> "despite all the housing that has been done, forty-two per cent of the
> people in Scotland live in houses of one or two rooms. I wish you to
> think of Church Extension as an expression of the religious wakening
> of the people today. The one great need is a recall to worship. Church
> Extension is a chief part of that recall. We have the responsible task
> as stewards of the talents entrusted to us to hasten the extension of
> Christ's kingdom."

VII

When the project of the Empire Exhibition of 1938 began to take
shape, John White saw an opportunity to make Church Extension more
widely known. The city of Glasgow had offered one of its finest parks,
Bellahouston, one hundred and fifty acres in extent, and only three miles
distant from the heart of the city, and amid its splendour of trees were
sites for the scores of buildings needed in so vast an enterprise. The
Exhibition was intended to foster trade and friendship within the British
Commonwealth of Nations; to show some of the progress made in those
lands to which Britain had brought trade and orderly government; to
reveal to the younger generation the immense potentialities of the United
Kingdom and the Empire; to stimulate productive work in Scotland;
and, by no means least amongst its ideals, there was an eagerness to draw
the attention of the world to the peaceful aspirations of Britain and the
Commonwealth. The first necessity was a large guarantee fund; it was
decided that the committee must have in hand at least a quarter of a
million sterling. This sum was subscribed within a week, and in a fortnight it was doubled. With a rapidly growing guarantee fund, the
Exhibition—the biggest held anywhere in the world since those at
Wembley in 1924 and 1925—began to take shape. And to John White it
seemed to be the duty of the National Church to provide religious services
for the visitors. At a meeting that was called nearly a year and a half
before the Exhibition was due to open, he unfolded the plan he had
devised. Not only should religious services be organised, but here was a
wonderful chance to interest hundreds of thousands of people from the
homeland and overseas in the National Church Extension movement.

> "Let me build within the Exhibition grounds," he said, "a
> complete set of church buildings and hall, similar to those that have

been set up in many places in Scotland, and it will show what we are doing to bring God into these new housing areas. It will interest people. It may stimulate many to help. It will show our friends from everywhere that the Church is alive to the needs of the time. Every day, our prayers will go up from that church. Among the multitudes who come as sightseers, some will surely remain to worship."

That was his first idea, and it was never lost sight of. He had to face some opposition. A professor at one of the Theological Colleges declared that "no ecclesiastical building is called for within the Exhibition grounds", and others were of a like mind. But John White was not deterred by criticism. Indeed, his idea was extended until in the end there was represented within their buildings all the main activities of the Church.

"The whole of our immense enterprise was created in Dr. White's room at 232 St. Vincent Street in Glasgow," wrote the Rev. D. W. Rutherford (later the parish minister at Aberdour in Fife), who participated in the work throughout the whole period of the Exhibition. "I well remember those early days before the Exhibition was open. Scores of problems seemed to pour into the office every day. All but the most trivial details had to be referred to Dr. White, and indeed it sometimes seemed that no detail was too small for him to scrutinise. He knew exactly what he wanted. The whole of our exhibit, the church, the buildings, the furnishings, the departmental displays—all had already taken shape in his mind. He was there in the office working among us every day. He surprised us with his expert knowledge of so many things. With a very firm hand, he dealt with the architects, the plumbers and joiners, the organ-builders, the designers, the decorators, the lighting experts. What an amazing gift for organisation he had. He was a man who instinctively looked ahead—and always with an eye to what was practical. If his life's work had been cast in another sphere, I am sure he could have controlled the greatest factory in the land. Because of his tremendous drive, our church and the other buildings stood there complete in every detail on the day the Exhibition opened, while many another pavilion still required the finishing touches. His primary aim was to demonstrate to visitors the 'Church in the Midst'—the extension church that was being planted in the midst of all those areas where so many scores of families were flocking to live in new homes."

John White had secured one of the finest sites in the Exhibition, and there the church was built near the trees that bordered the little Highland village, on the slope below the crest of the hill where the silver Tower of Empire rose three hundred feet. The church had its own tower, built in the Scots tradition with corbie gables. The cream-coloured walls emphasised the dark red of pantiled roof and the blue of window frames. In the circular panel of glass above the church door flamed the Burning Bush, emblem of the Church of Scotland since 1691, with the motto *Nec tamen consumebatur*—or, in the Scots tongue, *It lowed but was nane the waur*. With its stained-glass windows made by Scottish artist craftsmen, its floodlit ceiling, its Communion Table and pulpit and lectern fashioned from Scots oak, its silver baptismal bowl (a gift of Her Majesty the Queen, now the Queen Mother), the little kirk had simplicity and dignity. An adjacent cloistered garth with shady trees was a place for weary folk to rest awhile.

In what would have been the hall of an extension church was the pavilion with its many alcoves designed to hold the exhibits that told the story of the work of the Church of Scotland. The first of these was devoted to the children. One could see the methods by which young minds were drawn to what was pure and lovely and of good report. One realised, with a little flash of wonder, that the Church had Sunday Schools with more than three hundred thousand scholars and Bible Classes with a membership of ninety thousand, and that all but fifteen per cent of the total members of the Boys' Brigade in Scotland were connected with the Church of Scotland. In another alcove one could see how great was the Women's Home Mission work in the country. There was a panorama of a curing-yard at a fishing-port, with a drifter at the quayside, girls busy gutting and grading and packing fish, the Church rest-house with first-aid dressing station, and a Church Sister on her rounds. One realised, too, how the Women's Home Mission provided holiday homes for mothers who needed rest, services in summer camps and hospitals, all the tender human work that women's hands could do. An alcove contained a model of the Deaconess Hospital in Edinburgh—the only one in Britain supported by a Church—with its eighty-eight beds, twenty-six cots for children, and four thousand out-patients. Another feature of the Church's work that was little known to most of those who entered the pavilion was represented by a model of the farm which the Church of Scotland had established at Cornton Vale near Stirling. There were living-quarters for more than thirty farm workers—men who had been beaten to their knees by degradation or misfortune in city slums and who had been sent by the Church to work in the open air, to renew broken bodies and to come under the ministration of those who would help to renew their broken spirits. Indeed, the fact emerged that *the Church of Scotland was engaged in more social service work for the regeneration of body and soul than any other agency in the land*. Its thirty-five institutions ranged from homes for boys and girls to Eventide homes for aged folk.

On the overseas side, one of the most striking exhibits was in the double alcove where primitive Africa was depicted. You could see a land haunted by fear—a blazing village, toiling women, the Arab slave raiders driving off terrified native victims. The contrasting picture was of Christian Africa: natives engaged in farming, in trading, and in learning some of the benefits of Christian civilisation, with a school, a workshop, a hospital and ambulance, a church. But it was upon the work of the Home Board that John White wished the attention of visitors to be most closely focused. In a panorama of a Scots glen and mountains, he had set crofts on a hillside; on the lower ground he had shown tinkers' tents, a berry-pickers' camp, a youth hostel; in another place he had depicted a mining village. With its swift pictorial impact, it showed groups of folk to whom the Home Board ministered. A panel at one glance told of the great movement of people out from the city, and one could read the names of these new centres, from Drumchapel in the north-east to Castle-milk in the south-east. But the most vivid exponent of Church Extension was the kirk itself and those buildings joined thereto that had been erected where John White had wished them to be placed on that green slope amid the trees looking northward across the great city of Glasgow to the Highland hills beyond.

Folk worshipped in that kirk every day. Two services a day were held until the numbers became so great that a third service had to be added. Eighty Church helpers were on the rota for duty under the supervision of the Rev. James S. Taylor, and John White himself was seldom absent for long.

"Some wondered if we would not see so much of him," wrote Mr. Rutherford, "after the King and Queen had paid us an official visit and shown such fine interest in the work of the Church and in John White's plans for Church Extension. But soon such doubters were proved in the wrong. He was continually visiting us, or as we used to think *inspecting* us. He would drop in at the most unexpected times. I can never forget the day when we were secretly congratulating ourselves on the smart turn-out of all our exhibits in the pavilion. John White suddenly strode in, a figure of energy and enthusiasm. He raised his head, and I saw a cold eye fixed upon something on the window above. It was a cobweb. Then he looked at us, and we felt we were wilting under his reproving glance. He waited until that cobweb was removed. For at least a fortnight afterwards, the whole staff inspected every window first thing in the morning in case another cobweb could be detected. But I must not give a false picture of Dr. White, for his praise to us all was more than generous. Well do I remember, when it was all over, how he sat down and wrote a letter of warm sincere thanks to the hundreds of people who had helped. He made them all feel that they had played a part in making that little kirk and our exhibit one of the really outstanding things in the whole Exhibition. My own belief is that, in its own way, thanks to the inspiration of John White, it was a living centre of evangelism. Thousands upon thousands who were not connected with any Church visited us, were interested, saw the work that the Church was doing, and felt constrained to wait and worship with us in the sanctuary."

VIII

"It's the bairns we must think of!"

This was often John White's rejoinder when it was put to him that his exuberant efforts for Church Extension ought to be slowed down. At a General Assembly, when a member suggested that since many folk who lived in the suburbs could afford to run a motor-car they should be able to build their own churches, John White's answer flashed back that, as far as he could see, there were far more perambulators than motor-cars. He added that it was the occupants of these perambulators he was interested in. Dr. Robert Mackintosh and the Rev. Horace Walker, over a course of years John White's colleagues in Church Extension work, went with him to the dedication of many new churches. They have left it on record that they never saw him step into one of these churches without pausing to speak to the children first of all. It would have seemed that every time John White saw a group of children he was moved by the thought that here were the people of tomorrow, the people who would carry on the world's work, and so they were important in his eyes. Never did he condescend to a child, never did he talk down to one. They were, as it might seem, contemporaries: they thought the same clear, simple thoughts, they used the same simple words. Dr. Mackintosh once said:

"At Kirkcaldy Dr. White was opening a temporary hut as a make-do church. It only held about a hundred and fifty people and was crammed to the doors. Quite a number could not get into the dedication ceremony and some of the children were playing outside. As Dr. White was speaking, they began to get a little noisy. Inside the hut we could hear their voices. He stopped. Those who did not know him well probably wondered if he was annoyed. He was silent for a moment while the children's voices rang out more loudly than ever, then he said, 'Listen to the children—*they are the future!*'"

Dr. Mackintosh recalled another visit made with John White during a Christmas week. They had been attending a meeting, and they passed through a new housing estate on their way home.

"In the gloaming we could see the lights shining from a rough wooden building," said Dr. Mackintosh, "and I told Dr. White it was being used as a church for the time being. He ordered the chauffeur to stop. He got out and went over to the church. I followed. Inside, a young minister was holding a Christmas party for the children of that new housing estate. When he realised that it was John White who was paying him a visit, he was thrilled. We got a great welcome. To me the significant thing was that within a few minutes the children were all round Dr. White. They were pulling at his coat, clinging to him as if they had known him all their lives, eager for him to play with them. You could see at a glance that in John White these children had recognised a friend. . . . I thought then of some ministers and elders who had known the rough side of John White's tongue—maybe they deserved it, maybe not—and I thought how their hearts would have warmed to the man if they could have seen him at that moment, playing with these youngsters at their Christmas party, as happy as any of them, himself a child again. Here, I thought, is the real John White."

Not only was John White anxious that the Church should recognise her responsibility to the generations of the future, but he took every chance to inspire the children themselves with their own duties—their duties to other children, to their parents and teachers, to their Church. For those who were over Sunday School age, he established an association he called the League of the Lamp, and he asked the members of all Youth Groups to join. The membership fee, ten shillings a year, went to meet the cost of lighting the new churches, and it was always a member of the League who switched on the lamps for the first time.

One of the most notable enterprises of John White's first six years of Church Extension was the raising of money to build what became known as The Children's Church at Sighthill, Edinburgh. To begin with, a wooden hut seating two hundred was all they had for worship at this new housing area with a population of six thousand. It was known that another four thousand would soon be added, and John White and his helpers were inspired by the idea of encouraging the boys and girls of the Church of Scotland to raise the money to build the new church, which was appropriately to be named St. Nicholas. The plan was that each child would give a penny every four months. In one year alone, they raised over four thousand pounds.

Today, the Church of St. Nicholas stands at Sighthill, a permanent memorial to the affection and devotion of the children of the Church of Scotland.

Chapter XX

PEACE AND WAR

I

BY the time the First World War was a dozen years distant it was evident that there would be no fulfilment of the hope that the world would be a fairer place. For many people pleasure had become a cynical escape from reality; the old foundations were gone; the standards of morality and conduct of the age that had passed were arraigned as a code of hypocrisy; youth had been left bewildered; and the hunger at the heart of democracy was for leadership. The 'twenties had ended in an economic depression that seemed but the counterpart of a spiritual malaise. For John White personally, the great achievement and the hope for the future of the Church of Scotland had been the reunion of the two great Presbyterian bodies; but if this were to be perfected and to bring forth those fruits of the Spirit which had been its supreme purpose, he saw that the next decade would be a period of strain for both, a period in which charity would be needed in even greater measure than at any time during the long years of negotiation. Looking back, he was grateful that union had been completed before the new housing areas had spread themselves over the face of the land. It was among the folk who lived in these legions of new homes that John White's main work was now lying, but many other duties were continually pressed upon him. In 1937 he was to reach his seventieth birthday. In the nature of things, his body was now more vulnerable to fatigue, but he disliked to acknowledge it. The vitality of his mind was as lively as it had ever been, the ardour of his spirit as fervid, and he undertook tasks, many of them involving journeys and conferences and meetings, from which he had ample reason to be excused. Perhaps too many gallant crusades captured his imagination; certainly, many were the good causes that lay close to his heart.

He was one of the Presidents of Toc H. He was Vice-President of the Glasgow County Scout Council, and he was Chairman of the Glasgow centre of the Trinity College of Music, in which he took an enthusiastic interest. He was a Governor and later the Vice-President of the David Livingstone Trust; his admiration for Livingstone was too strong for him to decline any work on behalf of the national memorial for the man by whom "the Lord wrought great glory in Africa". He was appointed President in Scotland of the World Alliance for the Promotion of International Friendship through the Churches; and in those years when Hitler was raucously disturbing Europe, John White exerted all his strength to make the Council "more of a living power than it had ever been".

Early in his life he had become a Freemason, and indeed was a member of Kilwinning Lodge, the ancient home of Freemasonry in Scotland. When representatives of lodges all over the world assembled in Edinburgh to take part in the bi-centenary meeting of the Scottish Grand Lodge in the autumn of 1936, and the Duke of York, later King George VI, was installed as Grand Master Mason, John White agreed to preach the sermon at St. Giles'. Here was a God-given opportunity, he felt, to speak to his brethren from many lands. The healing of international strife, he told them, could be achieved only by a spiritual force making itself evident in brotherliness in the world.

> "But what is to be its inspiration, its dynamic? . . . It is no good merely saying it is our duty to be brotherly. Duty has a cold ring about it. Obligation is colder and harder still. The public platform has talked itself dumb about duty and obligation. The general conscience has not been sensitive to these appeals. Why? Because there is no passionate spiritual force behind this duty, no kindling love. The brotherhood of our Masonry requires the dynamic force of the fellowship of the Church of God. No other force can regenerate and unite society—nothing but a Freemasonry of God revealed in Christ."

Amid the disintegrating forces of the 'thirties, John White felt more than ever the need for the unity of every corporate Christian body in the land. He had been the first President of the Scottish Churches Council which had stemmed from the missionary campaign that had been a co-operative effort by many denominations after the First World War. With others he had felt the need for concerted action, or at least a unified declaration, on matters that touched the spiritual well-being of the people. Within the Church of Scotland he was always eager to give his support to any effort to quicken the Christian life; but he was not willing to rush headlong into evangelistic effort without preparation. At the time of the Mission of Rededication after the First World War, he had learned the value of preparing the way, and in the mid-'thirties he warned his colleagues of what seemed to him a too hasty attempt to launch a nation-wide campaign. He had returned from Tasmania to find such a Mission being planned to start with what he called "an impetuous rush". He attended an important conference and came away gravely dissatisfied:

"What is to be the main message of our campaign? 'Get on at once with the work,' some said, 'don't wait—we know the situation.' All this is very good, but it is vague talk. Was there ever any successful evangelistic movement in history that did not have a *special message* for its own day? Are we to prescribe without diagnosing? Is this not simply evangelical quackery? . . . I cannot forget the National Rededication Movement for which I laboured night and day. Despite all we did then, we did not do a tithe of what should have been done. The campaign never got launched throughout the nation. Nor can I forget the Forward Movement which was cradled in prayer but was started before the country had been properly prepared for it. It will be disastrous if we rush at this work without careful preparation, and then fail."

When the Recall to Religion was made in March 1937, John White gave it influential support; he wrote about it and spoke about it. The Home Board [1] of the Church of Scotland was deeply involved in it, and many presbyteries zealously took it up. In a speech to the General Assembly in May 1938, John White spoke of evidence of a reviving interest in the worship of the Church, of the good work being done by their Evangelism Committee, and of the conference for young ministers that had been held at Dunblane a few months before. "I left the conference," he said, "with the feeling that the Church has, in the ranks of its ministry, young men who are alive to the problems of the hour, to the part the Church is called on to play in the solution of these problems, and to the urgency of an evangelical leadership within the Church."

In the same year there was a change at The Barony which seemed for the moment to be disconcerting. The Rev. R. F. V. Scott, his colleague, was called to the important London charge of St. Columba's, Pont Street. This translation left a gap at The Barony which it would clearly be difficult to fill: nevertheless, in the conviction that there would be for "Robin Scott with his many great gifts" an opportunity for wider service,

[1] Under the supervision of Dr. White, the Home Mission Committee and others had been unified under the name of the Home Board, of which he was appointed first convener. He remained as such from 1936 to 1942 and thereafter was convener of the newly created National Church Extension Committee.

it was John White who had made the recommendation to his friend Dr. Archibald Fleming. Now returned from Australia, Dr. Boyd Scott again joined forces with him and put in a second period of service at The Barony. Meanwhile, the work which a young minister was doing in the centre of the coalfields of west Fife was becoming known throughout the Church; and in March 1939, the Rev. W. Roy Sanderson came from Lochgelly to be John White's colleague and successor.

Inevitably, it was a situation which required in the younger man the greatest charity and tact. Ordained forty years later than his eminent senior, he inevitably looked upon many things from a different angle: but John White saw in him a young minister who was supremely suited to handle the tasks of a church like The Barony with its congregation scattered throughout the residential districts of a great city. In Mr. Sanderson he knew he had found one of those young men who were "alive to the problems of the hour". In thanking him publicly for an outstanding piece of leadership, John White said: "The Church that will control the future is the Church that provides an educated ministry with a clear sense of how best to get its message across to the young in their serious perplexities."

The partnership proved to be all that both hoped and confidently expected. Their affection and respect for each other increased with the years and ripened into a fellowship of mind and spirit that was broken only by death.

II

"If a Christian cannot take sides in this war and strike with every atom of his energy, then a Christian is a being that, so far as this world is concerned, has committed moral suicide."

These words had been spoken by Principal James Denney in the General Assembly of the United Free Church during the First World War. Denney was a man John White had held in honour; the words had found an echo in his own heart. No more than fifteen years had passed since the end of a war that was to have ended war, when the cloud of international conflict had begun once more to darken the sky. The minds of men were troubled. What should be the Christian attitude to war? That every nation on earth might be grappled anew in a fight that would drain their very life's blood was a dismaying thought, but it was not the magnitude of such horror that pricked the conscience of many Christians. Was it wrong for a Christian to take part in an armed conflict, however small? Some thought, as did the Quakers, that it was. A Scottish Ministers Peace Group was formed; and at the General Assembly of 1933, in a speech of passionate sincerity, a member proposed an addendum to the Deliverance on the work of the Church and Nation Committee. War was an issue that must be squarely faced, he said: it was an issue on which the Church was being challenged by her Master. He believed that the whole possibility of Christian leadership in the modern world lay in the readiness of the Church to take her stand at the side of Christ and count the world well lost. Christ had refused to use the methods of the world to defend Himself, His friends, His cause; Christ had believed that they would overcome the evil in men only by being ready to suffer rather than betray the Divine love: take away from Christ that method of over-coming evil—and where is His divinity? Negative pacifism was not enough. Christ had not called them to passive resistance—it was to a new initiative of faith that would bring into the world the soul it so desperately lacked. "The worst service we can render our fellow men," the young minister said, "is to defend them or their just cause by methods which perpetuate the evil Christ was out to overcome." The seconder of the motion pointed out that the speaker represented a great body of young ministers and a great mass of young men and women in the country, and he called upon the General Assembly to give a clear opinion on the matter.

During his convalescence on Speyside, John White read the speeches delivered on that Wednesday, 31st May, and had noted with interest the words of three of his friends, Professor W. P. Paterson of Edinburgh University, the Rev. J. Pitt Watson, minister at Alloa (later professor at Trinity College, Glasgow), and Dr. Charles L. Warr of St. Giles'. Professor Paterson had been quickly on his feet after the addendum had been seconded.

> "We are all agreed that war ought to cease," he said, "and the Church is bound to give its heartiest support to all measures to that end. But we cannot take up the position that, horrible as the instrument is, war never has been, or will be, rightly employed for the restraint and the punishment of violence among the nations of the earth."

Mr. Pitt Watson begged the General Assembly to refrain from carrying it to a vote. If it approved of the addendum, it would stand committed to the pacifist position—and to the most radical statement of it. If it disapproved, it would "expose itself to the gravest misrepresentation upon perhaps the most serious public issue that confronts the Church and the Christian conscience at the present time". Dr. Warr said:

"We have been told there would have been no Christian faith at all in Scotland unless the Christian culture and civilisation had gallantly fought for its life. We are living in a world of men, and circumstances may arise when the way of the sword is the dark and terrible and only way left to a persecuted people to fight through to liberty, and justice, and everything that man holds dear. . . . Anybody who takes the slightest interest in the modern world knows that the storms are rising, knows that Christian culture and Christian civilisation again in this twentieth century are going to face threat and attack. I trust the Assembly will resist the appeal to sentimentalism that lies in this addendum. If the Assembly commits itself to the pacifist position, you will rue your action this day."

In the end, the addendum was remitted back to the Church and Nation Committee. That the question of the Church's attitude to war would be raised at the next General Assembly was certain, and many felt it to be imperative that the Church of Scotland take a stand and give help to those who looked to her for guidance.

When the Assembly met in 1934, John White made plain his own position:

"I hold in high respect many of the Pacifist Group. I should like to be a pacifist myself, but I cannot find any convincing argument in their memorandum. There is much in it we can sympathise with. They said that 'if war were to achieve any of its high avowed ends, some defence of it might be possible'. . . . Did not the last war achieve something? Did it not save the homes and altars of the Scottish Ministers Pacifist Group? We are told that modern war by its scale is different in degree and kind from the thing known as war in the past. Surely it is a fallacy for a Christian pacifist, or for any man, to reason from magnitude to ethics. Nor do I like the further argument that we have arrived at a higher plane of Christian ethics than the poor boys who gave their lives. It would be mistaken loyalty to those who fought and fell in the path of duty, the memorandum states, 'if we with our further light refuse to advance beyond the best that was visible to them'. It was certainly not intended, but I regard that to be an atrociously cruel statement. Do the writers of that sentence claim a higher ethical standard than Our Lord, who said, 'Greater love hath no man than this, that a man lay down his life for his friends'?"

John White repeated that, as a last resort, it might be a people's duty to take part in a war in fulfilment of its own destiny or to go to the help of a persecuted people.

In a speech that was frequently interrupted by applause, he told the Assembly that he was not putting forward what some might describe as only the Old Kirk view. He had taken the precaution of consulting Principal Martin, who was in touch with opinion among many in the old United Free Church. Principal Martin's health was beginning to fail and he could not come to the Assembly, but he had assured John White that their views on the vexed topic were similar. Professor W. P. Paterson had also written to say that he could not be at the Assembly: "I am a little anxious about this outburst of so-called pacifism, but feel sure that you will guide the Assembly to a finding that will be both Christian and statesmanlike." In the end, an amendment of John White's was amalgamated with the Deliverance. The Assembly recognised *the principle of the lawful employment of force upon just occasion, as an instrument for the restraint of wrong and the preservation of right and freedom in the world.* As to the individual conscience, the majority opinion was equally clear: "The General Assembly recognise that, in the event of war, conscience enlightened by the Holy Spirit must decide the individual's action."

That Germany was preparing for another war now seemed to many people certain; others indulged in what was commonly called wishful thinking. There was much talk of the international curtailing of armaments, and all the time the factories of Europe were producing instruments of destruction. War or peace: it was a topic of the hour, of the moment. Argument was rife; the correspondence columns of the newspapers revealed a wide public anxiety. The views of the Church of Scotland were discussed long after the Assembly had risen. In August, a minor bombshell burst in a London church, St. Martin-in-the-Fields, when a visiting preacher, Dr. Robinson of Chicago, spoke words that called forth headlines in the press. The report reached John White, on holiday at Speyside, and he despatched the following telegram:

The Clergyman in charge at
St. Martin-in-the-Fields,
LONDON.

Scottish newspapers report speaker in St. Martin-in-the-Fields yesterday as saying—"In May the General Assembly of the Church of Scotland voted overwhelmingly for war." This statement is so inaccurate as to be entirely false; please correct from pulpit tomorrow and give same publicity to withdrawal. From—Dr. John White, Mover of the Motion, and Leader of the General Assembly.

Grantown-on-Spey.

This telegram was another minor bombshell, and gave the press an excuse for further headlines. Reporters arrived at Grantown-on-Spey.

"I do not know Dr. Robinson," said John White to an interviewer. "He is credited with the discovery that the Church of Scotland needs a new conscience. He hails from Chicago, and is therefore entitled to speak on the great need of a new conscience. I am astonished at the constant endeavour of extreme pacifists to misrepresent the position taken up at the last General Assembly. St. Martin's would not wish, I am sure, to broadcast a false indictment of the Church of Scotland. Dr. Robinson is accurate when he says that the General Assembly voted against pacifists. He would have been correct to have said that only a very few voted for extreme pacifism. The vast majority voted for every endeavour to be made to further the cause of peace."

The Rev. Arthur Dolphin, in the absence of the Vicar, the Rev. Pat McCormick, and of Dr. Dick Sheppard, wrote to John White to dissociate the church of St. Martin-in-the-Fields with any statement made by Dr. Robinson, whom he described as "a very charming Theological professor (Presbyterian) and possibly well known to you". Dr. George L. Robinson, whose chair was in the Chicago Theological Seminary, said to a newspaper correspondent:

"I have nothing to withdraw. I said the General Assembly of the Church of Scotland voted against the pacifists, and it is up to Dr. White to prove that what I have stated is inaccurate. Ministers should have a higher standard than they showed at the General Assembly, for Jesus Christ did not die on the Cross with a rifle in His hand."

To this John White replied to an interviewer:

"I am only concerned with what this clergyman from Chicago is reported to have said, namely, that last May the General Assembly of the Church of Scotland voted overwhelmingly for war. He does not question the accuracy of that report. In my telegram to him, I challenge his statement as altogether untrue to fact. Dr. Robinson asks us to accept his revised statement, that the General Assembly

voted against the pacifists, as being quite the same as his former statement that the General Assembly *voted overwhelmingly for war.* It
would take a new logic as well as a new conscience to reconcile the
two. The first is true; the second is false. It is the second statement that
I ask be withdrawn."

When questioned about Dr. Robinson having said that Jesus Christ
did not die on the Cross with a rifle in His hand, John White told a
reporter: "Apart from the feebleness of the argument, some might think
it lacking in reverence. But it has to be remembered that many things
that would be regarded as irreverent in Scotland would not be so regarded
in Chicago."

The Rev. Arthur H. Dolphin from the pulpit of St. Martin's read out
the telegram of protest. "I read it in full," he wrote to John White, "and
most willingly. We are all most sorry you had cause to send the telegram.
But we know you will absolve us from any liability as to the statements of
visiting preachers." And so the dust settled on an unfortunate episode.
The reporters ceased to arrive at Grantown-on-Spey, and John White
was left peacefully to his holiday task of catching fish. His own comment
on the episode must be added: "There was at least one good result. The
local reporter had often come chasing after me on his old bicycle. Out
of what he had earned from the controversy, I am glad to say he was able
to buy a new one."

John White's attitude to war had not altered since the days when he
had denounced the aggressors in 1914, and he was still steadfast in holding
the same opinions when he spoke at the Rotary Club in Glasgow after
a second war with Germany was in progress.

"Pacifism should be silent," he said. "We are fighting for the
things that make life worth living, for everything that is symbolised
by our hearths and our altars—the spiritual values of life. . . . If
pacifism is not silent, it distracts the mind—or inflames it—at a time
when it is important that each and every one of us should devote our
entire energies to winning the war. There is not a single thing we
should do, or a single thing we should say, without having first asked
ourselves the question—Will this help to win the war? . . . It would
be a grave betrayal of our task and function as a Christian Church
to stand submissively aside. It would be to leave whole communities
without the Christian view of God and defenceless against the influence
of a crude materialism and of the new paganism of blood and race."

III

On the suggestion of John White in January 1939, the General Administration Committee established a committee on the Church and National Service. Many of his colleagues told him that there would be "peace in our time"; but he insisted that if a war with Germany was not certain, it was highly probable—it was so probable, in his view, that the Church of Scotland should make all possible provision to meet such an emergency. He drew up a memorandum covering what he considered the more important points.

Since ministers were not on the list of "reserved occupations", they could be called upon for service in the Armed Forces of the Crown. John White felt that arrangements should be made with the authorities for the retention of those whose absence would seriously impede the spiritual work of the Church. A call-up of all the younger ministers would be a disaster, but he felt that the clergy in general should receive training in air-raid precautions. While he was anxious that the Church should put at the disposal of the military and other authorities all the Church buildings that could be spared, he was determined that there should be no indiscriminate commandeering by officials. About these and other problems, he saw that the Church of Scotland should join with other denominations north and south of the Tweed in approaching the Government. He discussed matters with the Secretary of State for Scotland, John Colville, and had correspondence with the Home Secretary, Sir John Anderson, later Lord Waverley. The Home Secretary expressed his private view that it was of cardinal importance that the "spiritual ministrations of the Churches in time of war should be maintained", and clergy should not regard themselves as in any way obliged to undertake full-time service in any war activity except as chaplains; but he agreed with John White that they should be trained in civil defence, although they should not be called upon for duty in that work. His view was that, in time of war, the clergy should have the task of ministering to the comfort of those in hospitals and to the wounded and bereaved. If war should come, he said, it would be a war of morale and of will and of nerves, and the Church could contribute in no small measure to the maintenance of the necessary calm and courage. In this enlightened spirit did Sir John Anderson meet John White. It was at John White's suggestion that he travelled to Edinburgh to impart his views to the General Assembly of May 1939.

At the same Assembly, John White discussed the mobilising of the forces and resources of the Church if war should come. Sixty out of sixty-five presbyteries had formed special committees or appointed a member to the Assembly Committee. The work of sub-committees on manpower, church buildings, finance, was well in hand, and John White and his colleagues maintained close contact with service and civilian authorities. Instructions were issued on the holding of meetings in churches under A.R.P. conditions. Additional helpers were provided for religious work among the troops and women workers in factories and elsewhere. Three days before war broke out, a sub-committee with executive powers was established to handle the whole question of Church huts for the Forces. "We were on the field without a moment's delay," John White reported, "and the committee stood pledged to an expenditure of over fifty thousand pounds. The work increased so rapidly that a special committee on Huts and Canteens was formed."

The war service of divinity students had also been discussed at the Assembly. It had been proposed that the Church should claim their services so that they could receive full exemption. John White had refused to accept this, and would go no further than agree to seek guidance on it. He saw no reason why divinity students should not undertake combatant duties. He agreed with Professor Edgar Dickie of St. Andrews University that they were either conscientious objectors or they were not. If they were, there was machinery they could individually set in motion. If they were not, they should be classed with other students. At one of the universities, a number of divinity students prepared a manifesto in which they claimed that they should be retained to give spiritual consolation to the victims of air-raids. On this, Professor Dickie wrote to John White: "I am sure I could name a hundred elders, too old to serve, who could do that work far better than I could have done it as a divinity student—even with one war behind me! . . . I deprecate and deny the suggestion that a man cannot serve Christianity and the Church in the ranks of the Army." John White was glad to have these forthright words. In the National Service (Armed Forces) Act, which was passed on 3rd September 1939, ministers of religion were in fact exempted from service, and so were all theological students who had already begun their studies. This raised the question of students who had enlisted before they knew of the Government's decision: should they be given the chance to leave the Armed Forces and resume their studies? The decision was that they could do so, and even those taking an Arts course with a view to entering the ministry were excused. But the fall of France caused John White and his colleagues on the committee to think hard and quickly. On 26th July 1940 he wrote to Ernest Bevin, the Minister of Labour:

"The action of your Ministry in thus exempting these students was highly appreciated by the Church as an evidence of the high conception of the Church held by the State, and also as a recognition of the service which the Church could render at this critical hour by fortifying the heart of the community. Today, owing to the defection of France, the situation has changed. We have been driven to re-think the position in so far as these young men are concerned. I would ask if they should not be encouraged to take advantage of the choice given them and, instead of accepting complete exemption, offer for some branch of National Service. . . . With regard to students intending the Ministry but not yet entered upon their curriculum, I am of the opinion that they should be permitted, and indeed encouraged, to join up in one branch or another of the Forces. I am not only deeply concerned with the needs of the nation but also about the future influence of the young men who will be leading in the Church. *Their influence would be greatly strengthened by their National Service side by side with their brothers in the day of conflict.* . . . I ought to say that a great many of our young men have registered and are in service, and a number are giving useful help in huts and canteens."

The situation resolved itself. Few there were who did not respond to their country's need and leave their studies until peace should come again. Before long, it was not problems of exemption from service that engaged the minds and energies of John White and his committee. Indeed there were times when they had to act as a restraining and guiding influence on some who were eager to undertake national duties and relinquish tasks of importance. A notable achievement of the Church of Scotland in the Second World War was the work carried out overseas. Under the convenership of Dr. Charles L. Warr, the special committee on Huts and Canteens had organised an immense and intricate service which did an incalculable amount of good among the Forces in Britain and abroad. Dr. Warr's knowledge of the needs of those in the Services was based upon his personal experience in the First World War when he had been an officer in the Argyll and Sutherland Highlanders. He had known from the inside the life of a military hospital and a convalescent camp, for he had been dangerously wounded at the first battle of Ypres, and his memories of life at the front gave reality to all the appeals for help that passed through his hands. It is significant also that the man who was appointed General Superintendent of the work of the Church of Scotland in the British Expeditionary Force in 1940, and with the Allied Expeditionary Forces in north-west Europe after the opening of the Second Front in Normandy, had himself been a combatant officer in the First World War. Professor Edgar Dickie had served with The King's Own Scottish Borderers in Palestine and in France, had been wounded, and had won the Military Cross. Both were men after John White's own heart, for they had themselves carried out their own quiet ministry in camp and bivouac among their comrades in arms, and had returned to devote their lives to the service of Christ. It was well, said John White, that the Church of Scotland had men of such calibre in the long years of travail when the nations were locked in conflict.

IV

With the outbreak of war in September 1939, it seemed to many folk that an end must come to Church Extension. The nation must gather its strength for grimmer tasks: if Britain were to survive, her manpower and industries must be reorganised with one end, and only one, in view: what could new churches matter when a powerful enemy might soon be launching an attack upon the shores of the island fortress or dropping destruction from the skies?. . . .

So rife were the rumours that Church Extension was dead for the duration of the war that John White was hard pressed to check them. The editor of *The Glasgow Herald*, feeling that some official guidance should be given, asked him to contribute an article setting forth exactly what the position was. The opportunity was gladly taken to dissipate, as far as possible, some false notions. His first point was that Church Extension was not merely the erection of church buildings: it was a concerted effort in a parish to bring folk together in a Christian community. If there was no dedicated church building to worship in, they worshipped together in small or large groups—worshipped somehow, somewhere. They formed a community; that was the important thing. But it was utter nonsense to say that all work on their buildings had stopped. At least eleven were in the process of erection early in 1940, and the population they were to serve was about forty thousand souls. True, much more might have been undertaken but for the war, but new instructions had just been given for the building of four more hall-churches. And in the housing areas, evangelistic work was going ahead by clergy and laity. "Is Church Extension dead? There are difficulties," he admitted, "but Church Extension is very much alive and kicking."

The time was soon to come, however, when the building programme had to be curtailed. To secure permits for building of any kind became more and more difficult. These were issued by the Department of Health, and one of the main bottlenecks, to use or misuse a word that became the vogue, was timber. A Timber Economy branch had been established at the Ministry of Supply, and John White was warned that there would be an allocation only for "the completion of a small number of buildings which are already in an advanced state of construction". Thus John White and his colleagues were able to spend less than thirty-two thousand pounds during the whole of 1940. This did not go very far; and they were forced to cancel the building of a number of hall-churches and put up temporary structures instead. At the Assembly of 1941, John White was able to report that four halls had been completed and dedicated since the beginning of that year, and two more were nearly finished. With sorrow he said that many churches had been destroyed or damaged by enemy bombs, and some of these would be restored as soon as possible. But there was a bright side to the picture of the work in the housing areas: "Are you aware that within recent years our *new* congregations show a membership of nearly twenty-five thousand—our Sunday schools of thirty thousand?" On the other hand, he said, the fact must be faced that the membership of the Church of Scotland as a whole was declining:

"I believe that one of the reasons for this loss is the migration of Church communicants from the centre of large towns and cities to new housing areas. A sentimental attachment to the old church in the city, some distance away, leads to very occasional attendance, a slackening of interest, and a young family growing up without any church attachment. Twenty-one thousand communicants were lost to the Church in the last year, largely in this way. Here is one of the strongest reasons for my appeals for Church Extension."

Two problems closely tied up with Church Extension held his interest. He felt that more should be done to bring the students of Scotland's four universities within the influence of the Church. A young minister had been appointed as liaison officer with the Student Christian Movement, but this was not enough, and he began to turn over in his mind the ways and means of bringing the evangel into the midst of student life. For younger boys he saw the need for more clubs and community centres. In Glasgow, "he did a tremendous work in helping to found Church House Community Centre at St. Francis-in-the-East", to use the words of the Rev. Arthur Gray, who took charge of it, and later he drew up plans for starting community centres for youth in the south and other districts of the city.

V

The time came when it was almost impossible to obtain permission to put up new buildings. In 1943, speaking to the Presbytery of Inverness, he recalled the day when he had first appealed to the General Assembly for one hundred and eighty thousand pounds.

"Members listened to me with a smile," he said, "for the nation's trade had then been in the doldrums, and it had seemed wildly optimistic to ask for such a sum at that time. I agreed with the criticism," he added. "It was the very last hour I would have chosen for my appeal, but I told the General Assembly I believed it was the time God had chosen. And we got much more than I had asked for. We built fifty-five churches and halls, churches without halls, halls without churches. They cost nearly half a million, *and today we owe no man one penny.*"

Then he looked into the future. For the first time in history, the population of Scotland had passed the five million mark, and one million and a half of these folk were already living in new housing areas. It was the intention of the Government that another two million would migrate to new homes that were to be built for them, and most of them would consider that they were too far away from any existing church for convenience.

"With this enormous number of people in new homes, in new surroundings, what a chance there is for the Church to win them! If they have been indifferent to religion before, if the Church has failed to gain their allegiance, here is what I call a Second Chance. *But it may be the last chance for the Church.* A few years without Church ordinances will reduce most folk to paganism. . . .

"Remember, it is not an increased but a migrated population," he pointed out. "What we need is a better distribution of places of worship. Probably we could do with fewer churches and more church

349

workers: with fewer sheepfolds and more shepherds. At the same time, the poor districts with their reduced populations in town and city must not be deserted by the Church. On the contrary, our work in these areas must be even more thorough and aggressive.

"A tremendous responsibility rests on Church folk everywhere in Scotland to discharge the great task to which God has called his people. *It is the biggest single task that will face the Church of Scotland after the war.*"

On many occasions John White spoke along these lines with fervour, and the General Assembly of May 1943 supplemented the Church Extension Committee with a Commission for Church Extension Purposes. Thirty-six members were appointed, with John White as chairman and his colleague Dr. Robert Mackintosh as secretary. They estimated that, when it became possible to build again, one hundred and five new hall-churches would be required, and this would be but a meagre provision for a population equal to that of Glasgow, Edinburgh, Aberdeen, Paisley and Greenock. Taking the cost of building as about three times what it had been before the war, one million sterling would be needed for the work.

John White went to see the Secretary of State for Scotland, Tom Johnston, to talk about the sites of the new buildings they proposed to put up and to ask how the Church stood on the priority list for building. He said he realised that houses must be the Government's first concern, but the building of churches should be given an equally high place, for if housing schemes outstripped the provision of churches for the people, there was the risk of a whole generation being lost to the Church. Johnston, himself a churchman, was sympathetic, but there was little definite information he could give. The Department of Health had made some pronouncements about housing in Scotland, and John White went to an official and found that Scottish local authorities had the power to decide whether land for building sites would be either leased for a term of years, or, on the other hand, feud in the traditional way or sold outright. There was a dispute with the Glasgow Corporation on this point. Glasgow had offered sites to the Church of Scotland on a sixty years' lease, and said that if the Corporation wished to take over the site at the end of the period it would buy the church buildings at a valuation and the congregation would have to fend for itself. John White held that this was grossly unfair. What could be the market value of a church?

Certainly nothing that could be commensurate, after sixty years, with what it would thereafter cost to build a new one. If the Corporation gave them notice to quit at the end of the period, the congregation should be reinstated in another church. The Corporation disagreed.

John White thought matters over. He saw that he must have the heaviest backing he could get, and he decided to take the initiative and call together a conference of the Churches of all denominations in Scotland, throwing the net wide enough to include Roman Catholics and Jews. Their only hope of driving through the defences of an entrenched bureaucracy was to advance together. One of the first things this conference did was to denounce the injustice of the Glasgow Corporation for the stand it had taken about the leasing of sites for new churches after the war. The Glasgow Housing Committee agreed to receive a deputation from the new association of Churches. The result was the same. The land must be in public ownership, not in private hands, and John White protested that a Socialist-controlled Council was not judging the case on its merits. "The question was dealt with as a party issue, and it is difficult to see why party politics should have been allowed to enter into a question of this kind." He went again to see Tom Johnston and intimated that, since the Scottish Churches had received nothing but a stubborn refusal even to consider a compromise, he proposed to seek Parliamentary legislation to safeguard their position, and he would fight for an appropriate clause to be inserted in the new Town and Country (Scotland) Planning Bill.

Without delay he drew up a memorandum on the needs of the Churches and the proposed amendments to the new Bill, and this he sent to all Scottish members of Parliament. These included Walter Elliott, James Stewart, George Mathers (later Lord Mathers), Lord Dunglass (later the Earl of Home), J. H. F. McEwen (later Sir John McEwen), Ernest Brown, F. C. Watt, Advocate, Commander Galbraith, and James Maxton. With Maxton, John White had always been on friendly terms, and they exchanged half a dozen letters on church sites. Maxton said frankly he would be most disinclined to vote against the Glasgow Corporation, the majority of which were of his own political complexion, and he saw no reason why any Church should have a higher status over the question of sites for new buildings than Socialist clubs. He added that he had "sufficient faith in the eternal verities to leave the situation sixty years hence to be decided by my grandsons". John White, on the other hand, had had sufficient experience to know that if an unjust bargain were made today, the eternal verities might have very little chance to operate in sixty years. He was interviewed by the press in March of that year (1945), and said that he hoped that the Scottish Grand Committee would lick the new Bill into such a shape that it would help the cause of housing in Scotland. The Glasgow Corporation was still adamant in its refusal to agree to any compensation beyond valuation price if, at the end of sixty years, it gave a congregation notice to quit its own church. John White was to be the leader of the deputation elected by all the Churches in Scotland:

"I am proud," he said, "to head such a deputation to the Secretary of State. I do not think that in the Churches there has ever been such an expression of unity and unanimity for generations." The Secretary himself later stated that it was the most influential deputation that had ever appeared within the Scottish Office in his time.

A particularly heavy bout of letter writing followed. John White saw he would need all the support he could muster from the Socialists as well as from the Tories. He urged this upon George Mathers, Labour member for Linlithgowshire, a strong churchman and later to become Lord High Commissioner to the General Assembly. The decision of the Socialist members who were favourable to John White was that they would not attempt to vote in a group: better to leave it to the individual decision. John White was more than satisfied: "I do not wish the Churches," he said, "to be mixed up with party politics."

When the Scottish Grand Committee, debating the new Bill, came to the section that regulated the disposal of land by local authorities, there was discussion on whether such disposal "shall be by way of feu". In putting this amendment forward, Tom Johnston was but interpreting the unanimous demand of all the Churches of Scotland for security of tenure—a demand that would force the Corporation of Glasgow to come into line with all other municipal and county authorities. It was duly passed and became law.

In a letter to Sir James Simpson, John White wrote:

"I was indeed pleased. This is the fifth occasion on which I have succeeded in getting Parliament to move in the right direction. The secret of success is to be found in not forming a party to secure amendments in the House, but to do the business single-handed, drawing in support on all sides. If one forms a party, it is bound to be a minority party, and to be known as such in the House, and a minority party is always ignored there. I wrote to all the members of the Committee, and wrote very special letters to leading members of all political parties. At last, the Secretary had to give way. In his heart I knew he favoured the plea we had put forward. I had good help from Mercer Robertson[1] and Mackintosh."

VI

By 1943 John White had completed half a century of work in the ministry. Because his jubilee year had come at a time when so many of his people were harassed by the anxieties of war, he himself had "hoped the occasion would pass with as little fuss as possible". But in spite of his wishes, there were vivid demonstrations of respect and affection. He bowed his head and prepared to thole it all, but ended in enjoying it almost in a spirit of *fiesta*. He met old friends, recalled old battles, made many speeches and never failed to edge in a good word for Church Extension. At the special service held at The Barony on Sunday, 14th March, there came to honour him many of the leading men in Glasgow, including representatives of the Corporation and the Merchants and Trades Houses, of the Presbytery and the University, and of the Cameronians (which some called The Barony Regiment), with which he had been associated since his undergraduate days. The Conservative Club in Edinburgh gave him a dinner, and at the Jubilee luncheon of the Presbytery of Glasgow, Sir Hector Hetherington, Principal and Vice-Chancellor of Glasgow University, proposed his health in memorable words:

"You will observe how fittingly the Ministerial Jubilee comes," he said. "Here, just one hundred years from the great disruption, we hail the jubilee of one who led the Act of Reconciliation. So we rejoice in this occasion. We give thanks for all that Dr. White has been privileged to do. . . . There is no need for the language of eulogy. You, his colleagues, have known over many years that powerful, austere, trenchant and kindly personality. . . . In the reunion of the two great Churches, if any one man deserves the title of bridge-builder-in-chief, it is John White."

In the course of his speech, Sir Hector spoke of the mingling of the two processions at the union and the calling of John White by universal

---

[1] George Mercer Robertson, S.S.C., Solicitor of the Church and Legal Adviser to the General Trustees.

acclaim to be Moderator of the first General Assembly of a united Church of Scotland:

"That surely was the crowning moment of his life—an event unique in history, one which can never be repeated in his life or in the life of any other man. But his work did not end there. It was indeed a new beginning. Through the first years of difficulty and stress, he guided the Church; became the leader of its Assembly, the most influential of its statesmen, the Convener of its Home Board and of its Extension Committee, its spokesman on the Councils of the Churches furth of Scotland, and its trusted adviser in the thousand concerns of its work and witness.

"It is a grand life's work: and it is not yet over—not, I hope, by a long way. And what are you to make of it? It could have been done only by a man of quite unusual gifts. It wanted first a tough and strong and biddable body, capable of long labour and patient of fatigue. It wanted strength of mind, the power to choose the right ends of action and the means thereto. It wanted a home life of deep and quiet understanding and happiness; and above all it wanted a spirit of consecration. These things Dr. White has had—as well as his share of human sorrow. By them he has done his work."

Sir Hector said he had reason to refer to the John White entry in *Who's Who*:

"In the bare unadorned prose of that massive work is set out the roll of his offices and deeds, but it ends on a curious note. 'Recreation: fishing. Clubs: Conservative, Glasgow; Conservative, Edinburgh.'

"Fishing, I suppose, is right enough," Sir Hector agreed, "though I never could make much of it myself; in my experience, the other party to the sport seldom knows the rules. . . . But 'Clubs: Conservative.' I think there must be here some strain of fantasy. Here surely is something of a joke. This man of revolutionary energy, this builder of churches, this architect of the vastest change in the history of our Scottish Kirk, this missioner to the poor, this gadfly of our social conscience—sitting down from choice, not among the reformers, but among the Conservatives, Glasgow; the Conservatives, Edinburgh. I don't think they can have known very well what they were harbouring, though I am sure they liked him. And yet, you know, there is sense in it, too. For nothing is quite so formidable as the Radical who thinks he is a Conservative, and who therefore draws his power both from imagination and from tradition. And that, I think, is precisely Dr. John White.

"For our part, we know that though there are some things he has never sought to conserve—his own time and strength and labour—he *has* known how to conserve some of the best things of all—kindness and sympathy, the affection of his friends, and, above all, that inward dedication to his high calling which has been the secret wellspring of all his thought and speech and action. Sir, we salute you. Jubilee, Jubilate!"

Messages of kindly congratulation overwhelmed him during that exciting week. "I could not escape from the zeal of my friends," he said. He was touched by a gracious personal message from King George VI, a message in which the Queen joined. Letters or telegrams came from the Duke of Montrose, Sir Iain Colquhoun, Bt., of Luss, a former Lord High Commissioner to the General Assembly, from many former Moderators, from Dr. Charles L. Warr, Dean of the Thistle, from Principal G. S. Duncan, of St. Mary's College, St. Andrews, from his old friend Dr. Norman Maclean, and from many another. A message from his close colleague in the union negotiations, Dr. Alexander Martin, touched him deeply, ending as it did with a ringing cheer from the voice of one who at eighty-six was ten years his senior: "You are still a young man! The best is yet to be!"

One private celebration gave him great pleasure. This was the Family Gathering, as it was called, of Barony folk, with representatives from his former parishes of Shettleston and South Leith and an eager host of his old assistants and Church Sisters. Mr. Sanderson spoke of him then with filial tenderness as the father of the great Barony household. A beautifully bound volume containing many memorials, including an address from Barony folk, was presented to him. Dr. White himself gave them a cheque for fifty pounds—one for each year of his ministry—to be used to commemorate in some permanent form his association with the church and people. He wrote afterwards of that Family Gathering:

"I had an opportunity to acknowledge the aid my wife and I received from the faithful people of Shettleston, South Leith and The Barony; from a great band of three score assistants and loyal junior colleagues; from great companies of elders; and from troops of zealous and devoted workers. Very specially I desire to say again how much the latter years of my Barony ministry have been relieved of all parochial burdens and anxiety by my young colleague, Mr. Sanderson, whose loyalty has only been surpassed by his consideration and loving kindness. May a rich benediction rest upon you all!"

Of all the public marks of esteem shown to him, one for which he felt specially grateful was the gift of money that had been collected throughout the Church of Scotland. It was not for his own use but—what pleased him infinitely more—for the cause he had most deeply at heart. The next General Assembly was the occasion chosen for the handing over of this donation, and the whole of that great gathering stood while the Moderator, Dr. E. J. Hagan, spoke of how John White had put the cause of Church Extension on the conscience of the people and in the forefront of their interest. "You are a Prince of Israel," he said, as he gave John White a cheque for six thousand pounds to help an extension charge. After expressing his gratitude for the form and purpose of the gift, Dr. White added, amid the laughter of the Assembly, that he did not know the whole Church of Scotland had been behind the gift until he learned of it by chance one day: "I was asked to conduct a special service at which, I was told, 'a retiring collection will be taken to promote your own memorial'."

VII

Mrs. White had died in September 1942; and at the jubilee Family Gathering at The Barony, his friends were touched with sorrow when he spoke of how he missed the loyal support she had given him throughout his ministry. Her absence from his side was the only shadow cast upon the celebrations of his Jubilee year, which would also have been the year of their Golden Wedding. A naturally strong constitution, strained by work and anxiety in the First World War, had shown signs of weakness which her visits to Tasmania and her rest there in the sunshine had helped to hold in check. Her partial recovery had been due largely to her own determination to carry on in spite of pain and increasing weakness, but for some time before her death she had been able to move from her chair only with difficulty.

More perhaps than even John White himself had ever realised, she had been a counsellor to her husband. Part of the deep wound left by the loss of her affection and companionship was the loss of what he now realised to have been the advice of a far-seeing woman who knew the ways of the world. Her sons and daughter recall the wisdom she imparted to them in the day-to-day crises of their young lives. One of her sayings they never forgot was: "Fear nothing but fear." Another, not always easy to follow, was: "At a meeting when everybody seems to agree on something that you feel is wrong, do not keep quiet just to let things go smoothly through—you are not being true to yourself if you do not speak up." Still harder to follow was her advice on lending money: "Never lend to a friend, for you will likely make an enemy—in a real case of need, give it." It was said there could have been no more wonderful mother for boys. "She went fishing with us up the hill burns," wrote one of her sons, "while Pater was off to the big salmon pools. She could handle a gun; she could harness the pony; brought up on a farm herself, she taught us to love the country." Her family was said to have been of an elastic size, for her husband's assistants she treated as grown-up sons. When they all joined in making a presentation to John White on his first appointment as Moderator, they gave a gold cross to the Moderator's wife with the inscription: "To Mrs. White with much regard from the old assistants of Shettleston, South Leith and The Barony of Glasgow, 1925-6, the year of her husband's moderatorship of the General Assembly." In thanking them, John White said then: "Without her as my permanent colleague, my ministry would have halted on one foot."

She had brought many a fine gift to her task as minister's wife. One was the knack of remembering faces. Some, whom she had never known well, have told how she would meet them after a long lapse of years and would come out with quick friendly words such as, "Of course I remember you!—Shettleston Sunday School. . . ." She had a quite uncommon flair of making friends quickly and of keeping them. Friendship she prized as too great a gift to be allowed to grow dim, and amongst the highest and the lowest in the land she took pains to nurture those many friendships of hers, and found joy in them all. She had brought gifts in kind, as well as gifts of the spirit, to the aid of her husband in his life's work. Her private income, settled upon her by her father and considered handsome in those days, relieved the family of financial anxiety. It was not generally known how strong had been her father's support during the years of the Shettleston Church Case. The old Free kirkman had made common cause with his son-in-law in the fight with the heritors, had urged him to go through with it to the end, and had promised that if he should lose the case and have to face the law costs, which ran into many thousands of pounds, he would pay them himself rather than let the burden fall upon the Shettleston congregation.

In a tribute to her from the pulpit of The Barony, Mr. Sanderson, who knew the White's home as few others did in the later years, said that it had been she who had "made Dr. White's busy life possible. . . . And because she created a home for him, she was interested in the homes of others—and was thus welcome in every home she visited." Another friend wrote that "the salvation of a man of John White's ability and force was that he should have, early in life, some influence strong enough to hold him, tender enough to sweeten him—and that influence had been exercised by Margaret White".

Chapter XXI

THE GOVAN CASE

I

THE first clear picture John White received of a plan that had been forming in the mind of the minister of Govan Old parish church was in a letter written to him on 8th February 1938. The project laid before him by Dr. George F. MacLeod was something new in the history of the Scottish Kirk. It sprang from the heart of a great idealist, a man whose voice had rung out across Scotland with a passionate sincerity calling upon his fellow countrymen to dedicate their lives to God. His proposal was to establish a Brotherhood—a Brotherhood that was "not simply a Scoto-Catholic degeneration," as he put it to John White, "but a synthesis of all that had been and is best in the history of our Church". Its home was to be the sacred isle of Iona.

MacLeod had sprung from a family of great Scottish ecclesiastics, a family that had given many Moderators to the Church of Scotland. He is a grandson of Dr. Norman MacLeod of The Barony. His father, Sir John MacLeod, Bt., M.P., had been a good friend of John White's and had been of valued help at Westminster during the lengthy process of the passing through Parliament of the Church of Scotland Acts that opened the way to union in 1929 with the United Free Church. In the First World War, George MacLeod had served as a combatant officer in the Argyll and Sutherland Highlanders, had won both the Military Cross and Croix de Guerre, and had afterwards become honorary chaplain to Toc-H in Scotland. He had been a missioner in the lumber-camps of British Columbia; and after a few years as collegiate minister at St. Cuthbert's in Edinburgh, he had been called to Govan Old parish in 1930. A second son, he was later to succeed his nephew as the fourth baronet to the title conferred upon his father in 1924. He had always been known as a young man who was outspoken and impulsive, a man quick to acknowledge with penitence any word or action of his own that he may afterwards have regretted, a man of great generosity of mind and heart, who had endeared himself to thousands and who had collected some enemies by the way. His appeal to youth had a Celtic fervour that touched the emotions.

It was clear from the moment of its inception that in his new Brotherhood many young ministers would follow him with the same confidence that had inspired the men he had led into battle as an intrepid Highland officer.

Before the first step was taken, George MacLeod was anxious to assure John White that the Brotherhood, in spite of its suggestion of monasticism, would be strictly Presbyterian. He approached a number of men he hoped would become Sponsors, and he wished to have John White's name at the top of the list. He gave the names of others, and of one of them he wrote: "His is the only name redolent of cassocks—actually I contemplate that the Brotherhood in Iona would be dressed as fishermen!" The notes he sent formed a document of between four and five thousand words. He had been deeply moved by the problems with which John White had been faced in his great scheme of planting churches in the midst of the new housing areas. He believed that better results would come from a group effort in these areas than from the ministry of one man. He believed in what he called the Fellowship witness of the Church, but he did not think that Divinity Halls could adequately train men in the technique of Fellowship.

"This is not a peevish thrust," he said, "but the grave concern of many professors themselves. The fact is, that our curriculum was not constructed for that. . . . There has resulted for decades a plaint, now louder and now fainter, from year after year of students that, while there is nothing in the curriculum that should not be there, there is 'an additional something that has been left out'. . . . An experiment in the technique of fellowship within the Presbyterian witness and supplementary to the teaching of the Divinity Halls is necessary."

He could see on all sides the fading out of family prayers, the teaching of salvation through Creed and catechising fallen away, the discipline of kirk sessions attenuated, and the justification for comparatively infrequent communions (namely, that they should be exalted into holiness by preparation and thanksgiving) having proved ineffectual by the retention of the infrequency and the forgetting of the preparation. "The Scottish Sabbath languishes," he said, "and the disintegrating process gathers momentum." He made it clear that the purpose of the Brotherhood was to "preserve the essential truths for which the Reformers died. . . . What is required is an experiment, however small, that might begin to serve the housing areas, learn the technique of Fellowship, and investigate in its own life and worship how most richly to present to the modern day the active and latent vitality of Presbyterianism." And so he had turned to Iona.

> In Iona of my heart, Iona of my love,
> Instead of monks' voices shall be lowing of cattle,
> But ere the world come to an end,
> Iona shall be as it was.

That had been St. Columba's prophecy, and George MacLeod said that he knew enough about St. Columba to be certain that to read it in too literal a sense would be wrong. The Iona which St. Columba had known had been an up-to-date expression of religion for his own time. "He may have used coracles, but we can rest certain he would have taken a steamer had one existed." The Iona Brotherhood was to be of young men from the Divinity Halls, together with qualified artisans who would promise to serve the Brotherhood for a certain time. Everyone, both clerical and lay, would receive £50 a year and all found, and it was hoped that the community would be as far as possible self-supporting by the cultivation of a croft. Generally, it might be called the Presbyterian counterpart of Buckfast Abbey, in that the work would be "a community service for the glory of God and His Church, but the men would be under no vows and remain, in this aspect of their work, laymen". Those young ministers would be in Iona only during three summer months. In the winter they would work in couples in places where they would be urgently needed. They would return to Iona for one month the next summer ("to reset their compass") before they went back to a second year's work in a parish. After they had completed two years in the Brotherhood, they would be available as parish ministers. Twenty of them, together with twelve workmen, would be in residence during summer, and all would work on the restoration of the monastic buildings. When George MacLeod's plans had been completed, he hoped there would be some sixty men under training at Iona. Upwards of two hundred left the theological colleges each year, and George MacLeod felt confident that one in ten of them might wish experience in what he called "the technique of Fellowship within the Presbyterian witness".

His idea was that the Sponsors, with John White at the head of the list, would serve as an advisory committee in details of polity and practice. The very names of these Sponsors would indicate to the public that the experiment was backed by representative churchmen. Wooden huts would have to be built to house the Brotherhood before the monastic buildings were ready, the men would have to be fed, and their pay of fifty pounds a year would have to be found. "The whole scheme is an experiment," insisted George MacLeod. "and would depend for its essential life on the degree to which the Church feels it is really needed." He said he was prepared to act as leader, would expect no salary so long as he remained unmarried, and he proposed that his winter months be spent appealing for money to sustain the Brotherhood and pay for the necessary building, in addition to finding new recruits from the four universities. It would be vital that he keep closely in touch with those parishes in which his young men were busy on their evangelising task after the summer's training on the sacred isle. Since the Church of England had "tholed" for nearly a century a number of Anglican brotherhoods—though of a different kind—he felt that it was a reasonable risk for the Church of Scotland to take, a risk limited to five years as a start. If it failed, the Church must not be taxed with failure. He wanted a free hand and was prepared to "take the knock" if the scheme had to be abandoned. "I ask the Trustees and the Sponsors," he repeated, "to trust me personally that my purposes are utterly loyal to the Church of my fathers, and my supreme concern is the preservation of Presbyterianism."

II

The first meeting of the Iona Sponsors took place at the house of Dr. Charles Warr at Edinburgh on Thursday, 7th April 1938. The members of the Iona Cathedral Trust had approved of George MacLeod's plans, and all was set fair. The wooden huts were to be built, a water supply was to be brought down into the Abbey precincts, and an appeal was to be made for help to restore the monastic buildings.[1] George MacLeod asked John White to occupy the pulpit in Govan Old parish church on the first Sunday morning after the congregation had been told their minister was leaving them to go to Iona.

In the course of that sermon he said:

"Your minister has given strong reasons for the step he has taken. I share with you the regret that this great church, where his short ministry has been so blessed, is to be left without his zealous and

---

[1] The Abbey had been given by the 8th Duke of Argyll, accepted for the Church of Scotland by the General Assembly of 1900, and thereafter restored.

magnificent leadership. At the same time, what can one say, when he so sincerely believes that God wants him to do this thing on which he has set his heart? *What can we say but—God be with you!* . . .

"George MacLeod's scheme is for a settlement on Iona to train young men for the Home Mission ministry and in especial for service in Church Extension charges. Your minister wishes to try out his scheme. It has the backing of many within the Church who wish to see the experiment tested, who wish it well, and who may have something to say in directing the policy as well as commending the intention. It must be kept consistent with the government, worship, and doctrine of the Church of Scotland, and we are assured that what is proposed is strictly Presbyterian. . . . We are at present providing, through our Home Mission Committee, trained men and trained women to assist in such areas; but this new experiment may prove helpful in recruiting other trained licentiates to augment these forces, which are admittedly insufficient to deal with the situation as adequately as one could desire.

"Today, in wishing your minister well in this venture of faith, should the Presbytery release him for the work, I like to picture him as going out to that island, so rich in romance and tradition, in the joyous month of May, even as St. Columba in 563 landed on its shores and trained up a community of preachers and church builders in Scotland. The island of saints, the mother of churches, Iona will be a splendid setting for the experiment. Within the precincts of the sacred Abbey one trusts that, not only will the piety of the young community grow warmer, but that their patriotism will gain something of a new force as on the plains of Marathon.

"Dr. MacLeod takes this step on the eve of a celebration of the fiftieth anniversary of this church of Govan. He asks you to remember that this church was expressly built to inaugurate a new way of approach for the Church of Scotland to lay hold on the full ancient faith as it was once declared from Iona.

"I can recall the opening of this church on 19th May 1888, but more distinctly do I recall that day of sorrow ten years later—4th August 1898—when the Church and the city and the whole nation were shocked with the news of the death of John MacLeod. He was a great church builder in Govan parish; he was a Church statesman in his policy of Church reform and legislation; and he left his influence in a quickened consciousness of the vocation of the Church of Scotland as part of the Church Catholic, affirming its Divine basis, its super-natural life and its Heavenly calling."

Since Dr. MacLeod was not a member of the Assembly of 1938, he asked John White to commend the Iona scheme when it came up for decision. A person unnamed had handed out to the press the news of the proposed Iona Community, and this caused irritation. Someone had been too impulsive. The Rev. Arthur H. Dunnett, joint secretary of the Home Board, said that even the Home Mission Committee had not been con-sulted; nor was the General Assembly now being given an opportunity of declaring their approval or otherwise of the scheme. Nevertheless, he thought that "if it were within the power of any man to carry through such an experiment, it was Dr. George MacLeod, who had been able to make a world-wide public by means of the wireless and who had an extraordinary appeal to young people". He criticised as wildly exaggerated some of Dr. MacLeod's figures; it was sheer nonsense, he said, to say that if thirty new churches with one minister apiece were erected, each minister would be responsible for about forty thousand people. In addition, there were financial difficulties. The Iona brethren would mostly be sent to needy congregations, and it was hard to see how these could find the money to support them, as Dr. MacLeod proposed. "All I have seen of the scheme," he said, "suggests that Dr. MacLeod fears the hand of a constitutional body within the Church." But he hoped that they would welcome the splendid adventure even though Dr. MacLeod's method of setting out on it was not what some members might have wished.

John White said that it seemed to him that the Assembly was giving its unanimous blessing, and he thought Mr. Dunnett had been a little too severe. A dissenting voice shouted "No." To this John White replied characteristically: "*I* think so. I am not saying what *you* think." He pointed out that the Home Board had already been doing a great amount of the team-work proposed by Dr. MacLeod.

> "The Iona scheme has had its origin," he said, "in devising ways and means to help Church Extension charges in populous districts by means of team-work. . . . I hope the Assembly will give a very hearty blessing to what is a fine venture of faith. Someone said it may fail. Of course it may fail. But failure is not reproach when one is experi-menting in the work of God. Failure often shows the way towards success."

The project as sponsored by John White duly received the blessing of the General Assembly. Thanks to the generosity of Sir James Lithgow, Bt., the Glasgow shipbuilder, Dr. MacLeod found the money to begin his great experiment.

III

In the autumn, Dr. MacLeod, who had received a petition from members of the Govan congregation anxious to have him back, said he saw no reason why he should not return and at the same time remain leader of the Iona Community. If he were called back, he said, he would accept —unless the Presbytery thought it was against the best interests of the Church. On the feasibility of his return, the Business Committee of the Presbytery of Glasgow, with Dr. Alfred Brown, joint convener, in the chair, decided on 1st December 1938: "The Committee regards it as unconstitutional and contrary to the fundamental laws of the Church for a Vacancy Committee to submit as nominee to a vacant congregation the name of any minister who has other interests involving annual continued absences from his parish and also further frequent absences from his pastoral and pulpit duties." Rev. T. B. Stewart Thomson of St. Stephen's, Edinburgh, was called to fill the vacancy.

The outbreak of war in 1939 held up the planned development at Iona, but John White's interest in the project never flagged. On one occasion he felt constrained to tell Dr. MacLeod that Iona was suspected of harbouring "pacifists", and the Iona leader thanked him for the warning and said that he himself had heard rumours. He added that while pacificism was no definite part of the teaching in the Community, each man ought to have the right of deciding according to the dictates of his own conscience, therefore, pacifists were not barred from Iona. John White looked forward to the day on which the Community of which he was proud to be chief Sponsor would become, as he put it, "an integral part of the Church organisation, not an outside contributing agency working on a special scheme". As a first step, he suggested to Dr. Robert Mackintosh, Secretary of the Home Board, that something might be done to bring about a closer relationship between the Board and the work Dr. MacLeod intended to carry out through the Iona Community. "Would it not be possible for the Board," he said, "to enlist any help he and his Community could give, provided it was done as directed and planned by the Home Board? . . . It would provide the Iona Community with an opportunity of allaying these suspicions that are rife, and would make for peace and the enlistment of such forces as the Community can bring forward." But the closer co-operation did not, for a number of years, go beyond organised evangelistic enterprises on the invitation of kirk sessions.

In February 1948, Dr. T. B. Stewart Thomson having accepted a call to Dunbarney, Bridge of Earn, was duly translated to that parish, and Govan Old fell vacant once more. The Vacancy Committee had a list of seven possible ministers to consider for the charge, and Dr. MacLeod's name was among them. Although a decade had passed since he had gone from Govan, he was not forgotten in the congregation; and it was but natural that he should have had loyal friends among its members—friends who, since the charge was now vacant, would wish to have their beloved minister among them once more. But it is hard to imagine a more inauspicious start to the attempt to bring him back to his old kirk, for there followed a series of incidents that were to develop into a notorious dispute which became known as the Govan Case. There were sharp clashes at the Vacancy Committee meetings, discussions were heated, and some members indignantly resigned.

For two years Dr. MacLeod had been wondering "whether the next development of the parish-plans of the Iona Community would not best be served by an outright experiment with a Glasgow parish as the main sphere of the work", and when he was made aware of the discussions in the Committee, he felt that the members had an imperfect idea of the experiment he would try in the parish if he should be called to the Govan pulpit, and he felt obliged to complain to the convener. At three separate Committee meetings, the majority vote went heavily against the experiment he envisaged; his name was removed from the list; and the Interim Moderator was asked to write to two other ministers about the vacancy. Harmony, it seemed, had been restored.

While he was awaiting replies from the two ministers, the Interim Moderator received from Dr. MacLeod a copy of a Memorandum about a proposed Iona project in Govan. He read it in some perplexity. Dr. MacLeod, who was about to set out on a visit to Australia, explained that he had drawn it up and sent it to the Clerk of the Presbytery of Glasgow so that it would be available to the Presbytery if, in his absence abroad, Govan should put forward his name for the charge. He knew that his name was no longer on the Govan list, but he also knew that some members of the Vacancy Committee would have greatly liked to have him back in his old pulpit.

In the opening clause of the Memorandum, Dr. MacLeod said he would be prepared to accept a call to Govan on condition that he retained his connection with the Iona Community. In clauses that followed were details of his proposal to yoke Iona with Govan in a great missionary experiment. He pointed out that, in the ten years which had passed since the Community had been formed, the organisation had developed. It had now an assured annual income of over three thousand pounds; it had some twenty-five thousand pounds in hand for rebuilding purposes on the island, as well as a capital of twenty thousand pounds for work on the mainland. Dr. MacLeod had a full-time colleague, a full-time Master of Works on the island, and two full-time lady secretaries in Edinburgh.[1] Since he did not look on his leadership of the Community as an official Church appointment, he contended that there could be no objection in ecclesiastical law to his holding both posts—there was no "plurality". He said that it would be his "primary winter concern to rebuild Govan", and this rebuilding would be the Community's "most important experiment" on the mainland of Scotland. Out of his Govan stipend, he proposed to pay the salary of a full-time colleague in the parish who would officially be an ordained assistant. As to his personal absences, he said he would be away from Govan for no more than three months each year. "It is not an unknown thing," he added, "for ministers efficiently serving large charges in a Presbytery to be away for two months in summer, a fortnight after Easter, and a fortnight after Christmas. That is more than three months' absence," and he doubted if his own absences would even require Presbytery sanction. He would accept the call to Govan if the Presbytery placed it in his hands, because it would be good for both Govan and Iona and because he believed the Pearce Institute (an endowed community centre under the care of the minister and kirk session) "must be recovered as a strong point of Church activity".

When the Interim Moderator read the proposals of Dr. MacLeod in the Memorandum, he did not know what had been taking place, but learned later and recorded it for the benefit of the Probationers and Transference of Ministers Committee. Since his name was no longer before the Vacancy Committee as a possible occupant of the Govan pulpit, Dr. MacLeod had felt free to seek an interview with the convener of that Committee and discuss the proposals outlined in the Memorandum. Another member of the Committee whom he had approached and questioned on his adverse attitude to the Iona Community had been

[1] There were also, as Dr. MacLeod stated a little later, a full-time Publicity Manager and a full-time Publications Manager.

sufficiently impressed to go with four others to interview him. Unauthor-
ised by the Vacancy Committee, this had been a personal approach for
further enlightenment on the part of five members who had previously
voted against Dr. MacLeod. They had questioned him about the Community and the missionary experiment he had been eager to try in Govan,
and he had described with infectious enthusiasm his plan which their
adverse vote in the Vacancy Committee had killed. In the words of the
Interim Moderator in the vacancy, "they were converted".

At the mid-September meeting of the Vacancy Committee (the first
held for over a month), Dr. MacLeod's name was, for the fourth time,
brought forward. There was a startling change of front. An overwhelming
majority voted for the rescinding of the previous adverse decision against
Dr. MacLeod and his missionary experiment. "Anticipating such a move,"
stated the Interim Moderator, "Dr. MacLeod, before going to Australia,
had prepared the Memorandum." This was read over in the Committee
meeting and discussed, and the following motion was passed: "Having
heard the Memorandum of Dr. MacLeod, the Committee would be
agreeable, on these terms, to proceed to his nomination." The replies of
the two ministers who had been approached revealed little or no wish to
consider the Govan pulpit if it were offered to them: so far as they were
concerned, the way to Govan lay open to Dr. George F. MacLeod.

IV

The events of the next few months brought an increase of tension. The
unanimous opinion of the Presbytery's Advisory Committee on Vacancies
was that the list of duties of the leader of the Iona Community, which had
been supplied by the Community and published in a report to the previous
Assembly (before there was any question of a call to Govan), was so heavy
that it would not be possible for the Presbytery to sustain a call to a man
who had such a burden already on his shoulders. The congregational
and other parochial work of a minister in Govan, which had over two
thousand communicant members, was already formidable enough without
any additions. But the Vacancy Committee decided to reject this advice
and to proceed with Dr. MacLeod's nomination.

The matter then passed into the hands of the Presbytery's Business
Committee. Dr. MacLeod's Memorandum of August was studied. He
had made it plain that his acceptance of a call was conditional upon his
being allowed to retain the leadership of the Iona Community. The

Committee found itself reconsidering the same point of Church law as it had been obliged to do ten years before when there had been talk of Dr. MacLeod's return to the pulpit he then had recently left. The decision in 1938 had been that it was "unconstitutional and contrary to the fundamental laws of the Church" for a Vacancy Committee to submit, as nominee to a vacant charge, the name of "any minister who had other interests involving annual continued absences from his parish and also further frequent absences from his pastoral and pulpit duties". The Committee decided that it must reaffirm its previous decision. Dr. MacLeod was now in Australia, and it was felt that he should be informed of this with as little delay as possible; a cablegram was therefore sent to him by the Presbytery clerk, and an air-mail letter followed. Dr. MacLeod rejected the decision and replied to the clerk: "I hereby accept the call.[1] I have used no undue influence, either by myself or through others, to receive the call. As I am a member of the Presbytery of Glasgow, you already hold my Presbyterial Certificate and my Certificate of Status."

The Govan Vacancy Committee was informed by the Presbytery clerk that the nomination was invalid in the terms of the relevant Act of the General Assembly of 1932. This deals with ministers in employment that is not subject to the jurisdiction of the Church or who hold office under a religious society; and before Dr. MacLeod's nomination could be valid according to Church law, he must first resign the leadership of the Iona Community so that he could show himself to be free to devote all his energies to the ministerial work of the congregation and parish of Govan Old.

In a letter from Australia to the Presbytery's Advisory Committee, Dr. MacLeod said that he regarded Iona and Govan as complementary, not inimical. A responsible and efficient cure of souls in Govan must obviously be his first priority. This was equally essential, he stressed, for the sake of the Community. Few would continue to pay attention to Iona principles if the Community "failed to portray them efficiently" in what would become its most obvious mainland centre. He explained that the organisation had now settled down into a pattern. In its earlier years, the Community had been a "one man show": but he felt that now, after ten years, "if it cannot develop into a corporate responsibility, it stands condemned". His full-time colleague at Iona could undertake the general organisation there, and he proposed to make an "entire re-adjustment

---

[1] Dr. MacLeod meant that he was allowing his name to go forward for nomination; he had not by that time received the call.

that would be in favour of an efficient ministry in Govan, and the change would not endanger the Community". On his return home he preached at Govan on the first Sunday in December, and thereafter a ballot vote of the congregation was taken, and the call lay open for the signature of members. On 20th December, the day after the call was closed for signatures, Dr. MacLeod announced his acceptance of the call to Govan Old.

V

Since the Presbytery was informed that the papers relating to the Govan call were not in order, a committee was formed to investigate the whole matter. It was named the Special Committee anent Govan Old Vacancy. Fifteen members of Presbytery were on it, and John White was asked to be convener. It was a task little to his liking. With George MacLeod and his father, Sir John MacLeod, John White's friendship was of such long standing that he shrank from a commission which might even faintly mar a relationship he so greatly valued. He thought well before he accepted it. He felt it was his bounden duty to the Church to undertake it, and he hoped he might guide to a peaceful end an affair which had already aroused intemperate feelings and had caused grievous tension in a congregation which had been without a minister for nearly a year. It was in this spirit that he took up the convenership of the Special Committee anent Govan Old Vacancy.

It might have seemed to some that, in all charity, the new committee might well have done no more than to take note of the fact that, after having rejected Dr. MacLeod and his missionary experiment on three separate occasions, the Govan Vacancy Committee had changed their mind and by an overwhelming majority had accepted him and his project, and then have decided that if Dr. MacLeod felt himself Divinely guided and able to undertake the immense task which he had set forth in his Memorandum of August, he should be given every encouragement. The creating of the Iona Community had been a fine spiritual experiment, and John White himself had been its prime Sponsor: why not encourage another spiritual experiment which sprang from the very loins of the Community on the sacred isle? To be sure, there was that Church law of 1932. If it was a bad law, it should be rescinded. If it was a good law for ninety-nine out of a hundred cases, was this not the hundredth case where it should with Divine blessing be relaxed? But this was not Dr. MacLeod's contention. He held that his leadership of the Iona Community was not covered by the Act of 1932. His point was that he was not "employed" by the Iona Community. "I have never been paid a salary by the Iona Community and am not in receipt of one," he said, and argued that, before being called to a parish, the Act required that a minister should resign employment which is not subject to the jurisdiction of the Church or any office under a religious society or a charitable institution. The operative word, he declared, was *employed*, and he was not employed by anyone.

Since Dr. MacLeod took this stand, and took it firmly, the Special Committee found it necessary to consider its validity. With only one dissentient, it found that, without quibbling pedantically about the significance of the word "employed", the Act of 1932 had been framed and passed by the General Assembly to cover just such a case as the present one. The Law Agent of the Church, Arthur H. McLean, W.S., acting during a vacancy in the Procuratorship, advised that Dr. MacLeod had not been eligible for nomination because he had not produced a certificate of resignation as leader of the Iona Community. Until Dr. MacLeod gave evidence of his resignation, the Presbytery could not admit or induct him to Govan. It seemed that an *impasse* had been reached.

VI

John White and his colleagues noted in their report to the Presbytery that Dr. MacLeod, back from Australia, had preached at Govan on 5th December and thereafter a ballot vote of the congregation had been taken. While barely more than a couple of dozen votes had been cast against him, the total vote in his favour did not quite amount to twenty-five per cent of the membership, which was over two thousand. The signatures to the call were fewer than seventeen and a half per cent of the membership. The signatures to his call to Govan in 1930 had been more than two and a half times as many. The Presbytery was obliged by regulation to take into account the number of signatures when deciding whether a call should be sustained, for meagre support to a call might indicate a serious division in a congregation; and while there could have been little doubt about Dr. MacLeod's personal popularity among the majority of the congregation, there was also the question whether many doubted if Govan was a suitable place for the proposed Iona experiment and the harnessing of that project to the normal work of the congregation. The Special Committee decided to leave that matter an open question for the time being. Whether the

Presbytery of Glasgow considered that the nomination was valid under Church law was the point which had first to be settled.

In presenting the Committee's report to the Presbytery, John White pointed out that the Presbytery was

"not called upon to pass any judgement upon the work at Iona—may God prosper it and its chosen leader!—but to consider a call to that same leader to minister to one of our largest and most demanding parishes while he continues to occupy the post of leader of the Iona Community. The responsibility rests upon Dr. MacLeod. He must make up his mind whether he is prepared to accept the call to Govan—if the Presbytery places the call in his hands—or to continue his leadership at Iona. . . . Our high regard for Dr. MacLeod must not bias our judgement, nor must any critical attitude to the Iona Community affect our decision."

Of the report itself he said that to his knowledge there was nothing in it that could not be supported by documentary evidence.

When Dr. MacLeod rose to address the Presbytery, he declared that the status of the Iona Community was such that it could hardly be argued that it was fully covered by the phrase "outside the jurisdiction of the Church in the Act of 1932". He pointed out that the Community had effected scores of adult baptisms, and hundreds had been gathered into the Church's fellowship, all to the benefit of the Church of Scotland. While the ministers working for the Community were under the personal jurisdiction of the Church, he asked whether the Presbytery could be really happy to declare such a society *simpliciter* as outside the jurisdiction of the Church. He said he protested strongly against Dr. John White's view, and declared that it could not be compared as such with, say, the Glasgow City Mission. The Community was started with the sole purpose of training Church of Scotland ministers for work in the Home Mission field. It was an experimental group of ministers whose juridical relationship as a group was not yet clear, but the group was *de facto* within the Church. It was quite clear to him that the Act of 1932 was not designed to cover any such body as the Iona Community.

With this view, John White disagreed. Iona was not and never had been under the jurisdiction of the General Assembly. In his memorandum of the previous August, Dr. MacLeod had said there could be no plurality in holding the two posts because the leadership of the Community was *not* an official Church appointment. Moreover, said John White, "a call is a spiritual act, a symbol of God calling someone to particular work, and no man can accept that call with an amendment". The present report was but an interim report, dealing as it did entirely with documents. A subsequent report would be presented to the Presbytery after the Committee had conferred with interested parties.

On the Special Committee was a member who dissented from the decision that the Act of 1932 could be applied to the Govan Case. He had been greatly concerned about this and had consulted a lawyer, whose view had differed from the expressed opinion of the Law Agent of the Church of Scotland. That member of Committee spoke at the Presbytery meeting, and the same night he wrote to John White: "I did not consider myself to be at essential variance with you, and in speaking tonight I was less speaking against you than trying to shake the feeling of the Presbytery that the 1932 Act finished the case. . . . I felt that your opening speech lifted the issue and the Presbytery above faction, and for that I am glad indeed."

John White replied:

"This Govan business has been a worry to many folks. I hope it will not continue to be a worry to you any more. You have done your best in the interests of friendship and a wise finding. I am very sorry that, even in appearance, one should seem to be in opposition to Dr. George MacLeod, but I can assure you that I am whole-heartedly with him. But he cannot expect the Presbytery to appoint him to one of its most demanding parishes, calling for the full energy of a strong man, while at the same time he occupies the equally responsible and equally demanding office of leadership of the Iona Community. I wish he would make a decision. Unfortunately, the resignation of the leadership of Iona would be a disaster to the Community; and yet there is no reason why, if minister of Govan, he should not continue an interest in the Iona Community. But he cannot hold two full-time offices. He must decide."

VII

The reports in the press of the Presbytery meeting brought John White a sheaf of critical letters. Some were anonymous and abusive; some were written by those who had the courage to sign them. One of the latter gave both John White and the Glasgow Presbytery a trouncing. The writer said that there seemed to be a common idea among laymen that "there is a hard conservatism of opinion in the Presbytery which always stands in the way of eager and adventurous spirits for Christ". He said he had some uncomfortable thoughts about Church leadership:

"What right has anyone to try and cut down the work that God has called one to do? I would like to be sure in my own mind that all in the Presbytery were seeking only God's way and not their own way. . . . The kingdom of God will not be hastened by lengthy discussions on procedure and the turning of a phrase to suit one's own selfish viewpoint or intellectual vanity. Beware of being a stumbling block. I am sorry for the sake of the Church that the matter has been so badly handled."

John White replied by return of post:

"I regret that you have so much misunderstood the question before the Presbytery; and that you have then, without knowledge, proceeded to judge and condemn the Presbytery, attributing to the leaders of the Presbytery somewhat low and unspiritual motives: and the inexcusable criticism, so erroneous and unfounded contained in your sentence, 'There is a hard conservatism of opinion in the Presbytery which always stands in the way of eager and adventurous spirits for Christ.'

"It is also evident that you have not read the printed report of the Special Committee anent Govan Old Vacancy. There is not a single word in that judicial statement that entitles you to write a letter so devoid of understanding and Christian feeling.

"That report has to be examined by Dr. George F. MacLeod, and the Special Committee will see him before submitting a final report. . . . Is this a wrong thing to do? Does it justify your saying 'the matter has been badly handled'?

"You may not realise that the decision to accept or refuse the call to Govan rests with Dr. MacLeod; or that the Presbytery cannot, in view of Act IX Assembly 1932 proceed 'to admit or induct him' to Govan Old 'until he has given evidence of his resignation of the said office'—that is, of the onerous office of the leadership of Iona Community. I do not deal with one or two very unfair and most unjust personal references save to say—

(a) That I should be only too pleased to see Dr. MacLeod accept Govan.

(*b*) That as the chief sponsor of Iona Community—right from the beginning—I fear for the future of that 'experiment' if he should give up the Leadership and go to Govan.

(*c*) That your tortuous interpretation of my tribute to Dr. MacLeod, the work of the Community, and the prayer for its growth in influence and its religious contribution, is neither true nor charitable."

This at once brought a generous apology: "I realise that the tone of my letter was quite uncalled for, and I have to admit that I did not fully know the whole story." The writer said that his previous letter

"must have seemed an un-Christian attack on yourself . . . and the harbouring of such thoughts and their implications worried me considerably. The snippets I read in the press, taken from their full context, along with the gossip, was such that I did want reassurance that the interpretations arising in my mind could not be so. . . . I can well imagine how my words may have pained you who have worked so long and faithfully for our Church. I would thank you for putting things in their true perspective. I am glad to know that my unfair interpretations are unfounded. I do trust that my outburst will not cause you any further pain and that you will be able to accept this as my sincerest apology."

In a cordial reply, John White assured the writer that "not many are strong and big enough to write a letter like that which you have just sent to me. I thank you most sincerely. You can rely on the Special Committee which is in my charge doing everything free from bias to reach a settlement in this matter in the highest interests of the Church."

If all of those who harboured ill-feeling towards John White had written to him in frank terms of reproof, he would have had an opportunity to dissipate some of the innuendoes and cankerous criticism of himself and the Presbytery which were based so largely on "snippets from the press and gossip". Criticism of the Presbytery of Glasgow was not confined to laymen. One minister wrote to John White that

"a small group in the Presbytery seems to object to free discussion, especially if it be in opposition or in any way critical of committee decisions. . . . I have been perturbed at the increasing tendency in our Presbytery to take it for granted that committees have the power not only to consider the matters with which they deal but to make decisions that commit the Presbytery, sometimes without even informing the Presbytery. This, I am sure, is one of the reasons why some of our ablest men are shying clear of the Presbytery and its work. They are not willing to join in the chorus and fall in behind the Yes-men, and they don't seem to think it is worth while to run the risks involved in doing anything to oppose them."

John White answered some of these criticisms at the next meeting of the Presbytery when the second report of the Special Committee was presented. He spoke of the anonymous letters and postcards he had received. "I received many," he said, "telling me how the Church of Scotland ought to be run." He spoke of the purblind epistles about Govan, intolerant and opinionated. He spoke of several signed letters from the antinomian section of the community who believed that the law should, at times to be decided by them, be ignored. He spoke of some letters in which it had been suggested that the Presbytery should induct Dr. MacLeod to Govan for a limited period of years and then review the situation. "I know these are genuine proposals," he said, "but they are neither constitutional nor practicable." He spoke of other letters in which the Presbytery of Glasgow was vilified as a "reactionary body, out of touch with the needs of the day, which is restraining a young fresh leadership". This charge he hurled back at the heads of its authors.

"Nothing could be further from the truth," he declared. "The Presbytery of Glasgow is deeply concerned with every matter that affects the religious and social welfare of the city, and indeed the nation. Some of its most dynamic members are not even young members. The Presbytery of Glasgow never has had so many keen, mentally alert, spiritually sympathetic members as it has today. The criticism is a libel. It is based not on knowledge but on partisanship.

"It will save unnecessary correspondence," he went on, "if I say here and now that the decision to go to Govan rests with Dr. MacLeod. He could have been minister of Govan today if he had been willing to accept the call unconditionally, as any other minister accepts a call."

It had been proposed in the first report, and it was repeated now in the second, that the matter should be referred for decision to the General Assembly. To this, both Dr. MacLeod and the Presbytery agreed.

VIII

The reference was made to the General Assembly on Friday, 27th May 1949. The Assembly Hall was crowded. Counsel for Dr. MacLeod and for the Special Committee of the Presbytery of Glasgow spoke at the Bar of the Assembly. John White opened the proceedings by assuring members that he was not there to argue the case, but merely to place the facts before the members. Counsel could argue the case afterwards. He explained that Dr. MacLeod had said he would accept the call to Govan only on condition that he retained the leadership of the Iona Community. What was asked of the Assembly was a clear decision on Dr. MacLeod's eligibility.

The old point of dispute on "employment within the jurisdiction" of the Church was argued. Counsel for the Special Committee held that it had never been intended that the word employment, as mentioned in the Act, was being used "in any narrow, legal, pedantic sense, and the Act will be susceptible to very great and grave abuse if the narrow meaning were to be adopted". Counsel for Dr. MacLeod maintained that from the beginning the Church had accepted the fact that the Iona Community was under its jurisdiction, although it may never have passed any resolutions to that effect. The Iona Community had accepted the position that they were under the Church. The Church had accepted the position that it was over the Iona Community. Therefore Dr. MacLeod was not employed outwith the jurisdiction of the Church. Indeed, he was not employed at all. To have employment there must be an employer. There must be somebody to whom the employed person is responsible. Dr. MacLeod was responsible to nobody as leader at Iona. Therefore he was not employed within the terms of the sub-section of the Act.

The Convener of the Presbytery's Business Committee, in declaring that the Act certainly did apply to Dr. MacLeod, said it had been suggested that this was a special case—and should have special consideration. "It is not a special case," he said. "A Presbytery can be no respecter of persons or congregations. A Presbytery cannot turn a blind eye where Acts of Assembly seem to be flouted and broken."

The drama of that Assembly meeting touched those in the public galleries as keenly as ministers and elders on the floor below. Some felt that members were impatient with the legal argument and were eager to discuss whether the placing of Dr. MacLeod in Govan would be for the good of the Church. But the legal issue had to be determined first and could not be brushed aside in order to discuss the "practicability" of Dr. MacLeod's proposed return as minister to his old parish while he held the office of Iona leader.

By the time Professor Pitt Watson rose to support the speaker who had laid the case of the Presbytery of Glasgow before the members, the impatience of the audience was manifest. He said that he did not propose to deliver the speech he had prepared, but would put the case very simply. Was Dr. MacLeod, in his capacity as leader of the Iona Community, subject to the jurisdiction of the Church courts? Professor Pitt Watson asked the Assembly to note that, on the following day, it would be the duty of Professor Riddell to present the Report of the Committee *anent* the Iona Community: "What are the implications of that word 'anent'? Why was it used? How does it distinguish the Committee from other committees of the General Assembly?" The answer was that it was designed to keep the Assembly *in touch* with the activities of the Iona Community and to *inform* it about these activities. It had no control over these activities—nor, on its advice, could the Assembly exercise any jurisdiction over them. Professor Pitt Watson submitted that if, when the Deliverance on Professor Riddell's Report was dealt with, any member put forward a motion in which the Iona Community was either enjoined or forbidden to pursue any course of action, the decision from the Moderatorial Chair would, of necessity, be that of ruling the motion out of order and incompetent. Therefore the Act of 1932 applied without a doubt in the present case.

Whether it was a sound and practical project for the leader of the Iona Community to become minister at Govan was never discussed, for Dr. MacLeod was heavily outvoted on the legal issue. Afterwards, in an interview he gave to the press, he said: "It is only on the driest and most technical interpretation of the law that it can be maintained that the Iona Community is outside the jurisdiction of the Church." [1]

John White has left a personal note on what transpired at the General Assembly on 1949 after the defeat of Dr. MacLeod:

"It was declared by the Assembly that the Iona Community was outside the jurisdiction of the Church. As this finding—there could be

[1] Twelve months previously, Professor Riddell had written to Dr. White expressing his concern about a sudden and quite unexpected change in the attitude of the Iona representatives on the question of the Church's jurisdiction over the Community. They were pressing for it to be taken officially under the control of the Church. Professor Riddell had said he was not able to understand the reason for it, and he had refused to be hustled into advocating a course which, to his surprise, was being urged upon him with great persistence by the Iona representatives.

no other finding, it seemed to me—would be interpreted by many people as unsympathetic to the Iona Community experiment, and would do hurt to the Church, I resolved on a bold move. I had a Special Committee appointed by the Assembly on Tuesday, 31st May, to bring in a detailed scheme whereby the Community could be brought within the organisation and jurisdiction of the Church, and integrated with the life of the Church. It was carried almost unanimously; only six voted against."

IX

Inevitably, John White was pressed to accept the convenership of this committee, and with considerable reluctance he agreed. It seemed that at last the matter would be settled, and that a long, weary and unpleasant argument would be ended. But one week had hardly passed before his hope was broken.

Dr. George MacLeod drew up a new memorandum in which he discussed the feasibility of his return to Govan as parish minister. He argued that the scheme of duties which he had drawn up *was tantamount to his leaving his "employment" with the Iona Community.* He wondered if some accommodation could be worked out. He felt that the main opposition to his going to Govan as minister was coming from a certain number of members in the Glasgow Presbytery who did not want to see the Iona Community have a footing in Govan. If he did resign the leadership, he thought that the widest publicity should be given to the fact that he would remain an "active consultant to the Community". He said he would make no claim beyond that.

The Glasgow Presbytery agreed that a courtesy visit should be paid to the kirk session at Govan with the object of restoring harmony. Professor J. G. Riddell, the Moderator, said that there could be no doubt that the *jus devolutum* (by which a presbytery is empowered to intrude a minister on a congregation that has been vacant for more than six months) had come into operation, and since Govan had been without a minister for fifteen months, it was the duty of the Presbytery to find a minister as soon as possible to fill the pulpit. John White deplored the way in which some newspapers had handled the case; and unfortunately in some quarters, it was believed that Dr. MacLeod had been cast out of the Church—as if he were not eligible for a parish in Scotland.

"In this Presbytery," said John White, "I have made it clear, without any doubt whatever, that the decision whether Dr. MacLeod will go to Govan rests entirely with himself. I had hoped that the gracious act of the General Assembly (in bringing Iona under the wing of the Church) would succeed in allaying controversy. The religious life of Scotland must not be hindered by quite unjustifiable controversies among those who are all seeking the same end. Unfortunately, since the appointment of this *Ad Hoc* committee, I find some still saying that the Church is trying to hinder Dr. MacLeod's influence—and is doing so because Dr. MacLeod had been so forthright in his social witness in industrial parishes. That of course is sheer nonsense, and is not free from pride and prejudice. The Church has been strong in its social witness before the Iona Community was founded, and has never to my knowledge tried to hinder Dr. MacLeod from adding his witness to the social message of the Church."

And then, greatly to his dismay, John White learned that things had taken a new turn. Although Dr. MacLeod was prepared to give up the title of leader, he now stated his intention to be a good deal more than merely an "active consultant". He would take a continued interest in the Community; that had been agreed; but now when asked to interpret this, he said that he intended to retain a number of the more important duties he had performed as leader—in his own words, he would "maintain some contact with the Divinity Halls, speak in furtherance of the work of the Community, and attend the more important phases of the summer training on the island, as well as continue in advisory oversight of the Abbey building". These duties he laid down as his personal "interpretation of 'taking a continued interest in the Community' ". He amalgamated the points in a Declaration which he drafted, sent to the different Sponsors of the Iona Community, and invited them to sign it so that he could issue it to the press, if the Presbytery should appoint him to Govan, and it would thus be made widely known that, although he would no longer be called the leader, he would retain these particular duties. Understanding that such terms had been agreed upon, most of the Sponsors signed the Declaration. But John White himself, as chief Sponsor, refused to sign it: for he knew that the Presbytery's Special Committee would never agree to recommend Dr. MacLeod to Govan if confronted with a proposal that they could elect him only on the understanding that he be allowed to carry out certain stipulated duties for the Community. Dr. MacLeod insisted that these "essentials" should be officially understood by the Special Committee before any further step be taken, and he said he could not see how any committee or presbytery could deny to him what was "granted without question to other members of the Presbytery who are members of the Iona Community".

"We are back to the Memorandum," was John White's comment. "He has withdrawn that document only to bring forward the main heads of it." And he wrote to Dr. MacLeod:

"My dear George, I was sorry to get your letter dated 7th August—sorry, for it seemed to me that it opened up the whole question again and ran counter to Requirement Three in my letter, namely, that 'no condition be laid down regarding the acceptance of a call to a vacant parish'. . . . I am concerned and deeply anxious about the unwisdom of the last two paragraphs of your letter. May I say that, to my mind, they are not only unwise and controversial but are quite unnecessary. If you stand by them as 'essential' they will most probably lead to the dropping of your name from the list of persons duly qualified.

"I am sorry you should write as if the Special Committee and the Presbytery were endeavouring to limit your activities in Govan in any way. This is not so. You must know that neither can take any action on the matter of an experimental centre in Govan until the General Assembly have given their decision on the Report of the new *Ad Hoc* Committee. You have in your hands the clear statement that the Presbytery would exercise the same jurisdiction, and *you would have the same liberty in regard to non-parochial activities* as applies in the case of other ministers, the ruling consideration being the spiritual welfare and efficient service of the parish. So far from placing a limit on your non-parochial activities, the Special Committee have put on record that your continued interest in the Iona Community might be indicated, should you so desire, by your use of the title Founder.

"May I return to the last paragraph of your letter and ask you to consider well and reconsider what you lay down as 'essentials'. I quote it in full lest you have not retained a copy:—'I feel it equally essential that your Committee should officially understand the use of my spare time, as it is foreshadowed in the communication that would go out in the name of the Sponsors, as being not inimical to my work in Govan. I would of course prefer—in view of the public interest—that this communication be made part of the official report of your Committee to the Presbytery. But if this proves difficult, then it must be communicated to the Presbytery by some individual Presbyter who must be in a position to say that the Committee were cognisant of its contents before recommending my name.'

"The Special Committee," continued John White, "will no doubt consider this 'essential' as well as the other 'essential' with which I have already dealt. If however I may state my own personal opinion, I think it is a most inexcusable attitude to take towards a Committee acting under a specific Remit from the Presbytery to dictate what that Committee must report to the Presbytery; and then to say that, if the Committee does not accept your suggestion, you will arrange for a member of the Presbytery to raise the question and inform the Presbytery that the Committee was cognisant of the contents of the Sponsors' letter before nominating you, and that therefore it may be presumed to have agreed to its terms.

"Personally I do not think that the Special Committee has anything to do with the Sponsors' letter; nor will anything written by them affect the terms of your election—should the Committee agree, in face of what you say, to put forward your name to the parish of Govan.

"Might I ask for an early reply to what I have said in this connection, as it seems to me that almost everything depends on your answer: may you be wisely guided in your decision.

"All kindest regards, Yours sincerely, John White."

Professor Riddell, convener of the Assembly's Committee anent Iona, was in close touch with John White during the negotiations, and wrote to him:

"No liberty of action such as Dr. MacLeod speaks of has ever been accorded by a presbytery to any member of the Iona Community who is in charge of a parish in Scotland. . . . It is essential to make clear, as you have done, that this business of personal 'interpretation' of conditions, to be stated in open presbytery, is quite preposterous. It is, I suspect, an attempt to get the committee on the wrong foot by apparently yielding everything and then taking it all back by an ambiguous 'interpretation'. As far as I can judge from talk with members of Presbytery, it may not be easy to get the nomination approved at all. Certainly if there is any hesitation in his accepting the full requirements of the committee, it will be regarded as an attempt to get round the judgement of the Assembly and will be accordingly opposed."

Dr. MacLeod refused to move from what he called his "essentials" of his own continued connection with Iona, and he maintained that he was not putting them forward as "conditions" but merely as a statement of what he intended to do if he went to Govan, and he would not go to Govan if they were not accepted. John White wrote to him on 14th September asking him again if he would withdraw the two paragraphs of his letter of 7th August so that he could place the reply before the Committee; he said he would like by return to have a "yes" or "no". Dr. MacLeod's reply took matters no further. The Presbytery of Glasgow met on 4th October.

In considering the appointment of a minister under the *jus devolutum*, it is the duty of the Presbytery to seek a minister fitted for the ministerial tasks involved. The Presbytery is under no obligation to invite suggestions from the congregation, but as a conciliatory act the Committee had told the kirk session of Govan Old that names could be put forward. The Committee met the kirk session and the situation was fully explained; the members expressed their gratitude for the courtesy and consideration shown to them at this visit. The reception given to the Committee was very different from what might perhaps have been expected after Dr. MacLeod's warning to John White that if any other minister were appointed it "might create high trouble in Govan". It is inevitable that the membership of a congregation changes greatly in eleven years—in an industrial area between thirty and forty per cent might be a fair estimate—but Dr. MacLeod had still many loyal friends in Govan Old, and these deeply regretted that the months had slipped past in argument so that, under Church law, the congregation had lost the power to choose its own minister. In response to the invitation of the Committee, the kirk session put forward several names; Dr. MacLeod's was the one most favoured by the majority. The Presbytery was under no obligation to select any minister from the list if it considered none to be suitable; but John White was anxious to see Dr. MacLeod settled in Govan and the dispute harmoniously ended. He consulted with his colleagues, and at the Presbytery meeting on 4th October he said that they would consider the name of Dr. George F. MacLeod before the others suggested by Govan. Unfortunately, he continued, Dr. MacLeod had laid down some "essential" conditions that the Committee must accept before it nominated him and the Presbytery of Glasgow must accept before it elected him. "I am more than sorry that, after our patient efforts to make the rough places smooth, Dr. MacLeod has proceeded to make the smooth places rough. The

Committee can do no more. We have done everything we could do constitutionally. The decision rests with Dr. MacLeod."

John White made one statement in his speech for which he said he must personally bear responsibility:

"I am confident that if Dr. MacLeod, in accepting nomination to Govan Old as any other minister would be asked to accept it, should require an occasional short leave for work in Iona, or in connection therewith, the Presbytery would grant it with a benediction. But that is a very different thing from laying down conditions that he would retain some contact with the Divinity Halls, speak in further-ance of the work of the Community, attend the more important phases of the summer training on the Island, and continue in advisory over-sight of the Abbey building. The Presbytery has no wish to limit Dr. MacLeod's activities. But it cannot give him a roving commission along with his induction to a large and responsible parish."

Among the final words of the report of the Special Committee presented at the Presbytery meeting were these:

"The Presbytery will have fulfilled its responsibility if, as is now suggested, it leaves the issue in Dr. MacLeod's hands to accept, should he so decide, not in terms of his personal interpretation of any essential conditions, but in the spirit of the tradition of mutual trust and loyalty between Presbytery and Minister which is our heritage in the Church of Scotland."

In a statement he made a week later to the Presbytery clerk, Dr. MacLeod protested that all ministers of the Church were at liberty to establish an experimental centre of the Iona Community. To ask him to refrain meantime was to differentiate him from all other ministers. If this condition were imposed upon him while the *Ad Hoc* Committee deliber-ated, it would mean that *all* Iona experiments were suspended till the next General Assembly. What applied to Govan must be applied everywhere. He submitted that no decision of the previous General Assembly implied any "blame" to anyone who made an Iona experiment in any parish pend-ing the report of the *Ad Hoc* Committee.[1] He maintained that there was an invasion of the liberties of his private time, which had never been asked

---

[1] On 16th August, less than two months before, Dr. MacLeod had written to the Interim Moderator of the Govan vacancy: "I agree that the proposal to establish an experimenting centre of the Iona Community in Govan be held over pending the decision of the Genera Assembly on the Report of the new *Ad Hoc* committee."

of any other ministers in relation to their private interests, his own interest being in a purely private society. (He had already made this point in a letter to John White where he spoke of his continued connection with the Iona Community as "my private affairs in relation to a body outside the Church of Scotland".)

Dr. MacLeod wrote to John White saying that he "was entitled to put himself right with the public" since many Scottish newspapers said he had refused to accept Govan except on conditions. Was the necessity of informing the Presbytery of one's intentions, he asked, creating a condition? If so, it raised a grave spiritual issue. He closed thus: "With those kind regards which we mutually agree should continue whatever happens to this case!—I remain, Yours always sincerely, George F. MacLeod."

X

By the time the Presbytery of Glasgow met on 2nd November, the situation had in no way been ameliorated. John White was ill and unable to attend. The vice-convener of the Special Committee, Professor Pitt Watson, described what had happened since the last meeting. Correspondence was read showing that Dr. MacLeod had been offered the Govan charge "on the clear understanding that his acceptance of the nomination be unconditional" and that he "submit himself without reservation to the jurisdiction of the Presbytery" as any minister would be expected to do. By all members of the Committee except one, Dr. MacLeod's reply had not been considered to be unconditional acceptance. Professor Pitt Watson touched on the material points in Dr. MacLeod's protest that he had been unfairly treated. Dr. MacLeod had said he felt it incumbent upon him to do what he could to prevent the Presbytery of Glasgow from going down in ecclesiastical history as the only presbytery in modern times to have attached a condition to a nomination, and he gave notice of an appeal to a higher court against the findings of the Committee—whether or not it should hold up any further nomination of a minister to Govan Old parish church.

Professor Pitt Watson described this lodging of an appeal as "a very grave responsibility". He said that the appeal did not by law stop the Presbytery from placing another minister in Govan; but as Dr. MacLeod knew, it would in fact stop the Presbytery from so doing, for obviously there was little hope of making a successful approach to any other minister while this appeal to the Assembly was pending. Professor Pitt Watson spoke of the "confused and bewildered public" who were puzzled by the dispute: therefore, he said, let it be understood that the Presbytery had never sought to keep Dr. MacLeod from Govan. On the contrary: even although the last Assembly had decided against his eligibility, and the Presbytery had been free to seek another minister for the pulpit, they in fact had used every effort "to devise means whereby he could combine with the ministry of Govan his continued interest in the work of the Iona Community". The Presbytery did not impose conditions, but they required conditions to be withdrawn. In the proper exercise of their powers, and in conformity with the law and practice of the Church, they must insist that his acceptance of nomination be unconditional —and not by Dr. MacLeod's judgment, but by the judgment of the Presbytery.

He added that Dr. MacLeod had cited, as a parallel case, that of a minister who had been permitted to accept a prison chaplaincy in addition to his normal work in a parish. That was certainly not a parallel case, explained Professor Pitt Watson; it would have been so if the minister in question had intimated his acceptance of a call only on condition that he be allowed to undertake the chaplaincy.

John White's colleague at The Barony, the Rev. W. Roy Sanderson, moved as an alternative that, in essentials, Dr. MacLeod's letter was an unqualified acceptance, and that the Presbytery should proceed with his nomination. He said that they "had now come to a very small area of differences of opinion between Dr. MacLeod and the Church. The question is whether this area is big enough to justify us saying 'No'—not to Dr. MacLeod, but to Govan." On a vote being taken, the Presbytery of Glasgow decided, by two hundred and fifty-two votes to forty-five, that the letter was not an unconditional acceptance. The debate on the Govan Case had lasted three hours.

After the Presbytery meeting, Dr. MacLeod gave an interview to the press. He said he profoundly regretted that he was forced to dissent from a finding of Glasgow Presbytery, of which he had been a member for twenty years, but a condition had been attached to his nomination such as had been attached to no other nomination in the Church. For him to have acquiesced would have been to allow the possibility of that condition being added to the nomination of all ministers from that time onwards. It was easy for the Presbytery to say that it was only until the *Ad Hoc* Committee reported to the Assembly that he must defer an Iona Community experiment in Govan, but there was no certainty that the con-

dition might *then* be relaxed by the Assembly, and he might find himself
in a situation under which his Iona experiment in Govan would be suspended throughout his whole ministry there. Of all the ministers in the
Church of Scotland, he said, he thought it a strange condition to attach to
him alone.

When the statements which Dr. MacLeod had made were published
in Scottish newspapers, John White and Professor Pitt Watson felt obliged
to send a joint letter of protest to the press:

> "Dr. MacLeod's comment is open to censure," they said, "equally
> for its irresponsibility and its impropriety. The issues on which he saw
> fit to comment are *sub judice* in consequence of Dr. MacLeod's dissent
> and complaint against the Presbytery's finding in the matter of his
> nomination by the Presbytery to the vacant charge at Govan Old. As
> an appeal had been lodged by Dr. MacLeod before the Presbytery
> met, they were *sub judice* from the time the appeal was lodged. . . . In
> view of Dr. MacLeod's comment, we feel it our duty to point out that
> such *ex parte* statements, which can only be designed to influence
> public opinion, and to which the plain answer that might be given is
> not permissible until the matter comes before the superior court, may
> require to be brought to the notice of that court."

This letter appeared on 2nd November. On the day following, a letter
from Dr. MacLeod was published in the press to say that he was legally
advised that his comments to newspaper reporters had not been improper.
As to their being irresponsible, that was a matter of private opinion. "I
regret that Dr. White and Professor Pitt Watson," he wrote, "have concluded that my commonsense is so lacking as for me to do anything likely
to prejudice the hearing of my own case at a higher court." He went on to
say, however, that he was withdrawing his dissent and complaint because,
he had been informed, his case would not be argued at the Commission
of Assembly which was to meet in a fortnight's time, but would have to
wait until the following April when the Synod of Clydesdale would meet.
This would unduly delay the question of the vacancy in Govan. But
although he was withdrawing his appeal, Dr. MacLeod said: "I have in
no way departed from my strong dissent that a condition should have
been attached to my nomination which has been attached to no other
nomination in the Church of Scotland."

By this announcement in the press, the public learned that Dr.
MacLeod had finally given up all thought of returning to the Govan pulpit

in the near future and making his Iona experiment in the parish. To some people it seemed that this minister, who by his personality and distinguished service had created for himself a unique position in the Church of Scotland, had in the end failed to break down the unimaginative forces of law to win freedom to carry out the project on which he had set his heart and which had as its objective the furtherance of God's Kingdom. To others, it seemed that a long and tedious conflict had achieved nothing and had done irremediable harm, and that servants of the Church, who should all along have been conferring together in most harmonious goodwill, had wasted much time and energy in a dispute which gave some newspapers the kind of fodder for which their readers apparently hungered and which gave to non-churchgoing citizens a chance to disparage the Kirk.

Throughout the conflict, the greatest sufferer had been the parish church of Govan Old. For two years it was without a minister, and something of the bitterness that was felt in Govan can be seen in an extract from the minutes of the session which was sent to John White. The elders blamed "the unfortunate persistence in legal quibble on both sides", and to this John White felt obliged to reply:

> "I am at one with the Kirk Session in expressing relief that the termination of this protracted vacancy is now in sight. A careful examination of all the documents, from the time that the Vacancy Committee was appointed to the present, make it very clear that the Vacancy Committee and the Kirk Session are not altogether free from a large share of the blame associated with the vacancy."

That there had all along been differences of opinion in the congregation is evident. Meagre as was the number of signatories to the call to a new minister in February 1950, slightly more members signed it than had signed the call to Dr. MacLeod in December 1948.

The Rev. John Symington of Melrose had been chosen, and it was John White who had brought forward his name as a man with the qualities required to handle a difficult situation. Mr. Symington knew Govan well, for he had been an assistant under Dr. MacLeod nearly twenty years before. To his great satisfaction, John White was able to write on 28th August 1950 concerning the Govan dispute:

> "It ended to the great wonderment of Dr. MacLeod and the Kirk Session, and of many in the congregation, by the Presbytery

nominating and inducting the Rev. John Symington, minister of Melrose.

"I was very proud of my Presbytery committee, and not less pleased with the Presbytery, which stood firm and loyal behind the policy my committee outlined.

"We were impartial and sympathetic. But we could not change the constitution of the Church to suit the Govan-Iona ultimatum. We tried every road before we finally set aside the nomination of Dr. MacLeod.

"I have just received a message from Professor Riddell, who was taking services in Govan yesterday [Sunday, 27th August]. He was requested by the members of the Govan Kirk Session to convey their deep appreciation to me for what I had 'achieved for Govan in the recent controversy and for the splendid appointment made in nominating John Symington'."

XI

John White's further achievement was that of bringing into the Church the Iona Community, whose status had been so variously defined at different times by Dr. MacLeod. On the basis of the Report of John White's *Ad Hoc* Committee, the Assembly of 1951 appointed "as a governing body for the Iona Community, directly responsible to the General Assembly, an Iona Community Board which shall have within the Church a status similar to that of an autonomous Committee within the Home Department". Immediately after the Assembly debate, there was a meeting of the Iona Community, the Trustees and the Sponsors. John White was not present, and Dr. MacLeod wrote to him: "I was specifically asked to convey to you our appreciation of your Sponsorship, your chairmanship of the committee and your active interest through the years." Already in John White's hands there was a letter from Dr. MacLeod warmly inviting him to visit Iona during the summer months and to be the guest of his wife and himself. On 11th June of that year, John White wrote to Dr. MacLeod: "My dear George, There are many things I should like to write about, but one or two are essential, and the first is to thank you and the Community for the very kind recognition of anything I was able to do as a Sponsor and as chairman of the *Ad Hoc* Committee. . . ." Of all the many meetings, of Presbytery or Committee, or otherwise, which John White had attended since the beginning of the dispute, the one that gave him greatest satisfaction was that which was held in the hall of his own kirk of The Barony. It was a meeting of the Friends of the Iona Community. In warmly welcoming them, he said:

"I trust and pray that the Movement, initiated by one who bears an honoured name in the ministry of The Barony, will grow in strength and helpfulness and in coming years prove an invaluable asset in new avenues of witness and service. . . . Dr. MacLeod has asked me to say a word on the Home Mission side of the work.

"The Barony has always taken a special interest in Home Mission work. Norman MacLeod, the minister of The Barony, was the great leader of his time in the endeavour to vitalise religion and bring its spiritual power to touch every home in Scotland. He was indefatigable in his efforts to solve the problem of winning back those who had fallen away from ordinances. The Iona Community, founded by his grandson, has the same aim and works by new methods to achieve the same goal. Norman did not escape some strong opposition and criticism, and George F. has likewise been the object of some little fuss and fury.

"Then there was Donald MacLeod of 'The Park'—one of the able men of his time, one of the kindliest, one for whom I always cherished an affectionate and high regard. He was deeply interested in Home Mission work, was convener of the Home Mission committee, and introduced the Parish Sister to help to win back to the Church those myriads of our fellow countrymen who had lost touch.

"It was not possible, therefore, that George F. MacLeod—the grandson of The Barony and the grand-nephew of The Park—could escape the ancestral urge. A few years in Govan Parish brought him to a great decision. He had a vision of the needs of men and women in massed communities. He had a plan for bringing the Gospel of Our Lord to meet those needs. It was thus that there was born in his heart the idea of the *community*.

"I am proud of having been his first Sponsor. All through the storm and stress I have remained so. In many long drawn-out negotiations over Govan and the Iona Community, I trust I have been able to help in guiding things to the successful stage they have now reached.

"The Iona Community can give great help to the Home Mission work of the Church. It can do much to help in team work. It can do much by constantly stressing work on the parochial system. It can help by experimenting in ways not open to the regular ministry. It can help us out of ruts. I have always held that rutualism is more dangerous in the Church than the bogey of ritualism. . . .

"I look forward to the future of the Community. God prosper its work! May the Iona Community, now *within the Church*, be so guided and encouraged by God that it will prove a saving force in our land."

The Govan dispute had been the most bitter of all the disputes into which John White had been drawn. He had passed his eighty-first year when, with great reluctance, he became one of the central figures in a broil for which he had in no way been responsible. Old friendships meant much to him. For George MacLeod he had a deep personal affection; he knew him perhaps as well as any man did; he could appreciate with the best of good humour the many unusual facets of that unique personality; he loved the Celtic fire of the man, but he knew how often there were sparks of impulse and even irresponsibility that sprang from that fire; he respected him as a man of fine personal courage, who had been proved in the stress of battle, and who had not shrunk from facing a Presbytery and a General Assembly that voted heavily against him. John White had felt it to be his bounden duty to uphold the laws and discipline of the Church he served, and the fact that the man whose arguments he had been compelled to oppose was one for whose audacious evangel he had always had a deep sympathy had galled his very spirit. The two men had mutually agreed that nothing should endanger their friendship: and to the end, nothing did.

Chapter XXII

IN ALL THINGS DILIGENT

I

IN 1944 John White was already making plans for the post-war period. He roused the interest of the Presbytery of Glasgow in some of the problems that would have to be tackled when peace came.

"In many ways it will be a new world," he said, "and the salvage-heap is the place for any sermon that does not take into account the deep needs of a generation that has passed through five years of fierce and inhuman strife."

What action must the Church of Scotland take on the return of men and women from the Services?

"It might seem a little premature to talk about this before the War has been won, but we must think about it—we must guide ministers, office-bearers, congregations in welcoming them back to their homes. . . . We all know what happened at the close of the last war. Many of our young folks were shamefully neglected—they were left outside the industrial and economic life of the nation for which they had given their best years. We in the Church must see to it that this does not happen again. . . .

"Every parish must be organised, every home visited. Help must be given in every case of hardship or difficulty. Demobilised men and women will expect the Church to have a passionate concern for them. They will expect the same reality and efficiency they experienced in the Forces—and they will look for that fellowship in the Church which they had in the army, where comradeship is a religion. . . .

"It is in the Services," he continued, "that many young people have come into contact for the first time with religious teaching. They must be welcomed to our churches; they must be made to feel at home. The task will be a parochial one, and will call for a great pastoral effort."

He drew the attention of the Assembly in May to the problem:

"Has the Church a definite, relevant message," he demanded, "for those who will come back with victory from the jaws of death? . . . There have been serious stirrings in the minds of young men and women in these tragic years. There has been unsettlement, deep questionings. Have we in the Church something that will attract and hold them—something that will meet their needs?"

As convener of the Church and National Service Committee, he did all in his power to awaken every parish to its duty to those returning from war service. Every chaplain was asked to put men in touch with the ministers of their own parishes. The Second World War had hardly ended when John White was presiding at a large conference on the re-settlement of demobilised men and women. Representatives came from all the presbyteries, and there were officials from the Ministry of Labour and National Service. Even the consequences of casual and hasty marriages were discussed. John White said that the State departments had obviously done some wise thinking about the many problems that confronted those whose task was the reconstruction of the nation, but he criticised them for their failure to consult with the Churches before drafting schemes that dealt with human and therefore spiritual issues. There must now be the closest and most harmonious co-operation, he said, between the State departments and those who ministered to the nation in the social and spiritual interests of citizenship.

With enthusiasm he supported a scheme to win young people into the fellowship of the Church. With the co-operation of the Iona Youth Trust, the MacLeod Memorial Church in Glasgow was reconstructed to carry through a local experiment. At a meeting there of ministers and elders, John White spoke once again of the need of personal contact with every home through a parochial visitation. "Here in this enterprise of Mr. Sanderson's," he said, "is an indication that the Church is wide awake to the social and religious needs of the community, and is thinking and planning ahead."

Among the young folk coming home, he foresaw that a great menace would lie in the appeal of Communism, with its doctrine of an equal share of everything for everybody. In spite of the falsity of that doctrine and the almost fantastic inequity in the sharing out in the land where that doctrine had first taken a strong root, the very thought of a greater share for the underprivileged had the meretricious attraction of a mirage in a desert to a thirsty man. Professor Edgar P. Dickie, convener of the Church's Youth Committee, found in John White a strong bulwark for the Christian Action front against the challenge of Communism; and on behalf of the executive, he asked him to give his backing to their report in the General Assembly of 1949. "It looks as if a very great deal may hang on this issue for the future of Scotland," wrote Professor Dickie; and John White asked the General Assembly to set up a Commission to deal with the menace of Communism in the land. In that Assembly, he warned the Church and nation of what they would soon be facing.

"The problem calls for a special thinking department," he said. "The Church must be kept fully informed of the ways in which this new and self-confessedly atheistic movement can be met. We must have constructive and positive Christian action. As an economic interpretation of history and society, Communism leaves no room for religious ideas—no room for ideals or principles. It is a movement that is admittedly pagan. But note that it has an idealism of its own—which, its partisans say, will introduce the Millennium on earth. . . .

"We need a vital Christian evangelism that will carry our Christian principles into the factory, the market-place, the legislative chamber. This may lead in directions that will disturb our customary ways. But we must be ready for that. The problem of Communism is one that faces all the Churches of Christ. If there was a strong argument for Christian unity, it is in the menacing challenge of Communism that stands before every Christian fellowship in the world. If we are to defeat this menace that would destroy the freedom of the bodies and souls of men," he said, quoting some recent words of Lord Halifax, "the fire of our Faith and purpose must burn with as white a flame as theirs."

A crowded Assembly approved with a deep sense of urgency the setting up of a Commission of twenty-five, to examine the influence of "secular movements and philosophies and especially of materialistic Communism".

II

In his latter days, John White's thoughts were often with the future of the Church. He foresaw a shortage of ministers in the years immediately ahead, and this troubled him. The report of a committee appointed to look into the matter had shown a heavy decline in the number of ministers and probationers available for vacancies at home and overseas. He had hoped that the return of chaplains would help, but now it was clear that many of them would be required in the Far East and occupied territories. The suggestion was that congregations might be temporarily linked together until the supply of ministers increased, and presbyteries were recommended to appoint Lay Readers to help in suitable cases. John White put the question to the ministers and elders of the Church of Scotland: "How many young men of ability, with a promise of gifts of leadership and with a sense of vocation, have been guided to the service of the Church in the ministry?" The lack of ministerial manpower continued to distress him until the end of his days. He kept asking himself what future the Church could have unless young men came forward to fill the gaps. He believed that immense power lay in the hands of those who were already studying for the ministry. He accepted an invitation to have lunch with the students of Trinity College, Glasgow, and he addressed those who were studying in the University where he had studied more than sixty years before. He quoted the words of Marcus Dods, who, to a previous generation, had said he did not envy those who had to deal with the new situation that was looming up; but, added John White quickly—"Perhaps I *do* envy you! Perhaps, if I could, I would put back the hands of the clock and get alongside you now to face the future." He roused the enthusiasm of the students by his virile words.

"The Church is the biggest and most important reality in God's world. You are not called at any time to apologise for it. You are not called upon to justify it. Clever blue-prints are being issued to solve the world's situation, but they are like patent medicines. The Church, as the Body of Christ, is the one and only solution. In its message is the remedy for the ills of the day and the hope of the future. Against the Church, the very gates of hell cannot prevail. This is All Saints' Day. The heart is brave again and the arms are strong as we listen to the triumphant psalm of the multitudes by whom we are compassed about. . . .

"May I give you two thoughts that have often steadied me when I have been overwhelmed with the confusions and alarms of the world. First, God has put too much of Himself into this world to forsake it now. Second, it is not in the world that we have faith but in Him Who overcame the world."

He took the chance to emphasise that they were in the midst of an event without precedence.

"The mass atheism that is an integral part of Communism will never be stemmed by your preaching to a few folk in a church," he declared. "You must grapple with it, by personal touch, with the

many in their homes. You must get alongside them in their occupations. Mere denials are not enough. There must be something positive
in the appeal and the challenge. In season and out of season you must
fight this Godless movement that denies to man a soul and a striving
towards his Maker."

John White looked back on that luncheon with the students of
Trinity College as one of the most successful and satisfying meetings with
young men he had ever attended. He had lost none of his old joy in
responding to a challenge. With all the uncertainties that the future
presented, he was thrilled by the thought that the world was entering
upon a new age.

"After the First World War, when we looked forward to so much,
the coming of the Kingdom seemed to be stayed, and the love of some
grew cold. A new world will never be created by the destructive
efforts of fanatical dictators. The new age, when it comes, will be a
product of the forces of Christ working through His Church. . . .

"Is it coming now? Is the spirit of God brooding over the chaos
of the world today? Is He mothering a new order into being?

"Is it not possible that the tragic happenings of two world wars
are but the outward circumstance of one of the great creative moments
of history? If this be so, then it is surely a great privilege we enjoy.
We shall have been permitted to live in two ages. We shall have seen
the culmination of the one and the birth of the mysterious movements
of the other. . . . Mankind is being given another chance today. Let us
see to it that we do not slip back into a life of the jungle."

III

Throughout his whole life, John White was consistent in his preaching
and teaching of the value of the parish as an ecclesiastical unit. He had long
deplored the action of successive Governments for having so largely
destroyed the parish as the unit of civil administration. He had watched
the process of centralising, of taking the reins away from the hands of
those who knew local conditions; he had seen that process gain momentum
and the status of local authorities decline until Government departments
were in control. Once upon a day, the parish had the power to super-
intend education, but in 1872 the duty of providing a school in every
parish was taken from the kirk session and the heritors and handed over

to a School Board. In 1918, schools were grouped into large administrative areas, and eleven years later the Local Government Act killed off these local education authorities and set up statutory committees in county councils and the large burghs. The relief of the poor had once been the task of the Church, and she had encouraged thrift and Scottish independence, but the parochial board was given the place of the kirk session, and this in its turn was displaced in 1894 by the parish council, and later the Local Government Board took over most of the work. In the end, there was a plan euphemistically named National Assistance for the relief of the poor. It was the same in other spheres. The day came when the General Assembly of the Church of Scotland took serious thought on "the possible invasion of human rights and local independence by large-scale collectivism". The Assembly took note of the "continued disregard of Scottish sentiment, and the claims of Scotland as a nation in many matters which vitally affect the prosperity of the Scottish people", and declared their conviction that a lot of the centralisation must be undone if democratic development was not to be frustrated. One day John White was protesting to Sir John Gilmour, then Secretary of State for Scotland, that Whitehall had taken away the powers of parish councils. "I used to serve on the parish council at Shettleston," he said, "and while I was a member, our powers were taken away. Only sanitation was left us to attend to. Sanitation! . . . I resigned. I didn't mind being a Parish Councillor, but I refused to be a privy councillor. . . ."

After the union of the two Presbyterian Churches in 1929, there had been many changes in the ecclesiastical parish boundaries. By the time a decade had passed, many people feared that the parochial system—on which the Church's territorial ministry was based—had not been working as well as had been hoped. During the war, the Commission on the Interpretation of God's Will in the Present Crisis came to the conclusion that there must be a fresh emphasis on the importance of the parish as a unit in the Church. To study this, a committee was set up with John White as convener. He decided that the first step was to consult with presbyteries and enlist their interest. He divided parishes into four classes: Rural, Burghal-Landward, Towns (industrial and residential), and Cities. He sought information on whether the changes in parish boundaries had been of any value in increasing parochial visitation; he wished to know whether it had fostered a community sense; he particularly wished to know whether the Church's territorial system was proving to be effective, and he asked for suggestions that might make it better.

The response pleased him greatly. Out of sixty-six presbyteries, forty-four sent in full reports. The work of codification was onerous, and recommendations were set forth in detail. What John White had feared he now found to be true. In many towns, too often there was competition instead of co-operation between congregations; too often Church members recked little of their own territorial boundaries. Had the alteration of parish boundaries fostered a community sense within the area? Almost unanimously the answer was No. In large cities the parochial system worked badly. Of its working in rural parishes, there was little criticism. As he surveyed the reports of forty-four presbyteries, he was satisfied that some changes were necessary. The territorial system itself had not failed. He was convinced that parochial pride should be strengthened—that there should be a "more active ministering membership". It was his old cry. Kirk sessions and members must be brought—drastically if need be—to a fuller sense of their responsibility. "It is a big question," he said; "it is a fascinating question, but it is a most elusive question. The very constitution of the Church might well be affected before the necessary changes had been completed." More trained workers were needed:

> "but I would not advocate," he said, "an increased number of these to remain permanently in a parish, and I should like to see several mobile teams working under the Home Mission Committee to carry through an intensive visitation in chosen parishes. I once called these Flying Squads. Paratroopers, or Commandos, would be just as good a name, for the work would be militant and aggressive."

A number of presbyteries had recommended the grouping of parishes in large towns, and this would mean team work among the ministers. He said he would like to see Church Councils formed in boroughs where the population was under fifty thousand, so that there could be a unity of spirit and intention among the different congregations. Stricter supervision by presbyteries: that was a necessity. As he studied the reports, and began to draft suggestions and recommendations, he often found himself looking back to the year 1929 and the union of the Churches. When he asked himself whether his high hopes had been realised, he was compelled to admit that they had not. Before the union there had been much wastage of manpower and resources.

> "Have we been using our great united forces for the winning of Scotland? The Church is not infiltrating through the Community as

it *can* and as it *ought*. . . . We are all to blame. Too many of our good respectable Church folks still think of their own church as if it were a private religious club. They miss the main function of Church life and worship—to go out to their brothers and sisters and compel them to come in. As for the ministers, today they preach well and effectively, but a cordial wave of the hand from a motor-car travelling at thirty miles an hour is not in any sense an effective pastoral visit."

What gladdened his heart more than anything else in the parochial system was that, in spite of all difficulties, it was working better in those churches he had helped to plant in the new housing areas than in any other, either urban or rural.

IV

One of the causes into which John White threw himself with zeal was doomed from its inception because a recalcitrant Government department had already judged the issue: and the Church of Scotland was by no means the only body in Great Britain that suffered from that Whitehall decision.

When the Socialist Government decided to nationalise the railways, dismay began to spread among stockholders. Because of the "cheap money" conditions, it was realised that the compensation would be poor, and holders of railway stock would almost certainly suffer a loss of income. For a long time, this stock had been scheduled among the securities which trustees were permitted by law to hold, and considerable sums of money had been invested in it by the Church of Scotland Trust. Without delay, a sub-committee was formed to present a case to the Attlee Government. Contact was made with the Church of England, and a member of the Ecclesiastical Commission said he was confident that both the Church of England and the Church in Wales would join the proposed deputation and that the Archbishop of Canterbury would be ready to introduce it. Other Churches were quickly brought in, so that in the end the deputation included not only the Free Churches but Roman Catholics, Jews, and Quakers. The question arose: who would be the ablest man to lead the Scottish section of the deputation?

Dr. Robert Mackintosh of the Home Board conferred with Mr. G. Mercer Robertson, Legal Adviser to the General Trustees. It did not take them many moments to agree that the best man to tackle a Government department with hope of success was John White. But they knew he had been far from well in that winter of 1946. When Dr. Mackintosh went to see him in the New Year and put the proposal before him, John White shook his head: "I'm an old man," he said, "I shall be eighty this year. Don't you think I've led enough deputations to Whitehall? Let a younger man take it on."

Although they had many good younger men, Dr. Mackintosh argued, none had had his experience of handling Whitehall officials. John White admitted this, but said he felt it was high time that one of these younger men was sent forth to battle. It was difficult to counter such a sound argument, but Dr. Mackintosh stressed that a very large sum of money might be involved. What if the Church of Scotland should lose thousands of pounds annually in the years to come because some younger man had not presented the case forcefully and adroitly? "It's going to be a very hard fight," he added.

Dr. Mackintosh has described how, on hearing this last remark, John White sat up and looked at him keenly. "It's going to be a fight, is it?" he said. "Tell me more about it, Mackintosh. . . ."

From that moment onwards, there was never another word from John White about his being an old man. The thought of a fight on behalf of the Church of Scotland was like a tonic to him: as the eagle's, his strength was renewed. A few weeks later, he was in London leading the Scottish members of the delegation.

Under the nationalisation plan, a British Transport Commission was to take over all the railways in Britain on the first day in January in the following year. Reviewing the market value of Government securities at that date, the Treasury would decide on the compensation, and British Transport Stock would be issued. The book value of the Church of Scotland's holding was little short of one million two hundred thousand pounds; in addition, the endowments of many congregations were in the same stock. The Church had been warned that British Transport Stock might yield only two and a half per cent. This was discussed at the preliminary meeting held at Church House, Westminster, with Dr. Geoffrey Fisher, Archbishop of Canterbury, in the chair.

It was one of the most unsatisfactory meetings John White had ever attended. The representatives of many of the Churches had come without the necessary information; the Roman Catholics regretted that they could not supply details; the Church of England delegates, among whom were some members of Parliament, appeared to be filled with dismay at what the Socialist Government might do if the Churches protested too strongly.

One of the notable exceptions was the Church in Wales, whose delegates had come with statistics fully prepared. Impatiently, John White got to his feet and announced what the income of the Church of Scotland had been from railway stock, and gave figures of the loss she would suffer if no more than the proposed compensation were given. In the afternoon, the delegation went to meet Hugh Dalton, Chancellor of the Exchequer, at the Treasury.

It was obvious that Dalton was not impressed. He listened politely to Dr. Fisher; it was as if he could not do otherwise to the head of the Anglican Church. There were interchanges, all of them polite and inconsequential. It seemed to some who had travelled from Scotland that they might as well have stayed at home. And then John White rose. The Chancellor of the Exchequer was no longer merely polite. It was as if a strong hand had come down firmly upon his shoulder. Members of the delegation who had feared that their plea would end in smooth talk began to feel a great relief as they listened to John White talking to the Chancellor of the Exchequer.

The Archbishop had stated the main issue, he began, but there was a good deal more to be said and he intended to say it:

"My colleagues and I from the Church of Scotland have come a long way for this meeting. We believe that some of the proposals in the Transport Bill will seriously handicap important Church work in Scotland. We are here for one reason only. We intend to safeguard the religious activities of our Church. We do not discuss the political aspect of the Transport Bill. The Church of Scotland does not concern itself with party politics. We are not a political institution. Members of all parties are within the ranks of our Church. But whatever may be the political colour of individuals, we all believe that the scheme of compensation proposed in this Bill will be hurtful and in some ways disastrous.

"It will mean a lowering of the stipends of ministers in many parishes. Their present lot is hard enough. They must meet the high cost of living and heavy taxation. Some teachers, many doctors, all members of Parliament are millionaires compared with many of them. A parish minister has to meet claims on a stipend that compares unfavourably with that of many unskilled workmen. And the compensation terms you are offering will make it harder still for them.

"In addition, you will inflict suffering on those who receive grants from our Aged and Infirm Ministers' Fund, the Widows' and Orphans' Fund, and other funds that provide a meagre and inadequate allowance."

Then John White brought forward the cause which had for so long lain closest to his heart.

"In Scotland, we have undertaken many new tasks to meet the new day. I refer to Church Extension. This is a distinctive call to bring the ordinances of religion to the people in every parish of Scotland. The great migration to the new housing areas faces us with the duty of providing churches, hall-churches, halls, manses. We have already spent three-quarters of a million pounds on this work. We are appealing at this moment for another million. Even that will be inadequate. We are face to face with the greatest architectural task that the Church of Scotland has had to face in my lifetime. It is the largest change of its kind that has ever taken place in Scotland. It will be a calamitous thing if the Church is to be impoverished, as it will be by the compensation clauses of your Bill. Your proposals mean that we shall lose twenty-five per cent of our previous income from our railway stock, as well as many thousands of pounds invested by congregations throughout Scotland. These monies have been given in small sums by our faithful people all over the land, and you are taking away threepence in every shilling.

"Why did we invest it in railway stock? We had no option but to invest within the boundaries set us by legislative Orders and Trustee Acts. These investments were made in full confidence that we should have government protection, and I look to the government for a remedy to the serious situation that has arisen.

"A few days ago, the Minister of Transport described the Transport Bill as the biggest Socialist measure ever introduced before a democratic parliament, and he said, 'There is a body of opinion which says that *no compensation should be paid at all.*' I am glad the Minister added that he has never advocated confiscation. Indeed, he has said that the Labour party always stood for fair compensation—and I take that to mean twenty shillings in the pound. Addressing railway stockholders some years ago, I would remind you that Mr. Attlee uttered these words: '*We should like to make your securities more secure. I am a great believer in equity.*' Mr. Chancellor, we are not asking for greater security. We are satisfied with the security we have had. A twenty-five per cent drop in income would be rather too great a price to pay for what we do not need. I look to you to devise—as I am sure you can—some amendment to the compensation clauses that will meet the reasonable claims of the Churches and Charities."

John White then laid before Hugh Dalton two possible schemes by which the Churches and the Charities would not suffer the grievous loss which Mr. Attlee's Government was proposing to inflict upon them. The Chancellor moved uneasily in his chair as the speaker went forcefully on:

"Somebody has said that the government could not be expected to distinguish between one class of railway stockholder and another. That is a fallacy. As I have said, the Churches and Charities are obliged to invest within the limits of the Trustee Acts and Standing Orders. Many other bodies can invest as they like. We are not a commercial company. We do not invest to make a profit. The government has already recognised the distinction between the ordinary investor and the Church. We are exempt from Land Value Tax and from Income Tax, as well as from local rates on our buildings—in the same way as charitable institutions are exempt. . . . These are days when everything that can be done must be done to render the Church more efficient. These are days when nothing should be done to frustrate, or even curtail, the efforts of the Church. That is our case. That is our Claim of Right."

As a result of what John White had said, a promise was given that the Churches would be informed in good time before the compensation clauses of the Bill came before the House of Commons. Here was something definite which the delegates could take back to the Churches which they represented. Afterwards, in speaking about John White in the General Assembly, the Archbishop of Canterbury referred to this meeting with the Chancellor:

"I know now what Daniel felt like in the lions' den. This is even worse, because it is a den of theological lions, and my general impression from a distance has always been that of lean, hungry, voracious and slightly carnivorous theologians. Indeed, the kind of exemplar of your body I took from my friend, Dr. John White. I once went with him on a Delegation to the Chancellor of the Exchequer on Railway Stocks. I never wanted to be a Chancellor of the Exchequer!"

In reporting to the Church of Scotland Trust on his return, John White said that he hoped they had gained something by going south to the Treasury and presenting their appeal to the Chancellor. But just before the Assembly held in the May of that year 1947, he received a letter from Dr. Dalton, who said he had come to a decision. He did not, he said, propose to treat the Churches as privileged investors, and so far as he was concerned, the matter was closed. But it was not closed in Scotland. Headlines in the Scottish papers revealed the depths of feeling that the decision had created. The loss could not be less than twenty thousand pounds a year, apart from many thousands of pounds lost by individual congregations. Mr. William R. Milne, W.S., later Sir William Milne and chairman of the General Trustees of the Church, had been a delegate, and he told the Assembly:

> "Dr. John White put the Church's case very forcibly to the Chancellor. We were given an assurance that we should have the Chancellor's decision *before* the compensation clauses of the Transport Bill came before the House of Commons. *That promise was not fulfilled.* We feel that a definite promise of that sort should have been kept."

John White, who spoke after him, was even more severe in his criticism:

> "I found the Chancellor far more cordial and sympathetic than I had expected. But I recalled afterwards that Rob Roy used to smile when he was stealing cattle or—should I say—transporting stock." Laughter followed this sally, but there was an angry ring in John White's voice as he went on: "A promise was given—I have the words —that we should have Dr. Hugh Dalton's decision in good time, so that we could move amendments if we were not satisfied. We did not get his decision in good time. The Bill was passed in haste. The guillotine was used. Not a single reference to Scotland!" John White pounded angrily with his fist on the table as he cried: "This letter of rejection which I have here from Dr. Dalton means that he will not recognise that Churches and Charities do not invest to make profits. Churches and Charities had no option but invest within the limitations set by Trustee Acts and legislative rules. Where is the protection if a quarter of your income is taken from you?"

Warned by this bitter experience, the General Assembly authorised the Church of Scotland Trust to apply to Parliament for power to invest

404

in ordinary stocks or shares so that the income of the Church might be maintained. This power was obtained in 1948.

V

"In the case of adultery after marriage, it is lawful for the innocent party to sue out a divorce, and, after the divorce, to marry another, as if the offending party were dead.

". . . nothing but adultery, or such wilful desertion as can no way be remedied by the church or civil magistrate, is cause sufficient of dissolving the bond of marriage."

These sentences from the Confession of Faith of 1647, the chief subordinate standard of the Church of Scotland, were the only guidance the Church had had on divorce and remarriage for nearly three centuries. When it was felt that the time had come for a fuller statement to be made, the Assembly formed a committee to consider it, and in 1937 a pronouncement was made which removed many doubts about the Church's position. John White, a member of the committee, took a leading part in the debate and was responsible for killing an amendment which, if approved, might have left it an open question whether the statement in the Confession of Faith was still accepted by the Church. The Assembly declared that marriage was not a sacrament but a holy ordinance; the Church regarded it as a Divine institution to which life-long fidelity was demanded. The Assembly recognised that, since the Reformation, the Church had held it to be in accordance with the mind of Christ that the civil authority should have the power of divorce, and that, since 1573, either infidelity or desertion had been sufficient grounds for this, for if either of these had taken place the marriage had virtually been destroyed. It had been accepted as lawful for the innocent party to marry again; but a divorced person could not marry the one with whom adultery was proved to have been committed if named in the decree of divorce. Ministers were explicitly forbidden to marry any person who had been divorced for adultery or the person with whom adultery had been committed, even though the innocent spouse of the former marriage had died.

John White summed up the position of the Church briefly thus: "Ministers are forbidden to marry the guilty party. But it is lawful for the innocent one to marry another, 'as if the offending party were dead'."

Alarmed after the war at the immense increase in the number of broken marriages, the Assembly had asked the Church and Nation Committee to consider the whole matter afresh. When its report was presented in 1948, the Assembly reconstituted a special committee; and one morning, in the absence of John White, it appointed him convener, greatly to his annoyance when he learned of it. Professor Pitt Watson, he felt, was the man to handle the question.

It was a committee of distinguished persons. On it were the two eminent jurists, Lord Russell and Sheriff J. F. Strachan, K.C. (later Lord Strachan), Professor J. Pitt Watson, Professor M. G. Fisher, J. G. Kyd (the Registrar General), the Rev. Dr. R. F. V. Scott of St. Columba's, Mrs. George Duncan (the wife of Principal Duncan of St. Andrews), Dr. Dugald Macfarlane (a former Moderator), James Adair of Glasgow,[1] and many others. The report which they presented to the next Assembly was a treatise, historical, philosophical, ethical, that might have been prepared for some scholarly encyclopedia. On the practical side, the committee recommended that there should be a "panel"—perhaps an unfortunate word—to give advice to ministers before they came to a decision about persons who presented themselves for remarriage. The important thing was that it should be a central panel, not a presbytery one: John White was emphatic about this. The minister must submit all the facts for the judgment of this central panel; if he carried out a marriage against its judgment, he would come under the discipline of the Church. Furthermore, if there came before a minister a couple of whom one or other had been divorced, and they had already gone through a civil ceremony and now desired the blessing of the Church, the central panel must be given the chance to judge the case. Presbyteries were asked to discuss and comment upon these proposals.

The comments were not favourable. John White saw that the presbyteries were up in arms because they were being given no say in the matter. The central panel was not under the authority of any presbytery, and no presbyterial representative had a seat on it. Illness prevented John White from attending the committee meetings at which the new scheme was drawn up. He would have proposed, he said, that four presbytery members be allotted a seat on the panel, together with five permanent assessors to be chosen by the Assembly. What the committee decided was that certain cases should be judged by a presbytery panel, and it was hoped that this would go through under the Barrier Act and become the law of

[1] Later to become a member of the Wolfenden Commission on Vice, and to be a vigorous dissentient from its findings.

the Church. But among the presbyteries there was a heavy vote against
it, and John White's prophecy of failure proved to have been correct.
He put his finger on the trouble when he said:

> "Some champion of presbytery rises now and again to warn
> members that the supreme court of the General Assembly is becoming
> too dominant—that it is tending to engulf part of the constitutional
> functions of presbytery. . . . This fear of encroachment was expressed
> in recent meetings of presbyteries on the remarriage of divorced
> persons. Several presbyteries disapproved of the proposals, not on the
> merits of the scheme itself, but on the grounds that the General
> Assembly suggested a plan, which, they believed, deprived presbyteries
> of their rights and duty. It was completely overlooked that *this was
> a case calling for uniformity of treatment throughout the whole country.*
> This uniformity could not be reached by sixty-six presbyteries, or
> two thousand ministers, all acting on their own."

At the Assembly of 1951, John White spoke his mind plainly and said
that something would have to be done to amend a law, by which the
Church had been bound since 1566, that debarred one class of divorced
persons alone from remarriage. "This is where we stand," he declared,
"and we can't stand here any longer." He described divorce as a "septic
condition of too many homes in the land". In amending the provisions of
the Church, they must be careful that they would not be "smoothing the
path of those who, for reasons of social respectability, wished to be married
under the rites of the Church but without any expression of penitence
or any pledge to live a Christian life within the fellowship of the Church".

Without permanent assessors, he foresaw the danger that a remarriage
might be rejected in one part of the country and permitted in another.
Let the presbyteries be represented, he agreed, but there must be stability
and uniformity. After the Assembly, he sat down to write letters to the
members of his committee calling them together to hammer out a plan
which the presbyteries would accept and which might become a full
expression of the mind of the Church of Scotland. His work was cut short
by his death in August and Professor Pitt Watson was appointed convener.

The solution was to be long delayed. Towards the end of March 1956,
the report of the Royal Commission on Marriage and Divorce was
published, and the General Assembly committee studied it with care.
Unfortunately, "unresolved differences within the committee itself"
prevented it from expressing a common mind on the matter. Theological

issues were involved, and agreement on them had to be found before proposals could be made for any change in the law or practice of the Church. Professor W. S. Tindal succeeded Professor Pitt Watson as convener, and in 1957 the committee recommended to the General Assembly that the Church should, as John White had urged, cease to debar one class of divorced persons from remarriage while permitting it to others. It recommended that "the criterion should not be so much guilt or innocence but rather . . . the presence of sincere repentance, together with the resolve to enter upon a union that shall be in the full sense Christian". Some members of the committee would have liked to see the Church adopt the Scottish Episcopal and Anglican attitude and "refuse to celebrate marriage contracted after divorce in the lifetime of a former spouse". But the majority found that there was "warrant in the Gospel of St. Matthew (xix, 12) and in the teaching of St. Paul (I Corinthians vii, 15), together with the New Testament emphasis on repentance and forgiveness, for some relaxation of the marriage bond in certain cases". Nobody who was familiar with John White's thought could doubt that he would have agreed that sincere repentance should be given due weight in deciding a case for the remarriage of a divorced person. And in the report there was, among others, one contention of which he would fervently have approved:

"It is not to be thought that, because of certain offences, a marriage must be broken. Matrimonial offences of the gravest kind may be forgiven. Through grace a threatened marriage may be saved, but it is through grace rather than by law."

There was, however, one element in the report with which he would strongly have disagreed. He did not think it right that any difficult case should be decided by the minister to whom application for remarriage was made: for to throw such a responsibility upon the individual conscience of any minister was to burden him with perplexities that should be the concern of a central council of the Church, and it was only by establishing such a council that there could be any certitude that, throughout the land, there would be consistency in the approach to all cases.

VI

To the Assembly of May 1947 John White presented the only minority report to which he had ever put his signature. It was a one-man report, and he "submitted it with all respect" as a member of the Committee on the Place of Women in the Counsels and Councils of the Church of Scotland.

This report was in fact John White's strong protest against the decision of all his fellow members. Not one had he found to support him. Professor Daniel Lamont of New College, Edinburgh, who was convener, told the Assembly that the Committee could find no half-way house between the position women had always held in the Church and that of accepting them as full elders on a parity with men.

To this, John White replied:

"Whatever the views of the Assembly on the admission of women to the courts of the Church, I am sure it will not think it right that a question of such immense and immediate importance should be dismissed by a Committee in one line and five words. . . . There is not a single word of appreciation of the immense value of the work done by women in all departments of the Church, or of sympathy with their just claims of some recognition in the councils of the Church. This report of a line and a half has simply pulled down an Iron Curtain."

The scheme he put forward was designed to give women some definite responsibility in the conduct of the Church's affairs. He proposed that a number of women be elected to serve three years and to meet the kirk session at least twice every year, and together the two bodies would form a Parish Church Council which would advise on the life and work of the congregation and parish. They must never outnumber the elders, and certain things they must not touch—matters of Discipline, Sacraments, and Ordination. This Parish Church Council would elect a certain number of representative women to serve as members of the presbytery, and they could take part in all presbytery business except matters of Discipline, Sacraments, Ordination, and appeals from kirk sessions, although the presbytery could decide to give them a vote even on these matters. To the General Assembly, the presbyteries would send up a certain number of women members as Commissioners. John White had also put forward an alternative scheme which differed from the first in that the women representatives would be "Corresponding Members" of presbytery and the Assembly, as had already been suggested by the Woman's Guild. So that his proposal should be considered he urged that the General Assembly appoint a committee to discuss it and report to the next Assembly.

This was strongly opposed by Dr. J. T. Cox, who had for many years been Principal Clerk of the Assembly.

"We have all listened to an impassioned speech by Dr. White," he said. "A great part of it is irrelevant. I hope the Assembly will not be carried off its feet by the Doctor's eloquence. Why does Dr. White want a new Committee? Because the existing Committee unanimously disapproved of his scheme, and there is the off-chance that the new Committee will approve of it. Such procedure is entirely indefensible. In my long experience, I have never known such a demand with so flimsy a pretext. I am not in favour of women in the eldership," declared Dr. Cox, "although I believe it will come before very long. But I would like to see women enter the Church courts in a regular way, rather than by swallowing this unwholesome Church Court Mixture of Dr. White's."

In spite of these trenchant remarks, John White's proposals were approved by two hundred and sixty-two members; but these were outnumbered by nearly eighty. The question of women in the Church had come to a standstill.

The same question had been raised many times before and always with the same result. As far back as 1920, John White had made public his views on the ministry of women. His own home-life in his early years and after marriage had been sweetened by the devoted love of women of deep spirituality, and his attitude to them had instinctively been one of chivalrous respect and admiration. He had once asked: "Why is the act of the woman who anointed the Christ with the precious box of spikenard celebrated throughout the ages? . . . Because the fragrance of her ointment spreads through all lands and loses none of its sweetness; because she put the accent on the right thing by her simple act of pure and fervent love." Another of his dicta on women was: "The true woman has a special genius for discriminating between things that are merely desirable and those that are necessary: between things that are secondary and those that are primary in life."

Shortly before the Assembly met in May 1920, he published an article that attracted a good deal of attention. Writing of the movement within the Church, he said it was but part of a larger social process that was affecting the responsibilities of women in public service. The General Assembly had already placed on record their recognition that, since women occupied a place equal to men in the machinery of national government, it was high time the Church made a corresponding advance. It was by no means easy to embody that recognition in a practical scheme that would not "do hurt to honoured features in the life and constitution of the Church". He saw that there would be doctrinaires who would wish to continue the limitations that sex had imposed upon women's service, but the Church must be ready to overhaul its machinery. As far back as 1888, Dr.Charteris had succeeded in persuading the Church of Scotland to restore the ancient scriptural office of Deaconess as part of its organisation, and five years later Church Sisters—they were called Parish Sisters then— had been appointed to serve in populous and necessitous districts. Women's work in the foreign mission field was acknowledged throughout the world; and at home their talent and energies were co-ordinated in the Woman's Guild. In the work of the deaconesses, magnificent as it had been, there was nothing that could not have been undertaken by other laywomen; and it was John White's considered view that in the extension and development of the Order of Deaconesses lay the best hope of progress. From this view he never moved. He felt that by raising the qualifications of those who entered the service of the Church as deacon- esses—raising them academically to that of the level of ministers—the way would be opened eventually for their employment in higher spheres than before, so that one day the step could be taken to admit them as licentiates to preach the Word and eventually to full ordination.

The next move was made by the Marchioness of Aberdeen in 1931 when she petitioned the General Assembly on the opening to women of the diaconate, the eldership, and the ministry of the Church. Principal Martin had said that the Assembly found itself on that day in an un- precedented situation.

"Nothing less than a social revolution has come about in our lifetime, and almost all the other vocations and professions are now equally open to men and women. There are only two positions of great altitude, so far as I know, which are as yet barred to women. The one is a seat in the House of Lords, and the other," he said, with a glance towards John White, "is the convenership of the Business Committee of the General Assembly of the Church of Scotland."

When the laughter had died down, Principal Martin had added: "I do not wonder that some of us round this table feel that the ground is rocking and rumbling beneath us, and that Dr. White is asking in his heart—'If the foundations be destroyed, what shall the righteous do?'"

John White seconded Principal Martin's proposal that a committee be formed to consider the petition, but he added:

"After long years we have attained the Union of the Churches, and I believe that to grant the claim of the petition at the present juncture would jeopardise the unity of the Church. I am, however, strongly of the opinion that some further endeavour must be made to recognise the claim of women for a fuller share in the public work of the Church, with special bearing on the status and work of Deaconesses."

The committee left women's entry into the ministry an open question, but decided that there were "not sufficient grounds in principle for the discrimination of sex in eligibility for the eldership". As for the Deacons' Court, the committee recommended that women should be admitted on exactly the same terms as men.[1] This became the law of the Church in 1935, and so women were elected to those congregational bodies which deal with questions of management and finance. While this was a step in the right direction, John White was not satisfied. In putting forward the scheme of his Minority Report in 1947, he pointed out that there was nothing revolutionary about his proposals. It was a *via media* between the small group who believed that women should be elected to the eldership and those who believed that it would be against the teachng and spirit of the New Testament and would be too drastic a break from tradition. His view was that it was but a step, and not a very long one, from service on Assembly committees to service on Parish Church Councils. Already women could become members of any congregational committee formed to nominate a minister in a vacant charge: presbyteries had the power to add women to their committees: and nearly eighty women were already on Assembly committees. But in spite of his warm advocacy, he failed to swing round to his own way of thinking a majority of the Assembly. He was then in his eightieth year, and for as far back as most of the members could recollect he had been the dominating figure in every Assembly he had attended: for him to be outvoted in a cause of his own creating provided one of those rare exceptions that evoked comment even in the press. How many years were to pass before women were to be elected elders, to say nothing of their becoming eligible for the ministry of the Church of Scotland, was a question that nobody would then have attempted to answer.

[1] Membership of Deacons' Courts has no relation whatever to the Order of Deaconesses.

VII

For many years there had been controversy in the Church on the status of Deaconesses and Church Sisters and their relations with each other. After the union of the Churches in 1929, two committees had discussed the development of the Order of Deaconesses, but they did not arrive at a clear decision until 1933. For the next seventeen years, there was scarcely a General Assembly in which one aspect or another of women's service in the Church was not debated. Many had been confused about the separate existence of the two bodies of women workers. The Deaconesses and the Church Sisters were to a large extent doing the same work. Under their revised constitution of 1939, a Deaconess required higher academic qualifications than a Church Sister. John White and others had been greatly concerned at the falling away in the numbers of those who volunteered for this branch of Church work. Shortly after the union of the Churches, there had been sixty members of the Order; but after the Second World War had ended, the number on full-time duty as Deaconesses was less than a dozen. On principle, John White was against either of those bodies of workers absorbing the other. Nothing could make him relinquish the idea that in the Deaconess there was a potential minister of the Word; but it began to be widely felt that there was no other course but amalgamation. At last a scheme was worked out that satisfied him. The two would be linked together in one denomination using the older title, that of the Order of Deaconesses. What pleased him was that the Order would be divided into three groups. The first contained those who had previously been in the Order. Their work was to include that of assistants in parishes, with preparation for Holy Baptism, the instruction of candidates for Confirmation of Baptismal Vows, preaching and teaching, and other pastoral work. The same group included also those who might be appointed chaplains in universities and colleges, and teachers of religion. The course of study required of them would be at the same level as that of students entering the ministry, and it would be necessary to spend at least one year in St. Colm's College, Edinburgh. The second group, of which members had also to take a course in St. Colm's College, had tasks that ranged from probation work to personnel management. The third contained the Church Sisters, and for them a full two-years course at St. Colm's College was obligatory. After training and a successful period of probation, the presbytery could duly commission a candidate to the office of Deaconess. In discussing these three groups, John White made it plain that there had never been any difference in status between the old Order of Deaconesses and the Church Sisters; nor had there been a difference of status between them and ministers: "All were equally responsible before God as faithful servants in His Church. St. Paul has given his ruling on this, having told us to walk worthy of the vocation wherewith we are called, with all lowliness and meekness, with long-suffering, forbearing one another in love, endeavouring to keep the unity of the Spirit in the bond of peace." John White confidently believed that the new Order would give to women wide and responsible spheres of service in the Church, and for all who came forward there was a solemn dedication to its work as a Divine calling and a spiritual self-committal.[1]

The first service of this commissioning was arranged by the Presbytery of Glasgow to take place in Glasgow Cathedral on Thursday, 19th January 1950, and he was asked to conduct it. Part of the ceremony included the enunciation of the duties of the Order:

". . . to assist the ministers of the Church in nourishing and building up the flock; to commend the Gospel to those who are ignorant and out of the way; to teach the truths and duties of the Christian faith in school and college; to bring comfort and healing to the sick in body, mind, and spirit; to minister to women in the Forces of the Crown, in industry, in hospital, and in the home; and to care for the poor and needy, the perplexed and broken."

John White quoted some words of the Lady Grisell Baillie, who had been the first Deaconess and head of the Woman's Guild. When she was set apart as a Deaconess in 1888 by the kirk session of Bowden, she said it was a marked day for her. "I was very happy—only God knows how happy—to be permitted afresh to dedicate myself to His blessed service, and give myself wholly to the work of the Church, to make that my chief object in life, to be able to make my profession before many witnesses. What an honour to be counted worthy to be an office-bearer in the Church of my fathers."

"I speak to some," said John White, "who have served as Deaconesses; you will, I am sure, today re-dedicate yourselves to your sacred ministry. I speak to many Parish Church Sisters who have been set apart as such for manifold services, and who have now entered the

---

[1] The constitution of the Order was later modified in some of its details.

Order of Deaconesses. What shall I say in delivering this Charge from the Presbytery? . . . We are living in one of the great ages of history. It is also a difficult and critical age. It brings with it tremendous opportunities for the Church of Christ to inform it, to lead it, and to make it the finest era in all the history of the Christian Church. You and I have a great privilege in serving at this hour."

VIII

When Dr. Geoffrey Fisher, who had succeeded William Temple as Archbishop of Canterbury, preached a sermon before the University of Cambridge on 3rd November 1946, he made a call for Church unity that startled many thousands of churchmen not only in Britain but overseas. The sermon was widely reported in the press. When John White read of it he at once asked for a complete print so that he could study it in detail. The Primate was calling for "full communion" between the episcopal and non-episcopal Churches. John White remembered vividly how he and his colleagues, a dozen years before, had worked for unrestricted communion between the two Churches and for a free exchange of pulpits and how the Anglican and Presbyterian delegates had agreed in a fine harmony to recommend these ideals to their Churches. The talks, so far as they had gone, had been successful. In answer to questions put to him by his friend, Dr. Lauchlan MacLean Watt, John White wrote:

"It was not Union we sought, not federation, but an expression of Christian unity in a few sensible arrangements. The conference was unanimous in its six findings. The General Assembly of the Church of Scotland accepted the proposals with cordial unanimity, and appointed a small committee to carry through the findings in conjunction with a similar committee of the Church of England when that should be appointed. You know the result. The Anglo-Catholics shied. No English committee was appointed. There the matter stands."

Since then, as John White well knew, the Anglo-Catholic body had grown in strength, and he saw little hope of making further progress now. He could not ignore a declaration from Lambeth, made during the war on the newly united Church of South India, that the Anglican position was that "no clergyman who had not been ordained by a bishop should be appointed to any charge which had previously been Anglican except in the rarest circumstances". In the General Assembly of the Church of Scotland, this declaration had been denounced in strong terms: "We are bringing the Indians out of their own caste system into a system of ecclesiastical caste." However, since the Indian Churches were now autonomous and could snap their fingers at Canterbury, John White heard with satisfaction that the Indian Bishop of Dornakal had stated that "it should be clearly understood that the rite of mutual commissioning of presbyters and priests already ordained before union in no sense implies re-ordination because *all* have been ordained to be ministers of the Word and Sacraments in the Church of God". The Church of Scotland advised her missionaries in India that they should not acquiesce in any scheme of union in which the declaration of the Bishop of Dornakal was denied or impugned. That had been in 1944; but now in 1946, it seemed that the Archbishop's Cambridge sermon was turning away from sectarian discrimination and throwing open the door to a closer unity between the episcopal and the non-episcopal Churches.

As John White studied the sermon, however, he began to question how far open the door had been drawn by Dr. Fisher. "We are not yet ready for organic or constitutional union," he had said, and on this John White saw eye to eye with him. The Church of England had a complicated legal connection with the State, the Archbishop explained, and the State entered deeply into its machinery of government.[1] "The Free Churches would certainly not accept our establishment as it is," he said, "and the process of extricating the Church of England from what it was not desired to retain, and of accomplishing its transfer to a newly devised constitution, would be a work of even greater magnitude and difficulty than the scheme of reunion itself." Another reason the Archbishop gave was that "there are tensions within the Church of England itself which are not resolved. It has its own problem of recovering its own spiritual authority over itself and of re-ordering its own life. . . . But when it is thus engaged in a delicate task, it is unwise at the same time to involve it in questions of constitutional affiliation to other denominations." Dr. Fisher was here referring mainly to the cleavage in his Church which

---

[1] "The State recognises the Church of England as an integral part of the constitution of the realm. In this constitution, the authority of the Church lies not in the clergy in convocation nor in the laity in Parliament, but in both. Convocation can be summoned only by authority of a Royal writ. It cannot make provisional canons, constitutions, and ordinances without the Royal Assent and licence. . . . If it is God's will for us to be linked with the State, then we must accept the constitution which is agreed upon by both Church and State. To speak of a spiritual authority outside of this constitution is a pure myth invented not by the Church but by the bishops themselves."—*Secretary of the Church Society at Oxford, 21st October 1957*

the Anglo-Catholic movement had created and was steadily widening.[1] Nevertheless, he saw no reason why the Churches in this country should not "grow to full communion with each other. There can be a process of assimilation," he said, "a growing alike. . . . No insuperable barrier to full communion remains until we come to questions of the ministry and government of the Church." Here he was referring to the episcopate as manifested, among other ways, in ordination and confirmation by bishops. "There are requirements and functions," he said, "which Catholic tradition attaches to the office of a bishop which, if our aim is assimilation and full communion, must be safeguarded." There must be a *giving of episcopacy by the Anglican Church*, he said, and a *receiving of episcopacy by the other Churches*. What startled John White was the Archbishop's statement that, "the non-episcopal Churches have accepted the principle that episcopacy must exist along with the other elements in a re-united Church".

To this statement, John White quickly published a denial so far as the Church of Scotland was concerned. "We have made no such admission," he wrote in an article he was invited to contribute to *The Scotsman*. He pointed out that there had never been any occasion even to consider the question of agreeing to accept the principle that episcopacy must exist in a reunited Church; for in the negotiations which had come to a stop in 1934, organic union had not even been contemplated. The absorption of one communion with another had been far outside the scope of their talks. They had been aiming, he reminded his readers, at a "fellowship of many communions, fulfilled in a rich diversity of life and devotion". Presbyterians and Episcopalians would dwell together in amity in a larger unity without that unity being of a constitutional kind. But now the Archbishop of Canterbury was suggesting that the non-episcopal Churches should take the drastic step of adopting episcopacy: as he expressed it, "they should take episcopacy into their systems".

John White at once put the question in a letter to Dr. R. F. V. Scott of St. Columba's: "Is this to be a constitutional episcopate?"

There was little doubt about the answer to that. No modified form of episcopate, under whatever name it might operate, would be regarded by the Anglo-Catholic section of the Church of England as valid, unless

---

[1] The cleavage can be seen even in the Communion Service itself. Dr. Chevasse, the Bishop of Rochester, addressing the Rochester diocesan conference at Church House, Westminster, said on 21st November 1957: "How infinitely tragic that the one service which should unite us all, and at which every Anglican should worship happily, should instead divide us, even here in England, so deeply, disastrously, and antagonistically."

it were an episcopate reordained in the same manner as the English and Scottish episcopate, with the clear implication that Presbyterian ordination was imperfect.

"The Church of Scotland has always advocated inter-communion as leading to a closer fellowship," John White said. "But the Anglican Church's approach is now to seek agreement on the validity of ordination and of Church government." Would the Scots Kirk be prepared to cancel all that had gone before and tear up recommendations to which the Anglican delegates themselves had agreed in 1934? John White, for one, was not prepared to surrender a claim so manifestly fair to both, a claim in which no more was asked of the Anglican Church than what the Church of Scotland had already granted.

The next General Assembly agreed unanimously with his view. Professor Manson of Edinburgh University, convener of the Inter-Church Relations Committee, stated amid general approval: "While we cordially welcome the oecumenical spirit expressed in the utterance of the Archbishop, we record our conviction that a situation does not exist at present to which the particular proposals he makes can be applied." The General Assembly was not prepared to accept episcopacy in order to make communicants of the Church of Scotland spiritually fit to partake of the bread and wine of the Sacrament in an Anglican church.

In the Church of Scotland, there were comparatively few who saw any prospect of "episcopacy being taken into the system" of their Kirk. It was evident that the Archbishop hoped that his suggestion might seriously be considered, for in due course an invitation reached the Church of Scotland to join in talks, and John White was asked to lead the Scottish representatives, as he had done in 1932. He begged to be excused. But the leader of the Anglican delegation, the Bishop of Derby, in deference to him personally, sent to him an early draft of his proposals. Dr. Rawlinson wrote hopefully, but John White pointed out to him that a number of powerful men with perfervid Anglo-Catholic views were in a strong position in the English Church, and he told him that if he could persuade his own Church to obey the unanimous recommendations of the conference of 1934, he would be doing a great service. These recommendations were renewed and stressed by the Scottish delegates, but the Anglicans were compelled to give priority to the proposal of the Archbishop that the non-episcopal Churches should make the great and admittedly one-sided concession of adopting a form of episcopacy before there could be any serious talk of mutual communion. John White noted that the Church of England had clasped hands with the Old Catholic Churches on the Continent, and at the Lambeth Conference of 1948 it was conceded that "inter-communion does not require from either Communion the acceptance of all doctrinal opinion, sacramental devotion, or liturgical practice characteristic of the other, but implies that each believes the other to hold all the essentials of the Christian faith". Such a concordat could be reached with the Old Catholic Churches across the North Sea: but the same concordat could not, it seemed, be extended to their Presbyterian brethren across the Tweed. John White noted also that while the General Assembly went out of its way to deplore the promulgation by the Church of Rome of a new dogma declaring the Bodily Assumption of the Virgin Mary to be a belief which was necessary to all Roman Catholics for their salvation, and while the overwhelming majority of Anglicans also deplored it as having no basis in Scripture, many Anglo-Catholic priests accepted it with joy and taught it from their pulpits. This could not fail to widen the cleavage within the ranks of the English Church and, in consequence, make it more difficult for the Church of Scotland to foster relations with her so that they might, in the words of the Archbishop, "grow together".

To the same General Assembly which had deplored this dogma, the report of the joint conference on unity was presented. John White had been in no way responsible for it, but he had read it with interest and some dismay. He perceived that the old bogey was still showing its head—the bogey that had assumed in 1934 such a monstrous size in the eyes of the English churchmen that the talks had stuttered into silence—and it had grown still larger. The signatories had been forced to state that if it were held that Church of Scotland ministers be regarded as having been validly ordained, or that any communicating member had been validly accepted into membership of the Universal Church of Christ, it would "raise difficulties in the minds of a considerable number of Anglicans". This was but a euphemistic gloss on the fact—of which nobody was in any doubt—that validity was not admitted by the Anglo-Catholics and those with similar leanings. Anglicans who regarded this as an anti-scriptural piece of bigotry realised that their own members of the committee, only too aware once again of the growing dangers of schism within their Church. could do no more than make a few pious recommendations. One was that Church of Scotland ministers should be allowed to preach—but not to conduct a service—in Anglican churches, subject to prelatic consent. Another was that Anglican ministers, subject always to the consent of the

Scottish Episcopal Church, should be allowed to preach in kirks of the Church of Scotland. Yet another was that Church of Scotland members should be allowed, in certain exceptional circumstances, to take Holy Communion in an Anglican church. Always it was underlined that the permission of a bishop must be obtained, and the concession must not be taken as creating a precedent. But the Anglican delegates, foreseeing trouble, refused to recommend that *members of the Church of England should be permitted to sit at the Lord's Table in a Scottish Church where the bread and wine was dispensed by a Presbyterian minister.*

That could not be tolerated. The reason was plain. The Anglican Church had "never officially given sanction to their communicants to receive communion from ministers other than such as have been episcopally ordained". The delegates admitted that this rule had been broken, and without official censure: but it was only too apparent to them that what would seem in the eyes of all "Broad churchmen and Evangelicals" to be in conformity with God's will, would appear to the Anglo-Catholics as a partaking of communion from the hands of a heretic.

John White was never the man to mince words on matters of this kind. He rejected with scorn the term "heretic" as applied to himself either by Roman or Anglo-Catholics. And he stated with sorrow that the proposals of Archbishop Lang had been torn up by the new Primate and replaced by proposals of entirely different significance and implications.

The last sentence of the joint report was:

> "The meeting of minds was indeed such as to make the participants feel that despite the limited nature of the immediate proposals which at this stage they are able to put forward, the fellowship they have enjoyed together may be used of God as making its own modest contribution towards that closer unity for which the Churches they represent will ever continue to hope and pray."

No doubt the personal fellowship which each delegate had enjoyed was of a very delightful and informative kind; but however warm were the waves of *bonhomie* that flowed through their conferences, the position revealed by their 1951 report was that the Church of Scotland had come openly forward and laid down no conditions whatever on inter-communion and a mutual exchange of pulpits, holding before them the unanimous agreements reached seventeen years before, while the Church of England had stated that the Scottish Church could be permitted to take no further step until she had adopted some form of episcopacy and had nominated bishops whose ordination had been made valid by bishops of the Anglican Communion.

John White was reminded of some of the words of the Archbishop of Canterbury's sermon preached in 1946 as he sat in the Assembly of 1951 and listened to the address of Dr. Cyril Garbett, Archbishop of York. In his Cambridge sermon, Dr. Fisher had referred to the Church of England's "very complicated legal nexus with the State", and John White could only too well recall the legal nexus which had once existed between the State and the Church of Scotland. While the shackles that had bound the Scottish Church to Parliament had been broken, those of the English Church still remained. In his address to the Assembly, Dr. Garbett spoke of the report on the negotiations between the two Churches:

"I stand here with mingled admiration and envy, for I am addressing members of an established Church which has complete spiritual freedom. There is no other established Church in the world which has such complete spiritual freedom as your Church possesses. We in the Church of England, an established Church with great freedom in practice, nevertheless do not have the same kind of freedom that you possess. We hope that under the changing conditions of the twentieth century, Parliament may be prepared to give us a greater measure of freedom while we still remain an established Church."

To the Archbishops of both Canterbury and York, as they contemplated the doctrinal cleavage in the ranks of the Anglican Communion, it was patent that to obtain from Parliament spiritual freedom in as full a measure as was possessed by the Church of Scotland would present incalculable difficulties. And until this had been won from the State, there could be little hope of any long-term plan of organic union being carried out.

Shortly before the General Assembly had met, John White had addressed the Representative Church Council of the Scottish Episcopal Church. Manifestly, he said, Christian unity was the first and fundamental problem because it underlay all other problems.

"In Scotland there can be seen an increasing convergence of all the Churches, but it may be a very long time before any practical scheme can be framed for the organic union between a Church holding the historic episcopacy and a Church holding the historic presbyterate, *without greatly impoverishing the spiritual treasury of both.*

"Our first task," he insisted, "should in my view be the organic union of Churches of the same family."

Why think in terms of an organic union between Churches of different families while there were so many of the same family that stood apart from one another? [1] Could not the differences between non-episcopal Churches be more easily narrowed than the much wider divergence between the Church of Scotland and the Church of England? But if union among non-episcopal Churches were the first practical step to be taken, there must at the same time grow that fellowship of kindred minds in *all* the Churches that would prepare the way for a great advance towards a richer Christian unity.

> "More urgent, if it be possible, than even the social mission of the Churches is the present world situation. There is a call for unity in the Churches to heal the broken fellowships of the nations, and there is need to safeguard the Church of Christ against the alien atheism that is disseminated ruthlessly by an aggressive Communism. The present divisions in the Church of Christ throughout the world are a calamity, and rob the Churches of international political influence. So long as we are not at one, but at sixes and sevens, the world will not believe. How deplorable are the rents in the seamless robe of Christ!"

As John White looked into the future, hoping and praying with many another for the spiritual unity which the world so desperately needed, he failed to see any prospect of Christian fellowship at the Lord's Table being accepted by the Anglicans as the first step towards unity with any non-episcopal Church. They had firmly rejected this way of approach by saying that the only way was the way of episcopacy. As he tried to look realistically at the internal tensions within the Church of England to which the Archbishop of Canterbury had referred, he was forced to conclude that unless, by some miracle, there should be a change of attitude among the Anglicans, the Church of Scotland would have to decide whether she could turn her back upon her historic past, avert her eyes from the monuments she had set up to the martyrs she revered, and "take episcopacy into her system". Not until 1957 did the joint conference

---

[1] The Baptist Union had reported in 1937 that, if union with the Congregationalists and Presbyterians had been pressed to an issue, it would have split the Baptist denomination. The Congregationalists and English Presbyterians had resumed talks on union in 1948, and these had served but to stimulate the consciousness of each Church on the "specific witness" to which each had been committed.

succeed in producing a report which suggested possible means by which the one Church might take episcopacy into her system and the other take presbyterianism. This was commended to the careful study of all members of the Church and at once became a focal point of controversy, in which even the history of the Kirk itself was bent this way or that to support opposing contentions. For many months the correspondence columns of the press bristled with letters the majority of which condemned out of hand the idea of "bishops-in-presbytery" for the Church of Scotland, while most of the others pled for a measure of that calm consideration for which the General Assembly had asked. Many there were who would have been glad to hear the plangent voice of John White give an un-equivocal directive to those who were bemused by the Anglican demand that constitutional changes were necessary before Anglican communicants could be permitted to take communion from a Presbyterian minister, before Presbyterians could unconditionally take communion in an Anglican church, and before Church of Scotland clergymen could law-fully be welcomed on any occasion to an Anglican pulpit—in short, before there could be spiritual harmony between the two National Churches.

IX

In January 1946, Mr. Hay Downie, General Treasurer of the Church of Scotland, was able to report to John White that in the previous year more than one hundred and ten thousand pounds had been gathered for Church Extension. This was the first instalment of the million he had called for in 1945. The news heartened him, and he received enthusiastic letters, many of them from strangers. One was from his friend, the Rev. Joseph Gray, written from the manse at Old Meldrum: "The first Hundred Thousand! And well on to the second. A sign has been given you. Your sublime faith and gaiety of spirit, with the high levels to which you have lifted this great work, are bringing inspiriting results. Your strong lead has caught the imagination of the Church. A praying and giving people are behind you."

"A praying and giving people": that described the majority. But not all had yet been giving, and at the Commission of General Assembly, held in November, John White had astringent things to say about the non-givers:

"Two hundred and thirty-eight congregations of the Church of Scotland gave *nothing* last year to Church Extension. Of these, no less than one hundred and thirty-six have given not one penny since the work was begun thirteen years ago. I ask them to think again. I ask them to join with their brethren and share in the biggest Church job of their lifetime. If only the members of these two hundred and thirty-eight congregations could see with their own eyes the urgent need of a housing area with its teeming population, they would then become zealous enthusiasts."

He told the Assembly how he had been running bus trips to the new areas; and many who had been doubtful were now keen supporters. "I wish I could take eight bus loads of ministers, eighty loads of elders, a thousand loads of Church members! They would see for themselves what they were *not* supporting."

With pride he was able to tell of the success already achieved. "The five largest Sunday Schools in all Scotland," he said, "are in these new areas. The three largest Sunday Schools in Edinburgh, the three largest in Glasgow, the largest in Ayr, Dumbarton, Paisley, Dundee—all are in these areas. But the harrowing thing is that there is no room in the Sunday Schools for thousands of children who want to attend." He quoted a letter he had received from a minister: "We had to intimate last Sunday that we could take no more children into the Beginners or Primary departments. It was a hard decision; it caused heart burning, but we have no alternative."

By the end of 1947, he was writing to Mr. Hay Downie that, in his view, they were entering upon a new phase in their ten-year plan for the Ingathering of the Million. Enthusiastic congregations had completed, or almost completed, their task. The time had come, it seemed to him, when they should turn all their guns upon those congregations that had done little or nothing. The appeal to these apathetic ones should be intensified. At the same time, he had again the task of killing a rumour that Church Extension had closed down because of the Government's restrictions on building. As a deterrent to further rumour, John White published the news that eleven semi-permanent buildings had been put up during the past two years; that on 14th September 1948 he had laid the foundation stone of the first permanent building of the post-war years, a hall-church at Provanmill, in Glasgow; that the starting dates of another twelve permanent hall-churches had been fixed; that a further eight awaited permits for work to begin; and that sixty-five sites for hall-churches were being secured.

To encourage light industries in Scotland, where heavy industry had in the past been dominant, Sir Steven Bilsland (later Lord Bilsland) and others had succeeded in establishing new industrial estates; and as these developed, yet more houses would be required. With the increase of population in the pre-war housing areas, John White knew that what they had been able to provide there was now inadequate. Many temporary huts, accommodating two or three hundred, had already congregations that could fill them twice over, and to accommodate the worshippers two morning services had to be held. With the increase in the numbers of young folk, ministers and helpers felt impotent in the face of long waiting-lists, not only for Sunday School classes but in nearly all the youth organisations. At the Commission of Assembly held in November 1950, one can hear a challenging note in John White's words:

> "Are you aware that in many of our churches in these new areas there has been an overwhelming response to the call to worship? One minister wrote to me, 'I have never known anything like it in my former ministry.' Two recent reports in these newly planted kirks show that fifty per cent of new members in one, sixty per cent in the other, had not before been members of any Christian Church. Is that not significant? . . ."

Then he gave this warning:

> "Some gripping appeals are being made to these new communities. They are not appeals made by any Christian Church. They are from an opposing claimant that is not Christian, not even religious. By slow infiltration, it seeks to undermine the faith of the Church. It is the appeal from Moscow to the proletariat. It is absolute and confident as it rides the whirlwind and directs the storm. . . .
> "This is well known to many zealous and faithful churchfolk. They have been generous in providing the means of grace to those who have trekked to these new churchless areas. They have helped us to build sanctuaries—the safeguards that have kept Scotland a Christian nation in past days, and will prevent the children of today and tomorrow from being hurt by that poisonous breath of anti-Christ."

He asked the Commission of Assembly to consider what the position would be after the great transference had been completed. For the one and a half million folk who remained in the old residential areas, there would be some two thousand ministers. But what of the *three and a half million* in the new areas? Unless the Church put its best foot foremost, there would be only one hundred ministers for them.

"I know the good work that is being done by the Unions and Readjustments Committee," he said. "They have reduced redundant churches by no less than six hundred. That is a move in the right direction. But the sad thing is that we had built only fifty-six churches or hall-churches when the devastating hand of Hitler stayed our efforts. Nor did peace bring any easement. Shortage of material and labour made things even worse. What is the solution? We must build —build not only to catch up with the pre-War needs but to bring the means of grace to the folk who are coming to live in the half million new houses that are now going up to provide for migration.

"Meanwhile, every third child in Scotland is born and brought up in these new areas. When the migration is complete it will be seven in every ten. . . .

"I am sending out two thousand one hundred letters at once," he told the Assembly. "These will go to ministers asking them for a generous response before the end of this year. It is not those whose people have already given generously that I am trying to move. It is the others—those who are simply apathetic, those who have no vision, those who are satisfied to go stepping along in blinkers." And he repeated what he was never weary of saying: "This is the most important work for our Church and our nation in our lifetime."

At the beginning of Church Extension, city kirks helped these young congregations in the housing areas. But already the old order was changing. Some of the churches in the new areas were already in a position to help the older ones in the cities. John White quoted Dr. Mackintosh to show how one of these new churches had offered to give a hundred pounds a year towards the salary of an assistant in the city. Fourteen shillings of every pound of voluntary giving to the Church would one day come from these new areas.

"Be it noted that forty per cent of our congregations are declining," said John White significantly. "Of how many can it be said that they are holding their own? Another forty per cent. Of twenty per cent only can I say with certainty that they have a bright future. And most of these are among the new Church Extension charges. Does this not point the way for us? We must go forward with our work."

From the Rev. Ivan F. Tibbs, on the 17th May 1950, John White received a letter about the new suite of halls to be built at High Carntyne. The kirk session were eager to use the name "White Hall". The request revived old memories, for Carntyne had been part of John White's first parish of Shettleston, and in his reply he told how he had carried out his pastoral visitation on horseback in the northern parts of that large parish which became one of the most densely populated areas in Glasgow:

> "What a change has taken place in the last fifty-five years! While I was minister in Shettleston, I touched the beginning of the great problem which I saw the Church would have to face in the coming years. I built three churches then to meet the needs of that quickly growing parish. We have added many others in the subsequent years, including your own. It will be a great pleasure to see the completion of the suite of halls you so much need. . . . May I thank you and your kirk session warmly for the honouring suggestion that you use the name White Hall. Hitherto, I have refused all requests for the use of my name in connection with churches. I was asked to give permission at the time of the Reunion in 1929, when ministers had difficulty in finding distinctive names. Two generous citizens of Glasgow offered to build a White Memorial, but I thought that slightly premature, so asked them to put the money into the Church Extension fund. Your suggestion is somewhat different, and I have no hesitation in agreeing. I trust that you and your folk will be greatly heartened by the growing success of your great congregation."

In a letter written to him by Principal George Duncan of St. Mary's College, St. Andrews, one sentence has a special fitness: "And then, with the Union of 1929 accomplished, you were a lion-heart in the way you tackled Church Extension—*going in search of the people, as a living Church must ever do.*"

X

John White's battle with bureaucracy had not come to an end by his triumph at Westminster with the Town and Country (Scotland) Planning Bill. Indeed, it grew more intense after the Second World War had ended. Often he fought single-handed, writing letters to departmental heads or arguing with officials seated safely behind large desks; but sometimes he found it more effective to deploy a company of supporters gathered from Churches of all denominations and creeds.

Scotland had severely suffered from the bombs dropped by the Luftwaffe, and four hundred and eighty cases of damage to churches, halls, and manses had been reported by the time the war had ended. John White told the Assembly of 1946 that the War Damage Commission had paid the Church of Scotland nearly thirty-five thousand pounds compensation,[1] but he felt it was high time that the Board of Trade took steps also to pay compensation for the loss of their moveable property. Much of his strength during the next few years was expended in convincing officialdom, both in Scotland and in London, that the work which the Churches were doing throughout the land was of supreme importance to the future of the nation. He had many cheering words said to him during that period, but seldom could he detect any encouragement in the voice of bureaucracy. From overseas, gifts poured in to him to help the repair of damaged church buildings—gifts from South Africa, from the British West Indies and British Guiana, from New York. He spoke with particular pride of contributions from the Women's Missionary Society of the Presbyterian Church in Canada and of a generous donation from the Blue Mountains in New South Wales.

> "That donation came to me," he said, "from a minister who has a small beautiful church standing high in those great hills that are one of the most wonderful sights of Australia—but they do not surpass in beauty the action of these people who have asked that they might have a share in the rebuilding of our bombed churches here at home. . . . This practical sympathy from the Christian Fellowship in so many places is evidence of the growing unity of the Church throughout the world. I believe that a far greater spirit of Christian unity could be made manifest if the leaders of the Church were to act with courage and wisdom."

John White had begun his campaign as early as 1944 by asking the Minister of Works how soon the Scottish Churches Committee was to be informed that it would have a fair share of priorities in labour and materials for post-war building. He had had a conference with the Regional Controller, then with the Secretary of State for Scotland; and in June 1945, after pressure from John White, the Minister of Works had said that any labour they could spare was required almost wholly for

---

[1] The total sum which the Church ultimately secured was some seven hundred thousand pounds; but since nearly half of this was compensation for buildings that were not urgently needed, it was used for the erection of churches in new housing areas.

housing. The utmost that could be conceded was that, where the most urgent repairs were necessary to damaged church buildings, applications for a permit could be made to the Regional Licensing Officer, but in no case could he allow the cost to exceed one thousand pounds. It seemed that no more progress could be made for some time to come, but John White had no intention of bowing his head to any decision which placed the Church at a disadvantage and impeded her work.

Meanwhile, a minor skirmish was fought. This became known as The Battle of the Chairs. For the new Church Extension charges, many thousands of chairs were needed, and a thirty-three and a third per cent purchase tax had been put on them. One day John White learned with anger that cinema houses did not pay this purchase tax on new chairs, and at once he was up in arms. He protested and pointed out that the cinemas used chairs to gain profit while the Church did not. He was met by a shake of the head and a statement that "the Treasury would be most reluctant to recognise a privileged class". This stung John White into further action, and he replied: "The only privilege the Church has is the privilege of service." He proposed that, to keep the chairs off the general market, they should be stamped with a St. Andrew's Cross or the Church's emblem of the Burning Bush. "This was not accepted," he wrote at the end of the affray.

"I then suggested that the Church would give an undertaking that all chairs would be used exclusively for Church purposes. This too was refused. I then submitted a design of a Church chair with a book-box on the back; I was asked to make it a kneeling board. I pointed out that we did not kneel in the Church of Scotland. We used the Book, hence the book-box. Mercer Robertson was of immense help to me, so was our chair-maker in Glasgow. The press gave big head-lines to the controversy. I continued to hammer away at the officials. There was much letter-writing to interested folks in England and Scotland. At long last, the officials agreed to allow Church chairs, with a book-box, to be exempted from purchase tax. I have since wondered whether it was argument that won the day—or simply that the officials were tired."

That was in 1946, and towards the end of the year he was having another interview with the Secretary of State for Scotland about the "re-building of churches destroyed by the King's enemies" and of putting up hall-churches in the new housing areas. The latter, he said, would not be for Sunday services only; they would be used every day of the week as a community centre. But this argument held no appeal. The Secretary of State tried to convince him that the Ministry of Works was acting towards the building trade like a fairy godmother: "Just as a stream moves down to the sea and irrigates each of the banks," he said, "so the Ministry of Works has got to make certain that its forces are so spread that it gives the best benefit to the public."

"Yes," retorted John White brusquely, "but what if the hydro-electric people come in at the top and dam the whole show?"

He continued to put on pressure. Appeals were coming to him from all sides, and the burden of them was: "Can you help us?" Many ministers and elders seemed to think that he had magic powers by which he could persuade remote and indifferent officials to "do something". Other letters came from ministers who, with their kirk sessions, had struggled in vain to penetrate to any meaning that might lie hidden below the screeds of official jargon. John White gave Joseph Westwood, who had succeeded Tom Johnston at the Scottish Office, little peace:

"I am sending you a press cutting which states that the Regal Cinema at Hamilton, destroyed by fire in April, is to be reopened tomorrow, 3rd December. If this be so, it means that the cinema, burnt in April, will be resuming business almost without delay, while those churches completely blitzed five and a half years ago are being left in ruins." He demanded an explanation. The reply ignored damaged churches and blandly referred to the need for repairing the cinema roof to keep the weather from doing further damage. This made John White angrier still. "Profits are more important than religion! Amusement is more important than Christianity! I have done what I could," he cried in wrathful disgust, "and I am heart-sore at the outcome. It has been one long record of frustration."

Joseph Westwood again came under attack because he had promised after much persuasion to submit to the Ministry of Works a statement of the Churches' building needs. Had anything been done? No decisive answer could be got, and in desperation John White sent a telegram to Westwood. This he read to the Commission of Assembly on 5th March 1947, together with the reply. The Secretary said he regretted he was unable to give a decision on building permits for the Churches' programme because the matter required further consideration. Further consideration! John White told the Assembly that he had just read with amazement that a licence had been granted by the Ministry of Works to the Scottish

Tourist Board to spend nearly three-quarters of a million sterling to rebuild and redecorate hotels in Scotland:

"One must support the effort to put Scotland on the tourist map of the world," he declared. "We all agree about that. But surely one of the chief features of Scottish life and character is the Church which has written the finest pages in the history of the nation.

"Tourists will come to our renovated hotels on which there has been spent three-quarters of a million with the sanction of the Ministry of Works and of the Secretary of State for Scotland. They will, no doubt, see the historic places where Bruce and Wallace fought for liberty and independence, where Covenanters fought and died for the rights and freedom of the Church. And they will be shown our ancient places of worship. But if they also see the great housing schemes in our land, they will look for the Church in the midst. They will only notice the Missing Church. . . .

"They will learn that Scotland has now put everything before the Church. They will learn that the State, which once gloried in the Church and its great services for the community, cannot spare from housing, industry, cinemas and hotels, a single permit to build a House of God. It is not by this policy that Scottish freedom will be safeguarded. It is not by this policy that the best and highest interests of the nation will be secured."

XI

By the time the Assembly met in May, the situation had not altered, and John White read to the members a letter from the Scottish Office in which Westwood's private secretary had said that in the opinion of the Secretary of State still further discussions might be necessary. This meant, said John White, that they were no further forward than they had been eighteen months before. One who was present described the atmosphere in that Assembly:

"Dr. White read the letter from the Scottish Office slowly and with great deliberation, then turned to the Chair and declared, 'Moderator, when I received that letter I saw red.' This comment was greeted with loud applause and calls of 'Hear, hear' from all parts of the House. A member interjected a remark which was inaudible, and Dr. White said sharply, 'If you have anything stronger to say than I have . . .' The rest of his comment was lost in laughter. When it had subsided he continued, 'That letter is not worth . . . the paper it is written on.' The House endorsed Dr. White's views by another resounding outburst of applause. 'I wonder if I might call the Assembly to order and make this very serious statement,' Dr. White continued. 'Here is my finding on all this. For the first time in the recent history of Scotland, the Church's freedom to provide for the spiritual needs of the people is being hampered, if not altogether frustrated. Those in authority in the State claim the right to control the whole of our lives and activities, and to say whether the Church shall have an opportunity to make the most modest provision for the most important things in life for man and the nation. . . .

" 'Has Christianity failed? Does it serve no purpose to build Churches? Are we forced to leave everything in the hands of those economists and politicians who are making such a poor job of their task to redd up the mess the world is floundering in? Or shall we build the Church of God in the midst? Shall we declare to the people with sure confidence that this Church and its Message are essential to their spiritual well-being—that only in the Church can they find a solution to their most perplexing problems? . . . If we do not believe this, then Church Extension is but a waste of effort.' "

He added a personal word. He said that, for Church Extension, the great need was now for a man who could take full-time leadership in work that would last beyond his own years. In a few months he would have passed his eightieth birthday, and he had tried to find a younger man who would take over the work from his hands and carry it through after his days were ended.

"I have tried in vain to find him," he said. "It is not a task for one who has reached the twilight of life, and I still look for someone who will dominate the events that surround us—someone who will never let those events get the better of us. I thank the whole of the Church for its encouragement, its support, its affection. But above all, I thank God for the opportunity of service and the gift of strength to carry out His task, however imperfectly."

When he had finished his speech there was a burst of enthusiasm the like of which had seldom been seen or heard in the Assembly Hall, and the audience of over two thousand rose to applaud him. It was clear that the bow of burning gold must not be allowed to fall from his hand, and he went from the Assembly with strength renewed.

XII

His fiery speech that day, the talk it created, the publicity it received in the press, the outburst of popular feeling that followed—these had a greater effect than he had anticipated when he had risen to denounce government officials; to his demand for some assurance that the Church would no longer be ignored, he received a letter from the Scottish Office to say that the question had been examined and "the Minister of Works was now prepared, subject to certain conditions, to consider applications for building licences to cover Church work in Scotland costing in all not more than one million pounds".

Here at last was something reasonably substantial. If the sum, which must suffice for all denominations in Scotland, was not as large as John White would have wished, it was at least a beginning. The allocation must last for two years, and it must cover repairs and maintenance as well as all new erections. As for the dividing up of the building licences among the different denominations, the Churches must agree on that among themselves.

For this purpose, a committee was formed representing fifteen denominations, including Roman Catholics, Episcopalians, the Salvation Army, and Jews. It might have been thought that here was a fine subject for strife among the different bodies. The representatives asked John White to preside over them, and he accepted the chairmanship with some little wonder as to what the atmosphere would be. He found that his old apothegm was as true now as it had been during the union negotiations, that it was much easier for clergymen to agree about matters of money than on points of doctrine. In the committee there was the greatest harmony, and his own comment was:

> "We carried through the allocation of these building licences—
> I am proud to say it—in the most friendly spirit. There was unanimity.
> *I shall always regard this as a unique meeting.* I wish I could think it was
> full of promise for closer Christian unity amongst the Churches in
> days when Christian unity is the only way out of our troubles."

Ministers of Mr. Attlee's Government had confidently stated that building costs were expected shortly to come down. John White was told by the Scottish Office that this would be of great advantage to the Churches in the allocation during the next two years. In fact, the Government found itself powerless to stem the alarming rise in prices; and before the period had ended, building costs had risen by fifty per cent. To overcome this, John White did his best to persuade the authorities to put the Churches on the same basis as certain other bodies and allow them to repair war-damage to the cost of one thousand pounds apart from the allocation. They had already been granted a free limit of one hundred pounds, a paltry enough sum compared with the amount of restoration of war-damage that was still to be done. The new Secretary of State, Arthur Woodburn, sympathetic and anxious to press the case of the Churches, obtained some concession: so did his successor, Hector McNeil, a Glasgow boy who was then on the way to becoming a trusted leader in the Labour Party. The programme for that period of Church Extension included nine hall-churches for Glasgow and its satellite towns, five for housing areas located within a few miles of Edinburgh, three each for Dunferm-line and Ayr, two for housing areas near Dundee, and one each for Dumfries, Stirling, and Inverness: in all, twenty-five. This was greater than anything that had been attempted within any two pre-war years; and in the carrying out of the task John White depended largely upon his three colleagues, Dr. Robert Mackintosh, the Rev. Horace Walker, and Miss A. C. Veitch. Their loyalty to their chief and their whole-hearted devotion to the cause uplifted his spirit in these strenuous years, and both in the Assembly and in private he was quick to acknowledge his debt to them.

On Tuesday, 12th June 1951, representatives of all the Churches in Scotland once again met to divide among themselves [1] the permits which had been granted for building. With costs still rising, and licences still held at the million mark, there might have been contention in this meeting, but it was completely harmonious. At the close, John White was deeply touched by the gratitude expressed by his friends in those many denominations. The vote of thanks was proposed by Mr. Cohen, a Jew, and seconded by Mr. Lyons, a Roman Catholic. The opening prayer at that meeting, held at the offices of the Church of Scotland in George Street, Edinburgh, was to be remembered by those present as the last prayer any of them were to hear from John White's lips:

"Most gracious God, Who has called Thy Church out of the world to bring the world unto Thee, pour out upon Thy faithful people in

---

[1] The agreed allocation of the Church of Scotland was £446,000.

this and in all lands the spirit of power and of love and of a sound mind that Thy Church, bearing witness to Thee and Thy truth, may lead the nations to that promised day when nation shall not lift up the sword against nation, neither learn war any more. Guide us in our present tasks: grant us wisdom and patience: in Thy light may we see light clearly: in Thy service may we find perfect freedom. Amen."

A few weeks later, he was called to the greater service.

Chapter XXIII

THE MAN AND THE CHURCHMAN

I

IN the years that followed the end of the First World War, John White's activities brought him more and more into the public eye. It seemed to many people that his life was largely spent in hurrying from one appointment to another; and with his gathering fame it became inevitable that his speeches were reported, briefly or at length, in the press. A picture of him as an ecclesiastical statesman, a prince of the Church, was gradually being created. While many people had little idea of his deep spirituality, there were also many who were unaware of an aspect of the man on which the limelight never played—namely his life of carefully planned and intensive study. In all he undertook for the Church of Scotland, in his committee work, and in the larger schemes which he inspired and carried through, he was never satisfied until he had gathered and sifted and scrutinised every detail that bore on the main issue. Every task he treated with conscientious care. Many appeals were made to him for help in work that was outside the Church's main field. In the opinion of his friends, it was unfortunate that he responded so generously; and as he looked back on his life, he was forced to agree. To a young minister he wrote: "You are taking on far too much. I did the same myself and now I regret it. Every minister should have some blank pages in his engagement book. He must find time to read and to think." Except for the little volume of letters written from the war front, he never published a book; he even shook his head when it was suggested that he should print his sermons; but his writings would fill many volumes. To master a subject a man should write a book about it; this adage seems to have been his rule, for he could never peck at a subject or dally with it—he must settle down and get the same grip on it a man would require if he were preparing an article for an encyclopaedia. Towards the end of his life, he told of an old friend who had twitted him about his passion for sifting things out: "She ridiculed the painful detail with which my life had always been filled. If I were to ask you to tidy up the gravel round the house, she said, I believe you would take up every little stone and wipe it with a pocket handkerchief!"

It was this hard meticulous desk-work that so furnished his mind that in public he seemed to be omniscient, particularly on matters of Church polity and history. Among those whose lives and times he studied were great churchmen like Archibald Henderson, William Carstares, Thomas Chalmers, Professor Charteris: the subjects ranged from anthropology to the rôle of women in all eras of the Christian Church, the later social history of Scotland, the Reformation, Calvinism, and the relations of Church and State from Constantine onwards. The notes he made, some of them at considerable length, cover such subjects as the function of the Church, the Church and Science, early Evangelism, Hinduism, the Middle Ages, the Puritans, Trades Unionism. If he never seemed to falter in an extempore speech, if his brain seemed always to teem with ideas that were relevant (and at times irrelevant but beguiling), these triumphs, far more than most folk knew, were based on hours of persistent toil in his study.

His methods of work had become habitual in his undergraduate days. He had early learned the art of concentration. He saw that most students went to their work stone-cold and took half an hour or more to warm up to the point when their brains became fully efficient. To John White, bent always upon what was practical, this was a sorry waste of time. He taught himself to sit down to a task and put his brain into top gear with a minimum of delay. His long spells at his desk in the night hours remind one of the tireless vigils of Balzac. In the rapidity with which he absorbed fresh details when presented to him, he surprised some public men—such as Lord Birkenhead—who were themselves reckoned to have first-class brains. Often he left his colleagues in the Church amazed at his skill in disentangling a complexity of detail and in laying before them the salient points of a project.

When he had some particularly heavy task in hand and was able to clear the decks and concentrate upon it for a few days, he would go for peace and seclusion to Houndwood in Berwickshire. There, at the historic grey mansion, the home of his daughter, Mrs. Glen, he would find himself in an atmosphere where he could focus all his mind upon his task. He would wander in the lovely grounds deep in thought, and would work for many hours in a studio set aside for his use. Almost every year as the Assembly weeks approached, he would spend a few days at Houndwood preparing his speeches and refreshing his spirit at a home where welcome always awaited him in the deep green heart of the Merse.

Both in his study and out of it he had always worked himself to the limit. "Nobody ever heard him say he was tired," wrote one of his assistants. "I have sat with him in his vestry at The Barony, he upright in his chair—I never knew him to use the sofa—after a heavy day of committee work and other appointments. He must have left home at least fourteen hours before, but he would welcome a visitor as freshly as he would in mid-forenoon." In all that efficient organisation of his life, his fault was in his failure to relax. The daemon that drove him so ruthlessly left him little time in his earlier years to enjoy the full felicity of his family life. At intervals, after draining his strength too drastically, he broke down. His own illnesses he never seemed to have been able to understand. Enforced convalescence he found intolerably irksome: it seemed to him preposterous that he could not walk straight from his sick-room to a pulpit or a platform. Friends pitied members of his household when he was ill: it was well known that he was a bad patient, and over-estimated his own strength and was too ready, save in his later years, to brush aside the detaining hand of a doctor. He was over eighty when he wrote to a friend who was receiving medical treatment: "Don't take these specialists too seriously. They have too gloomy a view. If I had listened to them, I would have been on the shelf fourteen years ago. . . ." Such was the resilience of his spirit.

II

In April 1945, John White married Miss Anne Calderwood Woodside. Theirs had been a long association in the work of the Church. She had been a member of the headquarters staff of the Church of Scotland and had been appointed Organiser of the Church Extension movement. Very soon John White had come to depend upon her to smooth down difficulties and to keep him informed of the progress of events. In the great task he had undertaken, Anne Woodside by her enthusiasm and ability had made for herself a unique place as his personal assistant, and among her many tasks was that of addressing women's meetings and pleading the cause of Church Extension. She was a daughter of the manse and had been brought up to regard her duty to the Church as paramount. Her father, the Rev. David Woodside, D.D., minister at Woodlands United Free Church, Glasgow, was the author of a history of the United Presbyterian Church which has never been superseded. She was a granddaughter of Professor Henry Calderwood, who had occupied the chair of Moral Philosophy at Edinburgh University and whose influence upon those ministers who had studied under him had been profound and permanent. It was Professor Calderwood's wise words in season which had significantly pointed the way to Presbyterian unity in Scotland. Anne Woodside brought to the lonely house at Partickhill a new colour and warmth—and a great devotion.

More than had ever before been possible, there were afternoons when John White could relax. He would sit and look down over the valley of the Clyde from the height on which his house stood—the house with its steep garden and the rockery he had himself made—enjoying one of the occasional mild cigarettes he now permitted himself, but a wisp of a memory of the famous tobacco mixture that bore his own name.[1] He would dip into a favourite book—Amiel's Journal never lost its appeal for him—or he would meditate quietly or talk to his wife of some of the might-have-beens. Of none of these did he ever speak with the faintest touch of regret.

When Ramsay MacDonald had died in November 1937, John White had been pressed to allow his name to be put forward to represent the Scottish Universities in Parliament. It was widely felt that it would be a good thing for a prominent Scottish churchman to be one of the three University members in the House of Commons. Many considered that his close association with University life, as well as his "mastery of affairs and powerful personality", made him particularly suitable. The press took up the suggestion and supported it.[2] The opportunity of becoming a member of the House of Commons would have been tempting to many people, but John White saw that his duty to the Church lay in a very different direction. Some of his friends felt that a suitable appointment for him was the Principalship of St. Mary's College, St. Andrews. They hoped that, from the quiet haven in Fife, he would be able to carry out his work on Church Extension with more freedom than he could have had in Glasgow as senior minister of The Barony. The prospect of life in an old University had a special appeal to him, and he recalled how one of his early ambitions had been to follow an academic career in a theological college of the Church. The suggestion that he should become head of St. Mary's College seemed like a return to an early love. But John White

[1] He had even been ordered to stop smoking. In his own words, "the doctor said to me, you can choose between tobacco and Church Extension," and so his great collection of pipes was put away. He had immensely enjoyed the tobacco which had been blended to his own taste from five different kinds of leaf and was eventually placed on the market as "Dr. White's Glasgow Presbyterian Mixture—as smoked by the Prime Minister." It was through Lord Haldane that it came to the notice of Stanley Baldwin, who for many years smoked nothing else. "The mixture is one of my only claims to fame," said John White, "and I am sorry to say it always ends in smoke."

[2] Dr. White had received honorary degrees from three of the four Scottish Universities: D.D. and LL.D. (Glasgow), LL.D. (Edinburgh), D.D. (St. Andrews).

was essentially a Barony man, and it was his deep and abiding wish that he would be a Barony man to the end. Yet another might-have-been he would talk about in a whimsical vein. In the course of discussion about the reform of the House of Lords, some said that the Church of Scotland should be represented by at least one prominent clergyman: and John White had been asked if he would allow himself to be installed with Anglican bishops on the benches of the Upper House if such a reform should be accomplished. While he had no regrets over any of these, there were other projects he would fain have carried out:

"My way of life was so ruled," he said, "that my planning had to be set aside for some immediate task for the Church or for the country. As I look back now, I realise that this regret is very wrong. Our lives are in God's hands. It is His Will and purposes that we must obey, and not with demur but with readiness. Surely I have had abundant cause for thankfulness that I have been summoned to do something, not in my own strength and limited wisdom, but under Divine leading, to advance the business of the Church in which I am an ordained servant. This is a heartening thought that leads to a searching of the mind and to a deep sense of humility."

In these quiet hours of looking back, which always sweetened the tasks of the day, John White would sometimes contemplate the changes he had seen in his life. He followed a happy impulse to record some of them.

"I see a great difference in the dress of ministers," he wrote. "Often it is impossible nowadays to recognise by their dress whether a man is a minister or a respectable elder. Often the clerical collar is removed as being a class distinction—surely a mistake, since it is more a vocational badge. . . . I have seen many social changes which, I think, have affected church attendance. In my early years the velocipede was popular, then came the penny-farthing bicycle, then the safety-bicycle, and the motor-bicycle, and then the motor-car. What followed the motor-car? The week-end habit, the break-up of the unity of the home and the *occasional* attendance at church—and the excuse that there is really no time for church work. . . . From monarchies I have watched the change to republicanism and totalitarianism. I have seen the rise of many new ideologies. But to me more thought-compelling is the change I have seen from an unquestioning acceptance of the orthodox message of the Church to a secular rationalism,

Hedonism, and the New Psychology which appeared to succeed in their attacks on religion. In my years at the University, the Church was strong in the land. But a great and sudden change took place. The Church was soon in the Valley of Humiliation. In my Shettleston days the new rationalist was out-thinking the old champion of ortho-doxy. It was a hard time for the young minister. The attack grew worse when I was at South Leith. It reached its height in my early years at The Barony. All the forces that had been attacking religion and the Church seemed to gather strength. Then about the time of the Union, there came a recovery of the Church's prestige and influence. Men realised that the Church had something pregnant to say, some part in the shaping of the new age. Our theological writers began to provide for the masses a reasonable statement of the Christian faith in relation to the new scientific thought. Christianity had become intellectually respectable once more. A writer in the *Quarterly Review* actually said: 'The Reformation is nothing compared with what has been going on in the Church lately.' And I have seen in the last decade or so an even greater spirit of hope and enthusiasm in many depart-ments of life and thought in the Church."

III

There were those who said that John White was a High churchman. This reputation sprang from his anxiety that church services should be conducted with dignity and a vigilant regard for the long traditions of the Church of Scotland. On pulpit robes he placed stress; his gift to new assistants on their ordination had always been a stole. At the beginning of the century, he had introduced Holy Week Services at South Leith—an innovation that had startled many a staid Presbyterian. At The Barony, he gradually made the services more elaborate than they had been. The Amen was sung throughout; the Lord's Prayer and Creed were chanted; at the morning service there was also a prose psalm and an introit. As he thought fit, he would use a prayer from one or other of the Books of Common Order. When he began to make changes, he upset some of the more conservative office-bearers. One old elder waited upon him at the vestry: "Dr. Marshall Lang likit a high kind o' service," he said, "and we stoppit him. So did Dr. Martin and we stoppit him. Now, Maister White—"

"Just a moment, my friend," John White interrupted genially. "I don't want to prove you a false prophet."

Some years later, when the same elder was living on the outskirts of Glasgow and was too old to make the long journey to the centre of the city each Sunday, he wrote to John White:

"I much regret I cannot worship with you now, and how I miss your fine service at The Barony."

In his conduct of a Communion Service, his deep recognition of the awe and wonder of the Sacrament was felt with a sweet poignance by all who joined him at the Lord's Table. In the parish magazine in all his three charges, he wrote about the meaning of the Sacrament and strove to throw an intenser light upon it. At many of his Communion Services he would have no hymns sung: he preferred the psalms and paraphrases and, as one of his assistants has said, this did have a very real effect in introducing "a sense of tradition and of our spiritual ancestry". He greatly stressed the need for self-preparation before partaking of the Sacrament and the duty to join in the Thanksgiving afterwards. In his liking for the ancient ways in a church service, he had much in common with that friend of his earlier days, Professor Cooper of Glasgow. And along with this desire to return to something of the richness which had been lost in Puritanism and the revolt against episcopacy of the seventeenth century, there was a strong belief in the importance of the sermon. The minister must teach and expound, and he must fervently exhort. In both his hortative and his expository sermons, John White never failed to be forceful. To hear him preach was always something of an adventure: those in the pews never knew quite what to expect from him. Just as Dr. Joseph Parker's shout from the pulpit of the City Temple "God damn Abdul!" rang through London, so talk of John White's "Damn the Kaiser" sermon echoed around Glasgow. If some said he was more effective in the greater liberty of the platform than in the pulpit, his own Barony folk disagreed. Some of them still remember with gratitude a series of sermons he preached on the Lord's Prayer: a landmark in the life of sermon-tasting. A significant series on the Books of the Bible still lingers in the memory of some of the older members, particularly one on Isaiah that revealed the preacher's amazing insight into the mind of the prophet. When he felt it was his duty to admonish, John White preached (as was said) in a series of hammer-blows. From the pulpit he once said:

"Today we pray for the peace of the Church of Christ. We must be clear about the peace we want. There have been times of peace when the Church and the world made friends together, like Herod and

Pilate over a dishonoured Christ. Anything is better than such a peace of death. In this church of ours I see a vast amount of this peace of indifference . . . and it must be broken up."

At the same time, he warned his assistants that they must not say anything from the pulpit which they would be afraid to say to any individual. The person in the pew cannot rise and confute the preacher, so the preacher must not turn his pulpit into a Coward's Castle.

He prepared his sermons with great labour. He would rewrite some passages many times, and in his perusals of the final version he would mark with coloured pencils those phrases he wished to emphasise. Seldom did he depart from the carefully prepared manuscript; but when he did so it was because he was carried away—and then he would rise to the heights. At the opening of a new church at Greenock he became so impassioned by his fervour for Church Extension that he put his manuscript aside and preached a sermon that is still talked of.

> "I had been overawed by Dr. White's great reputation," said one of his assistants, "and when I heard him preach I was surprised that he made no attempt to be 'popular'. His sermon was powerful, it was direct, and you felt he had a tremendous grasp of New Testament doctrine. Every sermon I heard him preach was based on the fundamentals, but they all contained a living message for the times. 'Remember the needs of today,' he would tell us. 'I don't care whether your sermons are extemporaneous. That is a matter for you to decide. But they must be contemporaneous.'"

IV

John White had always been in favour of the Church of Scotland making a simple statement of her Faith. The substance of that Faith was contained in her Subordinate Standards: but these were not readily available to most members of the Church, nor were they easily understood by simple folk. He believed it to be the duty of the Church, in each new age of thought, to restate her Faith in terms of the needs of that age. The substance of it was unchangeable, eternal: but the presentation of it made in the midst of the troubles of the seventeenth century was not necessarily the best presentation for believers and sceptics in the conflicts of the twentieth. He became a member of the committee of the General Assembly appointed to restate the Faith, but the pressure of affairs prevented him from sitting on the sub-committee that hammered out the terms of the restatement, a task which took the best part of two years. Professor Hugh L. Mackintosh, the convener of the committee, wrote to him at the end of 1932, enclosing an advance copy of the draft, and begged him to attend the full committee meeting where it would be discussed. He assured John White that his presence would be a great help to them all: "If you are able to express general approval—no more could be asked at this stage—I can imagine nothing which would better enable us to make headway." John White had some minor criticisms to offer, but he was able to express a cordial approval of the work of the sub-committee, and the General Assembly commended it to all ministers and members of the Church as "an outline of the main articles of Christian belief suitable for the instruction of learners and for the help and guidance of believers". Thus a project for which he had pleaded throughout all his ministry came to fruition in 1935.

His own statements on doctrine made in the course of his preaching were marked by clarity and force. Confronted by the greatest mystery that mankind has ever sought to pierce, he refrained from speculation and his words came arrow-straight from heart and mind when he spoke of "the awful purity, the fatherly justice, the tender compassion of our God". He had little patience with some theologians who had been busily "putting God under enquiry", as he called it,

> "not a very exhilarating exercise for the believing Christian. . . . We are suffering a good deal from this perpetual analysis. We are constantly being told by these theologians that we are living in an age of cold abundant light. Probably this is true, for now and then we do see some ray or flash of it. But at times it does occur to me as I listen to some of the wireless talks that this is also an age of unmitigated twaddle."

He liked to answer in his sermons the questions put to him by individual members of his congregation. He felt that the doubts and difficulties of one were probably shared by others. When there was controversy in Scotland on the offering of prayers for the dead, he preached a sermon that went to the root of the matter. The sermon was reported in the press as a statement on a theme of topical importance, for there had been a "widespread and rapid revival of prayer for the departed", and John White said that it would be most unsatisfactory if it were left to rest on a basis of sentiment instead of on the solid ground of theology. In the vague conjectures of "a larger hope", he said we must not lose sight of the awful requisite of that holiness

"without which no man shall see the Lord. Only the pure in heart can see God. The first charge, then, on our prayers for the departed is that they may be cleansed from their sins and that they will be brought into complete conformity with the Will of Holiness. And there is not only God's Holiness but God's Justice to be thought of. . . . Our blessed Lord, we are taught, made on the cross a 'perfect and sufficient sacrifice'. Perfect and sufficient for what? For releasing men from the consequences of sin? Certainly not. Perfect and sufficient for acquiring grace to reinstate us in an effective Covenant relation with God so that we may work out the penalty of our sins. If it were not so, there could be no justice in the sacrifice of Christ. It would be pure substitution.

"It is here that the doctrine of the Atonement has been so terribly misunderstood," he maintained. "There has been inadequate teaching of the penalty due for sin. By far the greater part of the intellectual revolt against Christianity during the nineteenth century, and not a little of today, centres in the Atonement viewed as substitution instead of a process. If we are making use of God's Grace, we are 'working out our own salvation' with fear and trembling and also with contrition and suffering, with agony and with blood. . . . And what is begun here must go on after death until the uttermost farthing is paid—until the soul is holy and fit for God. What do we know of the sphere in which the work of perfecting is carried on? The Early Church spoke of this place as Purgatory because the first certain thing about it is that it is a place of purgation."

Those members of the Church of Scotland who sat at the feet of John White never had any doubt that his vision of the road to Paradise was not a primrose path.

V

John White will be remembered as a great churchman. He would rather have been born into the Church of Scotland, the Reformed and Presbyterian Church as by law established, than into any other branch of the universal Church. Anything which he regarded as a slight to her as the National Church of Scotland was to him like a physical hurt, and he became at once the Church's champion. He resented the blunders of officialdom in London which had on occasion given the Scottish Episcopal

Church precedence over the Church of Scotland. Some time before the Coronation of King George VI he was a guest of Archbishop Lang at Lambeth Palace, and there was much discussion on how many representatives of the Church of Scotland should be permitted to attend the ceremony. Cosmo Lang said: "I should be delighted, my dear White, if it were possible, to have you given a place in the service."

To this John White replied:

"I could not take part in the Coronation Service even if you could and did invite me. The bishops have to acknowledge the Sovereign as head of their Church. No Church of Scotland minister could do that. This is not a question of loyalty to the King, but of loyalty to the Head of our Church."

In the notes he made on their talk, he stressed that the Archbishop wholeheartedly agreed that the Church of Scotland should be recognised by a place in the Sanctuary. John White suggested that the Moderator and two ex-Moderators should have seats there, but this must not be a mere substitution for those Scots Kirk dignitaries who were by tradition always invited to the Abbey at a Coronation—the Clerks and Procurator. Cosmo Lang was sympathetic but did not have power to make any promise, and he suggested that John White should go to see the Garter Principal King of Arms at the College of Arms in Queen Victoria Street. This official told him that his wishes could not be granted, for all the bishops must be present, and to this John White replied: "Put some of the bishops out." The official then said that the English Royal Chaplains-in-Ordinary must be present.

"Put some of them out, too," said John White. "You have dozens of them. In the past, Coronations have been largely English ceremonies. There must be now a wider representation. The Royal Chaplains in Scotland must be included, so must the Dean of the Chapel Royal from His Majesty's Household in Scotland. I ask you to take note of what I am saying. Too often Scotland has felt she has had the cold shoulder on ceremonial occasions. If she does not have proper representation now, she will feel it deeply. I know you are in a difficult position, and I would not have your job at any price. But I am asking now for something that is of importance to the whole Scottish nation."

Sir Francis Wollaston, the Garter Principal King of Arms, was impressed by the fervour of John White's plea. Before they parted he promised to do all he could to put forward these requests in the proper quarter. John White left on the night train for Glasgow feeling that he had done what he could to win recognition for Scotland's National Church. Next day he received a telegram which read: "*All your demands granted.*"

Another of the clashes John White had with officialdom was over the date of the General Election in 1929. This had been fixed for a day in May while the General Assembly was sitting, and he protested. He roused the Presbytery of Glasgow to send a resolution to the Prime Minister and the Secretary of State for Scotland to object to the way the Church's interests had been disregarded. It had been suggested that the Assembly should meet on the day fixed at the previous Assembly, and should then adjourn for a fortnight so that the General Election and its repercussions would be a thing of the past. Another suggestion was that the Assemblies would rush hastily through their business and rise before the Election took place. John White said he hoped that the two Assemblies[1] would carry out neither of these suggestions.

> "The business of the Church," he said, "is not secondary to that of the State. In this year, above all years, it is of supreme importance. Nothing should be allowed to suffer from undue haste. The Assemblies cannot alter the date of their meeting, whereas the Government has a wide range of possible dates. It is inconceivable that they should disregard the wishes of the representatives of the Scottish Church. . . . It should be made quite clear that the commissioners who have been appointed are obliged to give regular attendance at the Assembly without regard to the election. Their duty is to the Church before any duty to the State."

If the Government persisted in their intention, he declared, then many ministers and elders would not be at home to vote.

The General Election was delayed to 30th May, the day after the Assembly closed.

John White was always very proud of the Church's ancient emblem, the Burning Bush. He studied the history of it, went through the old minutes of the General Assembly and found it was first used in the title-

---

[1] These were to be the last meetings of the two separate Assemblies before the Union.

page of *The Acts of the General Assembly 1690*, when Presbyterian government was restored in the Revolution Settlement. The design had been changed several times in early volumes of the same series, and now and again the motto NEC TAMEN CONSUMEBATUR had been rendered as NOT CONSUMED, a change of which John White did not approve. At the Union in 1929, D. Y. Cameron was asked to harmonise in a comely design the variants of the emblem used by the two Churches, and Sir David's new design was adopted by the union committee. Soon after the end of the Second World War there was a proposal that the Burning Bush be registered as the official emblem of the Church of Scotland and that the Moderator should have his own heraldic arms. The committee appointed to consider it rejected the idea, but under pressure a second committee was asked to give further thought to it. To the dismay of John White, the proposal was this time recommended to the General Assembly and a new design of the Burning Bush had been prepared. This was the occasion of one of the most incisive speeches he ever delivered in the General Assembly. He was over eighty, but he had lost none of his old force or raciness. Members could see he was in his best fighting form, and they leant forward to catch every word. Among those who did not enjoy his withering attack were the members of the committee who had recommended armorial bearings for the Church. At the first glance, said John White, the idea seemed harmless and innocuous.

"It is, in fact, no such thing. Far more is implied in it than meets the eye—far more than the proposers realise. We are told we should register it so that no other Church can use it. Why should another Church not use it? I should not object to this flattering compliment. The old Church of Scotland did not object to the Free Church using it. Nor do we object to the present-day Free Church using it now. Why should we? We are told some other Church might register it and so deprive us of our emblem. But we have used it without interruption for two hundred and fifty-seven years. No court in the land, certainly not the Lyon Court, could take it from us."

The Burning Bush is the emblem of the protecting power of God: he reminded members that it had been adopted after the bitter struggles of the Church in the seventeenth century when the blood of martyrs had stained the heather of the lonely moorlands. The Burning Bush with its motto had been deliberately chosen to mark the spiritual liberty the Church had regained.

"The earthly head of our Church of Scotland is not the reigning monarch, as with the Church of England," he said. "No more loyal subjects of the King exist in the land than members of this Assembly. As citizens, ours is an affectionate loyalty. But as churchmen, our first loyalty is to the General Assembly, which is the earthly fount of authority of our Church. The proposed armorial bearings can have no meaning whatever unless you wish to displace the General Assembly and substitute the King as the earthly head of this Church. Do you wish to do that?"

Impressively, he read the Act which vested authority in the Assembly, and then he asked:

"Is it possible that this Assembly will be a party to a proposal that would jeopardise a freedom won with so great suffering? Do you wish to see the Church with armorial bearings registered at the Lyon Court of Arms alongside corporations, boroughs, councils, and Episcopal Sees? In all these cases the insignia is but a fiction.

"Let us remain satisfied with the Armorial Bearings of the Epistle to the Ephesians! *Wherefore take unto you the whole armour of God that ye may be able to withstand in the evil day . . . having on the breastplate of righteousness . . . taking the shield of faith wherewith ye shall be able to quench all the fiery darts of the wicked. And take the helmet of salvation and the sword of the Spirit which is the Word of God.* There we have the spiritual power that makes the bush a BURNING bush!"

The proposal was dropped. The Burning Bush remained, not as a heraldic symbol but as an emblem of the protecting power of God.

VI

John White was a master of Assembly procedure. There was a time when he had hoped to become a Clerk of Assembly, but he was to find wider scope for his gifts. As chairman of the Business Committee of the General Assembly of the Church of Scotland, he was "leader" of the Assembly for the three years before the union; for two years, he shared the position jointly with Principal Martin; and thereafter, it was an exceptional year when he was not present to lead the House, and even when he was no longer officially the leader, he was still acknowledged to be the father of the Assembly in influence and personal prestige. In 1934 the

Moderator felt moved to pay him a tribute to which many another
Moderator would have gladly subscribed. "Very especially I am indebted
to the leader of the House, Dr. John White, who with sleepless vigilance,
patient thoroughness, wise guidance at critical moments, has kept the
business of the Assembly and myself in order." There were indeed members who felt that his leadership could be at times a trifle over-powering.
On one occasion when he rose and said, "I would not presume to *dictate* to
the Assembly, but—" the rest of the sentence was lost in a gale of laughter.
But few there were who could not agree that, by his guidance, the business
of the Assembly was transacted in a statesmanlike way and much time
was saved by his swift decisions and forethought.

"You are the only man to lead," D. Y. Cameron wrote to him.
"I find the clergy, as a rule, almost indifferent to anything outwith
congregational interests and untouched by the greater issues. The
closed door, the dust-sheets, the absence of the cross, wound me and
turn many of the finest spirits away from our national Church. Do
make the Assembly a place of spiritual power, not merely a chamber
recording what is already printed. *You* alone can do that. It is your
mission."

Sir David Cameron, who had given of his time and substance to the
Church, was one of her best-known and most respected elders. John
White's influence among the elders of the Church was noticeable, and
time and again it was seen that when he stood up to vote a great concourse
of elders followed him. Since they constituted half the membership of the
Assembly, he had a personal following of immense weight when it came
to a division.

"There are some men I always love to hear speak in the Assembly,"
he once said. "There are speakers you *can't* listen to, speakers you *can*
listen to, and speakers you *can't help* listening to. Some speakers hold the
Assembly, some the Assembly hold, some the Assembly cannot hold."
From the first day when he had risen to speak as a young minister he had
held the Assembly. Sir James Fergusson, Bt., Keeper of the Records of
Scotland, said of one Assembly he had attended:

"Of the speakers I heard there was only one real orator—and he
was that veteran, the Very Rev. Dr. John White. When he presented
the report of the National Church Extension Committee he broke the
Assembly's rule about the length of speeches by going on for about

thirty-five minutes. But it felt like ten—unlike the speeches of some people that last for ten minutes and feel like thirty-five. Dr. White was, if I may use the word, terrific. He swayed us, he inspired us, he lashed us. 'Men must come to believe,' he declared, 'that the Church is the greatest thing on God's earth—and that no one can afford to be outwith it.' That *was* a speech. There's something about Dr. White's delivery that makes you think of the weight and drive of history and tradition behind the General Assembly. The harsh strength of his voice, his burning eyes, his great sweeping gestures, and his long-drawn vowels somehow made me think of the giants of the past, men like Knox and Henderson and Peden. I could imagine Dr. White preaching in a conventicle, with the wind singing among the heather and the dragoons prowling beyond the hill. Like the stately procedure of the opening day, with the thrilling sound of two thousand voices uplifted in the one hundred and forty-seventh psalm to the tune of Dunfermline, he made the whole past of the Church of Scotland real and vivid: its struggles and its triumphs, its sufferings and its strength—the strength of the bush that burned with fire and yet was not consumed."

VII

When John White went to London at the invitation of Archbishop Lang to address the Lambeth Conference, he was asked by the Bishop of Gloucester if the Moderator of the General Assembly of the Church of Scotland was simply elected as a chairman.

"I was much concerned about what lay behind that question," he said afterwards, "and on my return I consulted with Church leaders and made an important change in the ceremonial at the opening of the Assembly. We arranged to have the Moderator *installed* in his office. It is now one of the most impressive functions of the opening day."

Prior to 1934, the new Moderator had taken his chair with a minimum of ceremonial, but on the installation of Dr. P. D. Thomson the ritual had a richer significance. After the new Moderator had been escorted through the midst of his brethren, who stood to welcome him, the retiring Moderator offered him the right hand of fellowship, then removed the Moderatorial ring from his own hand and placed it upon the index finger of the right hand of his successor in office. He then offered personal words of initiation and blessing and stepped down to allow the new Moderator to take his place. No longer could an English bishop have cause to ask whether the Moderator of the General Assembly was but an elected chairman. John White's description of the opening of each day's session shows his own reverence for the person and functions of the occupant of the chair of honour:

> "A visitor to the General Assembly is always impressed by the loud clear announcement made by the Assembly Officer—*The Moderator!* It means more than the entry of a presiding minister: it brings the whole Assembly to their feet in hushed stillness as they return the bow of the Moderator—a threefold salutation on his part to embrace all sections of the great Council of the Church."

He had decided views on the development of the supreme office to which a minister of the Church could be elevated. There was a day when his duties had been simple compared with what is now expected of him. In the eighteenth century, as often as not, he was a stern autocrat and permitted outspoken words only from those to whom he thought the brethren should listen. Today he has a gentle hand, and it is not often that he has to intervene sternly to keep order. Moreover, he is expected to have a working knowledge of the complicated ecclesiastical law and procedure. As John White said:

> "It is generally admitted by distinguished visitors—among them the leading members of the Houses of Parliament—that the conduct of our business is not surpassed by that of any other Council in the nation. We have had Lord High Commissioners who, prepared for a spell of boredom, expressed regret that their many outside duties deprived them of the pleasure of listening to more of the debates."

He was greatly concerned over the long and exacting programme of visitations and ceremonies now regarded as part of a Moderator's duty throughout his year of office. Looking back to the days before 1900, he pointed out that there were three Moderators for the various bodies that eventually united. He calculated that within the first half of the twentieth century the list of Moderators had been reduced by exactly seventy—

> "with a consequent loss," he added significantly, "in the superintendence of the Church . . . and in view of the immense pressure of responsible tasks a Moderator has now to undertake, he might be justified in refusing the invitation to moderate. I had this in mind when,

in 1924, I suggested to the General Assembly that the Moderator should be chosen not from the senior ministers of the Church—for whom it has become a premature and not merely a splendid form of Christian burial—but from the younger ministers, who are at an age of physical vigour."

He refrained from adding that his brethren must have taken his words to heart; for in the following year, a mere stripling of fifty-seven, he was elected Moderator.

Never the man to do things by halves, he made a more strenuous Moderatorial tour than any predecessor had ever done. He decided to make a special report on the matter to the next General Assembly, and as convener of the Church and Nation Committee he did so. He did not suggest that Moderatorial visitation should cease, but rather that it should be curtailed to a reasonable limit. What he proposed was a rota of Assembly Deputies, and that ex-Moderators should be specially commissioned by the Assembly and be given the duty of visiting the Synods which the Assembly might select. The Deputies, he felt sure, would be given a welcome hardly less cordial than that which he had received during his year of office. It followed that the functions of these Assembly Deputies would be, as he said, "more intimate in their nature and more restricted in their area than those of the Moderator of the year". That the visitation of presbyteries and parishes should be reduced was the last thought in his mind. On the contrary, he urged that it should be increased: "This would bring all parts of the great community forming the Church of Scotland into a clearer consciousness of their organic unity and would banish all sense of separation that comes through geographical apartness." He was deeply conscious, from his personal experience of visiting manses in lonely parishes, that too often "a depression is apt to accompany a solitary and unrecognised ministry in the distant outposts—and the Assembly Deputies would convey a message of cheer and stimulus from the supreme Court of the Church".

In John White's mind, the whole question of visitation by Assembly representatives was tied up with that of a closer superintendence of the work of the Church in parishes. He felt that this superintendence was urgently needed. He felt that presbyteries should exercise a close episcopal oversight of all the congregations within their bounds. He admitted that the weakness of the existing superintendence of presbyteries was that it was exercised by a plurality of individuals, with the result that the responsibility of taking the first step in a case where superintendence was required was not the responsibility of any one person: "Everybody's business is apt to be nobody's business."

There were times when he wondered whether this duty of super-intendence should be delegated in part to the synods. More than once the action of certain of the synods had roused his wrath. "There have been times," he wrote in 1937, "when instead of seeking to strengthen the synods I have wondered if it would not be better to scrap them as being a menace to the good government of the Church." Towards the end of his life, he gave a good deal of thought to the function of synods: he asked himself whether they could serve a more useful purpose than they had been doing. By an act of the Church, the moderator of a synod "*may* be appointed to visit, during his term of office, the various districts within the bounds of the province with a view to giving advice or stimulating interest in the work of the Church". Here was an opportunity for that superintendence which he had so vehemently urged.

"If that visitation has ever been carried out," he said, "I have never heard of it. How valuable it would be if the moderator of a synod were specially chosen with this great and important duty to discharge. . . . At the time of the union, I suggested that the synod should be desig-nated a Provincial Assembly. I said it should meet every autumn when the Life and Work programme for the winter is being drafted, and that a moderator should be appointed for not less than one year. . . . Has not the time come," he demanded, "for the Church of Scotland to ask itself in all seriousness whether there is not much in its organisation and its methods that calls for drastic revision?"

From his earliest days he had been an innovator. Just as, in his Shettles-ton ministry, he had accepted the new cycling craze and had met it by holding an early-morning service for cyclists each Sunday in the summer; just as he had been the first minister to take a magic lantern into a prison to add interest to a lecture; just as he agreed that the first Church service to be broadcast in Scotland would be transmitted from The Barony: so when mankind entered suddenly upon the new atomic age he took this miracle as the spearhead of a sermon broadcast on Remembrance Sunday in 1946. "The new world that is being thrust upon us will need a new religious outlook, a new intellectual outlook, a new social and economic and political outlook." The creation of this new outlook he regarded as one of the urgent tasks of the Church of Christ.

VIII

In advocating some of his proposed reforms, or in putting forward new ideas, John White has been criticised for going ahead without regard for the opinion of other people—of being swept on by his own enthusiasm. It was indeed fortunate for the Church of Scotland that he was thus carried away by his fervour for many of the causes he espoused. "When two courses are open," he once said to an assistant in a moment of ardour, "choose the more venturesome"; and one of the greatest of his own adventures which he began against the advice of many colleagues was the opening of the fund for Church Extension in the dark days of trade depression. He sometimes quoted Bernard Shaw's words, "The reasonable man adapts himself to the world, the unreasonable one persists in trying to adapt the world to himself; therefore all progress depends on the unreasonable man." And he would add: "I may be unreasonable, but—" and then he would make some formidable demand which he would proceed to prove was entirely reasonable and which could be fulfilled with a little honest effort. At a meeting after the dedication of a new hall-church, a speaker said with a twinkle in his eye that Dr. John White had a bee in his bonnet about Church Extension. John White interrupted: "You're wrong. I've got a whole skep of them—thank God!" That particular skep of bees hummed for many fruitful years.

Some said he had a bee in his bonnet about the architecture of the new churches and hall-churches that were being erected. This could be simple and functional, yet comely, he said, and he deplored the appearance of many modern churches which might be anything from a factory to a super-cinema. He had scrutinised with care the plans for the new Shettleston Parish Church, which is today a permanent memorial of his ministry there, and in 1933 he supported the formation of the Advisory Committee on Artistic Questions of which his friends D. Y. Cameron and Dr. Millar Patrick were the first joint conveners. When an architect came into his office in St. Vincent Street, Glasgow, to present plans for a new church, John White looked at them critically. On such occasions he did not pause to use soft words. "I don't like them," he said. The architect replied that, for his part, he thought his plans were rather good—they were tremendously modern and made you open your eyes.

"Precisely," said John White. "Tell me, young man, is the building you propose to put up going to look like a church? The other day I visited one of those you are supposed to have designed. Frankly, I looked around me and asked, 'Is this a church, or is it St. Enoch's Railway Station?' "

He had always a kindly eye for the doric simplicity of little country kirks of any denomination. To him the criterion was whether they were conducive to quiet worship. But the church that meant more to him than any other was The Barony. He loved every stone of it, and upon it he left his insignia in the form of some uncommonly fine stained glass, the work of the late Herbert Hendrie. Two windows he gave in memory of his daughter Margaret and two in memory of his son who was killed in the First World War; a fifth window, dedicated in 1939, marked the jubilee of the present building, and above and below the figure of St. Mungo, Glasgow's patron saint, are wrought the initials of John Marshall Lang, who built the church, and his own. A number of windows were given by other people at John White's request; and the magnificent chancel window of three lights was erected by his own effort to the former ministers of The Barony from the sixteenth century up to 1936. His own gift of money at the time of his ministerial jubilee, together with a subsequent gift, was used by Mr. Sanderson to replace a light in the Cunliffe Chapel by a window to the memory of John White's first wife, Margaret Gardner White. The War Memorial, unveiled in October 1921, was erected under his supervision, and indeed his conferences and correspondence with the architect, Dr. Macgregor Chalmers, show how keen was the interest he took in every detail. The great cross stands outside the church, looking down Castle Street, and in the Cunliffe Chapel is a plaque set on the wall with a sword and a wreath in bronze and the name of the fallen engraved upon a panel. Among his gifts to The Barony were a gold chalice and platter which had been presented to him by his assistants in 1925, when he first was Moderator of the General Assembly. Another gold chalice, presented by assistants on his jubilee in 1943, he also gave to The Barony for use in Communion Services held in the peaceful intimacy of the Cunliffe Chapel, which had always so movingly appealed to him for the celebration of the Sacrament. What he gave he gave with pride and with gratitude: for he was mindful always of what Barony folk had given to him in loyalty and affection. He was never surprised in his travels in many parts of the world to come across someone who had associations with his own kirk, and it warmed his heart to meet those who had been children of The Barony. On his return home he would tell in his sermons of these encounters and he would ask his folk: "Are we quite sure, all of us, that we appreciate The Barony as we should?" It would have been one of the great tragedies in his life if, when he was forced to give up his parochial work in 1935 in the interests of Church Extension, he had cut all ties with the church and with the congregation whose call he had been so proud to accept.

IX

By many people, particularly in his middle years, John White was misunderstood. His plain speaking was not to the taste of everyone, and he had a way of talking about sin that was like a sharp probe to the conscience. In the face of sheer stupidity or met by the delaying tactics of the obstructionist he could be withering. Not everybody knew of his tender side, of the warm generosity of his heart. It was as if some form of reserve would hold him aloof at times; and those who did not have the chance to know the man could never have guessed how fully he gave of himself where a lonely or a saddened heart hungered for some human touch. However terse were his letters on all matters of business, it seemed that he allowed his pen freedom when he was writing to offer solace or to revive hope. He would thus write to fellow ministers whom he knew but slightly, and he would write as a friend. "He had the gift of bestowing real friendship on the ordinary rank and file like myself," wrote a minister, "and one never left his presence without a deepening of the urge to do more and do better for the Church."

One very simple incident may perhaps show how he could be moved by a sudden impulse to perform a gracious and memorable action. A member of St. George's Parish Church in Edinburgh describes it:

"In the first Sunday of October 1932, our church was reopened after decoration, and the Rev. Dr. White officiated and preached the sermon. I admired Dr. White's preaching but thought he was stern to the point of harshness. Near the front, among the worshippers, was Miss McMeechan, a retired Church Sister, over eighty years of age. Dr. White had met her in his Home Mission work, and he noticed her among the worshippers. When he came down from the pulpit to give a special talk to the congregation he said, 'Before I give the address I should like to shake hands with Miss McMeechan, that valued servant of our Church.' He went to her and greeted her, and his kindly smile transformed his expression completely and revealed the kind heart of the man behind his stern exterior."

JOHN WHITE

Dr. George S. Gunn, today one of Edinburgh's most notable and scholarly ministers, tells of his experience at the General Assembly of 1945. He was due to present his first report as convener of the Foreign Mission Committee.

"I met Dr. White in a corridor of the Assembly on the evening before that report was due. 'Well, tomorrow is your big day,' he said to me. I replied that I anticipated it with great trepidation because I had never before spoken a single word in the General Assembly. 'Incredible!' he said. Next morning, before the debate started, Dr. White came round and sat beside me, and I felt he was doing this to sustain me before my ordeal. After a few moments he said to me, 'I could not get it out of my mind that you are to present one of the biggest reports of the Church and have never before spoken in the Assembly. I just want to let you know that I set aside time this morning to pray for you.'"

It was in quiet ways, in the midst of his bustling life, that John White was able to give comfort and a benediction: and he was conscious too that, in ways which he had never foreseen, God had directed him to His own ends. He recorded an incident in which he felt afterwards that he had been Divinely guided.

"One stormy night a gale was blowing and I had to make a visit in Black Street. As I fought my way along Parliamentary Road, which was lonely and deserted in that tempestuous night, a man staggered from an entry and began to walk, or rather stumble, close behind me. This gave me a very eerie feeling. Quickly stepping aside, I told him to go on ahead for I didn't like someone breathing down my neck. His answer came thickly, and I saw he had been taking too much drink. He must have recognised who I was, for he said, 'Please, Doctor, let me go on behind you. I can walk straighter when I'm close up to you.' The poor fellow had not been able to get along by himself in the storm. 'All right,' I said, 'I'm glad to know I can be of some help. Give me your arm and tell me where you're going to. . . .' It is not always the help one can give in big undertakings that one is proud to remember, but the quiet chance of giving direction and guidance—yes, and comfort and confidence—to the man who is down and out."

His heart was uplifted when he was told he had given comfort and confidence at a time of spiritual distress to a man who later became one of his own assistants. The Rev. John Swan has related how he had greatly wished to dedicate his life to the ministry of the Church but had lacked the courage to tell his father of it. He was then working in a business in which his father had a financial interest, and he was afraid that his father would strongly disapprove of his leaving it.

"One afternoon Dr. White came down to the West Church to speak to the young men. Well do I remember his text from the last chapter of Joshua, *Choose ye the one ye shall serve.* Dr. White told us that, when we had made a choice, we would usually find that the obstacles were but imaginary things that existed only in one's own mind. That very Sunday night, moved by the dynamic force of Dr. White, I spoke to my father. I told him I wanted to enter the ministry. To my surprise, he received the news with the warmest sympathy. Dr. White's words had been true. In many a vital choice, the obstacles against your going forward are of your own imagining. Here was one of his greatest gifts. I would not call him an imaginative man, but that tremendous force of his personality so very often, as I learned when I became his assistant, gave others the strength to do what they had been too timid or weak even to contemplate."

Many people have spoken of how he gave them courage. The Rev. A. G. Stewart of Troon wrote of his first contact with John White:

"I was an undergraduate at the time, and I met him on the summit of Cairngorm with a company of about twenty other people. Drenching mist blew up just before we hit the cairn and no one could see a yard, but they all rallied on call and soon we had reached it. With the help of my compass, Dr. White began to lead the party down the mountainside—down through two thousand five hundred feet of blinding, clinging curtains of mist till we emerged, all together, only five hundred feet above our base and dead on the line. . . . It was like that always with Dr. White in the Union Committee and everywhere else. All Scotland should sing the Te Deum and the Gloria in Excelsis for the greatest of her sons since John Knox."

In giving advice to his assistants, which he did like a father imparting worldly wisdom to a son, his apothegms were pointed and memorable. One was: "*Never take a weak case forward;* never shoot except to kill!" Another was a piece of advice he had himself received as a young minister from the lawyer who had opposed him in the Shettleston Church Case and who had taken a strong personal liking to him. It was guidance on the wise conduct of a controversy: *"Concentrate on your strongest point."* Never support your strong point with weaker ones, he said, for an opposing counsel would seize upon them, tear them to shreds, and your strongest one would be forgotten. Yet another was: *"In any conflict, try to keep a short front line."* He explained the wisdom of not attempting to advance on too wide a front unless one has overwhelming forces; by keeping a short front line, the objective might be attained. He gave this advice on handling a congregation: *"Keep them busy."* A congregation is never more harmonious, he declared, than when members are up to the neck in work. On the great task of Christianising the land, he insisted on the need for the closest contact in the fight against apathy and paganism and Godless Communism: *"You cannot fight from a distance, you must enter the fray with a short sword."*

At the same time, he had little relish for the rôle of adviser-in-chief to those who sought guidance on matters they should have been able to settle for themselves. When a minister came to him in some agitation and said that a senior elder had been criticising him bitterly for not doing enough work in the parish, and asked what he should do about it, John White replied: "You can do one of two things, my friend. You must either work harder—or pray that the Lord will remove your critic." He knew the elder by name, and happened to read of his death a little later. Meeting the minister, he greeted him with: "Well, I see you've been praying!"

He corresponded over a long period of years with a number of notable people who seemed never to let many months pass without posing a problem to him. Letters on Church and personal matters were frequently exchanged with his friend Lady Frances Balfour, a devoted member of the London church of St. Columba. The Hon. Victoria Bruce, daughter of his old friend Lord Balfour of Burleigh, was actively interested in social reform, particularly in improvements in prisons, and she found in John White a supporter whose personal experience as a chaplain at Barlinnie Prison and his knowledge of the seamy side of life were often of help to her in her work. Of the letters he received from Lord Elgin, many of them began, *"My* Moderator, I always come to you for advice. . . ." Their friendship had been cemented in 1925 when John White had for the first time been Moderator of the General Assembly while Lord Elgin was Lord High Commissioner. With many members of the Royal Family his association was close and personal, and his visits as a bidden guest to Balmoral were more numerous than the accustomed number paid by

Royal Chaplains in Scotland. "You are a prime favourite in that quarter," wrote one who was in daily touch with the Royal Family.

It would be impossible to complete any account of John White's friendships without a special mention of his relations with children. He took great pleasure in his many child friendships; and as he advanced in years, his response to children grew more and more quick and tender. Not that he was ever sentimental over them: he would never give a child too much rope—on the contrary, he believed in firm training and insisted on the value of Sunday School and Bible Class. "I sometimes think," he said, "that the modern plea for youth to have its way is far too strong. Nowadays, everything must be made attractive for the young. Everything must be made easy for the young. Discipline must be relaxed for the young. And all this is usurping the preaching of the Gospel."

To one of his granddaughters he wrote:

"I hope you will soon be coming forward to have your Baptismal Vows confirmed and to take your place at the Holy Table of Communion. Some folks call this 'joining the Church', but that is misleading, for you are already a member of the Church by baptism. You must however come forward and have confirmation. The first Communion is one of the most important steps in the religious life of a member of the Church. It should not be too long deferred. Sixteen or seventeen is a suitable age. If you read St. Luke, Chapter Two, verses forty-one to fifty-two, you will discover that Jesus at the age of twelve entered the Church. This may seem a very serious letter to you, but that is because it deals with a very responsible duty to be faced: but I do wish you a very joyous and gladsome time. . . . Goodbye and heaps of love from GRANDFATHER."

X

The Assembly of May 1951, the last which John White attended, was for him richly rewarding and inspiring. He had been too ill to attend in the previous year; and now when he rose to speak on Church Extension, he received one of the greatest ovations of his life. In the applause there was a spontaneous and generous warmth which revealed the affection of all for a trusted leader. He gave in many reports during that Assembly, including those on the Integration of the Iona Community with the Church, on the Remarriage of Divorced Persons, on Building Licences, and on War Damage. All this was a great strain to him, but he showed how gallantly he could respond to a challenge. He told the Assembly that, since the May of the previous year, he had spent over two hundred thousand pounds in building sanctuaries for the people, while twenty-two other buildings were in the course of erection, and the cost would be nearly three hundred and eighty thousand pounds. The million pounds for which he had already called would not suffice, he said: the Church must give more.

"I am thinking of starting a bricklayers' association," he added. "Each member will be asked to provide one brick every week. A brick costs twopence. If every member of the Church would give me a brick, it would amount in one year to more than half a million pounds! If one and all of us, fearing God and working hard, would grasp what is meant by Church Extension—not merely stone and lime, but sanctuaries for three and a half million migrants—there will be an abundant outpouring of riches for this great cause."

That he had stirred the Assembly was clearly shown by the response to his ringing words. Many who were never to see him again in the flesh carried with them a sharp memory of this aged but vital and dominating figure who, in his eighty-fourth year, could inspire and incite his hearers as vehemently as he had ever done in the days of his strength.

He had a good deal of work to do after that Assembly, and he was looking forward in August to a fishing holiday on Speyside with his wife. The day before he was due to travel north he told her he was not feeling well, and she helped him to settle down by the fire for a rest. When she was leaving the room he called after her: "I haven't looked out my fishing tackle. . . ." She assured him she would see to it. A few minutes later, something made her come hurrying back into the room—a room in which there was, as she expressed it, a terrible silence. John White had slept peacefully away. Speyside, where he had spent so many tranquil hours beside gleaming pools and rushets, had been among the last pictures in his mind. Quiet was the passing of a prince of the Scottish Kirk.

Indeed a prince of the Kirk: a well-kent figure among church-folk of many lands: but in any true assessment of him there must needs be a word about that which dwelt deep in the spirit of the man. "I can never forget that sense of faith which he always communicated to me," said the Rev. Roy Sanderson; "indeed he was a great churchman—but he was Christ's man first and foremost." Dr. Robert Mackintosh, one of the closest of all his friends, said: "I have known no greater man, nor have I known anyone with such humble and deep faith—those of us who knew him best knew how simple and strong was that faith." And it was in that God-given faith that lay the well-spring of his strength.

He has himself told how he received that gift of faith. His words were broadcast, and were permanently recorded so that they may be heard again by a listening people. On the first day of May, some three and a half months before he died, he was invited by the British Broadcasting Corporation to give a talk on the theme, "Why I Believe". He hesitated, then replied: "At first I was very much against it, as I do not like to open up the secret chambers for public inspection. I have reconsidered the matter, and I will do what I can."

Later, on Tuesday, 7th August, he telephoned to the Rev. Ronald Falconer, Organiser of Religious Broadcasting in Scotland, and said he was prepared to record this message on the following day. He spoke urgently; there must be no delay, he said. On Wednesday he arrived at Broadcasting House in Glasgow before the appointed hour and asked to be taken at once to the room where his words were to be recorded. Mr. Falconer described what then happened:

"I hurried to the studio, and there I found him already seated and at work on his script. He looked up and greeted me, then with a peculiar intensity added, 'I *must* do this talk—and at once!' From then until he left the building I was aware of a strange urgency in all he said and did —an urgency which his frailty of body made significant . . . the body so very frail—the mind and unconquerable spirit as alert and burning as brightly as ever!"

Of his own deep faith John White said in the course of that talk:

"It came to me as it does to most—in a flash and as a result of long and serious thought. I got moral certainty in place of a defective logical proof. *I met a Man.* ECCE HOMO! He did not speak to me in abstract syllogisms. He revealed the Grace and Truth of God in a human life. . . . Without Him I would still be groping. At that stage of my life I gave up the study of the law for the Gospel and entered the Church. In this change I was guided, compelled by that revelation of the Christ when He said: 'You have not chosen me—but I have chosen you!' . . . Life would be a tragedy—and a mockery of all that God has done for us in Christ—if life were bounded by this time and space world. I must believe that a new order of life will be mine. Eternal Life, which is something more than endless existence, is one of the most constant promises of the New Testament. It means a full life, spiritual felicity and an unwearied service. . . . The Christian is surely anchored to the steadfast rock of Christ's assurance: 'I am the Resurrection and the Life; he that believeth in Me, though he were dead yet shall he live; and whosoever liveth and believeth in Me shall never die. . . . I go to prepare a place for you, that where I am there ye may be also.' Yes, if it were not so, He would have told us."

"When Dr. White spoke of his belief in immortality," continued Mr. Falconer, "and read the triumphant death-defying words which we use so often in our Christian burial service, one knew that he was already of the Immortals. He was as moved as we were. . . . Twelve days later he entered into the Nearer Presence."

John White's recorded words were not broadcast until after his body had been laid to rest.

Those who had sat at his feet as members of the congregations to which he had ministered could never have had any doubts of the certitude of the faith which burned within him like an unquenchable flame. At Communion Services, in particular, they were conscious of it; and at the last Communion in which he took part at The Barony only a few weeks before his death, those who had gathered to join him in the Sacrament recalled how movingly he spoke the words of invitation to the Holy Table:

"Come unto Me, all ye that labour and are heavy laden and I will give you rest; I WILL REFRESH YOU. In His Name I invite you to do this in remembrance of the Christ; to hold Communion not with Jesus of Nazareth buried in the tomb, but with the Christ Who is our Resurrection and is at our side in this living and palpitating present year of 1951—with Him Who suffered for us, Who suffered with us, Who sorrows with us in our tribulations, Who will lead us through all to the JOY that endureth."

And then he prayed:

Be very near to us today: manifest Thyself to us in the breaking of Bread.

Thou art the Bread of Life: and yet Thou didst begin Thy ministry Hungering.

Thou art the Water of Life and yet Thou didst end Thy ministry Thirsting.

Thou Who wast led as a Lamb to the slaughter art our Good Shepherd:

Thou Who didst die for us all art the Giver of Life Eternal to them that believe.

And now what wait we for? Go with us to Thy Holy Mount:

May we behold Thy Glory:

May the Beauty of God's holiness be upon us.

It was decided to establish and furnish a chapel at The Barony in memory of Dr. John White, and the work was duly carried out. Everything in the chapel is closely associated with him. The stained-glass windows, the Holy Table, the Cross, the table lectern, the minister's chair, the sanctuary lamp, the Holy Bible, the curtains—all were given by his widow, by members of his family, by the Presbytery of Glasgow, by the present minister of The Barony and by its kirk session and its Woman's Guild. The Trustees of the National Memorial Fund, which was opened with His Royal Highness the Duke of Gloucester as sponsor, donated the plaque that bears the now familiar representation of his features and the following inscription:

TO THE GLORY OF GOD
AND IN MEMORY OF

JOHN WHITE, C.H., D.D., LL.D.
1867 — 1951

MINISTER AT
SHETTLESTON, SOUTH LEITH,
AND FOR FORTY YEARS AT
THE BARONY OF GLASGOW

MODERATOR OF THE GENERAL ASSEMBLY, 1925
MODERATOR OF THE UNION ASSEMBLY, 1929

APPENDIX

ARTICLES DECLARATORY OF THE CONSTITUTION OF THE CHURCH OF SCOTLAND IN MATTERS SPIRITUAL

I. The Church of Scotland is a branch of the Holy Catholic or Universal Church, believing in one God the Father Almighty, and in Jesus Christ His only Begotten Son Incarnate for our salvation, and in the Holy Ghost, three Persons in the Unity of the Godhead; owning obedience to its once crucified, now risen and glorified Lord, as the sole King and Head of His Church; proclaiming the forgiveness of sins and acceptance with God through faith in Christ, the renewing of the Holy Spirit, and eternal life; and labouring for the advancement of the Kingdom of God throughout the world.

II. The Church of Scotland adheres to the principles of the Protestant Reformation. The Word of God which is contained in the Scriptures of the Old and New Testaments is its supreme rule of faith and life. The Westminster Confession of Faith, approved by the General Assembly of 1647, is its principal subordinate standard, subject always to the declarations in the sixth and eighth Articles hereof. The government of the Church is Presbyterian, and is exercised through Kirk-sessions, Presbyteries, Provincial Synods, and General Assemblies. The system and principles of the worship, orders, and discipline of the Church are set forth in its authoritative historical documents.

III. The Church is in historical continuity with the Church of Scotland which was reformed in 1560, whose liberties were ratified in 1592, and for whose security provision was made in the Treaty of Union of 1707. The continuity and identity of the Church of Scotland are not prejudiced by the adoption of these Articles. *As national* it is a representative witness to the Christian faith of the Scottish people, and acknowledges its divine call and duty to bring the ordinances of religion to the people in every parish of Scotland through a territorial ministry.

IV. The Lord Jesus Christ, as King and Head of His Church, hath therein appointed a government in the hands of church office-bearers, distinct from and not subordinate in its own province to civil government. The Church of Scotland, while acknowledging the Divine appointment

466

and authority of the civil magistrate within his own sphere, and holding that the nation acting in its corporate capacity ought to render homage to God and promote in all appropriate ways the interests of His Kingdom, declares that it receives from its Head and from Him alone the right and power subject to no civil authority to legislate, and to adjudicate finally, in all matters of doctrine, worship, government, and discipline in the Church, including the right to determine all questions concerning membership and office in the Church, the constitution of its Courts, and the mode of election of its office-bearers and to define the boundaries of the spheres of labour of its ministers and other office-bearers.

V. The Church affirms that recognition by civil authority of its separate and independent government and jurisdiction in matters spiritual, in whatever manner such recognition be expressed, does not in any way affect the character of this government and jurisdiction as derived from the Divine Head of the Church alone and not from any civil authority, or give to the civil authority any right of interference with the proceedings or judgments of the Church within the sphere of its spiritual government and jurisdiction.

VI. The Church has the inherent right, free from interference by civil authority, but under the safeguards for deliberate action and legislation provided by the Church itself, to declare the sense in which it understands its Confession of Faith, to modify the forms of expression therein, or to *formulate other doctrinal statements*, and to define the relation thereto of its office-bearers and members, but always in agreement with the Word of God and the fundamental doctrines of the Christian faith contained in the said Confession, of which agreement the Church shall be sole judge, and with due regard to liberty of opinion in points which do not enter into the substance of the faith.

VII. The Church of Scotland, believing it to be in accordance with the will of Christ that His disciples should be all one in the Father and in Him, that the world may believe that the Father has sent Him, and recognising that other Churches, in which the Word is purely preached, the Sacraments are administered according to Christ's ordinance, and discipline rightly exercised, have richly contributed to the spiritual life of the nation, owns and declares anew the obligation to seek and promote union with these Churches; and welcomes conference with them on matters affecting the moral and spiritual wellbeing of the community, and participation by their ministers on national and public occasions in religious services conducted according to the usages of the Church of Scotland; and finally affirms the right to unite without loss of its identity with any other Church on terms which this Church finds to be consistent with these Articles.

VIII. The Church has the right to interpret these Articles and, subject to the safeguards for deliberate action and legislation provided by the Church itself, to modify or add to them; but the Church, as a branch of the Catholic Church, *unalterably adhering to the declaration of faith and duty set forth in the first Article hereof*, and solemnly recognising its sacred trust to defend and to transmit the faith once for all delivered unto the saints, declares that acceptance of the Word of God as the supreme rule of faith and life, and fidelity to the fundamental truths of the Christian faith which are founded upon the Word of God, and received in His Church, are essential to the continuity and identity of the corporate life of this Church. The Church also holds that Presbyterian Church government being agreeable to the Word of God and consonant with the religious traditions of the Scottish people is the only form of government of the Church of Scotland.

IX. Subject to the provisions of the foregoing Articles and the powers of amendment therein contained, the Constitution of the Church of Scotland is hereby anew ratified and confirmed.

PROPOSALS OF THE MINORITY

I. DOCTRINAL TESTIMONY

The Minority urged that the following should be part of the doctrinal testimony:

"The Church of Scotland is a branch of the Holy Catholic or Universal Church, believing and confessing unalterably that there is one living and true God; that there are three persons in the Godhead, the Father, the Son, and the Holy Ghost, and that these three are one God, the same in substance, equal in power and glory; and that the Lord Jesus Christ, being the Eternal Son of God, became man for our salvation by taking to Himself a true body and a reasonable soul, and so was, and continueth to be God and man in two distinct natures and one person for ever . . ." and so to the end of Article I.

II. NATIONAL RELIGION

The Minority urged that the following Article be inserted:

"The Church holds and confesses that it is its duty as national constantly to seek the support and aid of the State, and to labour for the advancement of Christ's Kingdom therein, and holding these views it values and maintains the ancient Statutory connection therewith, subject to modification or revision from time to time."

FIRST DRAFT, PREPARED BY DR. JOHN WHITE, ON WHICH THE ARTICLES DECLARATORY WERE BASED

The relations of the State to the Church are at present regulated by the Act of 1592 statute 116; the Act of 1690 statute 5; the Treaty of Union 1707 and relative Act of Security statute 6. From and after the passing of the Act confirming (endorsing) this Constitution, it shall be recognised that the Church possesses and enjoys thereunder in relation to the State and to the law all the liberty, rights and powers in matters spiritual herein claimed and set forth and that no limitation thereof is to be derived from any of the above mentioned or other statutes or laws affecting the Church of Scotland at present in force, such statutes and laws in so far as they may be inconsistent with said liberty, rights and powers, being repealed by the Act recognising this Constitution and declared of no effect.

1. The Church reaffirms and sets forth as a fundamental principle of its Constitution that the Lord Jesus, as King and Head of this Church, hath therein appointed a government in the hands of Church-officers, distinct from, and not subordinate in its own province, to civil government; that the civil magistrate does not possess the inherent right to exercise the powers God has given to the spiritual office-bearers in the Church concerning discipline, doctrine, worship and government.

2. The Westminster Confession of Faith adopted by the Church, ratified by Act 1690 c. 5, and approven by Act of General Assembly shall be, in so far as it sets forth the sum and substance of the doctrine of the Reformed Churches, being the fundamental doctrine of the Catholic faith, the public and avowed Confession of the Church. Recognising that the complete and exclusive jurisdiction in all causes concerning the faith is inherent in the Church of Christ, and that the Church's ultimate authority in all such matters is the Holy Scriptures and the Holy Spirit, the Church affirms its inherent right to declare the sense in which it understands its Confession of Faith, to modify its form of expression from time to time, or to formulate other subordinate standards setting forth the sum and substance of the Reformed Evangelical Doctrine, and to define its relation thereto; always in agreement with the Word of God and with due regard to the liberty of the individual conscience in points of doctrine which do not enter into the substance of the Faith. This power shall be exercised without any external interference, but always in conformity

with the safeguards for deliberate action and legislation provided by the Church itself.

3. The Church declares its freedom from all external authority other than the jurisdiction of the civil courts in relation to any matter whatsoever of a civil nature, and that its courts have the sole and exclusive right to regulate, determine and decide all matters spiritual within the Church, and their procedures therein, and regulations and decisions thereon, and are not subject to interdict, reduction, suspension, or any other manner of review by any court of civil jurisdiction. The expression "matters spiritual" includes all matters relating to the discipline, doctrine, worship and government of the Church of Scotland, and in particular all matters relating to the ministry, oracles and ordinances of God, the election, appointment and admission of ministers of the Church to the pastoral office, of the other office-bearers of the said Church to their offices, and their suspension and deprivation therefrom, the Constitution of the Courts of the Church and the admission of ministers and office-bearers to sit therein, the infliction and removal of Church censures, and generally all other spiritual matters.

4. There shall belong to and be exclusively vested in the Courts of the Church the powers at present vested in and exercised by the Lords of Council and Session acting as Commissioners for the plantation of Kirks and valuation of teinds viz.: to disjoin and erect parishes *quoad sacra* and to erect parishes without territorial districts; together with full power to transport churches, suppress charges, rearrange parochial boundaries, and otherwise deal with churches and parishes as occasion may necessitate.

5. The Government of the Church, as set forth in the Second Book of Discipline, and ratified by Act 1592, and again in 1690 and 1707, is by Kirk-Sessions, Presbyteries, Provincial Synods, and General Assemblies; and it shall be permissible for these Courts, each within its own province, to hold conference with any other Church of Christ in all matters affecting the religious state and morals of the people, and to associate with themselves, on public ceremonial occasions, representatives from other Churches.

6. The Church claims the inherent right to determine and regulate this Constitution, as duty may require, in dependence on the grace of God, under the guidance of His Word, and in conformity with the safeguards for deliberate action and legislation provided by the Church itself; such modifications and adjustments shall be consistent with the preservation of the identity of the Church as Presbyterian, Reformed, Evangelical, National.

Note (*a*). There shall belong to and be exclusively vested in the Courts of the Church the power to apportion and administer the endowments of the Church according to the needs of localities.

Note (*b*). In virtue of the provisions of the Act 1592 c. 116, the principles of common law, and in accordance with immemorial practice, Presbyteries are invested with civil jurisdiction subject to appeal to civil courts in questions relating to the patrimonial rights of the Church and the parochial buildings and property belonging to or destined for its use; this right belongs to them as bodies which by their constitution are entitled and bound to guard the rights of the Church, civil or ecclesiastical, within their respective bounds, and shall continue, unless in so far as affected by the Act, recognising this constitution.

INDEX

INDEX

INDEX

476

INDEX

INDEX